Athenian Comedy in the Roman Empire

Also available from Bloomsbury

No Laughing Matter, edited by C.W. Marshall and George Kovacs
Aristophanes, James Robson
Classics on Screen, Alastair Blanshard and Kim Shahabudin

Athenian Comedy in the Roman Empire

Edited by
C.W. Marshall and Tom Hawkins

Bloomsbury Academic
An imprint of Bloomsbury Publishing Plc

B L O O M S B U R Y
LONDON • NEW DELHI • NEW YORK • SYDNEY

Bloomsbury Academic
An imprint of Bloomsbury Publishing Plc

50 Bedford Square	1385 Broadway
London	New York
WC1B 3DP	NY 10018
UK	USA

www.bloomsbury.com

BLOOMSBURY and the Diana logo are trademarks of Bloomsbury Publishing Plc

First published 2016

© C.W. Marshall, Tom Hawkins and Contributors, 2016

C.W. Marshall and Tom Hawkins have asserted their rights under the Copyright, Designs and Patents Act, 1988, to be identified as Editors of this work.

All rights reserved. No part of this publication may be reproduced or transmitted in any form or by any means, electronic or mechanical, including photocopying, recording, or any information storage or retrieval system, without prior permission in writing from the publishers.

No responsibility for loss caused to any individual or organization acting on or refraining from action as a result of the material in this publication can be accepted by Bloomsbury or the authors.

British Library Cataloguing-in-Publication Data
A catalogue record for this book is available from the British Library.

ISBN: HB: 978-1-47258-884-5
PB: 978-1-47258-883-8
ePDF: 978-1-47258-886-9
ePub: 978-1-47258-885-2

Library of Congress Cataloging-in-Publication Data
A catalog record for this book is available from the Library of Congress.

Typeset by RefineCatch Limited, Bungay, Suffolk

Contents

Acknowledgements   vi

1. Ignorance and the Reception of Comedy in Antiquity
   Tom Hawkins and C. W. Marshall   1

2. Juvenal and the Revival of Greek New Comedy at Rome
   Mathias Hanses   25

3. *Parrhēsia* and *Pudenda*: Speaking Genitals and Satiric Speech
   Julia Nelson Hawkins   43

4. Dio Chrysostom and the Naked Parabasis   *Tom Hawkins*   69

5. Favorinus and the Comic Adultery Plot   *Ryan B. Samuels*   89

6. Comedies and Comic Actors in the Greek East: An Epigraphical Perspective   *Fritz Graf*   117

7. Plutarch, Epitomes, and Athenian Comedy   *C. W. Marshall*   131

8. Lucian's Aristophanes: On Understanding Old Comedy in the Roman Imperial Period   *Ralph M. Rosen*   141

9. Exposing Frauds: Lucian and Comedy   *Ian C. Storey*   163

10. Revoking Comic License: Aristides' *Or.* 29 and the Performance of Comedy   *Anna Peterson*   181

11. Aelian and Comedy: Four Studies   *C. W. Marshall*   197

12. The Menandrian World of Alciphron's *Letters*   *Melissa Funke*   223

13. Two Clouded Marriages: Aristainetos' Allusions to Aristophanes' *Clouds* in *Letters* 2.3 and 2.12   *Emilia A. Barbiero*   239

Bibliography   259
Index   291

Acknowledgements

This book developed out of a panel at the 2014 annual meetings of the American Philological Association on *Greek Comedy in the Roman Empire* in Chicago. We are grateful to the APA for the opportunity to develop this theme, to the panel contributors, and to the audience in attendance (three of whom have contributed to this collection). At Bloomsbury Academic, we have been very fortunate to work with Anna MacDiarmid, Alice Wright, and their team. Thanks are also due to Sebastiana Nervegna and Andrew McClellan. C.W. Marshall has been generously supported in part by the Social Sciences and Humanities Research Council of Canada and the Peter Wall Instutute for Advanced Studies at the Univeristy of British Columbia.

Note on transliteration and names

The works discussed in this volume were originally written in Greek and Latin, and most of them have titles in Greek, Latin, and English by which they might be commonly referred. We have chosen, therefore, to refer to ancient works by their common titles, rather than aim for strict uniformity of language. Further, the transliteration of Greek characters into English is not consistently practiced. While each chapter should be consistent with itself, we have not imposed a uniform format for transliteration and names, preferring to allow authors to present a format that they feel best communicates their material.

Every contributor to this volume has benefited from the continued publication of volumes of *Poetae Comici Graeci* (*The Greek Comic Poets*). This massive undertaking offers updated texts of the fragments of Greek comedy, as well as the testimonia about each author. Texts from these volumes are commonly cited in scholarly publications using the abbreviations *PCG* or K-A (the initials of the editors, Kassel and Austin). In this volume, fragments are labeled K-A (e.g. Eupolis fr. 16 K-A) and the volumes are labeled *PCG* (e.g. *PCG* VIII).

1

Ignorance and the Reception of Comedy in Antiquity

Tom Hawkins and C.W. Marshall

non medius fidius ipsas Athenas tam Atticas dixerim.
I would say that not even Athens itself was so Attic.

Pliny the Younger, *Ep.* 4.3.5

In a letter to his friend Caninius, the younger Pliny raves about a recent gathering, at which the impressively named but otherwise unknown Vergilius Romanus had given a reading of his latest poetry – his first foray into the realm of old comedy, *comoedia vetus* (*Ep.* 6.21.2). Among other details, Pliny tells us that Vergilius had presented his work to just 'a few people' (*paucis*), that he was already an accomplished author of *mimiambi* and comedies that rivalled Menander and others 'of that era' (*aetatis eiusdem*);[1] that he was a veritable Plautus or Terence; that he commended virtue and rooted out vice, using names both fictitious and real; and that he had lavished praise upon Pliny himself, perhaps adapting the self-promotion of many Old Comic parabases to the demands of Roman patronage.

Such information provides a rare glimpse into contemporary comic practice at Rome and the enduring influence of earlier eras, but its very rarity also makes this passage difficult to assess in broader terms. Does Pliny use *vetus* as a temporal or generic marker? Does this private reading imply that comedies of this sort were no longer staged? Was Vergilius' literary versatility the norm or an oddity? Was he composing in Greek or Latin? And can we deduce anything from the naming of the most famous poets of Greek New Comedy and Republican Roman Comedy compared to the absence of any expected Old Comic names? None of these questions have answers, and it was largely in response to this experience of ignorance that we were inspired to undertake this exploration of the reception of classical Athenian comedy in the Roman imperial era. We hope that this volume provides some answers to important questions about the influence and vitality (or decrepitude) of Athenian comic drama in the imperial era across an array of genres and media, and that our efforts inspire others to go even further in asking new questions and generating new insights on this topic.

Ignorance and misapprehension still dominate the subject of this collection. Many aspects of the reception of Athenian comedy in the Roman Empire have not yet been explored and we believe a collection of new studies from a range of theoretical approaches will benefit our field. In particular, we hope this project will appeal both to those interested in the afterlife of Greek comedy in the first five centuries CE and anyone concerned with the sources for the cultural and literary products emerging primarily in the Greek-speaking Roman world. For this reason, the personified *Agnoia* (Ignorance or Misapprehension) serves as a kind of muse for this project, and we see these chapters eroding the areas where she has the greatest sway. Agnoia herself also has a dramatic life, appearing as the delayed prologue in Menander's *Perikeiromenē* ('The Girl who Got her Hair Cut'). An illustration of her appears in a second- or third-century CE papyrus which we assume comes from this play (*P. Oxy.* 2652), and which has served as the cover image to this volume.[2] Her wide-eyed stare out from the papyrus holds our gaze and challenges the viewer to explain what she represents. If this does come from an illustrated edition of Menander, is the image of a soldier in *P. Oxy.* 2653 from the same play (and therefore a representation of Polemon)? Does her appearance reproduce details from an active performance tradition, or is the imagery independent, with the artist depicting erroneously the close-lipped mask characteristic of pantomime, the elite artistic entertainment of the empire? Is her simple and comparatively unadorned costume reflecting something in the play's text that no longer survives? By seeming to point at herself, Agnoia dares us to overcome ignorance itself in explaining the many unusual features of this exceptional pair of illustrations.[3]

The overview presented in the following three sections provides a chronological frame that allows us to consider the individual studies presented in *Athenian Comedy in the Roman Empire*. We outline the development of Athenian comedy from its inception until the death of Alexander; we provide an account of the transition through the Hellenistic and Roman Republican periods (which coincides with the development and spread of what comes to be known as New Comedy); and we then present some of the questions that dominate the study of the reception of Greek comedy in the Roman Empire to help position the original contributions in this collection.

Classical Athenian comedy (486–323 BCE)

The story of comic drama in Athens traditionally begins 2500 years ago in 486, when Chionides (Suda, *ad loc.*) presented an Old Comedy at the City Dionysia.[4] By *c.* 440 comedies were being staged as part of the Lenaea as well (*IG* II² 232.5), and from an early date both festivals probably were using the theater of Dionysus to showcase their dramatic competitions. Virtually everything that we know about classical Athenian drama derives (directly or indirectly) from these two festivals, at each of which five comic playwrights and their casts of actors annually competed. From this basic information, we can infer that there must have been hundreds of comic dramas produced in the classical era, of which we can talk about only a handful.[5] Yet this represents only a small part of the fuller story of early comic drama. Comedies were staged in Sicily earlier than they were at Athens, and similar traditions must have existed both throughout the Mediterranean basin and in a variety of smaller venues across Attica.[6] And thus our eleven complete plays by Aristophanes that span the years 425 (*Acharnians*) to 388 (*Wealth*) amount to a tiny slice of early Greek comedy and one that does not offer a representative sample of comic drama from this period.

From the evidence that we have, however, we can deduce a list of traits that delimit the shape of Athenian Old Comedy: individual playwrights composed a single play, which, if approved by the archon, was granted access into the competition at either the Lenaia or Dionysia; a selected play was assigned a chorus of citizens and a *khorēgos* (citizen-producer), who paid for the costuming and training of the chorus;[7] professional, male actors played the speaking roles, and wore elaborate costumes including masks and padded bodysuits with an attached leather phallus; plots tended toward the fantastical, rather than mythological or historical themes, but they took as their principal frame of reference the social, historical, and physical space of contemporary Athens; grotesque and sexual language and imagery were paired with sharp political satire of named and easily recognizable public figures; and plays were typically structured around an alternation of actor-driven, plot-driven episodes and choral interludes; of the latter, the three most prominent were the entrance song (*parodos*), the parabasis (in which the chorus interrupts the plot to speak as if with the voice of the poet about matters relating to comic dramaturgy, the greatness of the poet, the baseness of his rivals, the character of the audience, and political matters of the day), and the exit song (*exodos*). Although our evidence is incomplete and a great deal of variety existed within this broad superstructure, we can use this list of traits to demark the Old Comedy of Aristophanes, Cratinus and Eupolis (and their contemporaries) from other, later iterations of comic drama and as a benchmark against which to assess imperial receptions of the earliest phase of Athenian comedy.

In recent years, a spate of work on early Athenian comedy has helped contextualize Aristophanes more broadly. The continued publication of volumes of *Poetae Comici Graeci* (*PCG*) offers updated texts and textual analysis of all the comic fragments. Translations and commentaries on comic fragments are becoming easily available.[8] Mills and Olson have collected, edited, and analyzed the inscriptional evidence for the Athenian dramatic festivals.[9] The cumulative result of this work is that we now have a better understanding of Old Comedy beyond the Aristophanic witness than at any time since antiquity. What's more, the accessibility of many of these important scholarly tools means that the study of comic fragments is much easier now than ever before, which will encourage more and more individuals to pursue their study.[10]

The wealth of fifth-century evidence, centered around Aristophanes and primarily from the last quarter of the century, declines toward the end of the Peloponnesian War. Platonius, writing no earlier than the late Hellenistic era but perhaps much later, claims that politics and the theatrical license to abuse public figures precipitated the shift from Old to Middle Comedy. Although such neat schematizations were commonly used in antiquity, they are not always helpful for modern analyses, and this is particularly true in the case of 'Middle' Comedy.[11] Platonius describes this transitional period or sub-genre in terms of a diminished role for the chorus and a lack of overt political engagement. In particular, he points to the legend about Alcibiades murdering Eupolis in response to the playwright's effeminate portrayal of him in *Baptae*, and claims that this event marks a clear historical transition. But this explanation does not fit the evidence – most importantly, because Eupolis' death in 411, even if at the hands of Alcibiades, precedes the alleged decline of Old Comedy by at least a decade, and since Csapo has shown that 'what we normally think of as Old, Middle and New Comedy designate synchronic, not period styles'.[12] Such questioning of ancient categories has led modern scholars to debate the existence of Middle Comedy as a useful heuristic concept, since it certainly does not reflect a straightforward chronological development. Even if we accept some notion of distinct periodizations of Athenian comedy, and distinguish the careers of Antiphanes, Alexis and their contemporaries in the early fourth century as Middle Comedy, it is probable that they saw themselves as continuing and developing the traditions established by the previous generations of comedians. The lack of any complete example of a play that shares both the timeframe and the stylistic features that Platonius describes – with the possible exception of Aristophanes' *Wealth* (388) – means that our understanding of the period between Aristophanes and Menander remains woefully misunderstood.[13] For these reasons we have chosen to forgo references to 'Middle' Comedy altogether in favor of more precise and useful categories of analysis.

At the same time, however, the early part of the fourth century begins the era in which we can see the influence of Athenian comedy reach well beyond the stage.[14] From the fifth century, we find a very limited number of clues that, for example, suggest the impact of Old Comedy on tragedy, and Aristophanes tells us that bits of Cratinus had become standard repertoire at symposia (*Knights* 529–30), but otherwise we find little evidence of any wider influence of comic drama. But in the fourth century Plato and Aristotle bring comedy into the emerging realm of highly theorized intellectual discourse. Perhaps most importantly, Plato gives Aristophanes a prominent role in two texts: his *Apology* positions Aristophanes' *Clouds* as a key piece of evidence in the case against Socrates; and his *Symposium* situates philosophy as an intimate partner with both tragedy and comedy through the roles of Agathon and Aristophanes at the dinner-party to which the title refers.[15]

Two works by Aristotle have exerted more analytic influence on our understanding of comedy than any other, despite the fact that they are both now lost. His *Didaskaliai*, 'Production Notes', collected information from official records about the history of dramatic competitions at the major Athenian festivals and became the point of reference for the ancient system of dating that we still rely on today.[16] And although his second book of *Poetics*, devoted wholly to the subject of comedy, does not survive, we know a great deal about his general arguments, and he discusses comedy on other occasions throughout his corpus.[17] Thus, even though we have far more complete comic dramas from the fifth century than we do from the fourth, we can see comedy taking root more broadly in Greek culture during this period.[18] Storey has even gone so far as to suggest the influence of Plato propelled Aristophanes to become the face of Old Comedy rather than the more successful Eupolis and Cratinus.[19]

The inscriptional evidence from the fourth century shows several changes in Athenian dramatic practice that impacted the history of comedy. Most important is the increasingly common habit of restaging earlier plays. In the fifth and early fourth centuries, restagings at the major Athenian festivals were rare.[20] By 386, however, the Dionysia featured regular restagings of tragedies, and by 311 comedies were also being reperformed. Re-performances opened new theatrical possibilities, as we can see in Aulus Gellius' (second c. CE) story about a fourth-century actor named Polus who was playing the lead role in Sophocles' *Electra*: as Electra laments her brother's death, not knowing that he was actually still alive, and clings to the urn that supposedly contains his ashes, Polus' audience is also aware that the actor is holding the very urn containing the ashes of his recently deceased son (*Attic Nights* 6.5.7–8). This new habit of restaging fifth-century dramas is of obvious importance for a variety of reasons relating to canon formation, repertory and audience expectations, but in terms of the history of comedy, reperformance raises a specifically vexed question of terminology. When a bit of evidence refers to the performance of an old (παλαιά, ἀρχαῖα, *vetus*) or new (καινή, νέα, *nova*) comedy, how can we determine if the adjective is being used as a temporal or generic marker? Unlike tragedy and satyr drama, ancient classifications of classical Athenian comedy blur matters of periodization and generic nomenclature. In the didascalic inscriptions (based on and extending Aristotle's lost *Didaskaliai*), comparison with notices about tragedies and satyr dramas seems to ensure that *palaios* is used as a temporal, rather than a generic, term, but we should not assume a consistent terminological usage in different times and places.

As the restaging of fifth-century dramas became increasingly common, the didascalic inscriptions show that by 341 satyr drama had been separated from tragedy in the slate of competitive performances at the Dionysia (*IG* II² 2320). This might not seem to be a critical development in the history of comedy, but Shaw has shown that satyr drama, cut loose from the constraint of working in conjunction with tragedy, began to appropriate some of the distinctive traits of Old Comedy, particularly in terms of onomastic abuse, urban settings, metrical flexibility, paratragic engagement, and parabatic statements.[21] Yet the Old Comic aspects that Shaw finds in Agen's *Python* and Lycophron's *Menedemus*, for example, reflect a dynamic ebb and flow of generic horizons, and he goes on to show that this new direction in satyr drama may itself have been the result of a shift on the part of comic drama in the direction of satyr drama. This shifting of generic-performative territory raises a more subtle issue than the matter of nomenclature. Namely, how can we track the influence of a classical genre in the imperial era when the genre in question did not remain static?

Dramatic genres present a particular challenge in this regard, since they are structured around a mixture of parameters imposed by a festival program (e.g. the official labelling of a play as a tragedy or a comedy; the number of actors available; the presence or absence of a chorus) and other less rigid issues, such as a preference for urban or rustic settings, or mythological or political plot themes. The old chestnut of Euripides' *Alcestis* presents precisely this issue in a more familiar guise. Since that play was staged in the fourth position in a tragic tetralogy – in the position traditionally taken by a satyr drama – should we think of it more as a satyr drama that has cannibalized tragic dramaturgy or a tragedy that has supplanted satyric theater? Such reductive alternatives unnecessarily constrain both the role of the artist who brings a play to the stage and the role of an audience's generic expectations to participate in the production of meaning and the appreciation of generic dissonance, but they represent a necessary starting point for assessing the generic complexities of the shifting terrain of classical drama.[22] As we trace the development of Athenian comedy beyond the end of the fifth century, therefore, we need to be attuned both to the continued role of what passed for comic theater in any particular social context as well as the various strands of comic influence discernible in other modes of artistic expression.

Comedy in the Hellenistic era (323–31 BCE)

About the time of the death of Alexander the Great (323), trends in comedy again shifted toward a topical realism that drew upon romantic narratives that share narrative features with late Euripidean tragedy and which ancient commentators termed 'New Comedy'. Although the figure of Menander eventually became synonymous with this era of comic production, the careers of Apollodorus, Diphilus and Philemon also flourished at this time, and like Menander they too exerted a strong influence on the Roman comedy of Plautus and Terence.[23] Papyrus discoveries from the last century of many, often substantial, Menandrian fragments mean that we now have significant portions of six plays in addition to a great number of smaller fragments.[24] The best preserved is the essentially complete *Dyskolos* ('The Grouch'). There is less of *Epitrepontes* ('The Arbitrators') and *Samia* ('The Girl from Samos'), and less again of *Aspis* ('The Shield'), *Perikeiromenē* ('The Girl who Got her Hair Cut') and *Sikyonioi* ('The Sikyonians').

Menandrian New Comedy can be distinguished from its dramatic predecessors in a variety of ways. Compared to fifth-century drama, surviving texts suggest a diminished choral role, though this may reflect matters of textual transmission more than any real change in performance practices; the individual actors gained more prominence; characters came from a stock set of stereotypes, such as the 'angry father', and masks became more expressive as these roles become individuated. Compared to Old Comedy, the plots of New Comedy were typical and commonplace with generic settings, such as a farm, rather than the fanciful worlds of Aristophanes, and political satire and grotesque imagery were displaced by plots centered on romantic love and relationships among families and neighbors among whom the occasionally intervening divinities are not Olympians but minor gods and personifications (Pan, Chance, Ignorance). These traits help to distinguish New Comedy from its earlier comic forms, but lines of continuity are also evident. New Comedy's realism and its emphasis on family relations, for example, can be traced back to fifth-century tragedy, which often seems to be the point of reference for New Comedy's self-presentation.[25]

The conflation between Menander and New Comedy generally (and the concomitant occlusion of other authors) is itself part of the historical backdrop to our current endeavor. Philemon and Diphilus were Menander's two greatest rivals, and what we know of their careers diverges from the model of Menander in several ways. Whereas Menander was an Athenian citizen, part of a prominent family (his uncle was Alexis, another of the most prominent fourth-century playwrights) and preferred to stay in Athens rather than move to Egypt at the invitation of Ptolemy I, neither Philemon nor Diphilus were native Athenians. Philemon, who is said to be from either Cilicia or Syracuse, defeated Menander in competition several times with plays that were supposedly less refined than those of his rival, and he visited Alexandria at the request of Ptolemy II.[26] These anecdotes, however, highlight the difficulty we have in seeing through the layers of later pro-Menandrian bias: Gellius' claim that Philemon defeated Menander only due to underhanded tactics (*Attic Nights* 17.4) sounds suspiciously like a later writer trying to square his own tastes with the historical record of victories; and Plutarch's allusion to the mock execution ordered by Magas of Cyrene (*de cohib. ira* 458a, *de vit. mor.* 449e), after Philemon had been shipwrecked upon the king's shores, may be a fantasy that grew out of Philemon's mockery of Magas on stage (fr. 132 K-A) or an assimilation of Philemon into the theme of playwrights being attacked by their powerful targets offstage (rumors of Cleon suing Aristophanes, and Alcibiades supposedly 'dyeing' Eupolis in the sea on account of his depiction in *Baptae*, 'The Dyers'). Diphilus was from Sinope and died in Smyrna after a career spent mostly in Athens, and some of his works were adapted by Plautus (in *Casina* and *Asinaria*) and Terence (in *Adelphi*). In terms of dramaturgy he stands out, because several of his titles indicate plays centered on mythological burlesques of some kind (e.g. *Heracles* and *Daughters of Danaus*) and in his *Sappho* he presented the historically impossible scenario of Archilochus and Hipponax being rivals for the affections of Sappho.

These last points again raise questions about the relationship between comic genres and periodization, since mythical and historical themes do not fit with standard assumptions about the stock characters and realistic scenarios of New Comedy. We have already seen that in the fourth century satyr drama could adopt certain Old Comic traits, so it is possible that Diphilus' mythological plays have taken a cue from satyr drama. Similarly, the presentation of famous historical figures is most clearly known from Old Comic sources (Aeschylus and Euripides in Aristophanes' *Frogs* and Aristides, Miltiades, Solon and Pericles in Eupolis' *Demoi*). Although Menander eventually came to dominate thinking about New Comedy, we should bear in mind that other models thrived concurrently with his career.

The rough and perhaps semi-legendary outlines of the careers of these New Comic poets also reflect the changing dynamics throughout the eastern Mediterranean basin after the conquests of Alexander. The spread of Greek culture and the trends in festival patterns reflected in the epigraphic record show that entertainments of all sorts, including drama, were becoming wildly popular across the region during this period. During these years many new festivals emerge (some called *Dionysia* but others with names associated with other divinities or human patrons), as do the various unions (*synodoi*) of theatrical specialists (*tekhnitai*) under the patronage of Dionysus that organized the involvement of performers of all stripes at the myriad festivals that dotted the annual cycle.[27] With these changes, the Athenocentrism of our classical sources gives way to a model that looks much more like what we find in the imperial era.

With the death of Menander in 291 the era of clearly attested Athenian comedy essentially comes to a close, though inscriptional evidence (*IG* II² 2323) shows that comic competitions were still being staged at the Athenian Dionysia beyond the middle of the second century BCE.[28] In these later years, new plays continued to be produced, new poets were introduced, and old favorites were at least occasionally restaged.[29] From here, the story of Athenian comedy can be broken down into the overlapping themes of preservation and influence.[30]

The preservation of Athenian comedy derives from a desire to delimit and maintain the integrity of a fixed canon of plays. To some extent this impulse can explain habits of reperforming classical plays, though large-scale public performances were presumably not driven primarily by antiquarian interests. The history of comic texts in antiquity is difficult to discern, though Wilson notes that the Alexandrian editions presumably provided some uniformity as a basis for other copies.[31] More diffusely, the school curriculum, preferences for entertainment at dinner parties and scholarly activities worked together to develop an elite canon of taste and exclusivity. The typical school curriculum included comedy, with Menander (and Euripides) following close on the heels of

Homer, and with the more historically involved Old Comedy introduced to advanced students.[32] Menander's reputation for naturalistic depictions of everyday life, his clear and elegant Greek, and the continued staging of his plays must have contributed to his place in the educational canon and his continued popularity. Perhaps this combination of style and social location also explains the appearance from the first century CE onwards of lists of Menandrian maxims (often called *monostikhoi* or *sententiae*), many of which are clearly the product of school exercises.[33] Students who studied comedy as part of their education grew into the social set that tended to present bits of comic and tragic dramas at dinner parties, either as songs sung by the invited guests themselves or with performers brought in for private viewings. Pliny's decision to name two of his villas at Lake Como Tragedy and Comedy, based on contrasting analogies between the high vantage of the former with the 'high boots' (*cothurni*) of tragedy and the shoreline setting of the latter with the 'low slippers' (*socculi*) of comedy (*Ep.* 9.7.3) and the many theatrical mosaics and frescos from private homes in the Roman era offer easy examples of the deep connection between elite hospitality and the dramatic tradition.[34]

More rarefied scholarship on comedy begins early in the Hellenistic era with the polymaths assembled at Alexandria, though nearly all of these works are now lost: Lycophron, who was from Euboea and worked in Alexandria during the reign of Ptolemy II Philadelphus (reigned 283–246), was counted among 'the Pleiad' (i.e. the seven leading tragic playwrights in Hellenistic Alexandria); he organized and catalogued the comic texts held by the Library of Alexandria, and he wrote a nine-volume work titled *On Comedy*; Euphronius (probably from Cyrene and working in the third century) began the tradition of writing commentaries on individual plays (Athenaeus 11.495c), an intellectual endeavor perhaps already discernible in incipient form in the confrontation between Aeschylus and Euripides in Aristophanes' *Frogs*; another Cyrenean, Callimachus (310–240), produced the massive *Pinakes*, which effectively catalogued the holdings of the Library of Alexandria, and continued the Aristotelian work on dramatic chronology; Eratosthenes, also from Cyrene (*c.* 275–195) and who is perhaps most famous for his calculation of the circumference of the earth, wrote a single volume titled *On Ancient Comedy*; Aristophanes of Byzantium (*c.* 257–*c.* 185) edited the texts of Old Comedy and gave each a preface (*hypothesis*); he also seems to have begun the scholarly practice of working on Menander and may have edited his plays.[35] Such scholarly work continued beyond the Hellenistic era with the likes of Didymus, Varro, Quintilian, Plutarch, and Athenaeus, and the social location of comedy as a subject for these towering intellectual figures ensured the literary imprimatur of both New and Old Comedy in parallel to the continuing history of staged performances of comic dramas.

Whereas we have used the notion of continuity to refer to the enduring practice of staging comic plays and preservation to describe the social and physical contexts that served to maintain the prominence and knowledge of classical comedies, influence is a far slipperier and more sprawling category of analysis that resists many objective analytic criteria beyond the counting of recognizable citations. The most familiar case of classical Athenian comedy influencing the literature of the Hellenistic era is to be found among the works of the Republican Roman dramatists Plautus and Terence. These playwrights often loudly proclaimed their indebtedness to Greek New Comedy, and sometimes suggest that they have merely translated an old Greek play into Latin. Plautus' *Mercator* ('Merchant'), for example, takes its basic plot from Philemon's *Emporos* ('Merchant') and his *Casina* from Diphilus' *Klēroumenoi* ('Those Casting Lots'); Terence's *Eunuchus* ('The Eunuch') and *Andria* ('The Girl from Andros') emerged from Menander's plays of the same names. Decades of scholarship have been spent trying to discern Greek originals beneath the obscuring surface of these Latin works, but this inevitably comes at the expense of considering the Latin plays as Roman literary products that in the first instance were being addressed to Roman Republican audiences.[36]

Beyond these obvious (if hardly straightforward) cases of Greek New Comedy influencing Republican Roman comedy, instances of literary influence become more challenging to isolate. At one end of the spectrum, we can assume that classical Greek comedy exerted some influence at least indirectly on every author of the Hellenistic and indeed of the imperial era as well, but such a claim offers no useful critical insight. At the other extreme, we can doubt any assertion of influence that is not bolstered by such overt clues as quotations of comic material or references to comic playwrights, but such stringent parameters may lead to overlooking important connections. Influence, furthermore, is not always direct or linear. We have already mentioned the example of Plato's incorporation of Aristophanes into his *Apology* and *Symposium*, texts that were widely read and studied in the post-classical era, and similar extra-comedic avenues of influence can be found throughout antiquity. Theophrastus' *Characters*, for example, seems deeply engaged with the typicalized set of characters familiar from Menandrian New Comedy, but reaches beyond the world of the stage to the everyday world of Athens in its discovery of recognizable foibles that distinguish individuals.[37] Menander studied under Theophrastus (who was the successor of Aristotle as the head of the Lyceum), though the teacher outlived the student by a few years, and it is impossible to determine whether Menander's plays influenced Theophrastus' *Characters* or vice-versa. Influence is obvious, but the precise details remain elusive, and a common source could lie behind the *ethopoeia* (character drawing) of both Menander and Theophrastus.

Herodas, whose dates are uncertain but who almost certainly composed his *Mimiambs* in the later part of the third century BCE, presents a different version of the challenge of influence. Kutzko has shown that this fragmentary collection of poems draws together themes and structures borrowed from the Sicilian mimes of Sophron and Athenian comedy while also foregrounding the importance of Hipponax, who appears in *Mimiamb* 8 and whose choliambic meter is used throughout the collection.[38] Herodas' plan, that is, was not to continue the practice of composing recognizable comedies in the Athenian mode nor to preserve the legacy of Athenian comedy but, rather, to create something new in the mash-up of several literary models. Similarly, Horace's claim that Roman satire is built upon the legacy of Aristophanes, Cratinus and Eupolis (*Satires* 1.4.1–8) represents a manipulation of cultural authority and generic expectations rather than any sort of straight-forward assertion of a rigorously delineated literary genealogy.[39] These examples highlight the interconnectedness and partialness of literary influence, and they raise the possibility of indirect influence. For an imperial figure such as Persius, for example, how much of his engagement with Greek comedy is direct and how much is negotiated through his philosophical interests, which may have included Theophrastus, or his satirical debt to Horace's use of Old Comedy or to the choliambs of Herodas (and Hipponax) with which he composed the preface to his collection? For those authors in this volume who build their arguments around matters of literary influence, therefore, a basic challenge is to establish clear criteria by which comic influence can be recognized, defended and analyzed.

Athenian comedy in the Roman empire (31 BCE –)

Around the same time as the political changes that occurred following the Battle of Actium, as Rome was transformed into Augustus' principate and then the empire, and as the impact of Roman culture was disseminated across the Mediterranean basin and throughout Western Europe, we can document significant changes in the preferred forms of popular entertainment. Stone theatres continued to be built, leaving distinctive Roman architectural landmarks that distinguish the ambitions of an urban setting, a place wanting to be noticed.

Yet we have very little idea what sorts of performances took place in these venues. While musical and artistic contests did continue throughout the empire, and while plays did continue to be written and read (in turn shaping the literary output in other genres as well), it seems that the theatres were used primarily for the elite artistic medium of pantomime, a kind of masked ballet that focused on the mimetic dance of a single performer.[40] Pantomime flourished into the sixth century CE, and so shaped artistic tastes throughout the history of the empire. The mythological narratives of pantomime largely displace tragedy in the social and imaginative world of the Romans. The separate but related dramatic form known as mime develops from the specific kind of unmasked improvisatory street theatre of the Hellenistic era to a scripted literary form in the first century BCE, beginning with the authors Decimus Laberius and Publilius Syrus. In the empire, the use of the term *mime* broadened to include almost any performative genre, including (confusingly, at times) pantomime.[41] Both these genres were widely performed and remain inadequately understood today.

Where comedy as a theatrical genre fits within the literary and social practices of this world is the subject of *Athenian Comedy in the Roman Empire*. This is not a complete account, nor even a representative survey, but it does offer a number of new studies that complement what we know about comedy in this period. We choose to position these studies in terms of the reception of Athenian comedy – how the Romans (broadly conceived in political terms as those living in the empire and writing in Greek and Latin) understood, interpreted, and reshaped their own literary pasts.[42] A few scholars have considered these issues before (many of the same names recur regularly throughout the footnotes of the contributions here), but we are particularly heartened by the near explosion of new scholarship on this subject that has emerged since we first conceived of this collection early in 2013. In particular, the appearance of Sebastiana Nervegna's *Menander in Antiquity* (2013) makes easily accessible a wealth of material that was previously widely scattered. The publication of a number of handbooks and companions provides important groundwork for advancing that articulation of this history: in particular, *The Oxford Handbook of Greek and Roman Comedy* (2014) and *The Cambridge Companion to Greek Comedy* (2014) contain substantial sections on reception in the Roman period. These synthetic accounts (again, many of which are cited in footnotes here) demonstrate the degree to which the topography of this subject has changed in just two years. These works provide crucial detail to a general outline, and will facilitate more engaged exploration of this scholarly territory.

The place of Greek comedy in the Roman Empire is surprisingly free of the chronological distinctions that separate Menander from Aristophanes, as detailed in the historical survey above. This is, to us, unexpected: the division of Old and New Comedy (and the transition from one to the other, which can be given the label Middle) was reinforced by the scholarly attitudes that emerged in the early centuries CE. That it is not possible easily to separate studies in this volume focused on Old Comedy from those focused on New demonstrates that what was important was the larger conceptual category of Athenian comedy. Different sources may favor one over the other, but in the larger chronological sweep both periodizations remain relevant in different ways.

Another conceptual frame that might be employed foregrounds the place in society where awareness and knowledge of Athenian comedy emerges. Nervegna isolates three of these, when she (following a model articulated by Plutarch) discusses 'Menander in public theatres', 'Menander at dinner parties', and 'Menander in schools'.[43] Of course, the delineations between categories are highly permeable, and it is never long before enquiry along one path leads to many forking branches that demonstrate how deeply embedded ideas about Athenian comic theatre can be. These areas do provide some useful clusters for thinking about how comedy 'fits' into a larger cultural history.

Theatre

Though Athenian comedy was disseminated widely through performance in the Hellenistic period, evidence for the continued performance of these plays as plays in the empire is frustratingly hard to produce. Plays were performed, and existed as part of the larger performance traditions widely available. Many plays had been translated and adapted into Latin, generating a new comedic literature, as Greek comedy too continued to re-invent itself; and there are contexts where performance of excerpts of earlier comedies, at times set to music, seems to have emerged. At the same time, the Athenian plays were known, and live performance remains a plausible avenue for the dissemination of that knowledge. Yet we are tantalized by a frustrating lack of unambiguous evidence for reperformance of classical Athenian comedies at this time. Authors seem to assume that plays were still staged, but their assumptions are never unpacked to the degree that the modern theatre historian would like. Plutarch asks rhetorically, 'For what reason is it truly worth while for an educated man to go to the theatre, except for the sake of Menander?' (*Mor.* 854b: τίνος γὰρ ἄξιον ἀληθῶς εἰς θέατρον ἐλθεῖν ἄνδρα πεπαιδευμένον ἢ Μενάνδρου ἕνεκα), and this would seem to suggest that he could see Menander on stage in the first century CE. We are left wondering whether that's true, and how often he had the opportunities to see Menander performed on stage. Which plays were in the repertoire, and were they performed in Chaeronea, in Athens, in Rome, or elsewhere? Plutarch's comment answers nothing; it only points to how much we do not know.

Performances of comedies – both new compositions and restaged classics – did continue, though no imperial comedies survive with the exception of the Lucianic *Swift-foot*, a short piece consisting of fewer than two hundred lines of iambic trimeters that expects a performance context of some sort, but precisely what is not known.[44] Lucian emerges as an author who is especially clear about his debts to earlier comedy. Among imperial authors, Lucian foregrounds his use of Athenian comedy most prominently in his claim to have created a new generic amalgam that blends Old Comic wit and invective with the prose form and intellectual perspective of Platonic dialogue.[45] In a variety of texts, he engages with plots and scenarios recognizably modelled on classical Athenian plays, while also peppering his texts with passing references and allusions to both Old and New Comedy.[46]

Banquets

The presence of Athenian comedy at elite dinner parties is also attested widely.[47] Songs, performances of excerpts (by slaves, by hired performers, or perhaps by distinguished guests), and intellectual discussion could all include comedy in different ways. Athenaeus in his sprawling second-century work *Deipnosophistae* ('The Learned Banqueters') provides an extreme literary model of such a social context in which Athenian comedy is a constant point of reference. Many of the plays he cites are lost, and this fictional example provides a model against which we can hope to measure the more quotidian reality: what might someone attending a *cena*, *conuiuium*, or (Greek) *symposion* be expected to know or recognize from the literature of an earlier era? Dinner parties provided a private venue for comic performance to supplement the public venues described above, but for which documentary evidence does not exist. Additional information comes from these venues themselves, which can feature illustrations of Menander or Menandrian plays.

The most spectacular examples of these illustrations consist of mosaic floors of these dining rooms that represent scenes of actors from specific New Comedies, which at times are helpfully labeled with play title, character name, and even act number.[48] There is a so-called 'House of Menander' in Pompeii,

Mytilene, and Daphne (a suburb of Antioch on the Orontes), with similar mosaics found in Chania (on Crete), Zeugma (like Daphne in modern Turkey), Ulpia Oescus (in Bulgaria), etc. The representation of actors in performance would seem to support a living theatrical tradition. Unfortunately, in at least some of these examples, it can be demonstrated conclusively that the representation dates back to a Hellenistic illustration.[49] The continued interest in performed Menander might indicate his continued presence on Roman stages, but the specifics of the representation leaves the question open. Possibly, details provided in these mosaics are updated by the artist to reflect contemporary performance trends, but we cannot know.

These representations of performed scenes share important features with artistic representations in other media. Throughout the imperial period, artistic representations of masks and other accoutrements of theatre proliferate beyond the immediate reference to the theatrical event: emblems in the form of a comic mask are found on lamps, terracotta figurines show comic slaves seeking sanctuary on an altar,[50] wall paintings are adorned with theatrical scenes or settings; marble sculptures show an actor dressed for comic performance; fine metalwork and carved gems include scenes that reveal the personal attachment a Roman citizen might have with the comic theatre.[51] All of these document the notional importance, even centrality, of the comic theatre in everyday Roman life. Further, they share features with the illustrated tradition of performance of Roman comedy that survives in the manuscripts of Terence (and which also are based on an earlier theatrical tradition).[52] It emerges that thinking in terms of the influence of Athenian comedy on elite Roman dinner parties quickly spreads to other areas of cultural representation, and cannot be easily contained.

Education

A similar story emerges when considering the role of comedy in schools and in scholarship. Both Menander and Aristophanes were known (or at least knowable), as were the works of many of their rivals. Comedy was part of the school curriculum, and its speeches were used to help prepare orators.[53] The language and vocabulary used established a standard by which 'pure Attic' could be determined.[54] Greek literature in the second century CE in particular looked to classical Athens as a standard which should be emulated, and the impact of this interest in Athenian comedy affected all levels of the academic hierarchy. At one end of the scale, students would read Aristophanes (foregrounding *Clouds*, because of its relevance to Socrates); at the other end, learned commentaries were being written on Eupolis' *Taxiarchs* (1st c. CE?; Eupolis fr. 268 K-A, = *P. Oxy.* 2740) and *Prospaltians* (3rd c. CE; Eupolis fr. 259 K-A, = *P. Oxy.* 2813). Plays were being copied, edited, selected, and preserved.

Despite all the energy directed toward maintaining the social and intellectual prominence of classical Greek comedy, precious little has survived to the modern day, and the story of preservation must be paired with a history of loss, a history that must be deduced, as it were, from the negative space around evidence of preservation. Prior to the printing press, texts had to be copied by hand, and the entire corpus of ancient Greek comedy was simply too large to maintain.[55] Some texts were carefully preserved, as seen in the manuscript tradition of Aristophanes' surviving plays; others were excerpted into anthologies, making it difficult to know with certainty how many complete plays were still available to someone such as John Stobaeus, whose late antique *Anthology* includes selections taken from many Menandrian plays and quite a few by lesser-known figures such as Philemon. Galen (*On his own Books,* 17) still had enough material from which to compose separate treatises on political words in Aristophanes, Cratinus and Eupolis respectively, which strongly suggests that some complete plays of all three authors were still available. Yet by the early Byzantine era, it seems that Menander had largely disappeared and Old Comedy was quickly coalescing around a limited number of Aristophanic plays: the so-called Byzantine triad of *Clouds*, *Frogs*, and *Wealth*, with *Knights* also prominently attested. Papyrus evidence, preserved thanks to the dry climate of Egypt though often in a terribly fragmentary state, offers critical insights into the contours of this dwindling of the comic (and, indeed, classical) corpus, and it is from a series of papyrus finds that the extant corpus of Menander has grown enormously over the last century.[56]

Comedy as cultural literacy

These areas alone do not fully describe the place of Athenian comedy in the Roman Empire. As we have seen, none of these groupings creates a discrete set: each spills over, resisting classification and description. But comedy goes beyond this, serving as a familiar point of reference to the authors of the empire. Anecdotes continue to be told about comic actors from the classical period, and the 'idea of Menander' gains a cultural currency that would have been unimaginable to Menander himself. Comedy becomes an essential part of the basic cultural literacy of any educated person, and we should expect that most had heard stories about Aristophanes and Menander, as well as Eupolis, Cratinus, and others, and that they might quote lines in ordinary conversation being only barely aware of their source. When Julius Caesar or Saint Paul quote Menander,[57] it would be easy to assume an intimate familiarity with his plays. In each case, this is possible, but the quotation alone demonstrates no more than the established place lines of comedy might have in everyday speech.

Other imperial authors give clues about the status of comedy in this era via allusions to scripts or performances. The first-century CE literary scholar Quintilian, for example, speaks in glowing terms about the language of both Old Comedy (*antiqua comoedia*, with references to Aristophanes, Eupolis, and Cratinus) and Menander, who seems to have become the icon of New Comedy by this era (*Institutio Oratoria* 10.65–72). Three centuries later, in his self-abusing rant *The Beard-Hater*, the Emperor Julian compares himself to the titular grump of Menander's *Dyscolus* (342a) and later claims that the people of Antioch have heard of philosophers, such as Socrates, Plato, Aristotle and Theophrastus, only from their roles in comic parodies (353b).[58]

Many of the chapters in *Athenian Comedy in the Roman Empire* explore this wider position Old Comedy and New Comedy held in the living imaginations of Roman authors. They build on previous studies[59] and help describe the place comedy occupied in the Roman literary imagination, particularly when plays had transferred from the world of performance to a life beyond the theatre, beyond the dining hall, and beyond the schoolroom. The importance of these works is different for each author considered. Specific studies like these strive to expand the ways that the reception of comedy can be discussed. What emerges, though, is that tracing this history in the lives of Greek comedies, from four to ten centuries after they were first composed and performed, reveals a vast canvas that has only begun to be studied.

Notes

1 We might suspect that *mimiambi* here refer to typical Roman mime (a performance genre that falls outside the scope of this volume) if not for the fact that Pliny elsewhere praises another contemporary mimiambist by likening his verses to those of Callimachus or Herodas (4.3). It was this other poet, the consular Arrius Antoninus, who inspired Pliny's epigraph to this section.

2 Turner 1967 (= *MNC*³ 6EP 1): 'Thick hair, from which ringlets fall down by the side of the neck. Prominently circled staring eyes: they perhaps represent a mask but the lips do not appear to be open. A chiton clasped at the right shoulder, reaches below the knee and is caught up by a girdle. The bare right arm is bent upward at the elbow

and rests, with thumb extended, lightly on the chest. A cloak or scarf hangs down the left side from the shoulder, and a gathering of it is perhaps caught up by the left arm at waist level' (1967: 180).
3 There is a third papyrus from an illustrated Menander edition, *PSI* VII 847; see Bartoletti 1962 and Dedoussi 1980.
4 On the earliest history of comedy in Athens, see Storey 2010.
5 For a reassessment of the traditional notion that only three plays, rather than five, were presented annually at the Dionysia during the Peloponnesian War, see Csapo and Slater 1995: 107 and 135, where they print *P. Oxy.* 2737, fr. 1, col ii, 1–17, which claims that Plato Comicus' *Theater Police* (produced sometime between 427 and 413) placed fourth at the Dionysia.
6 Aristotle (*Poetics* 1449a-b) claims that the origins of comedy are not clearly known, but he points to Epicharmus and the shadowy Phormis as Sicilian examples of comic playwrights who preceded the rise of comedy in Athens. For the most recent discussions of early Sicilian comedy, see Bosher 2014; for Aristotle on comedy see Janko 1984 and Watson 2012; for performances at deme theaters in Attica, see Makres 2013: 81–6 and Paga 2010; for inscriptional evidence of comic performances outside Attica, see Csapo and Slater 1995: 44–9; for the iconographic evidence, see Csapo 2014, Taplin 1993, Nervegna 2014b and Slater 2014; for theatrical performances in Attica at the Rural Dionysia and Anthesteria, see Csapo and Slater 1995: 121–38.
7 Csapo and Slater 1995: 351–2 discuss the evidence for the recruitment of citizen choreuts (members of a chorus); as they show, participation in a chorus seems to have been considered a burden, and the *khorēgos* had a surprising range of coercive powers that he could use to ensure participation.
8 Henderson 2008; Most et al. 2013–; Nesselrath 2010; Olson 2007; Rusten 2011; Storey 2011. In addition, Storey 2003 and Bakola 2010 provide important monographs on Eupolis and Cratinus, respectively.
9 Mills and Olson 2012.
10 Dobrov 1995, Harvey and Wilkins 2000 and Biles 2014 exemplify this new potential for studying Athenian comedy beyond the few playwrights whose works survive intact.
11 Platonius (pp. 2–3 Koster = Storey 2011: vol. 1, 8–9). Story 2011: vol. 1, xvii succinctly presents the various ancient periodizations of Athenian comedy.
12 Csapo 2000: 121. For further debunking of the legend about Eupolis' death, see Storey 2003: 56–7.
13 Nesselrath 1990 offers the most thorough analysis of this period. He surveys the ancient and modern evidence (1–64) and argues for a temporal definition of Middle Comedy spanning 380–50 BCE, while admitting that the preceding years had led up to this period gradually (333–8). Csapo 2000 argues for a more gradualist

perspective in which elements of Old, Middle and New Comedy can be found throughout the entire period of classical Athenian comedy. Csapo and Slater 1995, e.g. 404, extend the period of Middle Comedy to *c.* 320. Arnott 2010, Shaw 2014: 106–22, and Sidwell 2014a: 60–78, offer the most updated discussions. On Alexis, see Arnott 1996a. See Rusten 2011: 434–576 for translations of the comic fragments from this period.

14 A similar process can be charted for virtually every other literary genre as well, since the surviving body of fourth-century Athenian texts show a high degree of cross-referentiality.

15 Clay 1975 discusses the theatrical aspects of *Symposium*; Platter 2014 analyzes Plato's engagement with Aristophanes.

16 We also hear of an Aristotlelian *Nikai*, 'Victories', though it is never cited in antiquity. Blum 1991: 31 suggests that the *Nikai* may have been an appendix to the *Didaskaliai*.

17 See Watson 2012 for a thorough discussion of Aristotle and comedy, and Janko 1984 on the second book of *Poetics*.

18 For a quick overview of the inscriptional evidence, especially the *Fasti* (*IG* II^2 2318), the Victors Lists (*IG* II^2 2325) and the *Didaskaliae* (*IG* II^2 2319–23a), see Csapo and Slater 1995 40–44; for a thorough discussion see Mills and Olson 2012.

19 Storey 2003: 4.

20 On fifth-century reperformance of tragedy, see Lamari 2014 and Biles 2006/7. Taplin 1999: 38 discusses early revivals of tragedy outside Athens. The reperformance of Aristophanes' *Frogs* is attested in the play's hypothesis (1c Dover). *Life of Aeschylus* (12) claims that the Athenians voted to restage his plays soon after his death in about 456 and that Aeschylus himself restaged *Persians* in Sicily at the request of Hieron of Syracuse. This second performance of *Persians* must have occurred between 472, when the play was debuted in Athens, and 467, when Hieron died. Bosher 2012 argues for the heterodox position that *Persians* was performed for the first time in Syracuse.

21 Shaw 2014: 123–48.

22 Marshall 2000.

23 Nervegna 2013 and Lape 2004 provide thorough and updated assessments of major issues relating to Menander. See Rusten 2011: 601–25, 660–704 for translations of the fragments of Menander's rivals (with valuable discussion still at Webster 1953: 125–83, 205–32).

24 The most recent major discovery was in 2003, when a 400-line palimpsest (that is, a text that remains partially visible after having been erased to make space for a different text) was found in the Vatican Library. The text, which is still unpublished, contains parts of *Dyscolos* and a previously unknown play called *Titthe* ('The Wetnurse').

25 Petridis 2010: 101: 'Tragedy seems to operate within New Comedy in ways comparable to the workings of epic myth in tragedy itself.' The foundational work on

Menander and tragedy is Katsouris 1975, updated by Petridis 2010 and Omitowoju 2010. Aristophanic plays such as *Acharnians, Thesmophoriazusae* and, above all, *Frogs* also use tragedy as a key point of reference, though Old Comedy often seems to be fifth-century tragedy's rival, whereas New Comedy is its heir.

26 Bruzzese 2011 is now the standard resource for all matters relating to Philemon.
27 Le Guen 2014: 362–7.
28 See Mills and Olson 2012: 76 for an assessment of the text; they conclude that the final entries on *IG* II^2 2323, which may extend as far as the 130s, must derive from the last years of the Dionysia's existence as a venue for dramatic competitions.
29 For Hellenistic restagings of comedies, see Nervegna 2013: 65–70 and Summa 2008.
30 Nervegna 2014a is structured around the claim that the 'ancient contexts of reception of Greek comedy' (387) were the theater, dinner party and school (following the structure of chapters in Nervegna 2013, which offers a focused treatment of the ancient reception of Menander). As this volume shows, the idea of artistic influence does not fit well with any of these three categories.
31 Wilson 2014a: 657.
32 Aristophanes of Byzantium ranked Menander second only to Homer (*IG* XIV.1183c = Test. 170c K-A); see also Statius *Silv.* 2.1.113–19 and Martial 14.87, 183, 184). For the pairing of Menander with Euripides, see Nervegna 2013: 9–10 and 110–16. For Menander's place in Egyptian education (the region from which papyrus finds permit the most detailed insights), see Cribiore 2001: 197–201.
33 For the collection of Menandrian maxims as a discrete corpus, see Liapis 2002 and Pernigotti 2008. Nervegna 2013: 201–51 and 2014a: 398–402 assesses the curricular role of classical comedy. Wilson 2014b: 427 notes that Aristophanes largely supplants Menander's place in the standard curriculum in late antiquity.
34 Nervegna 2014a: 395–8 discusses the literary sources for comic performances at dinner parties whereas at 2013: 120–200 she places much more emphasis on the host's theatrical décor. Hunter 2014: 379–84 addresses the social implications of Plutarch's comments about appropriate entertainments for dinner parties (*Sympotic Questions* 7.8). Tronchin 2012a and 2012b raises a cautionary issue – namely that Roman décor tended to emphasize eclecticism over spotlighting specific pieces. This suggests that we need to proceed cautiously when drawing conclusions about the presence of New Comic visual motifs (and the absence of Old Comic motifs) in Roman homes. At the very least, however, we can recognize that the aesthetic of New Comedy was among the many styles preferred by Roman tastes.
35 For early Hellenistic scholarship on comedy, see Lowe 2013.
36 For more on adaptations of Greek comedy at Rome, see Brown 2013, Petrides 2014, Fontaine 2014a, 2014b, and Ruffell 2014.
37 On Theophrastus and Menander, see Fortenbaugh 2003: 281–326; for a thorough analysis of Theophrastus' *Characters*, see Diggle 2004 and Millett 2007.

38 Kutzko 2012.
39 On Horace's claim, see Ruffell 2014b, Sidwell 2014b, Sommerstein 2011 and Nelson Hawkins, chapter 3 in this volume.
40 On pantomime, see Garelli 2007, Lada-Richards 2007, Hall and Wyles 2008, and Webb 2008: 58–94.
41 On the connection between Hellenistic and Roman mimes, see Panayotakis 2014; and for the most famous author of Roman mimes, Decimus Laberius, see Panayotakis 2010.
42 For an overview of Reception Studies as a sub-discipline of Classics, see Hardwick 2003.
43 Nervegna 2013: 63–119; 120–200; 201–51. See also Marshall, chapter 6 in this volume, for a discussion of Plutarch, *Mor*. 854 A-B.
44 If Lucian is not the author of *Swift-Foot*, it may have been composed by the fourth-century CE orator Libanius or his student Acacius. On this text see Zimmermann 1909.
45 See, for example, his discussion of the relationship between dialogue and comedy in his owns works (*Prometheus* 5; *Fisherman* 33).
46 For example, his reference to Aristophanes' *Clouds* (*True History* 1.25) and his introduction of a Menanderian prologue named Elenchus as a ventriloquized narrator (*False Critic* 4).
47 Jones 1991, 1993.
48 MNC^3 vol. 1: 85–96 provides an overview of these illustrations, with individual entries, esp. 6CM 1–2, 6DM 1–3, 6FM 1–2 and 5NP 1–30 (and see Green forthcoming). The bibliographies on the mosaics are extensive: see esp. Charitonidis, Kahil, and Ginouvès 1970, Gutzwiller and Çelik 2012 and Nervegna 2013: 136–69, and their bibliographies. Other studies include Abadie-Reynal and Darmon 2003, Balty 1995, 2004, Berczelly 1988, Bieber and Redenwaldt 1911, Bruneau 1970, 1972, 1984, Campbell 1988, Campbell, Ergeç, and Csapo 1998, Campbell and Stillwell 1941, Çelik 2009, Darmon 2004, Friend 1941, Görkay, Linant de Bellefonds, and Prioux 2006, Kahil 1970, Marx 1930, Nervegna 2010, Önal 2002, 2009, and see Dunbabin 2006, 2007, 2008, and 2010.
49 See Green 1985, Csapo 1997, 1999, 2014: 116–26, Bruneau 1999, Ferrari 2004.
50 See Webster 1995: vol. 1, 229–35.
51 Green 1994 105–71.
52 Wright 2006.
53 For education practices generally, see Morgan 1998 and Cribiore 2001.
54 Tribulato 2014.
55 Zimmerman 1998: 9 tabulates more than 2,300 plays by 256 known comic playwrights. Such specific figures are open to suspicion but they usefully provide a rough estimate of the overall number of plays that existed in textual form.

56 Bathrellou 2014 documents the many papyrus discoveries published over 40 years. For more on the history of the comic corpus, see Wilson 2014b for an overview; Nesselrath 2010 on fragments; Sommerstein 2010 and Wilson 2007 on Aristophanes; Blume 2010 and Handley 2011 on Menander.
57 Caesar: ἀνερρίφθω κύβος (Plutarch, *Pompey* 60.2.9, *Caesar* 32.6; Menander fr. 64 K-A; cf. Suetonius, *Julius Caesar* 32). Paul: φθείρουσιν ἤθη χρησθ' ὁμιλίαι κακαί (1 Corinthians 15: 33; Menander fr. 165 K-A).
58 On this passage, see Hawkins 2014: 291.
59 Fantham 1984, Bowie 2007, and Karavas and Vix 2014 are essential starting points. For an analysis of comic allusions in Greek novels, see Trzaskoma 2009, 2010, 2011, and Höschele 2014. Nesselrath 2014: 677–78 traces the influence of Greek comedy on the works of Clement of Alexandria.

2

Juvenal and the Revival of Greek New Comedy at Rome

Mathias Hanses*

This chapter examines how Juvenal's *Satires* respond to Greek New Comedy's enduring presence at Roman public festivals as well as to Menander's lasting literary influence on private recitations of new Latin poetry. I posit that Juvenal presents his poems as reacting to an ongoing influx of Greek comedic actors into the imperial capital.[1] These performers prefer New Comedy, in the original Greek, and especially the plays of Menander, which they stage in front of rapt mass audiences. According to Juvenal, their shows' extravagance has spoiled Rome and its traditional theatrical practices in two ways. First, the actors' excess has turned comedic performances from a wholesome experience into a corrupting influence. Second, the depravity has spread from the stages into the streets of Rome, with the ironic effect that comedy's comparatively innocent scripts – which were still being read, written, and recited by the elite – now no longer provide an adequate 'mirror of life' (the standard metaphor for the genre's role in ancient society).[2] New Comedy therefore needs to be updated, at least in its Latin and written form.

Accordingly, Juvenal's *Satires* set out to rejuvenate the Roman, literary branch of the Menandrian tradition through an infusion of elements recalling competing theatrical genres. The result is a literary version of Rome's varied festivals that merges New Comedy with elements not just from tragedy, epic, and elegy,[3] but also, and most prominently, the mime. The place that Juvenal's new, more 'mimic' literary comedy holds in the New Comic tradition is best understood as a re-boot of the *fabula togata*. Like the *Satires*, the *togata* combined an Italian setting with a distinctly Roman perspective at times quite hostile to the Greeks. Nevertheless, the genre remained firmly committed to its New Comic roots and claimed Menander as its ancestor.

Of course, as an appropriation, modernization, and Romanization of Menander that relies heavily on profanities borrowed from the stage, Juvenal's mime-infused literary *togata* avails itself of some of the same novel features that it criticizes. Considering that the satirist ultimately advocates a return to Latin comedy's Republican roots, this approach is hypocritical, and, I argue, deliberately so. It is through this and other obvious contradictions that Juvenal characterizes his satiric *persona* as the new *pater durus*, an exaggeratedly angry critic of contemporary *mores* whom we are not supposed to take entirely seriously.

I. Greek actors and Roman festivals

The Greek *comoedi*'s supposedly detrimental influence on Roman affairs is on fullest display in *Satire* 3. Umbricius, a stereotypically angry old man, leaves Rome in part because the Greeks that populate the city and its stages are so good at feigning emotion that Roman flatterers no longer stand a chance of advancement (Juv. 3.92–100):

> haec eadem licet et nobis laudare, sed illis
> creditur. an melior cum Thaida sustinet aut cum
> uxorem comoedus agit uel Dorida nullo
> cultam palliolo? mulier nempe ipsa uidetur,
> non persona, loqui: uacua et plana omnia dicas
> infra uentriculum et tenui distantia rima.
> nec tamen Antiochus nec erit mirabilis illic
> aut Stratocles aut cum molli Demetrius Haemo:
> natio comoeda est.

> We can praise the same things, but they are believed. Or is there a comic actor who is better [than the Greeks] when he stars as Thais or plays a wife or Doris who took off her *pallium*-cloak?[4] It really seems to be a woman, not a masked actor [*persona*], who is speaking. You would say that everything below the belly is empty and smooth and split by a fine crack. And yet, Antiochus will not be marveled at there [=in Greece] nor Stratocles nor Demetrius and effeminate Haemus. The whole tribe is a comedic troupe.[5]

According to Umbricius, Greek comedic actors have completely upstaged the local Roman talent. They specialize in New Comedy, as is apparent both from the performance practices Umbricius mentions (95 *palliolo*, as in *fabula palliata*; 3.96 *persona*)[6] and from the characters these actors play. Thais was the most famous incarnation of the Menandrian prostitute,[7] and she also appears in Terence's *Eunuchus*. The wife was another standard female type, as was the maidservant, who is called Doris in Menander's *Perikeiromenē*, *Kolax*, and

Enchiridion and here apparently takes off her *pallium*-cloak for work.[8] Antiochus, Stratocles, Demetrius, and Haemus infuse these New Comic roles with such realism that they take the city's audiences by storm, but in Greece, nobody would bat an eye at their performances. After all, everybody in the Greek East is a born liar and actor; 'the whole tribe is a comedic troupe' (3.100).

The problem that Umbricius sees in these Greek actors' success lies not only in their deceptiveness, but also in their lack of manliness. While Roman performers managed to preserve their masculinity when they played Doris or Thais in the Latin versions of Menander's plays, the foreign avant-garde's effeminate nature (e.g. 3.99 *molli*) makes the audience forget that there is a man behind the woman's mask. The *comoedi*'s softness thus turns the familiar plays into an unsavory experience that is liable to corrupt their audiences. This latter concern comes into sharper focus as Umbricius describes the life he envisions for himself in the countryside (3.168–78):

fictilibus cenare pudet, quod turpe negabis
translatus subito ad Marsos mensamque Sabellam
contentusque illic ueneto duroque cucullo.
pars magna Italiae est, si uerum admittimus, in qua
nemo togam sumit nisi mortuus. ipsa dierum
festorum herboso colitur si quando theatro
maiestas tandemque redit ad pulpita notum
exodium, cum personae pallentis hiatum
in gremio matris formidat rusticus infans,
aequales habitus illic similesque uidebis
orchestram et populum.

It is embarrassing to eat off clay dishes [at Rome], but you will deny this emphatically if you are suddenly spirited away to the Marsi or a Sabellan table, content there with a rough blue hood. There is a big part of Italy where, if we are honest, no one dons a toga except for his funeral. Even if at some point the grandeur of festival days is celebrated in the grassy theater and a well-known farce has returned to the boards, when the rustic child in the mother's lap gets scared of the pale mask's gaping mouth, you will see there the same and similar clothes worn in the *orchestra* and in the audience.

In Umbricius' rural Italy, the theater remains what it used to be in the days of Plautus, Terence, and Afranius. City audiences of the early Empire flock to the stone theaters of Pompey, Balbus, and Marcellus, but in the countryside, the stages are still wooden and a grassy hill provides the tiers. Old-style Atellan farces are still put on here (3.174–5 *notum / exodium*),⁹ and even the actors' masks retain their traditional effect. Rome's Greek performers are so malleable that they merge with the *persona* of Doris or Thais (3.95–6), but Italic masks are pale and rigid, separate from the actor. As a result, the actors intimidate the children in the audience with their severity rather than corrupt them with their effeminacy (3.175–6).¹⁰ Due to this positive influence, the rural Italians who populate Umbricius' fantasy recall the 'good old days' both onstage and off. The actors' modest garb is the same as the audience's (3.177–8), and Umbricius imagines himself at the table of an Italic household wearing the blue hood that marked a character as poor in Roman comedy (3.169–70). By contrast, the depraved performances of Greek comedy put on at Rome have contributed to turning the city's population into luxury-loving reprobates, as Umbricius laments throughout.

Umbricius' complaints about the Greek *comoedi*'s detrimental influence on city life presuppose a theory about the stage's ability to shape an audience's character that ultimately harks back to Books Two, Three, and Ten of Plato's *Republic* (376e–403c and 595a–608b).¹¹ Restrained forms of mimesis have a positive effect on the theatergoer's personality, whereas extravagant portrayals of (and by) questionable characters achieve the opposite. Of course, this view does not account for the inverse possibility that the audience's tastes may be driving performance trends. Unlike Umbricius, the reader of the *Satires* is aware of this alternative explanation. After all, old Umbricius has been a flatterer for longer than the Greek newcomers he criticizes (e.g. 3.92 *haec eadem licet et nobis laudare*, translated above), albeit an inferior specimen. In the end, art may simply be imitating life. Or, at the very least, the depravities of stage and street are mutually reinforcing.

Although this inherent irony undercuts Umbricius' credibility (as do the poetics of the satiric genre), *Satire* 3 does reflect (a version of) reality. The classics of Greco-Roman New Comedy were indeed still being staged at Rome's theatrical festivals.¹² Already in the late Republic, these performances had increased in spectacularity. For example, the opening of the Theater of Pompey in 55 BCE featured Roman comedies staged in a manner appropriate to 'modern' tastes.¹³ This led Cicero to complain that the exaggerated use of extras, animals, and expensive stage props spoiled all the fun (Cic. *Fam.* 7.1). Roughly contemporary, spectacular structures that may have hosted comedies include the (temporary) theater of Scaurus, featuring a stage of marble, glass, and gilded wood (58 BCE; Plin. *HN* 36.5.50, 36.24.113–15). The amphitheater of Curio of 52 BCE was constructed by joining together two moveable wooden theaters, both of which hosted dramatic *ludi* (52 BCE; Plin. *HN* 36.24.116–20). A few decades later, Horace lamented that his contemporaries continued to cram into the city's growing number of theaters for re-performances of plays by Plautus, Caecilius, and Terence (Hor. *Epist*. 2.1.50–62).[14] The trend continued at least to the turn of the second century.[15] Terence's *Eunuchus* was in fact so popular with Flavian audiences that Juvenal's contemporary Quintilian cites the play four times and describes the tones of voice, hand gestures, and nods that actors usually apply in its performance (Quint. 9.2.11, 9.3.16, 9.4.140, 11.3.182).[16]

Even more to Umbricius' point, Greek *comoedi* really did gradually 'Hellenize' these performances. In Greece and southern Italy, many playwrights continued to enter their own brand new New Comic pieces into competitions at festivals, and the material and papyrological record testifies to a strong commitment to Greek New Comedy in revived performances.[17] Nervegna recently demonstrated that the actors troupes' preference for Menander helped turn him into the provinces' most frequently staged comic author (comparable to his tragic 'colleague' Euripides) and contributed to his canonization as *the* representative of all New Comedy.[18] By the reign of Domitian, after a century of stabilized cultural exchanges between East and West under the *Pax Romana*, this theatrical trend had taken root in the city of Rome, along with the performers who participated in it.[19]

The inclusion of Greek New Comedy at the Roman *ludi* likely occurred gradually,[20] but by Quintilian's day, performances of Menandrian classics seem to have been commonplace. At *Institutio oratoria* 11.3.91, the rhetor condemns comic actors' excessive use of different voices:

> cum mihi comoedi quoque pessime facere uideantur, quod, etiamsi iuuenem agant, cum tamen in expositione aut senis sermo, ut in Hydriae prologo, aut mulieris, ut in Georgo, incidit, tremula uel effeminata uoce pronuntiant.

> Comic actors seem to me to be behaving really badly when they – even though they are playing a young man – speak in a trembling and effeminate voice when over the course of an exposition the talk of an old man comes up, as in the prologue to the *Hydria*, or of a woman, as in the *Georgos*.

Quintilian's dislike for actors changing voices in mid-speech when reporting another's words could stem only from performance. It is significant that he takes his examples from Menander's *Hydria* and *Georgos* without naming the playwright. He assumes matter-of-factly that his readers have seen these Greek New Comedies staged, and that they can identify their author. Quintilian also confirms that two of the actors mentioned by Umbricius regularly portrayed the standard types of Greco-Roman comedy, not in the relative privacy of an aristocrat's house, but at large-scale public events (Quint. 11.3.178–80). The elite attended these performances as well (178 *maximos actores comoediarum, Demetrium et Stratoclea, placere diversis uirtutibus vidimus*).[21] Demetrius excelled at playing divinities, young men, lenient fathers, good slaves, wives, and stern old women, and he was famous for grand gestures and exclamations 'for the theatrical audience's sake' (179 *theatri causa*). Stratocles played more vibrant characters, like angry old men, trickster slaves, parasites, and pimps, and his characteristic gait and swiftness reportedly suited him. So did his laughter, which sometimes did not fit the mask (*persona*) he was wearing, but Stratocles laughed anyway because he knew the public's taste (180 [*risum*] *populo dabat*).

Pointing out that Greeks were less likely to learn Latin than Romans were to learn Greek, Nervegna argues that Demetrius and Stratocles performed New Comedy in the original.[22] While we cannot be sure that this is true in the two actors' specific case, it is clear from Quintilian's comments that there really was a demonstrable trend to put on Greek New Comedies at Rome. This fashion can help explain the oft-noted but unexplained fact that early-imperial Latin poets mention Menander more frequently than Plautus and Terence.[23] While we have seen that Roman comedy did not fall out of favor, it seems that at least among the elite, Menander was growing *even more* popular than his Latin translators. The theatrical troupes' taste for *the* classic of Greek New Comedy seems in this case to have influenced the Roman elite's scholarly, literary, and educational preferences.[24] The shows also played to the Roman aristocracy's existing interest in the literary trends of the Greek-speaking provinces, where fifth- and fourth-century Athenian authors and playwrights were *en vogue*.[25] Quintilian himself notes the rise in Menander's relative popularity among his upper-class peers, remarking that Romans of the Republic preferred Plautus, Caecilius, Terence, and Afranius, while he believes that a far better education can be gained from a reading of their Athenian models (10.1.99–100). After all, Menander provides an 'image of life' (10.1.69 *omnem uitae imaginem expressit*), whereas Roman comedy 'limps' (10.1.99 *in comoedia maxime claudicamus*) behind the Attic playwright as 'barely a pale shadow' (10.1.100 *uix leuem consequimur umbram*).

Quintilian's characterization of Roman comedy as a mere shadow, or *umbra*, of its Athenian self brings us back to Juvenal's Umbricius. As the old man with the talking name departs from a city that increasingly favors Greek New Comedy, he turns into a personification of the genre's 'lame' Latin counterpart. From the moment he first says his good-byes, even his appearance is drawn into Juvenal's theatrical emphasis (Juv. 3.26–9):

> dum noua canities, dum prima et recta senectus,
> dum superest Lachesi quod torqueat et pedibus me
> porto meis nullo dextram subeunte bacillo,
> cedamus patria.

> While my grey hair is still new, while I am still in the first and upright stage of old age, while Lachesis still has threads to spin and I support myself on my own feet, not with a walking stick propping up my right hand, let us leave the fatherland.

Umbricius has been described as a reincarnation of the Roman comic parasite, a modern-day Curculio who – like his Plautine alter ego – laments the arrival of *Graeci palliati* competing for the attention of rich patrons.[26] The lines quoted just above suggest that this parasite leaves Rome as he is on the brink of turning into a *pater durus*, the angry stock type who prefers the old ways to the point of ridiculousness. On the stage, this character is white-haired and employs a cane. Umbricius may not need a walking stick yet, but the more he rants about his contemporaries, the more he runs the risk of turning into a *pater durus* in both attitude and looks. Like Roman comedy, Umbricius is acquiring a limp, and when compared to his Greek competitors, he too is reduced to a mere shadow. As a stand-in for 'old-style' Roman comedy, Umbricius is forced to leave.

Yet in his parting words Umbricius invites Juvenal to stop by at times and read him his *Satires* (3.321–2). There is a passing of the baton here, from Roman comedy to Juvenal's genre of choice. Juvenal's temper is not much different from Umbricius',[27] and he remains at Rome as the *pater durus*'s next incarnation, especially in the type's combination of traditional values with obviously exaggerated anger.[28] It is through the eyes of this re-booted *persona* that a new generation of readers will be able to glance into a 'mirror of life'.

II. Comic scripts, elite recitations, and a new *togata*

Juvenal's response to recent theatrical developments presupposes a distinction between comedic scripts as reading materials and their staging in Roman theaters.[29] Comedy's performative side – its music, costumes, props, sets, and apparently also the actors' aptitude at sexual innuendo however deplorable to the satirist – contributed to the genre's continued success on the city's stages, in Latin as well as increasingly in Greek. Quintilian, for one, implies that Greek scripts fared well too, recommending a thorough reading of Menander to his students. The texts of Roman comedy present a different picture, or so Juvenal implies.

The scripts of Plautine and Terentian classics still circulated in Juvenal's day, but while they were going to generate renewed interest later in the second century CE,[30] we have seen that they had at this point fallen behind Menander. In a similar trend, a steady but apparently not overwhelming number of the city's literati continued to pen new *palliata* plots and read them to colleagues, aficionados, and patrons mostly at private, salon-style recitations.[31] For example, Cicero's famous defendant Archias planned on composing a Latin comedy (Cic. *Att.* 1.16.15 *Caecilianam fabulam*), though it is not clear if he followed through. Horace's contemporary Fundanius wrote comedic scripts (Hor. *Sat.* 1.10.40–2 *libellos*; see also 2.8), as did an acquaintance of the Younger Pliny: The poet Vergilius Romanus composed and recited an Old Comedy featuring real-life Romans (including Pliny himself), several *mimiambi*, as well as 'comedies imitating Menander and others of the same age – you should number them among those of Plautus and Terence' (Plin. *Ep.* 6.21.4 *scripsit comoedias Menandrum aliosque eiusdem aetatis aemulatus; licet has inter Plautinas Terentianasque numeres*).

This passage once again attests to Menander's figurehead status and suggests that at least a small number of Roman intellectuals continued to follow their Greek counterparts' example of writing new New Comedies.[32] What is more, the 'Plautine and Terentian' plays of Vergilius Romanus seem at first sight to have been *palliatae*, but we should note that his 'Old Comedy' was set in Rome. Perhaps some of his Latin scripts in the style of Menander, Plautus, and Terence were as well. As such, they would be more appropriately labeled *togatae*. After all, grammarians and literary critics alike thought of this 'comedy in Italian dress' as the *palliata*'s Western equivalent and grouped both genres under the joint label of Roman *comoedia* (e.g. Euanthius, *De fabula* 3.5). *Togatae* were apparently more solemn than *palliatae* (Sen. *Ep.* 8.8; 89.7; Donat. on Ter. *Eun.* 57), focused on specifically Italian trades, and were critical of Greek and other foreign influences on Roman affairs (Afranius, *Togata* 232–3, 284 R³; Titinius, *Togata* 85, 104, 175 R³). Nevertheless, they retained many stock types of Menandrian fame, including parasites, pimps, and (Greek) prostitutes, at least one of whom was called Thais (Afranius, *Togata* 133, 136, 189–91 R³). The plots were similar to Greek New Comedy (with an added emphasis on marriage), and Afranius, the most famous writer of *togatae*, explicitly highlighted his reliance on Menander and Terence (among others; see Afranius, *Togata* 29 R³; Suet. *Vita Ter.* 7; Macrob. *Sat.* 6.1.4 = Afranius, *Togata* 25–8 R³). Accordingly, later readers thought that Afranius' *toga(ta)* would have fit Menander (Hor. *Epist.* 2.1.57; compare Cic. *Fin.* 1.7) and considered his plays a distinctly Roman addition to the New Comic tradition.³³

While Juvenal/Umbricius declares comedic performances too lascivious an influence on contemporary affairs, the satirist finds the Romans' comedic scripts too boring to justify their continued presence at elite recitations. In spite of some apparent similarities between *togatae* and *Satires* (e.g. stock types, Italian setting, xenophobia), he includes these comedies in a list of texts that his contemporaries enjoy writing and that he can no longer stand: 'Will I forever be only a listener? Will I never get revenge, even though I have so often been tortured by the *Theseid* of hoarse Cordus? Will this one have recited his *togatae* with impunity, and that one his elegies?' (Juv. 1.1–4 *semper ego auditor tantum? numquamne reponam / uexatus totiens rauci Theseide Cordi? / inpune ergo mihi recitauerit ille togatas, / hic elegos?*)

It is tempting to speculate that an author like Vergilius Romanus was the target of Juvenal's attack. Of course, Juvenalian scholars usually argue that the *togata* had long since fallen out of literary favor.³⁴ However, Juvenal criticizes this genre in the same breath as Flavian epic, and it seems unlikely that the one still existed while the other did not. It is true that we lack further evidence for contemporary *togata* writers, but the classics of the genre had remained popular among educated men at least as late as the Augustan era (Hor. *Epist.* 2.1.57). The last attested staging of Afranius' *Incendium* occurred at the emperor Nero's *ludi maximi*.³⁵ On this occasion, the stage building was stocked with luxurious household goods, and when it was set on fire, the actors' scrambling to save valuable pieces turned into part of the attraction (Suet. *Ner.* 11.2). After such a notable event, the *togata* is more likely to have fallen out of fashion gradually, rather than immediately. Whoever was reciting *togatae* in Juvenal's presence was probably beating a dying rather than a dead horse.

The prominent mention of *togatae* at the first satire's recitation of new poetry suggests that Juvenal sees his poems as improving upon literary comedies in the Menandrian tradition, especially those set in Italy and written in Latin.³⁶ After all, the other genres mentioned in this context (epic, elegy, tragedy) have long been shown to exert a formative influence on Juvenal's poetics,³⁷ and the satirist expresses his wish to supplant them all. Like contemporary scripts of Roman comedy, the *Satires* are meant for recitation, and as Juvenal points out early on, 'whatever men do – vows, fear, wrath, lust, joys, running back and forth – is the fodder of my little book' (1.85–6 *quidquid agunt homines, votum, timor, ira, uoluptas / gaudia, discursus, nostri farrago libelli est*). The satirist here appropriates the 'mirror of life' metaphor, usually applied to comedy, for the genre of satire. He does so in language recalling the prologue of Terence's *Eunuchus* (35–40), where the playwright describes comedy as dealing in various stock types – like the hapless slave, running about unsure what to do (*currentem seruum*) – as well as deception, love, hate, and suspicion (*amare, odisse, suspicari*).[38]

Juvenal's reclaiming and refashioning of Roman comedy consists in the addition of new types to the comedic cast. He retains the prostitutes, pimps, and parasites of the original, tweaks them slightly, and adds a fresh set of moralizers, informers, and hypocritical foreigners to the *dramatis personae*. Ironically, this update of literary Latin comedy includes elements from en-vogue genres like the mime, which share many features with the times' supposedly lewd performances of Greek New Comedy.[39] The satirist thereby undercuts his credibility. He calls the scripts of Roman comedy obsolete even as he advocates for a return to their traditional decorum. He condemns the transgressions of the stage in a text that itself relishes obscenity. In this manner, Juvenal emerges as his colorful ensemble's new *pater durus*, a character who, in his original incarnation, reprimanded a new generation for indulging in the same liberties he enjoyed when he was himself growing up.[40]

The contrast between Roman comedy's supposedly unsatisfying scripts, now no longer able to adequately reflect the city's increasingly debauched realities, and the *Satires'* new, mime-based approach, (re-)surfaces early in the first poem. The satirist watches his fellow Romans in a busy street. Here, 'the effeminate eunuch [who] takes a wife' (1.22 *tener uxorem ducat spado*) tops the list of Juvenal's countrymen who make it difficult not to write satire (1.30). The eunuch's marriage would have reminded imperial readers of Terence's *Eunuchus*, a play that has a young man dress up as a *castratus* so he can sneak into a brothel, rape the woman he is in love with, and ultimately marry her. We noted above that performances of the *Eunuchus* remained popular with Flavian audiences, so this Republican comedy could have provided an apt model for satiric commentary on imperial *mores*. However, while the *Eunuchus'* influence on the satiric scenario is evident, there is more to the story. The play's rape plot is offensive to modern audiences, but whatever the extravagances of contemporary performances, the script's ending in a 'functional' marriage probably struck Roman readers as wholesome.[41] By contrast, Juvenal is not talking about a costumed trickster in pursuit of what will ultimately turn out to be a suitable match, but about an actual *spado* who marries in spite of his inability to perform sexually. Life in the imperial capital no longer recalls a well-structured Republican comedy with a few indiscretions lining the path to respectable citizenship. There is no happy ending here, just absurdity and transgression.

In the mime, the stage provides a parallel for precisely this kind of travesty. Shedding the masks of Greco-Roman comedy and abandoning its scripts in favor of a stronger improvisational component, some mimes made the familiar stock types outright obscene. Many of these plays featured pimps, prostitutes, and tricksters, but also ample nudity and brutality. The *Laureolus*, for example, culminated in a crucifixion on stage.[42] Another popular scenario was the 'adultery mime'. Here, wives were caught cheating, and the plays starred real-life prostitutes who not only stripped, but even acted out these sexual scenarios on the stage. They thereby actually and gleefully broke the taboos that comedy's characters had only played with. After all, the institution of marriage remained intact in the vast majority of Plautine and Terentian plays.[43]

Pointing out that similarities to the mime are not fortuitous, Juvenal's list continues from the married eunuch to an informer so terrifying that even infamous Domitianic snitches like Baebius Massa and Mettius Carus fear him and appease him with gifts 'like Thymele secretly sent by fearful Latinus' (1.36 *ut a trepido Thymele summissa Latino*). We know that Latinus was a popular mime actor, and that Thymele was his 'leading lady'.[44] This means that Juvenal's two scared informers act like a character in a farce who sends his prostitute girlfriend to win over an enemy.[45] We thus find here another example of the transgressions of the stage rubbing off on society, and vice versa, to a point where the rules of traditional comedic scripts no longer apply.

This theatrical theme reappears in *Satires* 4 and 5. Here, Juvenal develops his new mimic stock types more fully, and in a setting uniquely appropriate to an updated comedy: the banquet. The humorous plays of Rome and Athens commonly culminated in such celebrations, and so does the first book of Juvenal's *Satires*. In the fourth poem, we read of the courtiers' dinner preparations, while in the fifth, it is the everyday client who is seeking a place at the table. The latter character revisits the comedic parasite. In traditional comedy, the patronage system still worked to the extent that the parasite was rewarded with copious amounts of food for his services. In contemporary Rome, every single citizen has been reduced to the state of a parasite – he even fathers 'baby parasites' (5.145 *parasitus . . . infans*) – and the system is broken.[46] The patrons indulge, but are increasingly unwilling to provide for their clients. If the trend continues, 'there will be no parasite anymore' (1.139 *nullus iam parasitus erit*). The reason why patrons starve their clients at dinner is, again, their desire to outdo at home what they watch on the stage. A real-life guest's 'whining gullet' is even more entertaining than 'any comedy or mime' (5.157–8 *quae comoedia, mimus / quis melior plorante gula?*).

Amid the old and new stock types of the *Satires*' banquets, Crispinus stands out as the money-belching, purple-wearing *scurra* of the Great Palatine (4.29–31 *tot sestertia . . . purpureus magni ructarit scurra Palati*). Crispinus is one of Juvenal's corrupt easterners, a prodigiously rich Egyptian immigrant in favor with Domitian. He is also a new, degraded kind of stock character reminiscent of the contemporary stage who found his way into the pages of Juvenal's 'script'. The noun *scurra* can just mean 'jester' more generally, but it also refers specifically to the clownish characters of the mime. Crispinus' indebtedness to innovative theatrical performances is further underscored by his 'entrance' at the beginning of *Satire* 4, right after Umbricius and traditional comedy limp out of town: 'Behold, it is Crispinus again, and I often have to call upon him to play his part' (4.1–2 *ecce iterum Crispinus, et est mihi saepe uocandus / ad partes*). The metaphor *uocare ad partes* dovetails nicely with the request not to 'read about', but to 'look at' (*ecce*) Crispinus, as one would in the theater.[47] As a decadent immigrant adulterer, Crispinus is no thoroughly developed individual, but a stand-in for a type of person that the satirist considers harmful.[48] The same is true of Domitian's hapless advisers. They star in the fourth *Satire*'s mock-epic description of the Emperor's inner circle debating heatedly how to cook a fish and thereby humorously illustrate larger points about common behavior at the court of a tyrant. They are a new kind of stock type, pioneered by comedy but spiced up by new performance practices and the mime.

In practice, this novel approach requires the satirist to enhance and foreground the carnivalesque side of his comedic characters. Comedy certainly has its moments where it subverts respectable types by highlighting their bodily functions and generally more physical side, but the mime – and satire – focus much more strongly on what Bakhtin called the 'material bodily lower stratum'.[49] Belches, farts, and explicit descriptions of sexual acts are on ample display, and as the satirist returns time and again to stage metaphors, he invites us to reflect on how different satire's new, more Bakhtinian and mime-based stock types are from their comedic ancestors.

In *Satire* 6, for example, we again encounter the entire theatrical cast of the first book. In another instance of life imitating adultery mimes, a 'colleague' of Latinus gets engaged (6.42–4).[50] Meanwhile, Thymele and other women swoon at the sight of pantomime dancers, gladiators, tragic and Atellan actors, and in an open breach of comedic decorum, they pay good money to have a *comoedus*' infibulation removed (6.61–75 *soluitur his magno comoedi fibula*). The *fibula*-pin was inserted into an actor's foreskin to prevent him from having sex, which was thought to ruin the singing voice.[51] The women want the actor's abilities restored, which makes for a fitting moment of meta-poetry in that they literally turn their attention toward the *comoedus'* lower stratum in ways that classical comedy did not allow.

This incongruity between the rules of traditional comedy and Rome's more mime-like realities surfaces repeatedly in *Satire* 6. At 6.184–99, Juvenal chastises older women for continuing to speak lasciviously as they did when they were young. To the listener, they are as enticing as comedic actors playing seductive roles. 'But', Juvenal warns them, 'don't fluff up your feathers: although you may speak more softly than Haemus and Carpophorus, your face still reveals your age' (6.197–9 *ut tamen omnes / subsidant pinnae, dicas haec mollius Haemo / quamquam et Carpophoro, facies tua conputat annos*). Or, to put it differently, their behavior recalls *comoedi* like Haemus, whom we remember from *Satire* 3, but on closer scrutiny, they are really just old ladies inappropriately dedicated to their men's crotch (6.192 *inguen*).

That this 'downward' focus resembles not the behavior of a character from an old-style comedy, but specifically of a transgressor from the contemporary stage, becomes apparent again in the Oxford fragment. Here, Juvenal describes a *cinaedus* who – while outwardly feminine – turns virile in bed: 'There, having danced "her" part, "Thais" takes off her mask and is revealed as a skillful Triphallus. Who are you laughing at? Save this mime for others!' (6.O.25-7 *exuit illic / personam docili Thais saltata Triphallo. / quem rides? aliis hunc mimum!*). The satirist will have us know, once more, that when we lift the traditional comedic mask[52] off his contemporary Romans, they emerge as characters from a mime.

In conclusion, the *Satires* portray comedic performances as spectacles every bit as depraved as the goings-on in Rome's alleys and palaces. As such, they still provide a 'mirror of life', but the satirist purports not to like the reflection he sees and blames it on the Greeks. He wishes that stage and street continued to resemble the glory days of Republican drama, but despairs of old-style comedic scripts' inability to speak to and rub off on a changed present. Accordingly, he sets out to claim the 'mirror of life' status for a different, but related branch of Latin literature: the *Satires*. Yet even as Juvenal's poems bring new life to Roman literary comedy in general, and to the *togata* in particular, the image in the mirror remains the same. His new *togata* is defined by a hefty dosage of transgressiveness from the mime and other contemporary stage shows.

While I have relied on examples from the first six poems to make this case, the *Satires'* meta-poetic dialogue with the stage is sustained throughout Juvenal's oeuvre. At 14.256–64, for example, the satirist casts his work as a spectacle that no theatrical festival can equal, no matter what genre is being put on (256–7 *monstro voluptatem egregiam, cui nulla theatra / nulla aequare queas praetoris pulpita lauti*). Juvenal proudly exceeds the *ludi* in spectacularity, then, as he competes with the stages' variety in the pages of his *Satires*. The angry *pater durus* may be trying to scare his readers straight, but ultimately, the image they glance at in the mirror is his own.

Notes

* I would like to thank Ruth Caston, Tom Hawkins, Toph Marshall, James Uden, and Katharina Volk for many helpful comments that significantly improved this paper.
1. Whenever I say 'Juvenal' here and throughout, I refer to the satiric *persona*, not to the poet himself. In no way do I mean to imply that the speaker's opinions are the author's own. On this subject, see e.g. Anderson 1982, esp. 293–361; Braund 1988, esp. 1–23; Braund 1996b.
2. The idea seems to have been pioneered by the Hellenistic scholar Aristophanes of Byzantium, who famously asked: 'O Menander and life, which of you imitated whom?' (Menander K-A test. 83 = Syranius' *Hermogenes* 2.23 Rabe Ὦ Μένανδρε καὶ βίε, πότερος ἄρ' ὑμῶν πότερον ἐμιμήσατο;). At Rome, the idea stuck beyond the fall of the Republic and well into the Empire (e.g. Cic. *Rep.* 4.11 = August. *De civ. D.* 2.9; Manilius 5.474–75; Quint. 10.1.69; Donat. *De comoedia* 5.1).
3. For epic in the *Satires*, see Winkler 1989; Henderson 1995. For tragedy, see Smith 1985; Schmitz 2000: 38–50; Keane 2003, esp. 265–74. For elegy, see Colton 1967; Watson 2007.
4. For the translation of this sentence, see the Σ, Courtney 1980 and Braund 1996a *ad loc*.
5. All translations are my own.
6. Jachmann's deletion of lines 95b and 96a, *mulier ... loqui*, if accepted, would remove the reference to the *persona*, but not the one to Doris' *palliolum*.
7. See e.g. Traill 2001.
8. Compare Courtney 1980 and Braund 1996a *ad loc*.
9. For imperial re-performances of *fabulae*, Atellanae as 'after-pieces' (*exodia*), see also Suet. *Tib.* 45, *Ner.* 39, *Galb.* 13, with Manuwald 2011: 169–77.
10. 'It is relevant to this reading that Greek terms for comedic masks include the noun μορμολυλεῖον (Ar, frr. 31 and 130 K-A "bogeyman face"). The traditional performance that scares children in the italic audience could therefore be a comedy.'
11. For this theory's popularity at Rome, see, e.g., Fantham 2002.
12. *Pace* Goldberg 2005, 52–114. Contrast also Ferri 2014, who does not believe that comedic re-performances had a significant impact on the literature of the late Republic and early Empire. For a counter argument, see e.g. Hanses 2014 and forthcoming.

13 So Shackleton Bailey 2001: 170–8 and Feeney 2006, *pace* Goldberg 2005. For the opening of Pompey's Theater, see also Dio Cass. 39.38.
14 *Pace* Goldberg 2005: 60, who argues that comedy here 'claims Horace's attention as a phenomenon of literary history, not as a contemporary art, for the circumstances of its reception were by his time quite different from the circumstances of its creation'. Critics of Goldberg's interpretation include Uden 2006 and Polt 2010: 1–2.
15 For further comedic performances occurring in the 'gap' between Horace and Quintilian, see my discussion of the *togata* below.
16 See esp. Müller 2013 with bibliography.
17 See C. P. Jones 1993; Nervegna 2007 and 2013, 63–119.
18 Nervegna 2013, 63–119.
19 So C. P. Jones 1993 with Suet. *Dom.* 4.4.
20 For an early example, see Cic. *Fam.* 7.1.3 with Shackleton Bailey 2001: 170–8.
21 For a further references to imperial intellectuals at large-scale comedic performances, see Dio Cass. 60.29.3 and Plut. *Mor.* 854a–b with Nervegna 2013: 99–110.
22 Nervegna 2013: 102–4.
23 Recently noted e.g. by Herrmann 2011: 28–32. Sample passages include Hor. *Sat.* 2.3.11; Prop. 2.6, 3.21.28. 4.5; Ov. *Am.* 1.15.17–18; Manilius 5.470–6; Pers. 5.161–74; Mart. 5.10.9.
24 *Pace* Fantham 1984.
25 For athletic and dramatic festivals as just as reinforcing of imperial Greek identity as the elite's literary preferences, see e.g. van Nijf 2000. Uden 2015, ch. 3 reads Umbricius' speech as a satiric take on the Romans' ongoing attempts at reasserting their own cultural dominance in response to the Second Sophistic. Uden's fascinating and nuanced study does not, however, discuss the Empire's taste for Menander. Other fruitful discussions of the cultural exchanges between Roman capital and Greek provinces during the Second Sophistic include Wallace-Hadrill 2008, esp. 17–27; Spawforth 2012; and Beard 2014: 91–5.
26 See Plaut. *Curc.* 288–95 with Uden 2015: 107–12, esp. n. 46.
27 For the similarities between Juvenal and Umbricius, see Fredericks 1973.
28 Compare Freudenburg 2001, who calls the satirist's angry *persona*'s seriousness into question and considers it a parody of the 'indignation industry' (239).
29 Note e.g. that the capital's extravagant performances make the actors rich, while the playwrights stay poor (Juv. 7.86–97).
30 See e.g. May 2006 and 2014 with bibliography.
31 Pliny mentions comedic performances as part of the nobleman's dinner entertainment and notes that he and his friends prefer them to the mime (Plin. *Ep.* 1.15, 3.1.9, 7.24, 9.17, 9.36.4); see esp. Jones 1991.
32 Note that Archias, the first exponent of exclusively literary Roman comedy, was Greek. A later example is Apuleius (*Flor.* 9.27 H, *Anth. Lat.* 712R, with May 2007: 63–71 and Nervegna 2013: 98).

33 Overviews over the genre and its reception are at Beare 1964: 128–36; Daviault 1981; Stärk 2002; Manuwald 2011: 156–69 and 261–7. Manuwald observes that the *togata* emerged from the Greco-Roman comic tradition as 'the result of differentiation [more] than opposition' (158).
34 Courtney 1980 *ad loc.* set the trend by dismissing the *togata* as 'virtually extinct'.
35 For an earlier re-performance, see Cic. *Sest.* 118.
36 It is not unusual for Roman satirists to define their genre against the backdrop of Greek comedy. Horace likened his *Sermones* to the Old Comedies of Eupolis, Cratinus, and Aristophanes, who spared no evildoer the criticism he deserved (Hor. *Sat.* 1.4.1–5). He also claimed that like the comedies of Terence, his satires are only superficially poetic (1.4.48–56). A few decades later, Persius also highlighted his poems' indebtedness to comedy. In keeping with the trend toward attributing greater prominence to Menander than to his Latin 'translators', he ventriloquized characters from the *Eunuchus* in their Greek, rather than their Terentian incarnations (Pers. 5.161–74). For the satirists' invocation of comic models, see also Leach 1971; Woodman 1983; Cucchiarelli 2001: 15–55; F. Jones 2001; Keane 2003; and Ferriss-Hill 2015.
37 See n. 3 above.
38 For literary recitations and their effect on, as well as treatment in, Juvenal's *Satires*, see F. Jones 2001; Mader 2007; Uden 2015: 94–104.
39 Compare here and throughout, Keane 2003, who argues that Juvenal 'exchanges satire's traditional affiliations with theatre for a more sensational form of entertainment' (265). However, Keane focuses on tragic elements in the *Satires*, not on the mime.
40 A good example is at Plaut. *Bacch.* 1079–83.
41 For New Comedy and its Roman translations as reaffirming of traditional values, see e.g. Plut. *Quaest. conv.*, *Comp. Ar. et Men.*; Konstan 1983: 15–32, 47–57, 115–30; Leigh 2004, esp. 312–13; but note the cautionary remarks of Brown 1990 as to the genre's somewhat greater complexity. A more thoroughly theorized discussion is at Lowe 2000: 188–221.
42 See Suet. *Calig.* 57; Joseph, *AJ* 19.94; Mart. *Spect.* 7; Juv. 8.187; Tert. *Adv. Valent.* 14; Σ Bernensis on Lucan 1.544; Wiseman 1985: 183–210; Fantham 1988: 157–8 with n. 27.
43 On the mime, see Reich 1903; Reynolds 1946; McKeown 1979; Fantham 1988; Marshall 2006: 7–12; Panayotakis 2010: 1–32; Manuwald 2011: 178–83. Rawson 1993 objects (unconvincingly, to my mind) to considering the mime 'vulgar'. The importance of adultery plots is perhaps best exemplified by Ov. *Tr.* 2.497–514. In Latin literature, references to the mime are sometimes hard to tell apart from allusions to the pantomime, a genre that had masked dancers act out varied sensual scenarios to hexameter lyrics and choral accompaniment. However, since pantomime plots were often erotic, the difficulty in distinguishing between the two genres need not have a big impact on our interpretation. On the pantomime, see esp.

Lada-Richards 2007; Hall and Wiles, eds. 2008. For its influence on imperial Latin literature, see most recently Lada-Richards 2013 with bibliography.

44 So Braund 1996a *ad loc.* See also Juv. 6.42–4, 66; 8.197, and Courtney 1980 *ad loc.*
45 Alternatively, we may observe that *ut a trepido Thymele summissa Latino* is Heinrich's emendation for the codices' *et a trepido Thymele summissa Latino*. If we retain the *et* of the original, we translate 'Massa fears [the informer] and Carus assuages him with a gift *and so does* Thymele secretly sent by fearful Latinus'. In this case, the mime actor himself would be scared, and he would be sending the actress to have sex with a real-life enemy. Either way, life in the streets of Rome has come to imitate the practices of the stage, and of the mime in particular.
46 On the parasite as 'a pathology of Roman patronage', see Damon 1997.
47 Compare Keane 2003: 257, who points out the character's indebtedness to the stage, but sees his roots in tragedy, another genre whose staging practices were turning ever more excessive.
48 The general nature of this type is further underlined by the fact that a Crispinus occurs in Horace's *Satires* as well, see Hor. *Sat.* 1.1.120, 1.3.139, 1.4.14, 2.7.45. His presence in Roman satire, as Braund 1996a points out *ad loc.*, is inevitable.
49 Bakhtin 1984[1965] *passim*, esp. ch. 6. On Juvenal and Bakhtin, see Hudson 1989 and Braund 1996a: 304. For the body's role in Juvenalian satire, see also Barchiesi and Cucchiarelli 2005.
50 On the man's identity and the mime scenario he finds himself involved in, see Reynolds 1946; Courtney 1980 and Watson and Watson 2014 *ad loc.*
51 See Celsus 7.25.2; Oribasius 50.11; Jüthner s.v. 'Infibulation', *RE* 9.2543–8; Watson and Watson 2014 *ad loc.*
52 *Pace* Braund 2004: 267, who thinks the Thais referred to here is not the Menandrian prostitute, but the lover of Alexander the Great. Compare Watson and Watson 2014 *ad loc.*

3

Parrhēsia and *Pudenda*: Speaking Genitals and Satiric Speech

Julia Nelson Hawkins

'[Denis] Diderot [in Les Bijoux indiscrets (1748)] provides the anatomical description of vagina as instrument à corde et à vent capable of emitting sounds . . . And, as Diderot makes clear, what speaks through her vagina is not the Body as such but precisely the vagina as organ, as a subjectless partial object'.

Slavoj Žižek, *Organs without Bodies*, 152

In his second satire Horace presents the image of a man named Villius arguing with his own penis:[1]

> *huic si muttonis uerbis mala tanta uidenti*
> *diceret haec animus 'quid uis tibi? numquid ego a te*
> *magno prognatum deposco consule cunnum*
> *uelatumque stola, mea cum conferbuit ira?'*
> *quid responderet?* (1.2.68–72).

> If this man's *animus* should see such great evils and say, in the words of his prick, 'What is it that you want? Do I demand a pussy descended from a great consul and veiled by a long gown, when my mojo [*ira*] is simmering?' How would the man respond?[2]

What are we to make of this image? In his commentary on the *Satires*, Porphyrio points to a Lucilian intertext for Horace's '*penis loquens*' (fr. 237: *at laeua lacrimas muttoni absterget amica*, 'But with her left hand my girlfriend wipes clean my *mutto*'s tears)', and Freudenburg follows Fiske in seeing a Cynic precedent in Bion's habit of endowing personified objects, such as *pragmata*, 'circumstances', with a speaking voice.[3] While Lucilius and Bion provide models of objects and ideas that obtain animate tendencies,[4] a weeping penis and personified abstractions cannot adequately account for Villius' throbbing cock (*muttonis ... conferbuit ira*)⁵ that is suddenly endowed with an *animus* and speech that manages to wed the salty oratorical style of Cato⁶ with the obscene word that was tantamount to *nefas* in oratory: *cunnus*.⁷ Prosopopoeia is often associated with Greek genres such as philosophical diatribe, yet Gowers rightly observes that Horace's genital personification transgresses even this model and ventures into the realm of parody.⁸ Obscene parody, particularly in combination with Horace's emphatic assertion of his satirical inheritance from Aristophanes, Cratinus, and Eupolis (Sat. 1.4.1–8, 1.10.15–20), opens a rich avenue of comparison between satiric speaking genitals and Athenian comedy.

As my epigraph makes clear, Žižek in *Organs without Bodies* sees Diderot's speaking vagina as emblematic of an aesthetic foundation for a new philosophy of 'revolutionary subjectivity'. Yet we have a much older etiology for Diderot's 'jewels' both in Aristophanes' images of speaking and volitional vaginas (as I will show) and in the speaking penises and pussies of Roman satiric writers.⁹ Indeed, Horace's depiction of a *mutto* endowed with an *animus* and an ability to declaim with abusive speech reverses the Homeric model of Odysseus' heroic exhortation to his *thumos* (which is explicitly parodied in Petronius' *Satyricon*, where the hapless hero addresses his penis in Homeric style) and presents a more radically bifurcated subjectivity. In Horace's formulation the *thumos / animus* – not the hero – is the subject who talks through the personified mouth of the phallus, and the result comes close to Žižek's model of the 'organ without a body':

> And one has to think of the phallus not as the organ that immediately expresses the vital force of my being, my virility, and so forth but, precisely, as such an insignia, as a mask that I put on in the same way a king or judge puts on his insignia – phallus is an 'organ without a body' that I put on, which gets attached to my body, without ever becoming an 'organic part', namely, forever sticking out as its incoherent, excessive supplement.¹⁰

Like Žižek's phallus-as-mask, speaking genitals in satire emphasize the incoherence of the idea of a unified subject with total freedom to speak and add another type of *persona* to the storehouse of character masks that satirists don.¹¹ In what follows I trace how genitals are linked to poetics and *parrhēsia*, 'freedom of speech', from Old Comedy to Horace, Petronius, and Martial through the image of sex organs that are either imagined to speak or that exhibit some other form of autonomous agency. My argument is that Aristophanes provides several precedents for speaking or volitional genitals and connects that genital speech to comic *parrhēsia*, and that Roman satirists then took up such imagery to express the limits of acceptable speech, *libertas*, in late Republican and imperial Rome.

Speaking genitals and *parrhēsia* in Aristophanes

In Horace's depiction of a talking penis, Gowers notices a 'possible pun on *mutto* and *mutus* (next to *uerbis*) . . .'.[12] Her suggestion of a joke that transforms what should be a 'mute' *mutto* into a 'verbose' *mutto* is supported by Aristophanes' portrayal of female genitalia in *Acharnians* and their connection to free speech. In this play we see what may be the inspiration for Horace's speaking penis in a scene involving a *khoiros*, both 'pig' and 'vagina', attempting human speech. When the Megarian attempts to pass off his pre-pubescent daughters as piglets for sale, Dicaeopolis disputes his claim that they are pigs and insists that they are instead 'human' (774 ἀλλ' ἔστιν ἀνθρώπου γε). The Megarian capitalizes on the semantic stretch of the word *khoiros* and switches to an obscene register, where the transaction morphs into one of under-age sex workers rather than piglets.[13] And in this scene, we hear a *khoiros* attempt to speak (777–82):

Μεγαρεύς	φώνει δὴ τὺ ταχέως χοιρίον.	
	οὐ χρῆσθα; σιγῆς ὦ κάκιστ' ἀπολουμένα;	
	πάλιν τυ ἀποισῶ ναὶ τὸν Ἑρμᾶν οἴκαδις.	
Κόρη	κοῒ κοΐ.	780
Μεγαρεύς	αὕτα 'στὶ χοῖρος;	
Δικαιόπολις	νῦν γε χοῖρος φαίνεται	
.	ἀτὰρ ἐκτραφείς γε κύσθος ἔσται.	
Megarian	Make a sound, little *khoiros*; You don't want to? You are silent?	
	Damn you! By Hermes I'll take you back home.	
Girl	'koi koi'	
Megarian	Is that a little *khoiros*, or not?	
Dicaeopolis	Now it seems like a *khoiros*;	
	but once it is grown, it will be a vagina.	

In this passage the Megarian passes off his daughters as pigs, but Olson notes that he tacitly switches to the pun on 'vagina' early on in the conversation (774),[14] which only becomes explicit once Dicaeopolis rebrands it a *kusthos* (783), a comic word that denotes female genitals. When the Megarian asks the *khoiros* to make sounds to prove that it was, in fact, a *khoiros* (777), he uses an imperative form of the verb φωνεῖν, which is not used of animal sounds until Aristotle. The initial reluctance of the *khoiros* to speak, perhaps a verbal play picked up by Horace with his juxtaposition of *mutto* next to *verbis* (*Serm*.1.2.68), highlights that the Megarian is demanding not just phonation but articulate speech from the 'genitals'. When it finally does make a sound, '*koi koi*' (780), the joke reaches an onomatopoetic level. Although Hesychius gives *grullē* (s.v.) as the porcine sound, '*koi*' is presumably an alternative, but more importantly it also sounds like half of the Greek word *khoiros*.[15] Given that φωνεῖν with an accusative can mean 'to call someone or something by name',[16] it is possible that the audience is being asked to reconfigure *khoirion* in 777 as an accusative direct object, rather than a vocative, as the Megarian tells the 'Pussy' to say its name. Later, the symmetrical mimesis between its name and its sound is even greater, when Dicaeopolis calls to it, χοῖρε χοῖρε, and it replies, κοῖ κοῖ (802–3). Thus we can conclude that we are essentially being presented with a vagina that simultaneously makes a pig sound and attempts human speech, uttering half of the word that reflects its own identity (*khoiros*).

We might expect to see even more of this genital prosopopoeia in the *Thesmophoriazusae*, since the plot revolves around grown women gathered together to celebrate an all-female ritual that embraces licensed obscenity and the display of phallic and vulvic models,[17] but we do not.[18] Although in this play Aristophanes does not depict sex organs that attempt speech, in two scenes he does correlate the *khoiros* with *parrhēsia* and depict a *khoiros* as volitional and locomotive, while presenting its sibling *posthōn*, 'penis', as having intelligence. After he has infiltrated in drag the exclusively female rites of the Thesmophoria, Euripides' kinsman Mnesilochus addresses the assembled women in an attempt to defend Euripides, and the women threaten to take retribution on his (in their opinion) outrageous claims by grabbing some hot coals and singeing his χοῖρον (534–40). Mnesilochus' response closely pairs his genitals and the right to speak freely:

μὴ δῆτα τόν γε χοῖρον ὦ γυναῖκες. εἰ γὰροὔσης
παρρησίαςκἀξὸν λέγειν ὅσαι πάρεσμεν ἀσταί,
εἶτ' εἶπον ἁγίγνωσκον ὑπὲρ Εὐριπίδου δίκαια,
διὰ τοῦτο τιλλομένη νμε δεῖ δοῦναι δίκην ὑφ' ὑμῶν;

No, no, ladies, please, not my pussy! Am I, when there's freedom of speech here, and when all of us here who are citizens are entitled to speak – am I, for saying what I considered to be right in defense of Euripides, to be punished for that by your plucking my hairs out?

(tr. Sommerstein)

While this *khoiros* does not speak, the juxtaposition of *parrhēsia* with *khoiros* is, I suggest, indicative of a fundamental link between comic licensed speech and genital obscenities. According to Varro obscenities do not belong in civic speech, but only on the stage: *Obscenum dictum ab scaena . . . quare turpe ideo obscaenum, quod nisi in scaena[m] palam dici non debet*, (*LL* 7.96: ' "Obscene" comes from *scaena*, "stage" . . . Wherefore anything shameful is called *obscaenum*, because it should not be said openly except on the *scaena*, "stage" '). In Mnesilochus' staged cry we hear the threat of violence to the vagina (which is really a phallus) as an assault on the liberty of the female's voice (which is really a male voice, both within the narrative as Mneslilochus and outside of it as the actor speaking). Part of the joke is that women were not citizens and did not possess *parrhēsia*, and thus Mnesilochus has essentially outed himself as a man by claiming the right that is only accorded to an Athenian male citizen.[19]

Earlier in the *Thesmophoriazusae*, we hear an explicit joke on 'vaginal volition' when Mnesilochus enters the Thesmophoria and prays to the patron deities, making a special prayer on behalf of 'her' children:

> καὶ τοῦ θυγατρίου χοῖρον ἀνδρός μοι τυχεῖν
> πλουτοῦντος, ἄλλως δ᾽ ἠλιθίου κἀβελτέρου, 290
> καὶ ποσθαλίσκον νοῦν ἔχειν μοι καὶ φρένας.

> And while we're at it let my daughter's pussy happen upon a rich man – but one who's a total moron, of course – and may the little pecker [of my son] be possessed of intelligence and common sense![20]

Mnesilochus prays that his/her daughter's *khoiros* (here, clearly a vagina) might marry a rich but foolish man, while he hopes that his son's little penis might attain wisdom (νόος) and sense (φρένες).[21] The joke is that Mnesilochus hopes that his son won't be duped by a money-grubbing wife, and that his daughter will be clever enough to be well kept by a senseless but rich husband.

Yet there is another level of comic sophistry at play in this scene: *noos* and *phrenes* are the faculties of intelligence in Plato's tripartite soul (later adopted by Galen's physiological system and assigned to specific body parts) that the lower registers of the appetitive soul do not possess (*Rep.* 439d), and in *Timaeus* they are precisely the attributes that the penis does not (and, by nature, could never) have (91a–d). In his physiological etiology for certain bodily organs, Plato provides a long description of the nature of the male and female genitals, claiming that the gods constructed a genital animal (91a2, ζῷον) which is external to the male but inside of the woman:

> And it was for this reason that the gods at that time contrived the love of sexual intercourse by constructing an animate creature (ζῷον) of one kind in us men, and of another kind in women; and they made these severally in

the following fashion. From the passage of egress for the drink, where it receives and joins in discharging the fluid which has come through the lungs beneath the kidneys into the bladder and has been compressed by the air, they bored a hole into the condensed marrow which comes from the head down by the neck and along the spine [91b] which marrow (μυελὸν), in our previous account, we termed 'seed'. And the marrow, inasmuch as it is animate and has been granted an outlet, has endowed the part where its outlet lies with a love for generating by implanting therein a lively desire for emission. Wherefore in men the nature (φύσιν) of the genital organs is disobedient (ἀπειθές) and self-willed (αὐτοκρατὲς), like a creature that is deaf to reason (ἀνυπήκοον τοῦ λόγου), and it attempts to dominate all because of its frenzied lusts. [91c] And in women again, owing to the same causes, whenever the matrix or womb, as it is called, – which is an indwelling creature desirous (ἐπιθυμητικὸν) of child-bearing, – remains without fruit long beyond the due season, it is vexed and takes it ill; and by straying (πλανώμενον) all ways through the body and blocking up the passages of the breath and preventing respiration it casts the body into the uttermost distress, and causes, moreover, all kinds of maladies; until the desire and love of the two sexes unite them.

(tr. Lamb)

Aristophanes and Plato present alternate perspectives on genital volition. Whereas the former presents an under-theorized model of genitals that can be discussed in terms of intelligence and speech, the latter dismisses such ideas by connecting the reproductive organs with the specifically irrational parts of the soul.

In commenting on the discussion of genitals in *Timaeus*, Helen King has shown that Plato's wandering womb does not so much reflect Hippocratic medical thinking (though it has typically been understood that way) as much as a wide-spread cultural tendency to describe both male and female genitals and other organs as autonomous, zoomorphic entities.[22] While the Hippocratics, then, do not endorse an independent wandering womb,[23] they do in fact explicitly describe the female body as having an upper and a lower mouth. As Dasen and Ducaté-Paarmann (241–2) have shown, there is a fundamental association in Greek medicine between the upper and lower mouths of the female body:

Like a human face, the womb has a mouth, lips, a neck, and shoulders. The uterus even has a kind of nose which smells and communicates with the nose of the top (cf. Byl 1995). This terminology, still in use today (*labia*, lips, *cervix*, neck), expresses hidden correspondences between the top and the bottom of the female body. Medical texts often refer to a direct communication, a *hodos*, between the upper and the lower ends. A change in the mouth of the womb transforms the top one. The loss of virginity can thus modify the girl's voice, which becomes deeper (Hanson and Armstrong 1986; King 1998: 28), or pain may be felt in the throat at the start of a menstrual period (*Coan Prognoses* 537=L. V, 706). Treatment can be applied to both mouths. To test the fertility of a woman, scented substances, such as garlic, are placed at the lower or top end of the channel. If the smell travels freely through the body, the woman can conceive ... As with Pandora, representing an insatiable belly, *gastēr*, associated with her bitch temperament, women have two corresponding mouths with similarly uncontrolled appetites.

If Plato did not develop the autonomous 'wandering womb' and 'irrational penis' theories, and they instead emerge from a long-standing societal attitude, then Aristophanes' independent *khoiroi*, half a century earlier, could be a personification of the wandering womb, while the verbal *khoiros* could be playing on the idea of a lower 'mouth'.

Ritual etiologies for the 'organ without a body': the phallus-pole and baubo

Evidence from Greek ritual adumbrates a wide-reaching system of practices and language surrounding autonomous genitals which further supports the idea that personified, speaking genitals are not so much a medical as a cultural phenomenon. Csapo argues that autonomous phallic representations are not only part of Dionysiac ritual and myth, but also a core feature of Greek drama: 'The phallus icon of Dionysus and the phalli carried in Dionysiac processions are always regarded as independent living organisms, of which the glans is a head, equipped with eyes and sometimes with (phallic, horse-like) ears and other animal attributes'.[24] The Dionysian phallus does not have a mouth (though some depictions give it wings, as if to suggest its autonomous movements[25]), because the phallus pole's symbolic role, according to Csapo, is to evoke penetration, arousal, and commemoration of the originary plague of priapism sent by Dionysus as punishment for the Athenians' refusal to welcome him and his emissary Pegasus of Eleutherai (Schol. Ar. *Acharn.* 243).[26] It does not, that is, represent speech.

In contrast, there is an etiological sex organ that does possess a mouth and that has a structurally parallel function to the phallus pole: Baubo is the female figure in terracotta finds who has the appearance of a hypertrophic vulva on two legs, but, in her masculine form, the word *baubōn* refers to a leather phallus, the same object, according to Olender, that Aristophanes' Lysistrata 'praises under the name olisbos' (*Lys.* 109).[27] There is some evidence that Baubo has an etiological connection to the Thesmophoria,[28] and, as many scholars note, she is for the most part interchangeable with Iambe – the etiological female figure for the genre of iambus.[29] The fourth-century terracottas of Baubo from Priene depict her as walking genitals, and her mobility, indicated by her legs, parallels the statues of phalli that the Athenians fashioned with moving parts and paraded through Athens.[30] In the *Homeric Hymn to Demeter*, Iambe made Demeter laugh by telling obscene jokes, and in other versions of the same story Baubo made her laugh by revealing her genitals (*anasyrma*);[31] one is a speech act, and the other a somatic gesture, but both function in a similar role to the phallus pole, in that they appease divine wrath with obscenity and are related to the etiology for the respective poetic genres of drama and iambus. Like Aristophanes' *khoiros* that, when asked to speak, attempts to squeal its own name, 'pussy', Baubo similarly stands in for a speech act that is only partial: it is her lower lips that speak – not with verbal language but by replacing (perhaps bypassing?) Iambe's spoken obscenities. If Baubo spoke, she would likely say her own name, like the Megarian's *khoiros* tried to do.[32] At the very least, we can see in Iambe/Baubo[33] and the phallus procession a cultural foundation for licensed genital obscenities in Aristophanes. Aristophanes' speaking and volitional *khoiros*-jokes are funny because they expand on the hilarity of a female figure revealing (or being made to reveal) her own sex organ, whether through speech (Iambe) or through visual display (Baubo).[34]

In comparing the differences between the etiologies of the phallus pole / Iambe-Baubo testimonia,[35] there is only laughter in the female etiology. What we see in Aristophanes, then, is the beginning of an exploration of this idea of volitional female genitals in the context of *parrhēsia*. Why not depict the penis speaking on stage? I suspect the answer is that male citizens were, by fiat of the *polis*, naturally endowed with *parrhēsia* and *isēgoria*, whereas females were excluded from both, so the cognitive dissonance involved in watching a vagina talk, wander around in search of a husband, or be positioned lexically next to the word *parrhēsia* in fifth-century Athens would have resulted in a greater incongruity for the (mostly male) audience, and therefore would have been funnier.

Roman receptions: Horace, Persius, and Juvenal

I believe it is due to the circumscription of *libertas*, Rome's closest approximation to Athenian *parrhēsia*, that Horace transforms Aristophanes' *khoiros*-that-squeals neologisms into the articulate *mutto* in the passage with which I began this chapter.[36] In Athens, having a penis and being free meant you had the right to free speech. But Horace claims to revive the free-speech spirit of Athenian Comedy in his *Sermones* (*Serm.* 1.4.1–5; 1.10.14–15) at a time when even a male as high born as Asinius Pollio protests that it is difficult to speak (or, more precisely, 'write') with impunity.[37] A closer look at the rhetoric of his speaking penis passage can now bear this out.

Horace's speaking prick in *Serm.* 1.2 not only seems at first blush to surpass the vagina's speech-act in Aristophanes – it speaks like an orator. The *mutto* uses a high-register, quasi-legal term *deposco*[38] when it harangues its possessor, reflecting tensions over masculinity and appropriate speech acts in the triumviral period.[39] The use of prosopopoeia in Roman literature is specifically tied, according to Quintilian, to the highest register of oratorical speech acts:

> A bolder form of *figure*, which in Cicero's opinion demands greater effort, is *impersonation*, or *prosopopoiiai*. This is a device which lends wonderful variety and animation to oratory. By this means we display the inner thoughts of our adversaries as though they were talking with themselves (but we shall only carry conviction if we represent them as uttering what they may reasonably be supposed to have had in their minds); or without sacrifice of credibility we may introduce conversations between ourselves and others, or of others among themselves, and put words of advice, reproach, complaint, praise or pity into the mouths of appropriate persons. Nay, we are even allowed in this form of speech to bring down the gods from heaven and raise the dead, while cities also and peoples may find a voice (tr. Butler).[40]

Cicero famously used the device to reify the *patria* and make it harangue Catiline at one of the crescendos of his first Catilinarian.[41] Horace uses the same rhetorical device, with an embedded oratorical watchword *deposco*, to conjure an image of a Ciceronian *mutto* that replaces the orator's *patria*.

But Horace also lays a verbal trap for the oratorical penis by having it violate Cicero's own standard of avoiding obscenity: Cicero asserts an orator should never use sounds that could evoke the word *cunnus* and orators should above all avoid obscenity and maintain a masculine, Attic purity.[42] In the *mutto*'s parody of the ideal Roman orator, much like Aristophanes' parodies of the Athenian demagogues, we see a satiric poet staging freedom of speech through the mouth of a speaking sex organ – and, here, one that speaks the other sex's sex. But Horace's penis reminds the reader that, for all of Horace's praise of Athenian onomastic comedy, the climate of free speech has changed, and even an articulate penis is foiled by the pressures of triumviral proscriptions, forcing the genitals to take over when the upper mouth is restrained (Pollio's words '*at ego taceo*' are relevant here).[43] In the *Epodes* restraint turns to impotence: throughout, the iambic collection's failure to 'get it up' becomes an organizational theme,[44] and Horace in *Epod*. 8 portrays his own *nerui*[45] as *inlitterati* (17: 'unlettered'), in a moment of impotence when faced with a sexually voracious woman who, like the *cunnus* in *Serm*. 1.2, is described as descended from a particularly threatening brand of nobility: a triumphator (*Epod*. 8.12).[46]

In this way, Horace ties the anxiety over triumviral strictures on free speech to a Greek-comic motif of speaking genitals that are staged by Aristophanes as a comic violation of the bedrock of Athenian democracy: male freedom of speech. According to Horace at *Serm*. 1.4.1–5, Eupolis, Aristophanes, and Cratinus used onomastic comedy for freely marking out (*multa cum libertate notabant*, 5)[47] the dregs of society: thieves (*fures*), sexual 'deviants' (*moechi*), murderers (*sicarii*)[48] and the notorious (*famosi*).[49] Horace even mobilizes a surgical metaphor at *Serm*. 1.10.14–15 to depict Old Comedy's efficaciousness: ... *ridiculum acri*[50] / *fortius et melius magnas plerumque secat*[51] *res*, 'Ridicule [the explicit mainstay of Old Comedy at line 16] excises great things more effectively and more swiftly than caustics'.[52] This therapeutic invective that is aimed at society looks back to Aristophanes' self-presentation as a civic healer[53] and functions to highlight Horace's palpable *lack* of any direct and meaningful onomastic agency, given the dearth of prominent, named individuals in the *Sermones*.[54]

In the Neronian period, Persius picks up on Horace's medicalized reading of Old Comedy by instructing that his readers approach his book with ears that have been cleansed (1.126 *uaporata* ... *aure*) by the vapors (1.126: *ferueat*)[55] that emanate from the more 'cooked-down / concentrated' (1.125 *decoctius*)[56] form of Old Comedy that he is presenting in his satire book.[57] Like his forebears, Juvenal also relies on the trope of invective therapeutics, casting an 'expert medical eye' across all of Rome and diagnosing its ills.[58] Persius and Juvenal share with Horace a healing persona;[59] both look to Horace and Lucilius as indigenous models of *satura*; both in their own way follow Old Comedy as models, but neither poet reprises the speaking genitals motif we see in Aristophanes and Horace.[60]

Petronius and the death of the speaking penis

Before Martial breathes new life into the *penis / cunnus loquens topos* and proliferates the image in a radically new direction, Petronius – the last major author to fall afoul of Nero after the Pisonian conspiracy and to be forced to commit suicide[61] – presents us with another variation on the speaking genital theme. After Encolpius suffers from a bout of impotence that resists cure, he harangues his own penis in a long, para-tragic speech. While the address to an uncooperative penis is a *topos* in Latin literature (e.g., *Priap.* 83[62] and Ov. *Am.* 3.7),[63] Petronius lingers on the penis' subjective reaction to Encolpius' verbal attack in a way that other such addresses do not and shows us the emotional state of his personified penis on trial and its subsequent, wordless death (*Sat.* 132.22–56).

Encolpius begins his speech, which Petronius variously refers to as an *oratio* ('oration'), an *obiurgatio* ('official rebuke'), and a *declamatio* ('declamation'), to his penis by deploying the language of the law courts in a scene that resembles the dog-trial in Aristophanes' *Wasps* in its use of bathetic personification[64]: he calls the offending member *contumax*, 'stubborn' or 'one who refuses to appear in court', because the *furcifera* ('pecker-head'), and *caput* ('head'), had earlier retreated, *confugerat*,[65] into Encolpius' insides, *uiscera*, to avoid punishment, *supplicium*; he then accuses it of 'slandering' his reputation, *traduceres*, and he demands that it defend itself by giving a verbal rebuttal, *Quid dicis ... Rogo te, mihi apodixis <non> defunctoriam redde*, 'What do you have to say for yourself? I submit that you return a proof that you aren't dead'. The *topos* of a personified penis that is called to testify in a law court looks back to the speaking *khoiroi* of the Aristophanes, but also provides a sharp distinction: whereas the Megarian in Aristophanes' *Acharnians* demands that a *khoiros* speak to prove its identity, Encolpius demands that his penis speak in order to prove its very existence. This court-room personification also alludes to the many instances of comic prosopopoeia in Old Comedy where staged personifications of things and concepts were common: Aristophanes personifies Demos in the *Knights* and Logoi in the *Clouds*; Eupolis personifies Persuasion (Peithô) sitting on Pericles' lips, an image much cited by Roman writers of oratorical theory,[66] and, perhaps most famously, Cratinus personifies Comedy as the poet's wife and Drunkenness as his mistress in the *Pytinē*, which Horace alludes to in the famous opening of his letter to Maecenas about the virtues of wine for poetic inspiration (1.19.1–3).[67]

But it is in Aristophanes' *Wasps*, when Bdelycleon stages a fake trial in order to cure his father of his jury addiction by calling dogs and a cheese grater to testify, that we find the closest parallel to Encolpius' oration to his penis. Bdelycleon calls the dog to the witness stand in language similar to Encolpius' demand that his penis give an account of itself: ἀνάβαιν', ἀπολογοῦ. Τί σεσιώπηκας; λέγε (944), 'Step up and defend yourself. Why are you silent? Speak!' The image also echoes the rudimentary speech of the *khoiros* in the *Acharnians*: both the defendant/dog and pussy/pig are commanded to speak and refuse, while both the prosecutor/dog and pussy/pig are given onomatopoetic 'speaking' lines: the *khoiros* says '*koi koi*' (*Ach.* 780), and the *kuōn* says '*au au*' (*Wasp.* 903) when cued. Petronius, however, does not allow Encolpius' penis to respond verbally. Instead, the reader is presented with the penis' stony emotional state and metaphorical death scene via allusions to Virgil's *Aeneid*:

Illa solo fixos oculos auersa tenebat,
nec magis incepto uultum sermone mouetur
quam lentae salices lassoue papauera collo.

That organ held its eyes fixed, with averted look
And its face was less moved by any of my speech
Than weeping willows as they bend
Or poppies with drooping necks.

Here Petronius compares his lifeless penis' eyes and face to those of Dido in the underworld after she has committed suicide and its drooping neck to that of the beautiful youth Euryalus as he dies on the battlefield.[68] In perfect old-comic fashion, Petronius mobilizes epic models in a bathetic moment to highlight the incongruity of a man talking to his penis.

Why might Petronius deploy this Old Comic and Horatian model of genital personification in his novel and not allow the accused member to speak? As with Horace, a reduced *libertas* is likely key. Ian Ruffell has recently argued that Old Comedy was primarily used among satirists 'to theorise *libertas* and negotiate their response to a political context that circumscribed just such freedom'.[69] This is certainly borne out by Rudich who sees a dissident dissimulation in Petronius' words and deeds (*dicta factaque*, Tac. *Ann.* 16.18.2), which Tacitus claims are characterized by *simplicitas*, 'frankness'.[70] For Rudich, Petronius' frankness and simplicity are hallmarks of his veiled dissidence toward the Neronian 'iron curtain' that crushed *libertas*. It is also the same word that Encolpius himself uses to describe the character of his address to his penis: *nouae simplicitatis opus*, 'an *opus* of new frankness'. Juvenal, writing a few decades later, claims at 1.151–3 that *simplicitas* is what enabled earlier satirists to attack prominent men by name and laments at 1.160–71 its loss in his own era, in which he claims only the dead can safely be satirized.

Skoptic prosopopoeia in Martial

Martial, writing in roughly the same period as Juvenal (late first century BCE), revives the Aristophanic, speaking genital motif in a new idiom. Aristophanes deployed the speaking *khoiros* as a joke, highlighting the lack of female *parrhēsia* in democratic Athens, and Horace presented a declaiming *mutto* to suggest that even elite males have reduced freedom to censure, while Petronius does not even name his *mutto* (Encolpius uses the euphemism *pudor* for his penis, 'because it is not *fas* to name you in serious matters', *Nam ne nominare quidem te inter res serias fas est*),[71] much less allow it to speak. This changes with Martial, who presents his longest skoptic prosopopoeia as a way to mock one of his sex partners, and he does so in an intertextual engagement with Aristophanes (7.18):

> *cum tibi sit facies de qua nec femina possit*
> *dicere, cum corpus nulla litura notet,*
> *cur te tam rarus cupiat repetatque fututor*
> *miraris? uitium est non leue, Galla, tibi.*
> *accessi quotiens ad opus mixtisque mouemur*   5
> *inguinibus, cunnus non tacet, ipsa taces.*
> *di facerent ut tu loquereris et ille taceret:*
> *offendor cunni garrulitate tui.*
> *pedere te mallem: namque hoc nec inutile dicit*
> *Symmachus*[72] *et risum res mouet ista simul.*   10
> *quis ridere potest fatui*[73] *poppysmata*
> *cum sonat hic, cui non mentula mensque cadit?*
> *dic aliquid saltem clamosoque obstrepe cunno,*
> *et, si adeo muta es, disce uel inde loqui.*

Since you have a face about which even a woman could find nothing to blame since no wrinkle marks your body, do you wonder why a fornicator so seldom wants you and comes again? You have a serious defect, Galla. Whenever I get to work and we go at it, your *cunnus* is not silent, while you are. Would that the gods would make *you* talk and *it* be silent! I am offended by the garrulity of your *cunnus*. I had rather you farted; Symmachus says that is healthy, and besides it makes one laugh. But who can laugh at the queefing of a stupid *cunnus*? Whose *mentula* and mind don't droop at the sound of it? At least say something and counter your clamorous *cunnus*; and if you are so silent, learn to talk out of it.

Like the Megarian's *khoiros* in the *Acharnians* that repeatedly says '*koi koi*' (five times) throughout the exchange, this *cunnus* is a chatterbox[74] (8, *garrulitate* can refer to the chatter of humans or animals). Galla's *cunnus* is not permitted a complete speech act beyond the onomatopoeic word / sound *poppysmata* – a Greek loan word that Aristophanes uses at *Wasps* 626 to refer to the smacking sound people make to ward off a natural disaster like lightning[75] and *Wealth* 732 to describe the sound Asclepius makes with his mouth when he calls his sacred snakes to come and lick Plutus' eyes. The comic poet Alexis even wrote a play with the name as its title (Ποππύζουσα, 'The Smacking Woman'). Like the '*koi koi*' speech of the Megarian's *khoiros*, this *cunnus* utters an onomatopoeic, comic sound that doubles as an articulate word.

In the other two instances it is used in Latin, '*poppysmata*' refers to the sound a priest makes during lightning (Plin. *HN* 28.25 and Juv. 6.584), and in Greek comedy the word seems to have a paratragic tone, all of which suggests that Galla's *cunnus* might be a bit full of itself, like Horace's *mutto* that declaims at *Serm.* 1.2. Furthermore, like Mnesilochus' wish in *Thesmophoriazusae* that his son's *posthaliskos* have intellect, Martial's own *mentula* is strongly correlated with his *mens* (cf. Mart. 11.78.2, *ignotumque sibi mentula discat opus*, 'let your *mentula* learn a task it does not know').[76]

What do we make of Martial's 'talking' *cunnus*? For one thing, we again see genital speech connected with the mouth's inability to persuade, though in Martial I submit that this is a different species of critique than the laments of lost *libertas* in Horace and Juvenal. Martial demands that the *cunnus* take over the task of being wittily seductive with words if the upper mouth can't produce the right speech. But Martial does not have much faith that the *cunnus* can succeed, as he brands it 'stupid' (11 *fatui*). The physician Symmachus takes on the role of Horace's *mutto* in *Serm.* 1.2, advising Martial to imagine the sound as a 'fart', because at least this is healthy and natural – a 'prescription' that comes off more as a chastisement of Martial for being too picky. Martial then wishes the woman's organ at the very least could make him laugh (10 *risum*), something that the Megarian's and Mnesilochus' *khoiroi* seemed easily to achieve. Martial wants more out of a *cunnus* than just animal sounds: he wants either silence or a joke.

Elsewhere Martial uses skoptic prosopopoeia in a similar, though less-developed fashion. At 3.72, Martial mocks a woman who is similar to Galla in 7.18: she is beautiful (7 *pulcherrima nuda es*), yet Martial assumes there must be some hidden, hideous blemish since she doesn't want to be naked with him. After the usual taunts that are typically tossed at the *uetula* scare-figures of satire, Martial ends with imagining her *cunnus* as having a mouth (6 'something protrudes from the mouth of your *cunnus*', *aut aliquid cunni prominet ore tui*), before concluding that her only vice, though deadly, is that she is characterized by 'stupid speech', *fatua*, like the *fatuus cunnus* of *Ep.* 7.18.11. In Book 11 Martial returns to Galla in a two-line epigram that reverses her portrayal of fatuousness in 11.19:

Quaeris cur nolim te ducere, Galla? Diserta es
saepe soloecismum mentula nostra facit.

You ask why I don't want to marry you, Galla? You're too eloquent, and my *mentula* often makes linguistic *faux pas* [*soloecismum*].

As Lavigne shows, Martial in Book 11 develops a sort of 'poetics of the gaffe', whereby women, like language, are the poet's media in a tongue in cheek silencing of anyone and anything that might rival his attempt at poetic and sexual mastery: 'the metaphoric use of solecism removes the poem from the realm of the simply obscene and requires the reader to reflect on the connection between poetry and sex'. He also shows that the inability to speak is operative in this epigram and throughout the collection: 'Within the logic of the poem, *soloecismum* is the metaphoric link between a tongue and a *mentula* through the image of the mouth that does not speak correctly ... First, as a foreign word, *soloecismum* is itself a solecism and, second, *mentula* can be seen as a misuse of diction. Martial is creating his own language by appropriating the rules of the misuse of language'.[77] Martial does not tell us if it is Galla's upper or lower mouth that is *diserta*, 'eloquent', but either way it is more of a compliment than his earlier complaints of her *cunnus* as stupid, *fatuus*. Furthermore, Martial here continues to make use of the *penis loquens* that is able to produce articulate, but ineffective speech. Like Aristophanes' penis in search of brains and Horace's 'illiterate' *nerui*, Martial's *mentula* makes intelligible linguistic gaffes.

At 11.58.11, however, Martial's cock speaks Greek in a decidedly Attic-comic key to his male lover who tries to bribe the poet with sex for money: *lota mentula lana*[78] / λαικάζειν *cupidae dicet auaritiae*, 'once my *mentula* has been wiped with wool [i.e. "once I have gotten off"], it will say "fuck off" to your cupidinous greed'.

The verb λαικάζειν is used nine times in the remains of Greek comedy,[79] yet, as Jocelyn notes, it does not appear in Greek historiography, oratory, or philosophical writings.[80] In this epigram Martial manages to trope not only the Greek precedent of using λαικάζειν in scenes of comic abuse (much as he did with *poppysmata* in 7.18), but he also pays tribute to the only other usage of the word in Latin literature: Petronius' freedman Seleucus, who, in the *cena Trimalchionis*, offers a morbid, pseudo-medical speech about the benefits of not bathing:

> *Excepit Seleucus fabulae partem et: 'Ego, inquit, non cotidie lavor; baliscus enim fullo est: aqua dentes habet, et cor nostrum cotidie liquescit. Sed cum mulsi pultarium obduxi, frigori laecasin dico'* (42.1–4).

> Seleucus took up his part of the story: 'I do not bathe daily, he said; for the bath is like a fuller: water has teeth, and it melts away our heart daily. But when I have imbibed a vessel of mead, I say "go suck it" to the cold'.

In Petronius obscene words are quite rare,[81] and Seleucus' obscenity, '*laecasin dico*', is de-fanged of any bite (despite the water's apparent teeth); the *ad hominem* aggression that characterizes the use of λαικάζειν in Greek comedy becomes in Petronius' hands banal chest thumping. Martial, however, reinscribes into λαικάζειν the Greek-comic precedent of attacking an opponent with sexually aggressive words and also combines it with personification of his penis, endowed with speech, but Martial's speaking penis accomplishes something very different from Horace's *mutto*. Horace's declaiming penis highlights his inability to satirize named targets, but Martial's obscenities tend to be part of a larger project of creating a debased persona that wants not so much to embody the constraints of speech placed on him by the regime as to celebrate his own ability to create poetry within such a society.

In his skoptic poetry, Martial finds it inevitable that 'poets are, or need to be, chronically *ill*'.[82] Rimell shows that Martial adopts the 'sick poet' trope that goes back to Roman Elegy, Horace, and even Plautine Comedy and drains it of any wit or romance. Martial depicts Rome as filthy, infected, and teeming with dirty bodies, both female and male, '[a]nd like their hypochondriac author, the epigrams are nervous about touching and being touched..., and Martial shows repeatedly how the epigrams themselves interact, rub off, "infect" each other'.[83] This is a very different Rome from Horace's swanky, louche bedrooms and dinner parties, and far from Aristophanes' symposiastic and litigious Athens. Yet on the other hand, the idea of an infection in the city connects Martial to his earlier satirical forebears.[84] Martial depicts himself as abject: Rome's illness is inescapable for Martial, and his own body is now caught up in the contagion, and Martial takes the anxiety expressed by his predecessors over the constraints on *libertas* and transforms them into a trope to be contrasted with his own chaotic mastery of language – Martial attempts to position his ineffective speech as indicative not of a *loss* of *libertas* and *simplicitas*, but as a tribute to what he attempts to portray as a more hopeful time under Nerva, as signaled elaborately in the introductory poems of Book XI. In this way, Martial's proliferation of personified sex organs is part of his Saturnalian vision of poetry that portrays itself as recovering some of the lost liberty and freedom to abuse that earlier satirists lamented.

Under pressure: male hysteria

I see the overall proliferation and development of skoptic prosopopoeia in Athenian Comedy and Roman satire as a result of what Neil Hertz has described as 'male hysteria' – an idea that Ellen Oliensis has applied to Horace's depiction of Canidia in the *Epodes*.[85] During times of extreme political pressure (he focuses on Revolutionary France, but his thesis could be applied equally well to the Peloponnesian War, the Roman Civil War, and the constraints of *libertas* in imperial Rome), Hertz argues that male hysteria creates an atmosphere in which political threats are seen as terrifying representations of grotesque female sexuality.[86] Tocqueville, for example, is prevented from entering the Chamber of Deputies, surrounded by guards, by a grotesque old woman selling vegetables who attacks him and provokes Tocqueville to shudder at 'the frightful and hideous expression on her face, which reflected demagogic passions and the fury of civil war'.[87] Similarly, du Camp portrays the painter Courbet as a violent revolutionary who was guilty (in the eyes of du Camp) of the destruction of the Vendôme column. This event shares important similarities with the mutilation of the *herms* during the Peloponnesian War: the destruction of these columns was connected with sexual debasement and identified as *damnationes memoriae* that led to revolution and bloodshed. In the former instance, the painter's subject matter in his controversial painting, '*L'Origine du monde*', and his revolutionary spirit went hand in hand: a reputedly vulgar painting of a naked woman's torso, focal point on the vagina, with arms and legs withheld from view by the borders of the canvas, revealed, in the words of du Camp in his four-volume denunciation of the *Commune*, Courbet's alleged moral abjection:

When one draws aside the veil one remains stupefied to perceive a woman, life-size, seen from the front, moved and convulsed, remarkably executed, reproduced *con amore*, as the Italians say, providing the last word in realism. But, by some inconceivable forgetfulness, the artist who copied his model from nature, had neglected to represent the feet, the legs, the thighs, the stomach, the hips, the chest, the hands, the arms, the shoulders, the neck and the head. The man who, for a few coins, could degrade his craft to the point of abjection, is capable of anything ... Thersites and Venus are thus equally beautiful simply because they exist; the humpback of the one is equal to the bosom of the other. This is the theory of impotent men, who erect their defects into a system; everyone knows the fable of the fox whose tail was cut off. [88]

Not long after the Courbet scandal, Sigmund Freud visited the Berlin Museum, where he saw on display for the first time the Baubo statuettes from Priene. Freud describes them in detail in his writings.[89] Bonfante suggests that it was these statuettes that inspired Freud's diagnosis of a young man who, every time his father came into the room, would see a face where the sex organs should be.[90] As I have suggested, this is not a new hysteria: Aristophanes, Horace, Petronius, and, to some extent, Martial have shown that speaking sex organs are especially prominent examples of constrained and debased speech on the comic stage, the satirist's page, or the pornographer's celluloid in times when satirists feel their speech is under threat, either by governmental censorship (as with Horace and Petronius) or real or alleged new-found freedoms (as with Aristophanes, Martial, and twentiethth-century pornographic cinema).

Notes

1 Gowers 2012: ad loc, notes that Villius is the lover of Sulla's daughter, Fausta. I am grateful for helpful comments from and discussions with the editors, Toph and Tom, as well as many others, including Dana Renga, Elizabeth Sharp, David Smith, and especially Don Lavigne.
2 On this passage, see Harrison 2007: 89: '*Animus* here echoes the Homeric *thumos* in internal debate scenes, and the lofty language of 1.2.70 (*magno prognatum deposco cunnum*) stresses the epic origin of this scene'. See also Hooley 1999, who describes this 'chat' between a Roman male and his penis as refiguring elegiac love poetry in a satiric vein, and Sharland 2010: 110–114, who reads the penis as adopting the persona of 'polemic moraliser.' All translations are my own unless otherwise noted.

3 Freudenberg 1993: 24–5. Armstrong 1989: 35 claims that 'Horace's talking penis is apparently unique in ancient poetry, although Lucilius (fragment 237) had been gross enough to picture one weeping'.
4 The type of prosopopoeia that Freudenburg and Fiske adduce as models is most frequently associated with ancient diatribe: Gowers 2012 s.v. 68–72.
5 Curran 1970: 234: '[T]here is metaphor in "ira" and even in "conferbuit", but the fundamental notion is the literal physiological sensation of heat and angry throbbing.'
6 Gowers 2014: ad loc., notes that 'The penis's aggressive diatribic manner evokes the robust Cato figure of 31–5'. As we will see below, the image of a penis endowed with reason wittily transgresses the first principle of Platonic medical physiology in the *Timaeus*, where genitals are described as the epitome of irrationality and animal instinct.
7 For *cunnus* as obscene, see *Brutus* 154; if we said it the other way, the letters would run together in a rather obscene way'); cf. *ad Fam.* 9.22.
8 On diatribe and the idea that Horace's penis evokes the figure of Cato, mentioned in lines 31–5, see Gowers 2012 ad 68–72 (p. 106). In fourth-century comedy, the image of the speaking anus appears (Eub. fr. 107 K-A. Cf. *AP* 11.415), though I consider this to be a different phenomenon altogether than speaking penises and vaginas.
9 Lucilius' image of a weeping penis, for example, finds a precedent in Ar. *Th.* 1187: . . . κλαῦσί γ' ἂν μὴ 'νδον μένῃς. Cucchiarelli 2001 revolutionized studies of Horace's *Satires* by showing how Aristophanes' *Frogs* is an important model, not only for the journey narrative of *Sat.*1.5, but also for Horace's appeal to Old Comedy in *Sat.*1.4 and his overall meta-poetic program of what Gowers calls, following Cucchiarelli, a satire that is 'slimmed down' (cf. Gowers 1993: 126 on Euripides slimming Aeschylean tragedy at Ar. *Frogs* 940). More recently, McNelis 2012: 252–64, has shown that Persius and Juvenal both adopt and adapt the Aristophanic motif in the *Thesmophoriazusae* of an effeminate poet who dresses in drag and spies on women's rituals.
10 In his attempt to re-think Deleuze's call for a 'body without organs' via Lacaniansim, Žižek 2004: 87 posits instead a model of organs without bodies, and I reproduce this passage here within its larger context for clarity's sake: 'If a king holds in his hands a scepter and wears the crown, his words will be taken as the words of a king. Such insignia are external, not part of my nature: I don them; I wear them to exert power. As such, they "castrate" me: they introduce a gap between what I immediately am and the function that I exercise . . . In this precise sense, far from being the opposite of power, it is synonymous with power; it is that which confers power upon me. And one has to think of the phallus not as the organ that immediately expresses the vital force of my being, my virility, and so forth but, precisely, as such an insignia, as a mask that I put on in the same way a king or judge puts on his insignia – phallus is an "organ without a body" that I put on, which gets attached to my body, without

ever becoming an "organic part" namely, forever sticking out as its incoherent, excessive supplement'.

11 For persona theory in Roman satire, see Kernans 1959, Anderson 1982, Freudenberg 1993, Braund 1996, and Keane 2006.
12 Gowers 2012 *ad loc.*
13 See Platter 2002, 88–9 on obscenity and 'Megarian humor'. See Lloyd 2003: 1–13 on 'semantic stretch'.
14 Olson 2002 *ad loc.* notes that Aristophanes' use of οὗτος χοῖρος at line 774 is 'the first-still tacit – acknowledgement of the fact that χοῖρος in this scene means not just "[female] piglet" but "pussy"'.
15 Hesychius' ὑῶν φωνή ('pig sound') is presumably connected to Plutarch's Gryllus, but that name itself surely builds upon a traditional representation of a pig's grunt. For similar puns involving a change in aspiration that allows a person's name to be read as a sex organ, see Rosen 1988: 32–3 on Bupalos as 'bou-phallos' (bull-phallus) and Shaw 2014: 126–7, who reads Harpalus Pallides, a character in Python's satyr play *Agen,* as 'Harphallos Phallides'. This also shows that a Greek ear would likely hear a punning connection between aspirated and unaspirated forms of a consonant. Compare with Fontaine 2010: 79 n. 84, who argues that Ballio in Plautus' *Pseudylus* should be read as Phallio, suggesting 'phallus'.
16 S.v. *LSJ* II.c.
17 Henderson 1991: 15: 'Likewise at the Thesmophoria, where the ritual obscenity was thought to derive from the good-natured jesting of the maid, Iambe, which cheered up the grieving goddess *(h.Cer.* 202 ff.). Baubo, the "orphic Iambe," cheered up the goddess by actually exposing herself; she may be connected with the ὄλισβος (dildo) of Herod. 6.19. We find companies (ὁμιλίαι) of obscenity-hurlers at the Syracusan Demeter cult'. On the display of phalli and vulva at the Thesmophoria, see Halliwell 2008: 165, 174–6.
18 Henderson 1991: 87.
19 On *parrhēsia*, see Halliwell 1991, who insists that comic freedom of speech had a special status in the 'democratic organization of classical Athens precisely because it belonged closely together with ritual or festive (Dionysiac) celebrations'. See also Sommerstein 2004; Saxonhouse 2006, esp. 129–37; Rosen 2014a.
20 See Olson 2004 *ad loc.* for a discussion of the son, rather than the daughter, as the probable referent of ποσθαλίσκον.
21 Elsewhere Aristophanes uses πόσθων as a term of endearment for a boy (Ar. *Pax* 1300).
22 See King 1998: 222–5, for an excellent discussion of this passage. King warns us that Plato's description of the womb does not cohere with Hippocratic physiology, and she stresses that 'analogies comparing certain parts of the body to living creatures is common' (223). In their refutations of the 'wandering womb' theory, both Galen and

Soranus mention that 'some' still espouse it (*ibid.* 224), showing that it continued to be a popular idea into the imperial period.
23 King 1998: 224.
24 Csapo 1997: 260.
25 Csapo 1997: 269–75 provides evidence that part of the phallus procession involved 'moving parts' that allowed the out-sized cult penis to bob up and down and simulate penetration of the riders.
26 On the evidence for the plague as priapism, see Csapo 1997: 267.
27 Olender 1990: 84.
28 Halliwell 2008: 165.
29 Halliwell *ibid.*; Rosen 2007: 47–57.
30 See Diels 1907.
31 See Halliwell 2008: 265, esp. n. 25.
32 Examples from 1970s pornographic cinema offer instructive parallels to Aristophanes' attempt to demonstrate what a talking vagina would say: 'The Speaking Sex' (*Le sexe qui parle*) is a French porn film released in 1975. Foucault uses the phrase in his 1976 landmark volume of *The History of Sexuality* to critique society's seeming obsession with talking about sex. In the film, a young woman who is compelled to seek fulfillment in extramarital affairs finds that her vagina is endowed with speech and begins to confess her sordid experiences to her husband. The film ends with the disease spreading to her husband, whose penis begins to speak up. The 1972 film *Deep Throat* also depicts a woman with an insatiable 'medical' condition: her clitoris is located in her throat. The plots of both films hinge on the conflation of the lower, genital mouth with the oral mouth. See Garrigou-Kempton 2010; Williams 1999: 1–33; Cryle 2001.
33 Halliwell 2008: 165–75, discusses the difficulties of dating Baubo evidence, but also clearly shows how Baubo became assimilated into the older Iambe traditions.
34 On the importance of Iambe and Baubo for Horace's depictions of Canidia in the *Sermones* and *Epodes*, see Gowers forthcoming, Barchiesi 2009, Oliensis 1998: 64–101.
35 Csapo 1997 and Halliwell 2008: 161–6, have published the majority of the testimonia.
36 Lape 2004 and Fontaine 2010 are the best treatments of the intervening years between Aristophanes and Roman Comedy. Rudich 1993: xvii succinctly describes the rupture in Republican traditions of *libertas*: 'As Tacitus makes clear, the boldest champions of the Republic "perished on a battlefield or in the course of proscriptions" (*Ann.*, 1, 2). Furthermore, the Senate underwent at least three substantial purges (28 BC, 8 BC, and AD 14) with Augustus in the capacity of censor. Finally, the traditional institution of patronage, based on the ethics of reciprocity, played a crucial role in the process. Standing at the top of the power pyramid, the

emperor possessed multiple means to act as supreme patron in regard to the members of the upper classes, promoting their careers and bestowing upon them benefactions and rewards in the form of ranks, offices, decorations, or even financial assistance. In consequence, a new nobility, often recruited from municipal and even provincial gentry, filled vacancies and largely replaced the old'.
On *libertas* in Horace, see Braund 2002; Gowers 2002; Henderson 1994; Feeney 1992; Lowrie 2008.

37 *Pollio, cum fescenninos in eum Augustus scripsisset, ait: at ego taceo. non est enim facile in eum scribere qui potest proscribere* (Macrobius 2.4.21: 'When Augustus had written Fescennine verse against him, Pollio said: "But I am silent. For it is not easy to write against one who can proscribe" ').

38 Cicero uses the word at least twenty times in a legal context, e.g: 'The Martial legion and the fourth legion had devoted themselves to the authority of the senate, and had devoted themselves to uphold the dignity of the republic, in such a way that they demanded Caius Caesar for their commander' (Cic. *Phil.* 11.20.14–18: *legio Martia et legio quarta ita se contulerant ad auctoritatem senatus et rei publicae dignitatem ut deposcerent imperatorem et ducem C. Caesarem.*). Livy similarly uses the word primarily in legal contexts.

39 On anxieties of masculinity in Horace, see Gowers forthcoming.

40 Quint. 9.2.29–32: *illa adhuc audaciora et maiorum, ut Cicero existimat, laterum, fictiones personarum, quae prosopopoiiai dicuntur: mire namque cum uariant orationem tum excitant.* [30] *his et aduersariorum cogitationes uelut secum loquentium protrahimus (qui tamen ita demum a fide non abhorrent si ea locutos finxerimus quae cogitasse eos non sit absurdum), et nostros cum aliis sermones et aliorum inter se credibiliter introducimus, et suadendo, obiurgando, querendo, laudando, miserando personas idoneas damus.* [31] *quin deducere deos in hoc genere dicendi et inferos excitare concessum est. Urbes etiam populique uocem accipiunt.*

41 *Cat.* 1.7.18: *quae tecum, Catilina, sic agit et quodam modo tacita loquitur: nullum iam aliquot annis facinus extitit nisi per te ... haec si tecum, ita ut dixi, patria loquatur, nonne impetrare debeat, etiamsi uim adhibere non possit?* 'For She [the fatherland], o Catiline, thus pleads with you and in a certain way speaks silently to you: "For so many years now no crime has existed except through you ...". If the fatherland spoke thus to you, as I have said, should she not get her wish, even if she were not able to apply force?' See Stroup 2003; Habinek 2005: 35, 51, 55; Gowing 2005: 118; Hine 2010: 213 for the use of personification in Roman oratory.

42 See note 6 above and Connolly 2007: 214–23, as well as Worman 2008: 62–120.

43 Hawkins forthcoming offers an important account of the complex way that authors and crowds managed to work around obstacles to free speech in imperial Rome.

44 Gowers forthcoming; Henderson 1987 and 2009; Fitzgerald 1988; Oliensis 1998: 64–101.
45 Cf. Watson 2003: 307 on the probability that *nerui* refers solely to Horace's penis and not to 'penises' in general. *Nerui* also clearly means 'a penis' at *Epod.* 12.19 (referring to Horace's own penis). See Watson 2003: 42: 'In personifying his *nerui illitterati* (cf. *eneruet* 2), Horace does not simply project himself as a crass sensualist: he becomes as it were, an appendage of his penis, a self-categorization that is of course nullified by the consummate artistry of *Epode* 8. And that artistry is abundantly on view in the final couplet, which, with its Aristophanic blend of crudity and subtle humor, is emblematic of the *Epode* as a whole'.
46 See Mankin 1995 *ad loc.*, on *imagines . . . triumpmhales* (*Epod.* 11–12) as a gloss for *triumphatores*. Impotence is also a steady theme throughout much of the iambic corpus: Hipponax seems to have suffered it (see Rosen and Keane 2013), and the Mnesiepes inscription claims that the Parians suffered a bout of impotence (ἀσθενεῖς] εἰς τὰ αἰδοῖα) – after accusing Archilochus of saying something 'too iambic' against Dionysus.
47 'Ferris-Hill 2015: 5 argues that the word *notabant* "Romanizes" Eupolis and Aristophanes, placing them in the role of the Roman censor, the highest office of the *cursus honorum.*
48 Freudenburg 2001: 17–18 notes that Horace is being deliberately misleading, as Aristophanes does not point out murderers in his extant plays.
49 Ruffell 2014: 294 sees this passage as intentionally distorting satire's relationship with Old Comedy and interprets Horace as claiming that Old Comedy mocked *exempla*, rather than named individuals, but I do not see Horace's lines as mutually exclusive with onomastic comedy. True, Horace does not name any of Aristophanes' targets, such as Cleon, but Aristophanes did claim that, for example, Cleon was a thief and a sexual deviant.
50 *Acer* is used throughout Cels. *De Med.* to describe astringent and sharp medicine and is contrasted with *lenis*, which is used to describe "gentle" medicine; e.g., 2.12.2d4 and 2.12.2e2.
51 For *seco* as a surgical word, see Bramble 1974: 36, who was the first modern critic to see a programmatic use of disease imagery in Persius' portrait of the satirist as one who surgically strikes 'at corruption, directing it, like the *sermo* envisaged by Cicero at *de Off.* 1. 136, *ad urendum et secandum* ["in order to cauterize and cut"], to diagnose, and perhaps heal, the vices of society'. See most recently Sommerstein 2011 for Horace's engagement with Aristophanes.
52 As Ruffell 2014a notes, Horace does an about-face over a decade later in the *Ars Poetica*, where he claims that Old Comedy's *libertas* led it into vice (*uitium*, 283) and that its force (*uim*, 282) had to be curbed by law (*lege*, 283).
53 Bakola 2008: 22–3.

54 On Horace's response to triumviral constraints on *libertas*, see Gowers 2002 and Henderson 1998. On Horace's constant redirection of sightlines of abuse in the *Epodes* see Nelson Hawkins 2014.
55 On the use of hot vapors in Roman medicine, see Cels. *De Med.* 2.17.1.3, 4.9.1.3, 6.8.1 and *infra*.
56 On decocted medicines, see Cels. *De Med.* 2.12.2e1, where Celsus describes how to cook down certain herbs like mallow to use as an enema for purging.
57 Gowers 1993, 19, 73, 75, 137, discusses the close connection between culinary and medical images in Roman satire. Barchiesi and Cucchiarelli 2005: 218–19 make the argument that there is a fundamental connection between healing and satire and describe Persius as a poet 'who resorts to dietary and curative imagery more often than any other satirist . . . One can easily see how Persius turns a physician's eye on poetry itself by exploiting the physiological connection between the poet and his verse'. They also note an interesting bodily intertext with Aristophanes' *Thesmo.*: 'There Persius uncovers the remote origins of his "diagnostic" procedure in Greek Old Comedy, by re-adapting that scene of Aristophanes' *Thesmophoriazusai* where the playwright Agathon's effeminate verses effect the sexual arousal of his listeners. To conclude his performance Agathon tells his audience: "it is necessary that what one writes should resemble what one is" ' (2005: 167).
58 Barchiesi and Cucchiarelli 2005: 219.
59 Though, as Braund 1996 shows in her exploration of persona theory, the healer is only one of many personae that the satirist dons like a mask.
60 For Juvenal, the answer may point to style and thematics, but the question is more difficult for Persius, who was not averse to obscene words: See Kenney 2012: 134: 'Juvenal on the whole steers clear of the sort of outright coarse vulgarity affected by Persius at 4.35–41, avoiding the words generally considered gross which were freely used by his contemporary Martial and even occasionally by Horace (Courtney 1980: 45–6)'. See also Cucchiarelli 2012: 168–9: 'As for Juvenal, there certainly doesn't seem to be in him any particular interest in comedy, and it is undeniable that here Juvenal wished, more so than Persius, to distance himself from Horace's model'. McNelis 2012: 256, however, provides an important corrective: 'Although Juvenal nowhere makes an explicit declaration of the importance of Greek Old Comedy for his verse, he similarly draws upon that tradition (or at least upon the Roman uses of the Greek comic poets) to explore the relationship between poet and audience from a sexual perspective'.
61 Rudich 1993: 144–9. There is evidence that Persius' freedom of speech was greatly constrained out of fear of Nero as well: 'the *Vita* of Persius says explicitly that the allusion to the myth of Midas at the end of his *Satire* 1 was edited posthumously out of fear of Nero' (Richlin 2012: 479).
62 From the *Virgilian Appendix* (Büchler, pp. 151–3 Oxford). See Richlin 1992: 114–15, for a discussion.

63 Richlin 1992: 116 and Adams 1982: 29–30.
64 On Greek models for Petronius, see Barchiesi 1999, who points to recently discovered fragments of Greek novels as important models for Petronius, but he also cautions that these finds also provide a means of also recognizing how much of the Greek novel Petronius did *not* use.
65 Cicero uses *furcifera* (*Vatin.* 15.16; *Pis.* 14.9; *Deiot.* 26.1), and it is used several times in Plautus and once in Horace (*Serm.* 2.7.22). Cicero also uses *confugo* to describe someone defending himself in courts (*Ver.* 2.3.191). Cf. Quint. *Inst.* 6.1.4, where he describes the use of *confugio* in legal contexts.
66 Ruffell 2014: 291.
67 *Ibid.* 298. Dover 1958: 235, characterizes personification as a bedrock of Aristophanic comedy: 'Few people have been so ingenious, or so rash, as to find *allēgoria* in Aristophanes. On the other hand, if "allegory" is used, as it has commonly been used since the eighteenth century, to mean simply the personification of qualities, acts, and situations, Aristophanes is pre-eminently an allegorical dramatist'.
68 Ausonius (fourth century CE) takes up where Petronius leaves off in his pornographic section of the *Cento Nuptialis* – a Fescennine send-up of Virgil's *Aeneid* which was purportedly in honor of the wedding of Gratian and Constantia, daughter of Constantius II and son of Valentinian. In it, the poet describes the deflowering of a bride on her wedding night in graphic language mixed with quotations of Virgil's *Aeneid*, one of which is also an allusion to Euryalus' death (A. 9.434). See McGill 2005: 113.
69 Ruffell 2014: 275.
70 Rudich 1993: 291. Cf. Lape 2004: 1–39, who offers a different sort of 'dissident' reading of Menandrian comedy, where the plays can be read as responding to the reduction of personal freedom after the loss of Greek democracy: 'Menander's comedy is constituted by countervailing narrative trajectories to reproduce and resist the civic social order' (12).
71 Encolpius here seems to be following the Ciceronian injunction against using genital obscenities in oratory; see n. 6 above.
72 Symmachus is the terrible doctor who kills patients rather than heals them at Mart. *Ep.* 5.9 and at 4.6.70.6.
73 At *Priap.* 39.8, we see a 'non-fatuous' *cunnus*: *si qua est non fatui puella cunni*, 'if there is any girl with a smart vagina'.
74 *Chatterbox* is the name of a 1977 American comic porn film, in which a young hairdresser named Penelope discovers that her vagina, later named 'Virginia', can talk and becomes a singing and talk-show celebrity, driving Penelope to despair, as she is silenced by her lower mouth. See Rees 2013: 562–76. Both *Chatterbox*'s advertising poster and that of the 1975 French porn film, *Le sexe qui parle*, display heavily

lip-sticked lips in the shade of red, engaging with the now iconic image of the red lips from the 1975 film *Rocky Horror Picture Show*.
75 Philocleon, rejoicing in the thundering din of the courtroom, compares it to the lightning of Zeus, which causes the rich people to smack their mouth and shit themselves.
76 Martial's 'deaf *mentula*' at 9.37 contrasts with 7.18's chattering *cunnus;* at 9.37.9–10, Martial focuses on Galla's ugliness and claims that, although his *mentula* is deaf, nevertheless its one eye can still see how ugly her *cunnus* is. See Richlin 1992: 67 for a discussion of the passage. At 1.58.3, his penis protests, *queritur*, over the high price of a prostitute.
77 Lavigne 2008: 287, n. 22.
78 On *lana* instead of *laeua*, see Kay 1985 *ad loc.*
79 Ar. *Eq.* 167; *Thesm.* 57; *Ach.* 79, 537; Pherecr. fr. 159.2 K-A; Cephisod. fr. 3.5 K-A; Men. *Dysc.* 892; *Peric.* 485; Strato Com. fr. 1. 36 K-A.
80 Jocelyn 1992, 14.
81 Smith 1975 *ad* 42.
82 Rimell 2008: 21. See esp. 'Contagion and Copyright: the City as Text', 19–50.
83 *Ibid.* 24–5.
84 Barchiesi and Cucchiarelli 2005.
85 Hertz 1983. Hertz takes the idea of male hysteria from Freud: a fear of castration from a sexually aggressive (and repulsive) woman that is sublimated into 'a similar panic, perhaps when the cry goes up that throne and altar are in danger' (Freud 1963: 215). On Oliensis' use of Hertz, see 1998: 7–8.
86 Hertz 1983.
87 *Ibid.* 173.
88 *Ibid.* 172 and 169. This painting has a long history of causing controversy and titillating the intelligentsia: Jaques Lacan – the last private owner of the painting – secretly bought it after World War II and installed it in a private room of his country home, hidden behind a screen and almost never displayed to visitors (Barzilai 1999: 8–18). Fellini unveiled it to the world, however, in one of his advertising posters for *La città delle donne* (1980), 'City of Women', which is a riotous and carnivalesque re-reading of Aristophanes' *Thesmophoriazousae*. In the advert poster, Courbet's nude is used though also defaced: the poster shows a hand-drawn circle around the woman's vulva with an arrow pointing to the words 'center of the world'.
89 See Bonfante 2008: 2 n. 6.
90 *Ibid.* 2–9.

4

Dio Chrysostom and the Naked Parabasis

Tom Hawkins*

Compared to the rollicking fun of Lucianic satire or the broad literary sweep of Athenaeus, Dio Chrysostom (c. 40–c. 110 CE) might seem to be an improbable player in the story of Athenian comedy's imperial afterlife. At one point he has the young Alexander tell his dad Philip that of all the poets, only Homer has the nobility and grandeur befitting a king, and the prince includes Archilochus and the comic poets as examples of verse that is only useful 'for laughter or mockery' (Or. 2.4–6: γέλωτος ἕνεκεν ἢ λοιδορίας). In the *Euboean Discourse* Dio asserts that the poor should be kept from serving as tragic or comic actors, since such activities are unbecoming of self-respecting and free individuals (Or. 7.119–20).[1] And in outlining a course of study for a patron interested in dabbling in the life of a public speaker, Dio praises Menander's elegant style and dismisses Old Comedy completely (Or. 18.6–7: ἡ ἀρχαία κωμῳδία).[2] Yet even this praise for Menander seems to be poorly supported in Dio's own writings. Aside from this passage, he mentions Menander by name only in a glancing reference to a statue of the playwright in Rhodes (31.116) and quotes a single pair of securely attested lines of his poetry (fr. 298.6–7 K-A at Dio 32.16).[3] By contrast, Dio quotes or alludes to Euripides scores of times, and he rarely goes more than a few paragraphs without engaging somehow or other with his beloved Homer.

Yet in two public orations, Dio draws more overtly on comic material, and he leans heavily upon this comic influence in articulating a persona through which he can harangue his audience to good effect. This divergence from his usual habits has been noted before but never deeply analyzed.[4] I suggest, therefore, that in his *Alexandrian* and *First Tarsian* orations (*Orations* 32 and 33) Dio turns to comic poetry specifically in order to replicate the admonitory and advisory role of the comic poet found in most Aristophanic parabases. The outrageous plots and costuming of Old Comedy hold no interest for Dio, but in these speeches in which he upbraids his listeners with the stated goal of helping them improve themselves, the parabatic voice offers an apt and effective model. With the other trappings of Old Comedy cut away, these speeches take on the feel of extended and isolated parabases.

I pursue this idea that Dio has composed two naked parabases in three steps: first, I discuss the parabasis itself both in its classical instantiation and in a few apposite comments from Dio's era; second, I devote the bulk of the paper to analyzing Dio's two speeches in terms of the influence of Old Comedy; and finally, I conclude by suggesting a few ways in which Dio's parabatic maneuver can be understood as stretching and updating the classical function of the parabasis.

Parabases in Old Comedy and beyond

After singing a quick *kommation* (510–17) the chorus of our extant version of *Clouds* addresses the audience in the first person singular: O spectators, I will speak (κατερῶ) truthfully to you ... (518).[5] On this line the scholiast comments that 'the parabasis seems to be spoken by the chorus, but the playwright introduces his own persona'. This fits with Pollux's succinct definition of the parabasis: 'whenever the chorus comes forward and says whatever the poet wants to say to the theater' (4.111). Although this was not always the way parabases worked, the shift from plural to singular at *Clouds* 518 and the need for later ancient explanation of that shift highlight the striking theatrical effect of an Old Comic parabasis.[6] The parabasis interrupts the plot and frequently disrupts the characterization of the chorus, who speak directly to the audience in stylized and standardized ways (both in terms of meter and content). Through the parabatic voice, the poet praises and justifies himself, derides rivals, flatters and teases the audience and offers seemingly serious advice on political issues of the day.[7] This last theme is nowhere as prominent in our evidence as in the case of *Frogs*. Because of the advice he gave in that parabasis, Aristophanes was given an olive crown and an official commendation, and the play itself was granted the unusual honor of being re-staged.[8]

It is useful to recognize, however, that the word parabasis is not itself part of the vocabulary of old comic poets but only of later ancient critics and commentators. Aristophanes refers to 'the anapests' or speaks of 'turning aside' (*sc.* to the audience) by means of the verb *parabainein*. Particularly interesting in this regard is the scenario in the first two lines of the parabasis-proper in *Peace*, where the chorus claims that 'the bailiffs ought to thrash any poet who, coming forward during the anapests (παραβὰς ἐν τοῖς ἀναπαίστοις), praises himself before the theater' (734–5). As this passage makes clear, the self-conscious language about the parabasis was couched in terms of an intersection of a metrical context and a physical movement. Yet although it may seem that matters of content and propriety are at stake in the apparent contradiction of a poet chastising other poets who praise themselves at a point in the play seemingly designed for self-praise (compare similar sentiments at *Ach.* 628–9 and *Knights* 507–9), such comments may also serve to highlight the disruptiveness of the parabasis. Certainly the parabasis is something of a grand and standardized aside, but the verb *parabainein* means not only 'to step aside' but also 'to transgress', a definition we can find both prior to Aristophanes and in non-parabatic portions of Aristophanic plays.[9] As Biles has shown, whatever the exact history of the development of the Old Comic form, the parabasis was conceptualized not just as an aside but as a creative act of transgression (against rivals or theatrical traditions) that asserts the playwright's own authority and artistic vision.[10]

Biles' argument about the parabasis as a locus of creative transgression suggests that highly formalized approaches to Old Comedy may overlook innovations in the name of imposing order. It is with this in mind that I suggest we can find parabatic language outside the formal boundaries of parabases.[11] For one thing, our knowledge of the parabasis relies so heavily on Aristophanes, that it is at least possible that the Aristophanic parabasis was not the norm. Eupolis fr. 192 K-A, for example, comes from the parodos of *Marikas*, yet both Storey and Bakola have recognized the parabatic tenor of these lines, and Bakola has argued that here Eupolis vaunts himself as a teacher of the *polis* in direct contrast to Aristophanes' bid to be its healer.[12] This long fragment preserves parts of an ancient commentary on the play and thus includes both bits of text and fragmentary explanatory comments. From this we can recognize that Eupolis' chorus undermines the claims of Aristophanes-the-healer by stating that 'the diseases return' (7 πάλιν ... νοσήματα ὑποτροπάζει); then that the audience, like students, 'have been let out of school for a long time' (13 πολὺν πολλοῦ χρόνον καὶ τὸν δ' ἀφεῖσθε), a comment explained as coming from the language of school teachers (14–15 ἡ δὲ μεταφορὰ ἀπὸ τῶν γραμματοδιδασκάλων); and finally the speaker tells the audience to 'wipe it clean' (18 ἐξαλείφετε), which is glossed as 'ready your writing tablets' (19 λέαινε τὰ δέλτους), showing that Eupolis-the-teacher is ready to succeed where Aristophanes-the-healer had failed. Parabatic moments can appear in other parts of a comic play.

Unfettered by formal constraints, parabatic speech can be found even further afield. Pollux, in the same passage cited above, mentions the seemingly nonsensical idea of tragic parabases (4.111):

τῶν δὲ χορικῶν ᾀσμάτων τῶν κωμικῶν ἕν τι καὶ ἡ παράβασις, ὅταν ἃ ὁ ποιητὴς πρὸς τὸ θέατρον βούλεται λέγειν, ὁ χορὸς παρελθὼν λέγῃ. ἐπιεικῶς δ᾿ αὐτὸ ποιοῦσιν οἱ κωμῳδοποιηταί, τραγικὸν δ᾿ οὐκ ἔστιν· ἀλλ᾿ Εὐριπίδης αὐτὸ πεποίηκεν ἐν πολλοῖς δράμασιν. ἐν μέν γε τῇ Δανάῃ τὸν χορὸν τὰς γυναῖκας ὑπὲρ αὐτοῦ τι ποιήσας παράδειν, ἐκλαθόμενος ὡς ἄνδρας λέγειν ἐποίησε τῷ σχήματι, τῆς λέξεως τὰς γυναῖκας. καὶ Σοφοκλῆς δ᾿ αὐτὸ ἐκ τῆς πρὸς ἐκεῖνον ἁμίλλης ποιεῖ σπανιάκις, ὥσπερ ἐν Ἱππόνῳ.

The parabasis is another one of the choral songs in comedies, when the chorus comes forward and says whatever the playwright wants to say to the theater. Comic playwrights generally do this, but it is not tragic. Yet Euripides has inserted them into many plays. In *Danae* he made the chorus of women say something on his own behalf, and completely forgetting their womanly voice he made them speak as men in their bearing. And Sophocles does this out of rivalry with him on a few occasions, as in *Hipponous*.

Cairns argues that Pollux's reference to tragic parabases most probably points not toward any formal structure, such as we find in so many Aristophanic plays, but, rather, to moments in Euripidean and Sophoclean tragedy when he sensed an intrusion of the poet's own voice and thoughts.[13] In the case of Sophocles' *Hipponous* we know too little about the play to evaluate Pollux's claim, but imperial recollections of Euripides' *Danae* are more tantalizing. Seneca quotes (in Latin) part of Ixion's speech about his lust for gold (fr. 7 Karamanou = 324 Kannicht) and claims that the audience was so outraged at Ixion's statements that they interrupted the show until Euripides himself came on stage to beg them to withhold judgment (*Letter* 115.15).[14] Plutarch preserves a rebuttal to such reactions in which Euripides claims that he 'didn't let Ixion leave the stage until he was bound to the wheel [sc. on which he would be punished forever in Hades]' (*Mor.* 19e).[15] The combination of Pollux's comment about a tragic parabasis in Danae, Seneca's account of Euripides coming on stage in the middle of the play to defend his narrative, and Plutarch's version of just such a Euripidean defense is a striking coincidence, and it could be that all three pieces of evidence allude to a single shared cultural memory about this play. Although I agree with Cairns that the idea of an actual Euripidean parabasis modeled on what we know from Aristophanic comedy is highly improbable, Seneca's anecdote amounts to a fantasized staging of such a moment that is motivated by an ethical expectation imputed to tragic audiences.

Shaw has shown that in the fourth century, satyr drama could also adopt recognizably parabatic language. Although the evidence is extremely limited, he finds such parabatic moments in a fragment of Astydamas *Heracles* (*TrGF* 4), described by Athenaeus as a satyr drama (496e), and in an unattributed satyric fragment, datable on metrical grounds to the Hellenistic era (*TrGF* 646a).[16]

Non-dramatic examples of parabatic speech can be adduced as well. On different occasions Kahn has compared the myth at the end of Plato's *Gorgias* and the central digression of *Euthydemus* to Aristophanic parabases, and various scholars have found similar parabatic moments in other Platonic texts.[17] Whereas the idea of a Platonic parabasis depends heavily on a reader's willingness to find such a thing, since Plato offers no overt clues of parabatic influence, we find clearer philological markers for a prose parabasis in two comments by Aelius Aristides in his response to an unnamed person who has accused him of inappropriately inserting words of self-praise into a speech in honor of Athena. Far from denying the basic point, Aristides admits that he had praised himself extemporaneously and asserts that such flourishes are both perfectly acceptable and as old as Hesiod (28.21 Keil = 49.360 Dindorf):

ὁ μὲν μεταξὺ τὸν ὕμνον ποιῶν ταῖς θεαῖς τοῦτο ἐντέθεικε τὸ ἔπος, ἐγκώμιον ὡς εἰπεῖν ἑαυτοῦ· ἡμεῖς δὲ τοὺς εἰς τὴν θεὸν λόγους καθαροὺς καθαρῶς ἐξεργασάμενοι μικρόν τι περὶ ἡμῶν αὐτῶν ἄγραφον παρεφθεγξάμεθα.

While composing a hymn to the goddesses, [Hesiod] inserted this line [=*Theog.* 22] as an encomium, as it were, to himself. But having piously finished my pious speech to the goddess, I said a little unscripted something about myself.

Although Aristides does not clearly mention a parabasis here, Sifakis has shown that his use of *paraphthengesthai* in these lines closely parallels his use of *parabainein* in a subsequent passage that overtly deals with comic and tragic practices (28.97 Keil = 49.387–8 Dindorf)[18]:

καὶ κωμῳδοῖς μὲν καὶ τραγῳδοῖς καὶ τοῖς ἀναγκαίοις τούτοις ἀγωνισταῖς ἴδοι τις ἂν καὶ τοὺς ἀγωνοθέτας καὶ τοὺς θεατὰς ἐπιχωροῦντας μικρόν τι περὶ αὑτῶν παραβῆναι, καὶ πολλάκις ἀφελόντες τὸ προσωπεῖον μεταξὺ τῆς Μούσης ἣν ὑποκρίνονται δημηγοροῦσι σεμνῶς·

You could see the judges and spectators granting the comic and tragic playwrights as well as their actors the chance to step aside and say something about themselves, and often they remove their mask in the middle of the play they are acting and speak openly.

Thus, it seems that Aristides here equates parabatic speech with insertions of self-praise in any genre. Although such a claim may seem to be an oversimplification in terms of our analysis of Old Comedy, for my purposes it shows both that the parabasis continued to be a topic of more than antiquarian debate into the imperial era (even a full generation after Dio) and that it could be conceived of in terms of a plasticity that transcends literary form.

Aristides' claim that parabatic speech involves stepping out of character to speak openly parallels another comment about Old Comic parabases from Plutarch, an exact contemporary of Dio. In a discussion of the best music for sympotic entertainment, Diogenianus rejects Old Comedy and goes on to praise Menander effusively (*Mor.* 711f–712a = *Table Talk* 7.8.3):

> τῶν δὲ κωμῳδιῶν ἡ μὲν ἀρχαία διὰ τὴν ἀνωμαλίαν ἀνάρμοστος ἀνθρώποις πίνουσιν· ἥ τε γὰρ ἐν ταῖς λεγομέναις παραβάσεσιν αὐτῶν σπουδὴ καὶ παρρησία λίαν ἄκρατός ἐστι καὶ σύντονος, ἥ τε πρὸς τὰ σκώμματα καὶ βωμολοχίας εὐχέρεια δεινῶς κατάκορος καὶ ἀναπεπταμένη καὶ γέμουσα ῥημάτων ἀκόσμων καὶ ἀκολάστων ὀνομάτων·

> Of comedies, the old form is ill-suited to men in their cups on account of its disjointedness. Because their vehemence and excessive frankness in the recited parabases are stark and intense, and the indifference to raillery and foolishness is dreadfully immoderate and crass and replete with unsuitable words and lewd expressions.

Diogenianus' rather effete rejection of Old Comic grit offers an extreme take on parabatic license, yet it fits broadly with Aristides' description of parabases as featuring the blunt words of the *koryphaios* himself, rather than the scripted comments of a character in-role.

The evidence here surveyed from the imperial era suggests that parabatic speech could be understood as transcending generic limitations and that it typically featured some combination of self-praise and blunt but licensed critique. If such an intersection proved too intense for Plutarch's Diogenianus as he lounged among his friends, for Dio, it offered an ideal gambit for haranguing the people of Alexandria and Tarsus.

Dio's naked parabases

Dio's *Orations* 32 and 33 were delivered to large audiences in Alexandria and Tarsus, respectively.[19] The *Alexandrian* (*Or.* 32) is clearly delivered in the city's theater, and there is good reason to believe that the *First Tarsian* (*Or.* 33) was similarly presented at the main urban theater.[20] Moreover, in both speeches Dio chastises the citizenry so forcefully that one might wonder how an audience would sit through such gruff treatment. In the *Alexandrian*, Dio harangues the people's preference in and comportment at public entertainments (particularly athletic and musical performances) in the aftermath of a riot that had gotten so out of hand that the military intervened (32.70–4); he also accuses them of licentiously throwing themselves into frivolous matters while altogether ignoring anything of actual importance. In the *First Tarsian* he has a go at the people of the Cilician capital for making some particularly unpleasant nasal sound (ῥέγχειν) that Dio associates with a catastrophic slide into the dissolution of gender norms and which, he claims, singles Tarsus out for abuse (λοιδορία) from its regional rivals, who call the Tarsians a bunch of Cercopes (33.38).[21] Dio concludes the speech with a sarcastic claim that the men of Tarsus are virtually 'complete and, in accord with nature, androgynes' (64 ὁλόκληροι . . . καὶ κατὰ φύσιν ἀνδρόγυνοι), language that clearly alludes to Aristophanes' speech in Plato's *Symposium* where our ancient *physis* is described as being 'complete' only during the existence of the 'hermaphroditic gender' (189e ὅλος . . . ἀνδρόγυνος).

The theatrical setting and low-register subject matter bring both these speeches into the very general neighborhood of Old Comedy, but to bolster my claim that Dio constructs a specifically parabatic voice for himself I will show that in these two speeches Dio draws himself into an updated but still recognizable version of the playwright, who uses the parabasis, in part, to give useful advice and instruction to the citizen audience.

Dio refers to comic material more often in the *Alexandrian*, but it is early in the *First Tarsian* that he offers his most programmatic account of his relationship to comedy. He begins the speech by wondering what the people might possibly expect him to say (33.1–5). He fears that they want to hear themselves and their city eulogized and claims that he has nothing to add to what many have said before him. Furthermore, he warns that such flattery leads to self-satisfaction rather than critical reflection. He then contrasts medical performances that aim to dazzle an audience with the often unseemly work of practicing physicians, whose aim is to heal the sick rather than impress spectators (6–7).[22] Next he warns that philosophers, unlike eulogists and medical showmen, are best left alone, lest they deliver a performance that the people would not want to hear. At this point he offers a history of comedy (9–10):

σκοπεῖτε δὲ τὸ πρᾶγμα οἷόν ἐστιν. Ἀθηναῖοι γὰρ εἰωθότες ἀκούειν κακῶς, καὶ νὴ Δία ἐπ' αὐτὸ τοῦτο συνιόντες εἰς τὸ θέατρον ὡς λοιδορηθησόμενοι, καὶ προτεθεικότες ἀγῶνα καὶ νίκην τοῖς ἄμεινον αὐτὸ πράττουσιν, οὐκ αὐτοὶ τοῦτο εὑρόντες, ἀλλὰ τοῦ θεοῦ συμβουλεύσαντος, Ἀριστοφάνους μὲν ἤκουον καὶ Κρατίνου καὶ Πλάτωνος, καὶ τούτους οὐδὲν κακὸν ἐποίησαν. ἐπεὶ δὲ Σωκράτης ἄνευ σκηνῆς καὶ ἰκρίων ἐποίει τὸ τοῦ θεοῦ πρόσταγμα, οὐ κορδακίζων οὐδὲ τερετίζων, οὐχ ὑπέμειναν. ἐκεῖνοι μὲν γὰρ ὑφορώμενοι καὶ δεδιότες τὸν δῆμον ὡς δεσπότην ἐθώπευον, ἠρέμα δάκνοντες καὶ μετὰ γέλωτος, ὥσπερ αἱ τίτθαι τοῖς παιδίοις, ὅταν δέῃ τι τῶν ἀηδεστέρων πιεῖν αὐτά, προσφέρουσι μέλιτι χρίσασαι τὴν κύλικα. τοιγαροῦν ἔβλαπτον οὐχ ἧττον ἤπερ ὠφέλουν, ἀγερωχίας καὶ σκωμμάτων καὶ βωμολοχίας ἀναπιμπλάντες τὴν πόλιν. ὁ δὲ φιλόσοφος ἤλεγχε καὶ ἐνουθέτει.

Consider this example. The Athenians were used to hearing obloquies about themselves, and, by Zeus, they crowded into the theater with the express purpose of being abused. Having set up a contest with a prize for those who were best at it – they did not come up with this idea on their own but acted on the advice of the god – they used to listen to Aristophanes, Cratinus and Plato [Comicus] and did not punish them at all. But when Socrates, with neither set nor stage followed the instructions of his god, without any vulgar dances or prattling, they couldn't take it. Those comic poets being distrustful and fearing the populace began to flatter it as if it were a tyrant, nibbling on easy targets with a laugh, just as nurses, whenever they have to give their wards something unpleasant to drink, smear the cup with honey before they hold it out to the children. So the comic poets did no less harm than good, by enflaming the city with effrontery and jokes and foolishness. But the philosopher censured and rebuked.[23]

Here we see both an explanation for Dio's disdain for comedy, since it eventually slouched into sycophantic praise, and a historical through-line of the benefits of well-considered civic chastisement (λοιδορία) that passed from comedy to Socratic philosophy. Dio, of course, has positioned himself as the heir to that tradition of ethical abuse.[24] The reduction of Old Comedy to nothing more than its abuse of the audience represents a willful oversimplification that only someone who disliked the genre could imagine, yet this also helps us to see what Dio found valuable (at least in its early instantiation) in it. Since the parabasis, and in particular the syzygy, was the Old Comic structure best suited for extended civic critique (as opposed to the myriad passing quips), it seems most probable that Dio has here charted a genealogy of parabatic speech that moved from comedy to philosophy and which he now makes use of in the theater at Tarsus.[25]

Although the rest of the *First Tarsian* contains less overtly comic material than does the *Alexandrian* (though in 33.64 he does quote Aristophanes fr. 587 K-A just before calling the Tarsians a bunch of androgynes), I have suggested elsewhere that Dio may have structured the entire speech upon the model of Cratinus' *Archilochoi*, and I will briefly summarize that argument here.[26] Beyond the mention of Cratinus at 33.9 as part of the early generation of comic poets who offered substantive abuse of Athenian audiences, Dio has constructed his critique of the Tarsians around the poles of Archilochean abuse and Homeric praise, an opposition found in various sources but which seems to have appeared most explicitly in Cratinus' play. Furthermore, Cratinus was remembered by later antiquity as someone who vaunted the ethical value of *loidoria*, much as Dio does in the *First Tarsian*.[27] Among the few fragments that we have of Cratinus' play, we find a reference to the Cercopes (fr. 12 K-A), who also make an appearance in Dio's speech at 33.38.[28] In the *First Tarsian*, then, Dio speaks from an ethical position that must have paralleled the voice of Cratinus' chorus, which spoke on behalf of Archilochean poetics, and his admonitory tone of civic chastisement is most closely paralleled in our extant sources by Aristophanic parabases. In dispensing with the frippery of Old Comic costuming and the outlandishness of its plots, Dio preserves the ethical *loidoria* of the comic parabasis, which Socrates took over from comedy and which Dio, in turn, claims to have inherited from the philosopher. Whereas the early comic poets had sought to improve Athens with licensed abuse and Socrates had attempted something similar with his unprepossessing conversations, Dio now applies his parabatic speech for the betterment of Tarsus, lest their louche ways end up undermining the city's prominent status in the organization of the eastern part of the empire.

With Dio's use of Old Comedy in the *First Tarsian* now clarified, we are in a better position to assess what he does in the *Alexandrian*, and I will examine the first thirteen sections of this speech in greatest detail, since it is in them that he constructs his parabatic voice before moving into the heart of his message to the Alexandrians. He begins with something of a parabatic opening, as he tries to get the citizens' attention (32.1):

Ἀρά γε βούλοισθ' ἄν, ὦ ἄνδρες, σπουδάσαι χρόνον σμικρὸν καὶ προσέχειν; ἐπειδὴ παίζοντες ἀεὶ διατελεῖτε καὶ οὐ προσέχοντες καὶ παιδιᾶς μὲν καὶ ἡδονῆς καὶ γέλωτος, ὡς εἰπεῖν, οὐδέποτε ἀπορεῖτε· καὶ γὰρ αὐτοὶ γελοῖοί ἐστε καὶ ἡδεῖς καὶ διακόνους πολλοὺς τούτων ἔχετε· σπουδῆς δὲ ὑμῖν τὴν πᾶσαν ἔνδειαν ὁρῶ οὖσαν.

> Could you be serious for a moment and give me your attention? Since you're constantly playing around and not paying attention and you never get enough, so to speak, of joking and merriment and laughter. For you yourselves are mirthful and merry, and you have many ministers of such things. But I see in you a total lack of seriousness.

Dio here brings his own seriousness to the Alexandrians' natural blitheness in a way that suggests the creation of a comical *spoudogeloion* meeting of the minds.

He next introduces the idea of a chorus (32.2) with the initially surprising contrast between the virtue of a chorus working in perfect unison and the virtue of an audience being united in perfect silence. Yet this comparison to a chorus, spoken in the theater by a single performer, serves to cast Dio's speech in a more dramatic light – something that he will build upon in the next several sentences.[29] Although he does not specify what sort of chorus he has in mind (and on the surface his point is more about the logistics of choral performance in general than any particular genre), he nevertheless gives a hint that he is thinking specifically of a comic chorus. For after a few more comments about the Alexandrians' devotion to jokes and horse-play, he gives an amazing four-line send-up of Homer (4). He slightly misquotes each line, adapting it to his context, and, more impressively, he jumbles together lines culled in sequential order from different books! He takes line 261 from *Il.* 24 and line 262 from *Il.* 16 and inserts between them lines 263–4 from *Od.* 18 (deviations from Homer underlined):

μῖμοί τ' ὀρχησταί τε χοροιτυπίῃσιν ἄριστοι,	(– *Il.* 24.261)
ἵππων τ' ὠκυπόδων ἐπιβήτορες, οἵ τε τάχιστα	(– *Od.* 18.263)
ἤγειραν μέγα νεῖκος ἀπαιδεύτοισι θεαταῖς,	(– *Od.* 18.264)
νηπιάχοις, ξυνὸν δὲ κακὸν πολέεσσι φέρουσιν.	(– *Il.* 16.262)

The best mimes and dancers move in time,
and riders on swift horses, who most quickly
rouse a great uproar among the illiterate audience,
the fools!, and bring common ruin to the many.

This manipulation of Homer is typical of Dio's close engagement with those beloved poems, but the specifics of retooling Homeric lines into a playfully configured passage of pseudo-Homeric poetry owes a debt to Old Comic treatments of hexametric material (he later presents a thirty-six-line Homeric *cento* that produces a similar effect at 32.82–5). Platter devoted a chapter to the carnivalesque reworkings of Homer in Aristophanic plays, and he concludes that 'resisters of epic-oracular authority turn hexameter poetry into a lingua franca that increases its base while reducing its rhetorical effectiveness'.[30] I would turn that comment around in this case and suggest that Dio here increases the rhetorical effectiveness of Homer's words by shifting their tone to fit the tenor of his speech.[31] That is to say that he comically distorts Homeric material in order to cast his oration as a comic presentation, since (he claims) his audience only understands tomfoolery and monkey-business. Dio Portrays himself as an oratorical master of comically distorted Homeric poetry.

After more commentary on the Alexandrians' misdirected attention to unproductive entertainments, Dio makes his most explicit connection between his words and Old Comedy, by contextualizing his own *parrhēsia* in terms of this commendable (classical) Athenian custom: 'that they let their poets put to shame not only individuals but even the city as a whole, if they were behaving at all badly' (32.6 ὅτι τοῖς ποιηταῖς ἐπέτρεπον μὴ μόνον τοὺς κατ' ἄνδρα ἐλέγχειν, ἀλλὰ καὶ κοινῇ τὴν πόλιν, εἴ τι μὴ καλῶς ἔπραττον). This discussion of Old Comic license parallels comments by Horace (S. 1.4.1–5), and Dio ensures the generic specificity of his reference by quoting overtly political bits of Aristophanes (*Knights* 42–3) and Eupolis (fr. 234 K-A), while saying that these passages were merely two among many that could be found 'among the comedies'.

The problem here in Alexandria, Dio says, is that 'for you there is neither any such chorus, nor poet nor anyone else, who will reproach you in a spirit of good-will and lay bare the failings of the city' (32.7 ὑμῖν δὲ οὔτε χορός ἐστι τοιοῦτος οὔτε ποιητὴς οὔτε ἄλλος οὐδείς, ὃς ὑμῖν ὀνειδιεῖ μετ' εὐνοίας καὶ φανερὰ ποιήσει τὰ τῆς πόλεως ἀρρωστήματα). Dio presents himself as the person to fill this need for a comic poet or chorus, and in the next sentence he even suggests that the city should sponsor a festival in honor of such a person's arrival. This comment, akin to Aristides' parabatic insertion of self-praise (28.21 Deil = 49.360 Dindorf, quoted and discussed above), makes a rhetorical bid to have his audience understand his words as deserving of the same classical-era Athenian license enjoyed by the Old Comic poets, particularly in their blunt civic critiques found in the parabasis.

Keeping in mind what he says about the connection between comedy and philosophy in the *First Tarsian* it comes as little surprise that immediately after positioning himself as fulfilling Alexandria's need for a comic poet or chorus, Dio suggests that this need may have arisen from the collective failure of the city's philosophers. Even the local Cynics, who ought to be able to cow people into better behavior, have actually made the situation worse, because their constant and ineffectual bawling on street corners has made them something of a laughing-stock (32.9). And generally speaking, those few who have used frank speech (παρρησία) have done so too rarely, too briefly and with a goal of upbraiding rather than instructing (11 λοιδορήσαντες μᾶλλον ἢ διδάξαντες), i.e. with *loidoria* that is not ethically directed. These statements cut in several directions at once. Dio seems to suggest that even in Alexandria both comedy and philosophy have the potential to effect positive change, though each can also fall short, as Old Comedy eventually did in classical Athens and philosophy has now done in Alexandria. On this reading, we might be able to detect a cross-generic issue of public comportment that is critical to one's ability to benefit the city. In the *First Tarsian*, Dio points to a slide among the comic poets from harsh abuse toward flattery; in the *Alexandrian* he calls out philosophers for refusing to engage the public at all, for doing so by 'stringing together jokes, lots of gossip and those down-market calls' (32.9 σκώμματα καὶ πολλὴν σπερμολογίαν συνείροντες καὶ τὰς ἀγοραίους ταύτας ἀποκρίσεις); or for offering epideictic oratory or their own doggerel instead of anything of philosophical substance. Perhaps, then, any city would benefit if both the comic poets and philosophers did what they were supposed to do. On the other hand, this highly normative position (as if there were clear and universally-accepted job descriptions for comic playwrights and philosophers) also smacks of the sort of commentary we hear from Aristophanes about his rivals. If we were to trust Aristophanes' witness, we'd be forced to conclude that rival poets, such as Cratinus, were simply bad, rather than understanding Aristophanes' badinage as part of the process of creating an authorial persona in aggressive dialogue with others.[32] Thus, Dio the philosopher masquerading as comic poet may overplay the casting of blame in order to set himself up more dramatically as the savior of the city.

Finally, Dio contrasts this image of the failed philosophers of Alexandria with his own unimpeachable intentions, since he plays the part of Socrates by claiming that he has been inspired to speak this way to the people of Alexandria by a *daimonion* (32.12), that term that is often translated as the 'genius' of Socrates (e.g. Pl. *Ap.* 40a; X. *Mem.* 1.1.2), and Dio connects his personal experience of this *daimonion* with the religious landscape of Alexandria by essentially conflating his divine inner voice with Serapis, whose most famous cult center was in the city. In light of the comic atmosphere of this part of the speech, this combination of a Socratic *daimonion* and a reference to traditional Alexandrian cult can even be understood as replaying a basic tension in Aristophanes' *Clouds* in a more positive and productive register.[33] This clear (if syncretized) allusion to the divine inspiration for Socrates' career completes the picture of Dio as someone who has stepped forward to fill the valuable social role of the comic poet presenting a salutary parabasis while also having the wisdom and daring of the Socratic parrhesiast.

These first thirteen sections form something of a complete exordium (though the introductory remarks actually continue through 32.32), as can be sensed in Dio's strong transition when he takes up a new topic: 'first of all …' (14 πρῶτόν γε ἁπάντων).[34] In this opening part of the speech, which makes up slightly less than ten percent of the entire oration, Dio establishes his authorial persona, which consists of the parabatic voice of Old Comedy with an infusion of Socratic inspiration. From here, the intensity of comic engagement recedes, and Dio moves into broader discussions of the Alexandrian's reactions to musical and athletic spectacles. Yet he continues to use more comic imagery than is his usual wont. This comic material can be quickly summarized: At 32.16, he quotes Menander fr. 298 K-A. At section 21, he includes a line that has, at times, been understood as a comic fragment.[35] In section 29, there may be an allusion to *Knights* 396. At 31, he presents the opinion of some unnamed person that the Alexandrians care only for 'lots of bread and seats at the races' (πολὺς ἄρτος καὶ θέα ἵππων), which so closely parallels Juvenal's *panem et circensis* that one might wonder if Dio is drawing upon a stock satirical quip.[36] Section 71 contains a clear allusion to *Acharnians* 616–17. Sections 84–5 include the long Homeric mash-up mentioned above.[37] At 86, Dio claims to be quoting a comic line when he recites a slightly adapted version of Euripides' *Hecuba* 607 (= *adesp.* 153 K-A): ἀκόλαστος ὄχλος ναυτική τ' ἀταξία, 'unrestrained mob and naval disorder', where the last word in the Euripidean line is ἀναρχία. Von Arnim (1898, *ad loc.*) bracketed the entirety of Dio's comic reference here, on the assumption that he had mistaken Euripidean tragedy for comedy and then misquoted it, yet I think it more probable that Dio refers to a comic send-up of the Euripidean line or is himself providing a comic twist (something made slightly more probable because of his attribution of the line to 'one of the comic poets' rather than giving a specific source). As he builds toward the conclusion of his long speech, Dio references the humor of seeing a drunk Heracles on the comic stage, which allows him to connect the Alexandrians to this image through Alexander's claim to be, like Heracles, a son of Zeus (though Dio goes further by suggesting that the locals more closely resemble drunk Centaurs or Cyclopes, 94–5). And finally, within a few breaths of the end, Dio draws loosely upon *Peace* 1–18 to compare the Alexandrians to Attic dung-beetles, who, though they are surrounded by the sweetest honey in the world, prefer their coprophagic fare (98).

This list of comic allusions, some less secure than others and scattered over a very long speech, testifies to the sustained importance of Dio's comic self-construction in the *Alexandrian*. And in both this speech and the *First Tarsian* he makes it patently clear that the most valuable part of Old Comedy derives from the productive chastisement that is delivered for the benefit (ὠφέλεια) of the city (cf. *Frogs* 1054–5). Both of these speeches therefore appropriate the parabatic voice independent of the larger comic context, as Dio focuses his invective on the moral correction of his theatre audience.

Dio's parabatic strategy

Why does Dio adopt such an unusual strategy of self-presentation in these two orations? If we were dealing with Lucian, such parabatic speech would hardly need an explanation, but Dio is a very different figure, whose tastes typically veered away from Aristophanic comedy. I suggest that we can explain the striking emphasis on comic material in the *Alexandrian* and *First Tarsian* in terms of a network of issues relating to antiquarianism, the role of local performance in the 'global' Roman world, and tensions between Roman hegemony and the power of the lone sage.

The issue of antiquarianism is predictable enough for someone writing in Dio's era, and his ambivalent discussions of Old Comedy reveal the basic framework of this dynamic. Classical Athens was the bygone era of record in which we can see such laudable and now regrettably defunct traditions as the comic license to abuse individuals and the city as a whole; yet Dio shows us that prior to the dereliction of Old Comedy the playwrights had already betrayed the original spirit of their duties. This deployment of comic material is in line with Whitmarsh's discussion of literary mimesis as an active and creative process of identity formation that simultaneously asserts a historical continuity while drawing attention to points of discontinuity.[38] This tension allows Dio's allusions to the classical past to serve as protreptic fodder in Alexandria and Tarsus without having them devolve into cultural nostalgia.

Such nostalgia for classical Athens might have had a place among some of the literati of this period, but many of the people who crowded the massive theaters of Alexandria and Tarsus must have had a strong sense of their own civic identity that did not fit well into sweeping analyses of Hellenism and Romanization across the empire. Thus the visiting speaker had to find a way to treat the civic population on its own terms, rather than merely as a manifestation of a Greco-Roman template. This must have been a particularly tricky issue in speeches such as these, since they reject the easy option of lavishing praise upon the city and its people and instead upbraid the habits and behavior of the citizenry. Here the recourse to a parabatic voice offered a twofold advantage. First, it allowed Dio, who was from Prusa in Bithynia (modern Bursa in northwestern Turkey), to speak to the people of Alexandria and Tarsus as if he were their fellow-citizen; and second, Dio's abuse becomes more tolerable to the local population inasmuch as it suggests a patina of festival license and an intention to benefit rather than simply deride. Dio's parabatic performances foster a sense of local intimacy in a world in which elite performers regularly crisscrossed the empire.[39]

Finally, Dio's parabatic voice suggests a role for himself as an influential speaker who can stand somewhat aside from the hierarchical relationship between these major provincial cities and imperial authority. It has long been suspected that in both speeches Dio is serving as an emissary of the emperor (whether Vespasian or Trajan), but even if such an idea could be confirmed, his personal intervention in civic affairs should not be wholly subsumed into the duties of an imperial delegation.[40] In both speeches Dio constructs a persona that expects nothing in return from the city but which is bold enough to risk giving offense by speaking abuse intended to help the audience. Such assistance may mimic imperial interests in civic orderliness, but it fits more closely with the constructive and educational aims of Aristophanes' *Frogs*. By resuscitating the persona of an Old Comic *koryphaios* delivering a parabasis, Dio creates a theatrical space in which to offer his harsh critiques. Conjuring a scenario in which a playwright is licensed to abuse his fellow citizens in classical Athens, Dio asserts a pedagogical agenda and persona through which he hopes to improve the behavior of the people of Alexandria and Tarsus. The Roman emperor may have enjoyed a virtual monopoly on most official mechanisms of control, but Dio's self-presentation at Tarsus and Alexandria makes the claim that cities enduring a crisis of values still needed to find a wise and persuasive individual who was willing and able to stand up and speak the truth as the Old Comic poets had once done in classical Athens.

Notes

* I would like to thank C.W. Marshall and David Smith for their valuable input on early drafts of this chapter.
1 The poor are also to be kept from participating in mimes or working as dancers (*orkhēstai*), choristers (*khoreutai*) except in the sacred chorus, kitharists or auletes. This list provides a useful synopsis of contemporary modes of dramatic performance.

2 The entirety of Dio's advice on this topic is: καὶ μηδεὶς τῶν σοφωτέρων αἰτιάσηταί με ὡς προκρίναντα τῆς ἀρχαίας κωμῳδίας τὴν Μενάνδρου ἢ τῶν ἀρχαίων τραγῳδῶν Εὐριπίδην· οὐδὲ γὰρ οἱ ἰατροὶ τὰς πολυτελεστάτας τροφὰς συντάττουσι τοῖς θεραπείας δεομένοις, ἀλλὰ τὰς ὠφελίμους. πολὺ δ' ἂν ἔργον εἴη τὸ λέγειν ὅσα ἀπὸ τούτων χρήσιμα· ἥ τε γὰρ τοῦ Μενάνδρου μίμησις ἅπαντος ἤθους καὶ χάριτος πᾶσαν ὑπερβέβληκε τὴν δεινότητα τῶν παλαιῶν κωμικῶν…, 'And let none of the intellectuals chide me for preferring Menander to Old Comedy or Euripides to the old tragedies. For doctors do not prescribe the most expensive remedies to their patients but, rather, the best. It would be a mighty labor to enumerate all the benefits of these authors. For Menander's portrayal of every character and pleasure altogether surpasses the cleverest of the Old Comic playwrights…'. Note that Dio seems to contrast the singular (τῆς ἀρχαίας κωμῳδίας) with the plural (τῶν ἀρχαίων τραγῳδῶν) to distinguish between the genre of Old Comedy and the era of the 'earlier' tragedians. Since by this era Menander and Euripides are the predictable choices to represent their respective dramatic modes, Dio's *sophōteroi* must amount to a pedantic few. For a similar preference for Menander, see Paus. 1.21.1 and Marshall's discussion of Plutarch in chapter 7 of this volume.

3 *Or.* 7.143 may contain an allusion to Menander's *Samia* 387. It should also be kept in mind that some of Dio's unidentified comic quotations could be by Menander.

4 For example, Nervegna 2013: 51: 'Getting ready to lecture the Alexandrians on morality, [Dio] presents himself in the role of an Old Comedy poet and praises the Athenians for allowing comic poets to expose both individual citizens and the entire city'. Hunter 2014: 384–6 pairs Dio's *Alexandrian* and *First Tarsian* in terms of their use of Old Comic tropes and structures.

5 The *kommotion* is the sung introduction to the parabasis and is one of the seven constituent parts identified by Pollux (4.112): *kommotion*, *parabasis* (the section which seems to have given its name to the entire parabasis), *pnigos/makron*, *ode*, *epirrhema*, *antode*, *antepirrhema*.

6 Hubbard 1991: 220–5 shows that after 420 the author's persona intrudes less overtly into parabases.

7 Sifakis 1971: 37–51 maps out the various messages that could be conveyed in each section of the parabasis.

8 *Testimonia* 1.35–9 K-A; Hyp. 1.c Ar. *Frogs*. Dover 1993: 73 dismisses 'Weil's lamentable emendation' of parabasis to *katabasis* ('journey to the underworld').

9 For example: A. *Ag.* 789: δίκην παραβάντες, 'having transgressed justice'; *Birds* 331–2: παρέβη μὲν θεσμοὺς ἀρχαίους / παρέβη δ' ὅρκους ὀρνίθων, 'he transgressed the ancient laws / he transgressed the avian oaths'.

10 Biles 2011: 12–55.

11 I recognize that this statement risks circularity, but an approach to parabatic speech modelled on Rotstein's cognitive methodology in her work on iambic poetry (2010: 3–60) would, I think, support my suggestion here.

12 Storey 2003: 206; Bakola 2008: 22–3. And compare Bakola 2010: 29–59 on 'quasi-parabatic' comments in Cratinus. I print slightly simplified versions of the text in *PCG*.
13 Cairns 2005.
14 Karamanou 2006 *ad loc.* explains that Seneca mistakenly attributes these lines to Belerophon.
15 Hunter and Russell 2011, *ad* 18d and 19e believe that Plutarch is referring to Ixion's role in Euripides' *Ixion*, though the matter is not certain. Ixion is a problematic character wherever he might appear, but it would be surprising nonetheless to find separate anecdotes about objections to Euripides' treatment of him in different plays. It is more probable that both Plutarch and Seneca are referring to Ixion's role in Euripides' *Danae*.
16 Shaw 2014: 133–6, who confronts the various claims that each of these fragments derives from fifth-century Old Comedies.
17 Kahn 1983: 104 and 1998: 325; Fendt 2014: 126 compares *Republic* to an extended and particularly complex parabasis; Arieti and Barrus 2010: 11–12 claim that *Protagoras* includes a central parabatic scene (from Socrates' threat to abandon the conversation until the entrance of Alcibiades), though I am skeptical of this assertion, since they seem to conceive of the parabasis too narrowly as a temporary interruption of the main narrative. Platter 2006: 94–8 offers insightful comments about the parabasis in general and a useful comparison of the relationship between author and spokesperson in Old Comic parabases and Platonic dialogues; he does not, however, suggest that any Platonic text specifically includes parabatic speech. In chapter 8 of this volume, Rosen suggests that Lucian's *The Dead Come to Life* draws upon recognizable conceits of an Old Comic parabasis.
18 Sifakis 1971: 64–6.
19 Both of these texts have received careful scrutiny in recent years, and debate continues as to whether these speeches were composed under Vespasian or Trajan. In line with the most recent assessments, I accept a Vespasianic date for both, though my arguments here do not hinge on this point. For overview, updated arguments and bibliographies relating to the *Alexandrian*, see Kasprzyk and Vendries 2012; and for the *First Tarsian*, see Bost-Pouderon 2006: 7–40 and 141–79. *Orr.* 32 and 33 are so similar in tone and style that one might imagine that they were composed by Dio as a pair (though Jones 1978: 41 in noting their similarity rejects the idea that this implies that they were written in the same period.)
20 *Or.* 32 references the theatrical setting several times; for the setting of *Or.* 33, see Bost-Pouderon 2006: 7–40. Lemarchand 1926: 125–6 suggests that *Or.* 33 is a humorous Cynic diatribe that was never presented in Tarsus at all; this point has not been taken up by more recent scholars.
21 What exactly Dio means with the word ῥέγχειν has been a matter of frequent debate. Kokkinia 2007 surveys the state of this issue and lobbies for the idea that Dio is speaking of flatulence. 'Cercopes' is the universally accepted emendation of κερκίδας, 'rods' in Dio's text.

22 For Dio's self-presentation as a doctor in the *Alexandrian*, see Kasprzyk and Vendries 2012: 158–61.
23 This is Dio's only reference to Plato Comicus by name; Aristophanes appears again only at *Or.* 52.17; and Cratinus at *Or.* 56.2.
24 Brancacci 2000 assesses Dio's Socratic self-presentation. It is also clear that Dio sees Archilochean *iambos* as the precursor to Athenian comedy, a topic I have discussed at length in Hawkins 2014: 186–215, and which Dio makes explicit (*Or.* 2.5). At 33.11 Dio contrasts Homer and Archilochus as the originators of ethical *loidoria* and empty flattery, respectively.
25 The sequence of parabatic songs consisting of the ode, *epirrhēma*, antode, and *antepirrhēma* is called the epirrhematic syzygy (συζυγία refers to any group of things that have been 'yoked' together). For the audience's expectations relating to this portion of the parabasis, see Marshall 2014: 132–3.
26 Hawkins 2014: 203–5.
27 Cratinus, *test.* 17 and 19 K-A preserve the later memory of Cratinus' ethical *loidoria*, and these passages are discussed by Rosen 1988: 40–1 and Bakola 2010: 75–8, who connects this motif with Dio 33.12.
28 Although these imps who tried to pull one over on Heracles are not exclusively comic figures, they seem to have been most at home there. Hermippus (frs 36–41 K-A), Plato Comicus (frs 52–3 K-A) and Eubulus (frs 95–7 K-A) all produced plays called *Cercopes*. Archilochus too seems to allude to their story in fr. 178.
29 Kasprzyk and Vendries 2012: 131–2 discusses the implications of delivering a speech about theatrical matters in a theater, and they acknowledge that Dio's citation of Aristophanes' *Knights* imbues the oration with a comic tone, yet their analysis of his manipulation of tropes of praise and blame never touches upon the parabatic dimension of his words.
30 Platter 2006: 142.
31 Kasprzyk and Vendries 2012: 144 claim that Dio here turns himself into an 'anti-Homère', but his manipulation of his Homeric model is not simply a negation but, rather, a positive and creative adaptation (if intentionally hackneyed) in the style of an Aristophanes.
32 See Biles 2011.
33 On the role of *Clouds* in imperial literature, see Barbiero, chapter 13 in this volume.
34 Although the exordium proper seems to end at 24, Kasprzyk and Vendries 2012: 115 rightly speak of 'une sorte de second exorde (25–32)'.
35 Kock included the line in his edition of comic fragments (*adesp.* 1324), but Kassel and Austin did not include it in theirs and in their *comparatio numerorum* list it as *adesp. iamb.* 29 Diehl.
36 In theory, one author could be drawing directly on the other. Chronology suggests that it is somewhat more probable that Juvenal would be drawing upon Dio, and

Latin authors tend to be more open to admitting a debt to Greek sources than the other way round. For the possibility of Greek borrowings from Latin, Courtney 1980: 624–9 offers a useful model for sorting the atmospheric or commonplace from specific allusions. Dio's comment may be a stock element of elite criticism of spectacles more generally. Such a wider view contextualizes Dio's comments within the long history of such aristocratic disdain for spectators' passionate engagement (cp. Dio's own similar comment at *Or.* 66.26).

37 Dio attributes this cento to 'one of your meager [σαπροί] poets' (81), and Kasprzyk and Vendries 2012: 143 note that *sapros* is a strikingly Aristophanic term of abuse.
38 Whitmarsh 2001: 47.
39 Kasprzyk and Vendries 2012: 123–6 discuss Dio's use of Aristophanes' *Knights* as a basic template for addressing the theater audience as if it were equivalent to the politically empowered *demos*.
40 For the debate over dating these speeches, see n. 17 above.

5

Favorinus and the Comic Adultery Plot

Ryan B. Samuels

Favorinus of Arles, the friend of Plutarch, student of Dio Chrysostom, professional rival of Polemo of Laodicea, and frequent interlocutor of Gellius' *Attic Nights*, is described in contemporary sources as a eunuch or hermaphrodite who was nonetheless accused of adultery with the wife of a Roman of consular rank.[1] Favorinus himself even reportedly publicized the allegation as the second of his 'three paradoxes' reported by Philostratus roughly a century later.[2] The composite picture furnished by contemporary testimony to his incomplete or ambiguous genitalia at birth, effeminate voice, and lack of facial hair offers little reason to doubt the historicity of Favorinus' condition,[3] and a medical diagnosis of Reifenstein's syndrome has been proposed.[4] The biographical tradition of Favorinus' alleged adultery, however, conforms suspiciously closely to a traditional comic plot, the transvestite comedy in which a male seducer infiltrates female space in the guise of a woman or a sexless man. The report in Philostratus of the self-avowed 'three paradoxes' is only one indication, supported by other circumstantial evidence, that Favorinus actively incorporated the comic tradition of transvestite and eunuch adultery into the self-fashioning of his own public persona. In this chapter I show that Favorinus cultivated the image of a eunuch adulterer in order to re-appropriate that comic stereotype from his rhetorical rivals who exploited his indeterminate gender in order to call his manhood into question.

I begin with a brief overview of cross-dressing in Athenian drama to highlight Menander's introduction of the device into the comic adultery plot and establish the classical template for later adaptations of that motif in the imperial period (I). I next provide a diachronic survey of scientific and pseudo-scientific sources on the sexuality of eunuchs from the classical through Byzantine periods (II) in order to discuss the relationships between anatomical and biological realities and cultural prejudices in the literary development of two seemingly contradictory archetypes in this single figure: the pathic castrate and the potent penetrator in disguise. I then survey transvestism and eunuch adultery in the literature of the Second Sophistic (III) to situate these themes synchronically within discourses of gender and sexuality contemporary with Favorinus. I next take a narrower focus on declamatory themes (IV) to illustrate ways that professional sophists like Favorinus and his rivals would have encountered and used the figure of the eunuch in rhetorical education and performance. The final section (V) considers the evidence for Favorinus' own contribution to the construction of this aspect of his biographical tradition.

I. Transvestism, eunuchism, and the comic plot in Athenian drama

Menander wrote at least two plays involving male infiltration of female space through disguise: the early *Androgynos* (50–6 K-A), adapted by the Roman comedian Caecilius (fragments 7–8 Ribbeck), and the later *Eunouchos* (137–49 K-A),[5] familiar from the extant Latin adaptation of Terence.[6] In the lost *Androgynos*, the young lover appears to have disguised himself as his own sister in order to gain access to the daughter of his curmudgeonly neighbor. In the Terentian *Eunuchus* and presumably in its Menandrean model the mischievous youth Chaerea disguises himself as a eunuch, presents himself as a gift from his brother Phaedria to the courtesan Thais, and after being admitted in this way to the women's quarters of the brothel, rapes Pamphila, a freeborn daughter of Athenian citizens whom Thais had hoped to return to her parents with her virginity intact (*Eunuchus* 653–67). *Casina* of Plautus, based on a Greek original by Menander's contemporary Diphilus,[7] puts a clever twist on the transvestite plot, in which the cross-dressing is usually a male stratagem to gain access to the women's quarters. In this play the initiative comes from the matron Cleostrata, who dresses the male slave Chalinus as the slave girl of the play's title and sends him to a darkened bedroom of the neighbor's house to present himself to her awaiting husband, the philandering *senex amator* Lysidamus.

Transvestite intrusion into gendered space figures prominently in plots of Athenian drama prior to Menander, but seduction or rape is not the primary motivation. In the *Thesmophoriazusae* of Aristophanes (411 BCE) Euripides, assisted by the cross-dressing tragedian Agathon, shaves and dresses his kinsman as a woman in order to infiltrate the exclusively-female Thesmophoria, where the women of Athens are planning their revenge against Euripides for his misogynistic depiction of female characters. In the *Ecclesiazusae* (391 BCE), on the other hand, the women of Athens dress as men in order to sneak into the assembly and pass a measure transferring control of the state over to themselves, although in general male-to-female transvestism is the norm on the Attic stage.[8] Aristophanes' contemporary Eupolis famously lampooned Alcibiades and his associates as transvestite worshippers of the Thracian goddess Cotyto in *Baptae* ('Dyers', 76–98 K-A, 416 or 415 BCE), for which the biographical tradition says that the controversial politician murdered him by throwing him from a ship in Sicily during the Peloponnesian War.[9] Outside of comedy, male surveillance of women's rites motivates the plot device in Euripides' *Bacchae* (405 BCE), in which the Theban king Pentheus, egged on by Dionysus, dons feminine costume in order to observe the Dionysiac ritual of his female relatives.[10] Menander is thought to have modeled his *Androgynos* upon the similar plot of Euripides' lost *Skyrioi* (date unknown) about the draft-dodging, transvestite Achilles hiding among the girls on Scyros; in the action of both plays an infant appears to have been conceived as a result of the ruse.[11] In Euripides, however, avoidance of military service rather than intercourse with Deidameia, which apparently preceded the action of the play,[12] was the goal of the subterfuge.[13] Thus it seems that cross-dressing in advancement of the sex plot was a Menandrean innovation, as was the substitution of eunuchism for transvestism in the later *Eunouchos*.[14]

At the subconscious level of artistic creation a folkloric and possibly even Indo-European paradigm for stories of transvestite and eunuch seduction or rape cannot be excluded, but exact parallels and direct links are elusive.[15] Besides the story of Achilles on Scyros, the nearest correspondence to this pattern in Greek mythopoetics is a version of the Daphne story in which the smitten Leucippus disguises himself as a girl in order to join her misandrist train of hunting nymphs, though this tale is attested only in literary sources that postdate Menander.[16] The postclassical popularity of Menander ensures that in subsequent Greek (and Roman) literature instances of seduction or adultery involving transvestism or eunuchism inevitably evoke his plays as the model for this literary motif.[17]

II. Ancient sources on the sexuality of eunuchs

An unsystematic vocabulary of Greek and Latin terms denoting ambiguous, incomplete, or absent male genitalia was used more or less interchangeably to embrace what today would be considered a variety of different conditions or gender statuses.[18] The biblical idea that some men are born eunuchs, some are made eunuchs by others, and others make themselves eunuchs for God (Matthew 19.12), is perhaps the most familiar ancient acknowledgement that conditions described as eunuchism could be congenital, as in the case of Favorinus,[19] or acquired (through compression [θλίψις, θλάσις] or surgical removal [ἐκτομή] of the testicles),[20] whether under compulsion or voluntarily.[21] The majority of eunuchs in Greek and Roman antiquity were slaves or freedmen who had been castrated in early childhood.[22] Scholars have plausibly speculated that the original use of castrated slaves as guardians of royal harems in the courts of the ancient Near East had been designed on analogy with techniques of animal husbandry to ensure, by sterilizing potential reproductive rivals, the king's paternity of all offspring of his wives and concubines.[23]

After eunuchs began to be employed as personal servants of affluent women in private Greek and later Roman households starting, to judge from Menander's *Eunouchos*, in the late classical and early Hellenistic periods,[24] impotence was inferred from infertility, and it was widely assumed that castrated males would not, or at the very least could not consummate heterosexual desires, even if they did experience them.[25] The early medical sources believed that castrated males were rendered not only infertile but also asexual (lacking desire) and impotent (unable to achieve erection).[26] If eunuchs were sexualized in classical Athens, given their assimilation to women and boys, the desire attributed to them was to be penetrated.[27] Due to the proverbial smoothness of eunuchs and the belief that effeminate men practiced hair removal out of a desire to play an unmanly or age-inappropriate (i.e. passive) sexual role,[28] this stereotype of the pathic eunuch survives in one strand of satirical and moralizing literature and tendentious historiography and biography contemporary with Favorinus as an extreme version of the superannuated catamite (παιδικά, *puer delicatus*); childhood castration was thought by some to be a more permanent way than depilation to keep a beautiful youth in a state of perpetual adolescence and sexual availability.[29]

Another strand of this same literature, however, taken up by patristic authors in later antiquity, depicts some eunuchs as not only willing but also able to satisfy a woman.[30] Most studies of eunuchs in antiquity sharply distinguish prepubertal castrates and individuals castrated after puberty, attributing to the ancients a belief that the former would not develop the sexual function of men, but the latter would not lose it.[31] Scientific and medical sources do not make this contrast in these terms before the Byzantine period.[32] The distinction between impotent, prepubertal and potent, postpubertal castrates, like the idea that women prefer sex with eunuchs as a prophylactic measure against pregnancy,[33] is a commonplace of satirical and moralizing texts.[34] As a literary figure the penetrative eunuch likely reflects irrational male anxieties about unsupervised female sexuality more than the lived experience of most authors,[35] especially since postpubertal castrations could never have amounted to more than an insignificant minority of total orchiectomies until modern times with the advent of castration as a form of rehabilitation or punishment of sex offenders and treatment of prostate and testicular cancer.[36] A medical text of uncertain date spuriously attributed to the Aristotelian commentator Alexander of Aphrodisias (early third century CE) comes closest to the explanation of the satirists: Posing the question, 'Why do some eunuchs desire sex in some measure and sometimes experience lust?' (Διὰ τί ἔνιοι τῶν εὐνούχων ποσῶς ἀφροδισίων ὀρέγονται καὶ ἐρῶσί ποτε;), it answers, 'Because they had their testicles removed or crushed long after puberty and are, as it were, "half eunuchs"' (ὅτι πολὺ παρὰ τὸ ἡβάσκειν ὠρχοτομήθησαν ἢ ἐθλάσθησαν καὶ ὥσπερ ἡμιτελεῖς εἰσιν εὐνοῦχοι). The text goes on to explain, however, that although men castrated in sexual maturity have the hotter livers (θερμότεροι τὸ ἧπαρ) and enlarged *vasa deferentia* (σπερματικὰ ἀγγεῖα) of adult males, they are unable to achieve erection, because they have lost the 'swelling spirit' (οἰδίσκον πνεῦμα) generated by sperm, 'and the seminal ducts have contracted and been blocked as in children' (*Problemata* 1.9 Ideler ὡς ἐπὶ παιδίων δὲ τετύφλωνται αὐτῶν οἱ σπερματικοὶ πόροι συμπεσόντες).[37] Although the image of sexually frustrated 'half eunuchs' (ἡμιτελεῖς ... εὐνοῦχοι) is more pathetic than threatening, what this text with its clinical tone and technical terminology shares with the less sober nightmares of the satirists and moralizers is the suspicion that despite their effeminate exterior some castrates are, at least to some extent, like the disguised youth of the transvestite adultery plot, really men in eunuch's clothing.

Intact males wedded to traditional notions of masculinity interpreted this gender indeterminacy as the outward manifestation of a deceitful nature.[38] The Second Sophistic was a heyday of physiognomy, the pseudoscience that considers the physical characteristics and external deportment of an individual as reflections of his or her inner character.[39] Polemo of Laodicea was its preeminent practitioner:

> Cognovi igitur eunuchos gentem malam esse libidine et omnibus moribus effeminatis instructam. Scias autem mutari eunuchi ab hominibus castrati figuram et colorem et corpus quae habebat antequam castratus est; contra iis qui sine testiculis nascuntur res alias esse diversas ab eorum proprietatibus

qui castrantur. Itaque perfectior in malo nemo est quam qui sine testiculis nascitur.

> (*De physiognomonia* 1.162.21–164.8 Förster, trans. Hoffmann from the Arabic)

I have therefore realized that eunuchs are an evil tribe, furnished with lust and all manner of womanish ways. You ought, however, to know that the shape, complexion, and body that a eunuch who is castrated through human intervention had before are changed; on the other hand those who are born without testicles have characteristics that are different from the qualities of those who are castrated. And so no one is more completely evil than he who is born without testicles.

In other words castrated eunuchs are rendered bad through human intervention, but born ones are worse, because they are pure evil by nature from the very beginning. Polemo was of course describing his personal enemy, the congenital eunuch Favorinus.

III. Transvestism and eunuch adultery in the literature of the Second Sophistic

The womanizing eunuch is a particular species of a more general stereotype recognized by scholarship as the 'effeminate adulterer.'[40]: This figure's habitual invasion of the women's quarters actually assimilates him to the inhabitants of that feminine space, as it is perceived to reflect not a hypermasculine sexuality in accordance with a modern, heteronormative morality but rather an inability or refusal, considered effeminate, to control his own pleasures.[41] In the classicizing cultural milieu of the Second Sophistic, in which newer literary forms such as comic dialogue and the novel were developed out of creative imitation of canonical texts, authors, and genres, it is not surprising that the transvestite plot of Athenian comedy provides authors such as Favorinus and his rivals a literary frame of reference for their competitions over cultural authority, intimately bound up as it was with traditional notions of Greek manhood.[42] In live theater the tradition survived and flourished in contemporary mime and pantomime, where the adultery plot, transvestite burlesque on mythological themes, including Achilles on Scyros, and the self-emasculating, transvestite priests of Cybele known as *galli* were well represented on the popular stage.[43] Although *galli* personified passive or receptive homosexuality (κιναιδεία) from their first appearances in Greek and Roman literary sources of the Hellenistic and Republican periods,[44] beginning in the first century CE satirical and parodic texts start to attribute heterosexual activity to them.[45] As a constructed identity achieved through body modification, the figure of the *gallus* provides Greek and Roman authors with a convenient locus in which to play with social and anatomical conceptions of gender and sexuality. In Lucian's aetiology of the Syrian branch of the cult the courtier Kombabos secretly castrates himself as insurance against suspicion of adultery when the king Seleucus orders him to escort the queen Stratonike to the Holy City (*De Syria dea* 19–27). In the fragmentary 'Iolaus Romance', preserved on an Oxyrhynchus papyrus from the second century CE (*POxy.* 3010), a youth appears to have prevailed upon a friend to learn and teach him the secrets of these castrated priests in order that he may approach the object of his desire disguised as a eunuch; scholars have recognized the parallel with the comic plots of Menander's *Androgynos* and *Eunouchos* (and Terence's *Eunuchus*).[46]

Elsewhere in the Greek novel, Achilles Tatius turns the Menandrean sequence of disguise, access, and seduction or rape on its head in *Leucippe and Clitophon*: The transvestism comes after a liaison rather than before, and the disguise is not a male stratagem designed to gain access but is instead the idea of the married Melite, a sexually aggressive older woman, who is inspired by the story of Achilles on Scyros to help her younger lover, the protagonist Clitophon, escape undetected (6.1.3). Clitophon earlier rebuffed her advances because he was mourning his beloved Leucippe, whom he presumed dead, but submitted to Melite after she taunted him out of sexual continence, a masculine virtue in Greek eyes, by calling him a eunuch, a hermaphrodite (ἀνδρόγυνος), and a woman (5.22.5, 5.25.7–8); Jones highlights the irony that by giving in to Melite in an attempt to prove his virility, Clitophon effectively demonstrates the feminine lack of self-control traditionally associated with these figures.[47] Heslin describes how the Roman poet Statius, a century or so earlier, similarly assimilated the transvestite Achilles on Scyros to the original *gallus* Attis (*Achilleid* 1.624–36; cf. Catullus 63.50–73); as Heslin notes, the clever slave Parmeno in Terence's *Eunuchus* had suggested the stratagem of disguise to the young lover Chaerea with a backhanded compliment about his suitability for the role: 'Besides, your youthful beauty is such that you could easily pass for a eunuch!' (Terence, *Eunuchus* 375: *praeterea forma et aetas ipsast facile ut pro eunucho probes*).[48] The false eunuch as effeminate adulterer has a long pedigree, and its reflexes in Greek and Roman authors as different as Achilles Tatius and Statius derive ultimately from a common source in Menander.

The mirror image of the effeminate, receptive male or passive homosexual is the masculine, insertive female or active lesbian, who plays the male role in sexual intercourse by penetrating her sexual partners with her oversized clitoris, an artificial or prosthetic phallus, or her tongue.[49] This figure too appears in a contemporary instance of the transvestite plot in the *Dialogues of the Courtesans*,[50] for which the comedies of Menander provided the primary source material for settings, situations, and characters,[51] although Lucian adapted them to his own purposes.[52] The fifth dialogue consists of a conversation between two courtesans, Klonarion and Leaina, in which the former peppers the latter with curious questions about her client Megilla, described as a 'terribly manly' (5.1 δεινῶς ἀνδρική), rich lesbian from Lesbos, and especially about the practicalities of female-female intercourse, which Leaina coyly refuses to divulge in explicit detail. Klonarion asks whether Megilla is an ἑταιρίστρια (5.2), a Platonic *hapax legomenon* glossed by the lexicographers as τριβάς and defined by Klonarion as 'one of those virile women who refuse to have it done to them by men but instead themselves have sex with women just like men' (τοιαύτας ... γυναῖκας ἀρρενωπούς, ὑπ' ἀνδρῶν μὲν οὐκ ἐθελούσας αὐτὸ πάσχειν, γυναιξὶ δὲ αὐτὰς πλησιαζούσας ὥσπερ ἄνδρας).[53] Leaina ambiguously answers, 'something like that' (τοιοῦτόν τι). She tells Klonarion how Megilla threw a drinking party with another rich lesbian from Corinth named Demonassa and invited her (Leaina) to come and play the cithara. After the music and drinking the three were engaging in foreplay, when Megilla removed a wig to reveal a bald scalp, close-shaven in the manner of a male athlete, and asked, 'Leaina, have you ever seen such a handsome youth?' (5.3 Ὦ Λέαινα ... ἑώρακας ἤδη οὕτω καλὸν νεανίσκον;). Megilla's name, she said, was Megillos, and Demonassa was her wife. Leaina laughed and asked:

> So can it be then, Megillos, that you'd been a man all along without us knowing it, as they say Achilles was hiding among the maidens, and you have a man's you-know-what and do to Demonassa what men do?
>
> Οὐκοῦν σύ, ὦ Μέγιλλε, ἀνήρ τις ὢν ἐλελήθεις ἡμᾶς, καθάπερ τὸν Ἀχιλλέα φασὶ κρυπτόμενον ἐν ταῖς παρθένοις, καὶ τὸ ἀνδρεῖον ἐκεῖνο ἔχεις καὶ ποιεῖς τὴν Δημώνασσαν ἅπερ οἱ ἄνδρες;
>
> (5.3)

When Megilla answered that she had something even better, Leaina asked if she was a 'hermaphrodite' (Ἑρμαφρόδιτος) with 'both sets of genitalia' (ἀμφότερα), to which Megilla replied that she was 'all man' (5.3 τὸ πᾶν ἀνήρ). In answer to the question whether she had undergone a sex change like Tiresias (5.4), Megilla explained to Leaina, 'I was born female like the rest of you, but I have the mind, sexual appetite, and everything else of a man' (5.4 ἐγεννήθην μὲν ὁμοία ταῖς ἄλλαις ὑμῖν, ἡ γνώμη δὲ καὶ ἡ ἐπιθυμία καὶ τἆλλα πάντα ἀνδρός). Asked if sexual appetite (ἐπιθυμία) was enough, Megilla told Leaina that if she 'put out' (πάρεχε), she would find out that she had 'something just as good as what a man has' (5.4 ἔχω... τι ἀντὶ τοῦ ἀνδρείου). Won over with begging, fine clothes, and expensive jewelry, Leaina gave in and 'received her like a man' (ὥσπερ ἄνδρα περιελάμβανον), while Megilla 'did [it to her]' (ἡ δὲ ἐποίει). When Klonarion eagerly asks what Megilla did and how, Leaina tells her, 'don't ask for details, it's embarrassing' (5.4 Μὴ ἀνάκρινε ἀκριβῶς, αἰσχρὰ γάρ). This final absence of a definitive answer to the question with which the dialogue began destabilizes the regular categories of active and passive, penetrative and receptive, male and female more than any of the expected solutions could have done by neatly assigning Megilla and Leaina to 'butch' and 'femme' roles.[54] In a similar way Lucian cleverly uses the transvestite plot to problematize issues of gender, sexuality, and gendered space. With the setting of the symposium Lucian establishes the scene in a traditionally male sphere; although all present were women, only Leaina, as musical and sexual entertainment, belonged there according to classical Greek protocol. As Megillus, however, Megilla presents herself as a rightful occupant of that space. Her removal of her feminine 'disguise' and her 'exposure' as a 'male youth' (5.3 νεανίσκον) mirror the traditional Menandrean scenario of *Andrygonos* and *Eunouchos*. In this case, however, the 'revelation' raises rather than answers the question of her 'true' gender: Is it Megilla or Megillus? Leaina's naïve questions, informed by mythological exempla, about Megilla's possible statuses as a transvestite (Achilles), hermaphrodite (Hermaphroditus), or transitioned transsexual (Tiresias) exhaust the options for non-binary alternatives acknowledged by the mainstream culture. There is no legendary precedent for Megilla or a Greek term to denote the identity that she describes and modern society would call transgender: Her gender identification as a man does not correspond to the female sex that she was assigned at birth.

Lucian's *Eunuch*, a lampoon of Favorinus, thinly disguised as one Bagoas, the namesake of the Persian eunuch beloved of Alexander, consists of a dialogue in which 'Lycinus' (Lucian) reports to his interlocutor about a trial at which he was present. A dispute had arisen over the succession to the chair of the Peripatetic school in Athens, which brought with it an imperial stipend of 10,000 drachmas. The finalists for the position were Diocles, a dialectitian, and Bagoas the eunuch. In answer to the charge that his unmanly condition precluded him from participation in philosophy and tutelage of the young, Bagoas even adduces the precedent of 'a certain Academic eunuch from the territory of the Pelasgi, who shortly before our time attained fame among the Greeks' (7 τις Ἀκαδημαϊκὸς εὐνοῦχος ἐκ Πελασγῶν τελῶν, ὀλίγον πρὸ ἡμῶν εὐδοκιμήσας ἐν τοῖς Ἕλλησιν), all but naming Favorinus. Bagoas concluded his defense of eunuch philosophers when 'a third party' (τρίτος ἄλλος) stood up and offered an ironic argument on his behalf: Despite his smooth cheeks, woman's voice, and eunuch-like appearance, if Bagoas were stripped of his clothes, he would prove to be 'all man' (πάνυ ἀνδρεῖος),[55] as rumor has it that he was caught in the penetrative act with a married woman but escaped conviction for adultery by appealing to the impossibility of eunuch sex; the judges, moreover, could not believe the indictment when faced with the sight of him.[56] The couple caught in flagrante and the cuckolded husband taking the adulterer to court are stock situations of the imperial adultery mime.[57] The allusion here to the indictment and acquittal of Favorinus as it has been preserved in the Philostratean biographical tradition is unmistakable. But whereas Philostratus attributes the report to Favorinus himself, Lucian, thinly disguising himself as the unnamed 'third party' at the trial, cites anonymous gossip (οἱ περὶ αὐτοῦ λέγοντες).[58]

IV. The eunuch adulterer in the rhetorical tradition

Anderson has noted the formal resemblance of the trial in Lucian's *Eunuch* to a school theme,[59] and several scholars have speculated that Favorinus is the inspiration for a declamatory theme attested by Hermogenes: A man is defended against a charge of murder for killing a eunuch whom he caught in adultery with his wife.[60] The case, which occurs in the context of a discussion of definition (ὅρος), is one in a series of examples in which both sides agree upon the facts but disagree on their definitions.[61] The law at issue, that a husband may kill an adulterer (μοιχός) whom he catches in the act with his wife, is borrowed from Lysias 1.[62] The twist in this instance is that the deceased is found to be a eunuch. The dispute over definition then concerns whether or not a eunuch may be considered an adulterer according to the letter of the law.[63] If not, the husband is guilty of murder; if so, he should be acquitted. The accused, therefore, must either prove that the eunuch was capable of adultery, as strictly defined in the sense of penetrative intercourse, or otherwise argue that, even if he was physically incapable of the act because of his condition, he was still guilty of adultery under a broader definition and liable to the penalty prescribed by the law.[64] The underlying premise of the charge of murder, that a eunuch cannot possibly perform the act of adultery, is indeed reminiscent of the defense against the charge of adultery taken by Bagoas (Favorinus) and the reasoning followed by the judges according to Lycinus in Lucian's *Eunuch*.[65]

Comparison with another allegedly historical episode of gender-bending adultery, the *Bona Dea* affair of 62 BCE in Rome, shows that both the forensic scenario outlined in the declamatory theme of Hermogenes and the biographical tradition of Favorinus' adultery conform to a shared comic pattern. In December of that year, P. Clodius, quaestor-elect for the following year, was caught in drag in the home of C. Iulius Caesar, *pontifex maximus*, at an official celebration of the rites of the *Bona Dea*, in whose worship all males, human or animal, were forbidden to participate. Cicero's reference to the incident in his correspondence and in the *De haruspicum responsis* and the fragmentary *In Clodium et Curionem* are silent on Clodius' motive, but later tradition states that he was pursuing a liaison with the absent Caesar's wife, Pompeia. A special court was appointed by the Senate to try Clodius for sacrilege (*incestum*, ἀσέβεια), of which he was acquitted. Most interesting for comparison with the case of Favorinus is an extant fragment of Cicero's speech against Clodius and Curio: 'But if it had been determined that it did not appear that a man had gone where he had gone' (fragment 5 *Sin esset iudicatum non videri virum venisse, quo iste venisset*). In other words, as the Bobbio scholiast explains, Cicero insinuates that Clodius was acquitted of sacrilege not because he was innocent of the act but because the judges did not consider him a man. This is the same satirical logic that Lucian presents for Favorinus' acquittal of adultery. Focusing on the extant fragments of the *In Clodium et Curionem* that highlight the details of Clodius dressing in women's garb in preparation for his scheme, Geffcken showed Cicero's debt to comic descriptions of feminine couture and similar transvestite dressing scenes in Aristophanes' *Thesmophoriazusae* and Euripides' *Bacchae*.[66] Cicero's knowledge of and fondness for Greek and Roman comedy has been well documented and studied, as has its influence upon the characterizations and narratives of his speeches.[67] It is not hard to imagine the basic outlines of the rest of the lost speech, including the costumed infiltration of the women's rite and quite probably an exposure in the Menandrean and Terentian manner.[68] A brief look at Plutarch's version in his life of Caesar, more or less repeated in his life of Cicero, reveals all the ingredients of such a comedy: a nocturnal women's religious festival, an absent husband, an overprotective mother-in-law, a secluded wife, and a beardless youth in drag, aided by a conspiring nurse (Plutarch, *Caesar* 9–10, *Cicero* 28–9).[69]

The eunuch in love, moreover, is one of many declamatory themes based upon character types from classical comedy and one that Favorinus may have performed. Although the specific terminology varies between 'declamation' (μελέτη, *declamatio*), 'imitation' (μίμησις, *imitatio*), 'personification' (προσωποποιία), 'character' (ἦθος), and 'characterization' (ἠθοποιία),[70] the general outlines of fictive or ethical declamation in Greek and Roman rhetorical education are remarkably consistent between the first centuries CE and late antiquity.[71] Student declaimers are assigned 'themes' (ὑποθέσεις, *positiones*) and 'characters' (πρόσωπα, *personae*) based on clearly defined 'types' (ἤθικα), many of them familiar from New Comedy, such as the farmer or rustic, the rich man, the miser, and the coward.[72] This scholastic exercise influenced literature of all types. The formula 'What would so and so say?' (τίνας ἂν εἴποι λόγους, less often τί ἂν εἴποι;) provides the organizing principle behind an entire series of the so-called 'declamatory' epigrams of the *Greek Anthology* (9.449–80), the first of which is based on the paradoxical theme of 'Love in love' (Ἔρως ἐρῶν). The prompt most often situates a familiar figure, whether a named individual from classical Greek history and legend or an ethical type, most often borrowed from comedy, in a situation likely to elicit strong emotion or a reaction illustrative of character (ἦθος). For the declamations of the ethical variety, the combination of type and circumstance is often paradoxical, as for example 'What would a whore say upon gaining self-control?' (Libanius, *Ethopoeiae* 18 Förster τίνας ἂν εἴποι λόγους πόρνη σωφρονήσασα;).[73]

The Greek novel as a genre is especially full of monologues of this type. An example that clearly draws on motifs in New Comedy occurs in *Daphnis and Chloe* (4.16.2–4), when the parasite Gnathon, overcome with lust for the beautiful youth Daphnis, entreats his patron for assistance, favorably comparing the object of his desire with the usual obsession of his ethical species, food.[74] The literary model for speeches of this type was Menander, whose ancient reputation for realism was inextricably connected to this notion of rhetorical appropriateness of speech to a diverse but limited array of familiar types.[75] In an academic setting the success of such a speech was gauged by the 'appropriateness' (τὸ πρέπον, *decor*) of its manner of expression, likened to the 'interpretation' (ὑπόκρισις, *actio* or *pronuntiatio*) of an actor, to the manners or 'character' (ἦθος, *mores*) expected of its assumed speaker, the circumstances (καιροί, *res*) set by the theme, and the emotion (πάθος, *adfectus*) likely to be elicited from that type of character under those circumstances.[76]

Of particular interest for the purposes of this discussion is the theme of the eunuch in love. Transmitted among the 'Preliminary Exercises' (προγυμνάσματα) of the fourth-century rhetorician Libanius is a short *ethopoeia* based on the prompt, τίνας ἂν εἴποι λόγους εὐνοῦχος ἐρῶν; ('What speech would a eunuch say if he fell in love?').[77] Amato attributed the piece on stylistic grounds to Severus, who was a student of Libanius.[78] The speaker self-identifies as a eunuch castrated after birth, both impotent and infertile. Comparing this short piece with a fragment attributed to Favorinus and previously identified by Barigazzi as belonging to a philosophical work on Socratic *erotodidaxis*, Amato considers the latter to be instead an *ethopoeia* on the same theme, the eunuch in love[79]:

> Some affliction has fallen upon my soul, and what it is I do not know. The initiated say that it is love. Malicious and irrational divinity, you have attacked an infirm body that cannot bear you. I yield to you, divinity, I surrender the battle to you. I am not your soldier.
>
> χάθος τί μοι προσέπεσε τῇ ψυχῇ, καὶ τί μέν ἐστιν οὐκ οἶδα· ἔρωτα δὲ αὐτὸ λέγουσιν εἶναι οἱ μεμυημένοι. βάσκανε δαῖμον καὶ ἀλόγιστε, ἀσθενεῖ προσελήλυθας σώματι φέρειν σε μὴ δυναμένῳ· ἐξίσταμαί σοι, δαῖμον, παραχωρῶ σοι τῆς μάχης· οὐκ εἰμί σου στρατιώτης.
>
> (Favorinus, Fragment 18 Barigazzi = 111 Amato)

The sources that mention Favorinus' sexual proclivities hardly create the picture of someone inexperienced in matters erotic,[80] but it must be remembered that this is role-play. The initial failure to diagnose the symptoms of love correctly is a commonplace of this genre.[81] The emphasis, moreover, upon impotence in the face of desire in the texts of both Severus and Favorinus is not inconsistent with comic stereotypes: In Terence and perhaps his Menandrean model, upon learning that the putative eunuch Chaerea has violated her mistress Thais' ward Pamphila, the maid Pythias exclaims that she 'had heard that eunuchs were huge lovers of women, but impotent' (*Eunuchus* 665–6 *at pol ego amatores audieram mulierum esse eos maxumos, | sed nil potesse*).[82] If, however, Philostratus is to be believed, and Favorinus embraced a eunuch identity and promoted the adultery charge as a centerpiece of the biography that he presented to the public, this fictional exercise in the character of an impotent eunuch could not have been without some degree of self-reference,[83] even if only of an ironic kind. On the other hand, it would not always have served Favorinus' purpose to publicize his sexual prowess; impotence, after all, to go by the admittedly suspect testimony of Lucian, was supposedly the cornerstone of his defense against the adultery charge (*Eunuchus* 10).

V. Comic eunuchism and sophistic self-fashioning

Lucian's *Eunuchus* has been read as a satire on the professional feud of the previous generation between the hypermasculine Polemon and the sexually ambiguous Favorinus.[84] Philostratus says that the quarrel grew out of the intercity rivalry between Ephesus and Smyrna, the former championing Favorinus and the latter Polemo, continued in Rome as eminent Romans became partisans of one or the other sophist, and ultimately descended into a battle of invective speeches (*Lives of the Sophists* 490–1). The screeds have not survived, but the broad outlines of the debate, if that is not too elevated a description for *ad hominem* attacks, may be speculatively reconstructed from contemporary testimonia and titles of lost works. Philostratus indicates that not all the insults were slanderous, opining that the combatants demeaned themselves, 'for outrageous personal abuse, even if it happens to be true, does not absolve from shame even the one who speaks about such things' (491 ἀσελγὴς γὰρ λοιδορία, κἂν ἀληθὴς τύχῃ, οὐκ ἀφίησιν αἰσχύνης οὐδὲ τὸν ὑπὲρ τοιούτων εἰπόντα). Comparison of the 'facts' of the Philostratean life with the abuse leveled at Favorinus in Lucian's *Eunuchus* and Polemo's *De physiognomonia* suggests that among other things Polemo likely ridiculed his enemy's beardlessness, lack of testicles, and alleged history of eunuch adultery.[85] Philostratus presents Polemo as a master of invective (*Lives of the Sophists* 543), and cites a declamation still extant in his day entitled 'The Adulterer Unmasked' (542 ὁ ... μοιχὸς ὁ ἐκκεκαλυμμένος) as an illustration of his skill in this style. Philostratus gives no context for the initial composition and delivery of this piece, but if it was already among the greatest hits in his repertoire, its polemical potential in the feud with the eunuch adulterer Favorinus would have been obvious. Favorinus on the other hand in his lost treatise *On the Lifestyle of the Philosophers* (*Suda* s.v. Φαβορῖνος = Phi 4 Adler Περὶ τῆς διαίτης τῶν φιλοσόφων) may have defended his own claim to the pursuit of philosophy despite his smooth appearance by attacking philosophical hypocrisy in the familiar satirical figure of the 'bearded philosopher', whose solemn avowal of devotion to manly virtue in public does not square with the enthusiastic pursuit of a debauched (i.e. effeminate) lifestyle in private.[86]

A remark of Polemo presents Favorinus as a kind of transgressive insult comedian who incorporated his unconventional appearance into his act: 'Cutting such a figure as this, he would make insulting jokes, and whatever he had in mind he tended to do' (*De physiognomonia* 1.163 Förster *Forma tali praeditus ioco utebatur ludibrioso et quidquid animo volvebat facere solebat*). Two generations earlier in his discussion of humor in oratory Quintilian gave an example of unexpected or paradoxical jokes (παρὰ προσδοκίαν),[87] attributed to a presumably eminent person whom he left unnamed out of 'respect' (*vercundia*): 'You are more lecherous than any eunuch' (*De institutione oratoria* 6.3.34 *libidinosior es quam ullus spado*). This joke, which precedes Favorinus' lifetime, points to the comic genealogy of Favorinus' second paradox, whereby he fashioned the sexual and gendered aspects of his public persona from the familiar stereotype of the eunuch adulterer. There are, however, indications that his response to the charge of adultery changed over time to suit different circumstances and agendas. Independently Lucian's *Eunuch* is suspect, but together with corroborating information from external sources, after allowance for the exaggerations and distortions of satire, it can have some evidentiary value for the reconstruction of the events and personalities that it satirizes. 'Bagoas' (Favorinus) is said at his trial for adultery to have pled not guilty on grounds of impotence (10), but the attacks of 'Diocles' (Polemo) upon his masculine qualifications to teach and practice philosophy presented him with a rhetorical conundrum: 'He thought it was not safe to confirm the charge of adultery, but he also did not consider this accusation to be useless to the present contest' (11 οὔτε συγκατατίθεσθαι τῷ περὶ τῆς μοιχείας ἐγκλήματι καλῶς ἔχειν ᾤετο οὔτε ἀχρεῖον αὐτῷ τὴν κατηγορίαν ταύτην ἐς τὸν παρόντα ἀγῶνα ἡγεῖτο εἶναι). Ultimately the absurd outcome was that 'Diocles' persisted in accusing his opponent of adultery, even though the charge confirmed the virility that he sought to deny 'Bagoas'; 'Bagoas' in turn 'played the man' (ἀνδρίζεται) and 'stayed busy with the case' (διὰ χειρὸς ἔχει τὸ πρᾶγμα) in order to show that he was a fully functional male (13). The report of Philostratus is less colorful but more plausible: Favorinus acknowledged but neither confirmed nor denied the charge, volunteering only that he had been accused but not convicted, and left the details of the affair to the imagination of his public.

The most substantial extant work in Favorinus' own words is the *Corinthian Oration*, transmitted among the works of his teacher Dio Chrysostom (*Discourse* 37), a speech delivered in protest of the Corinthians' removal of an honorific statue that they had earlier erected to him; the action appears to have been taken in response to rumors of a falling-out between Favorinus and the emperor Hadrian.[88] Despite some textual difficulties in the transmission it is evident that the speech was a virtuoso piece of self-praise in which the orator put his own statue on trial and alternated between advocating for it and ventriloquizing in its voice on his own behalf.[89] Favorinus describes his statue as a monument to cultural mobility and the triumph of culture over nature in his successful self-transformation from native Gaul into honorary Hellene through Greek education and mastery of the Greek language ([Dio Chrysostom] 37.25–7). A slander, however, about a trivial transgression of which he has not been convicted (32) has threatened to undo all his success:

> Consider: think back to yourselves whether anything of the sort has been done by him in your city. And yet you dwell in a city that is most sensuous of all that are and have been, but still you have heard nothing, and I would say confidently that no one else among the Greeks has either. Then do you think that he who has lived decently in Greece amid greater license and permissiveness has changed in Rome in the presence of the emperor and the laws? But that is like one saying that an athlete behaves himself when he is by himself but breaks the rules in the stadium in the presence of the referee.

> Οὐ σκέψεσθε; οὐκ ἀναμνησθήσεσθε πρὸς ἑαυτούς, εἴ τι τοιοῦτον αὐτῷ παρ' ὑμῖν πέπρακται; καίτοι πόλιν οἰκεῖτε τῶν οὐσῶν τε καὶ γεγενημένων ἐπαφροδιτοτάτην, ἀλλ' ὅμως οὐδὲν ἠκούσατε, θαρρῶν δ' ἂν εἴποιμι ὅτι μηδὲ ἄλλος τις Ἑλλήνων. εἶτα τὸν ἐπὶ τῆς Ἑλλάδος ἐν πλείονι ἀδείᾳ καὶ συγγνώμῃ κοσμίως βεβιωκότα, τοῦτον ἐπὶ τῆς Ῥώμης παρ' αὐτὸν τῶν ἄρχοντα καὶ τοὺς νόμους ἡγεῖσθε μεταβεβλῆσθαι; ἀλλὰ τοῦτό γε παραπλήσιόν ἐστιν, ὥσπερ ἂν εἴ τις τὸν ἀθλητὴν φαίη καθ' αὑτὸν μὲν εὐτακτεῖν, ἐν δὲ τῷ σταδίῳ καὶ παρὰ τὸν ἀγωνοθέτην πλημμελεῖν.
>
> (34)

The alleged crime was apparently of a sexual nature. The mention of Roman laws must refer to the *lex Iulia de adulteriis coercendis*. Commentators have not accepted Favorinus' denial at face-value.[90] The silence around the nature of his alleged offense is more conspiratorial than embarrassed. The reminder of Corinth's historical reputation as a center of prostitution and the cult of Aphrodite in the description of the city as 'most sensuous' (ἐπαφροδιτοτάτην) subtly indicts the citizenry of hypocrisy.[91]

An epigram from the *Greek Anthology* spuriously attributed to Meleager but recently assigned to Favorinus' contemporary Strato claims that Favorinus could also speak in less oblique terms about his sexuality[92]:

> You don't believe that Favorinus fucks? Disbelieve no longer: He told me himself that he fucked with his own mouth!

> Εἰ βινεῖ Φαβορῖνος, ἀπιστεῖς· μηκέτ' ἀπίστει·
>   αὐτός μοι βινεῖν εἶπ' ἰδίῳ στόματι.
>
> ([Meleager], *Anthologia Palatina* 11.223)

The joke hinges on the double meaning generated when the instrumental dative ἰδίῳ στόματι ('with his own mouth') is understood with the verb εἶπ(ε) of the main clause ('he told me') or the infinitive βινεῖν of the indirect statement ('he fucked'): By an ambiguity of word order the penetrating eunuch is restored to his conventional, subordinated role as *fellator* or *cunnilingus*.[93] The evidentiary value of such a hostile piece of testimony as this may be questioned, but the humor only works if at some point and in certain circles Favorinus actually did claim to be capable of 'playing the man' (Lucian, *Eunuchus* 13).

In the *Corinthian Oration* Favorinus attributes the 'slander' (32 διαβολῆς) at the root of his troubles to the disapproval (ψόγος) of enemies who object to his 'sensuous eloquence' (33 περὶ τοὺς λόγους ... ἐπαφροδισίαν). Philostratus says that Favorinus 'charmed' (ἔθελγε) the masses of non-Greek-speaking Romans (τῆς Ἑλλήνων φωνῆς ἀξύνετοι) 'with the sound of his voice, the expressiveness of his gaze, and the rhythm of his speech' (*Lives of the Sophists* 491–2 τῇ τε ἠχῇ τοῦ φθέγματος καὶ τῷ σημαίνοντι τοῦ βλέμματος καὶ τῷ ῥυθμῷ τῆς γλώττης);[94] the crowds were especially enchanted by his musical perorations, which they called the 'song' (ᾠδήν). Philostratus reports in the immediately preceding life that Dio's 'persuasiveness was such as to charm even those without a thorough understanding of Greek culture' (ἡ πειθὼ τοῦ ἀνδρὸς οἵα καταθέλξαι καὶ τοὺς μὴ τὰ Ἑλλήνων ἀκριβοῦντας), including Trajan, who allegedly said to him, 'I have no idea what you're saying, but I love you like myself' (488 τί μὲν λέγεις, οὐκ οἶδα, φιλῶ δέ σε ὡς ἐμαυτόν).[95] Despite their similarity the two passages have important differences that throw into relief a contrast between two styles of eloquence. Favorinus' Roman audience did not understand his language, whereas Dio's could not follow his argument due to an incomplete familiarity with 'Greek culture' (τὰ Ἑλλήνων);[96] Dio cast his spell through persuasion (πειθώ), Favorinus through sound rather than sense.

From contemporary and later descriptions, it appears that Favorinus was the master of a style of oratory maligned by traditionalists and advocates of a sparer style as effeminate, Asiatic, ostentatious, and sung; rhetoricians from Quintilian to Favorinus' own teacher Dio liken its practitioners specifically to eunuchs.[97] The association of sophists and eunuchs is a contemporary commonplace,[98] of which Favorinus himself is the supreme example, but one wonders whether Dio wrote the *Fourth Kingship Oration* before or after he encountered a certain smooth young philosophy student from Gaul with a rhetorical bent and a flair for theatrics[99]:

> '... A great mob of foolish people such as this you might sometimes find attendant upon the so-called sophists, and you will realize that a sophist is

no different from a licentious eunuch'. And hearing this, [Alexander] wondered in what respect [Diogenes] had likened the sophist to a eunuch and asked him why. 'Because', he said, 'the most shameless eunuchs claim to be real men and lust after women, and they sleep with them and harass them, but nothing comes of it, even if they associate with them night and day'.

> τοιοῦτον εὕροις ἂν καὶ περὶ τοὺς καλουμένους σοφιστάς πολὺν ὄχλον ἐνίοτε συνεπόμενον ἀνθρώπων ἠλιθίων· καὶ γνώσῃ ὅτι οὐδὲν διαφέρει σοφιστὴς ἄνθρωπος εὐνούχου ἀκολάστου. καὶ ὃς ἀκούσας ἐθαύμασε κατὰ τί τὸν σοφιστὴν εὐνούχῳ παρέβαλεν, καὶ ἤρετο αὐτόν. ὅτι, εἶπε, τῶν εὐνούχων φασὶν οἱ ἀσελγέστατοι ἄνδρες εἶναι καὶ ἐρᾶν τῶν γυναικῶν, καὶ συγκαθεύδουσιν αὐταῖς καὶ ἐνοχλοῦσι, γίγνεται δ' οὐδὲν πλέον, οὐδ' ἂν τάς τε νύκτας καὶ τὰς ἡμέρας συνῶσιν αὐταῖς.
>
> (Dio Chrysostom 4.35–6)

No wonder Philostratus remarks that the student could not have been more different from the teacher (*Lives of the Sophists* 492).[100] In his speech 'Against Those Who Burlesque the Mysteries of Rhetoric' (Κατὰ τῶν ἐξορχουμένων) Aelius Aristides makes explicit the comparison between eunuchs and crowd-pleasing Asianist orators who deliberately cultivate an effeminate style in a way that evokes Favorinus' pride in his second paradox, that 'although he was a eunuch, he was tried for adultery' (Philostratus, *Lives of the Sophists* 489 εὐνοῦχος ὢν μοιχείας κρίνεσθαι):

> Then they act just as if some hermaphrodite or eunuch were not to blame physical disability or misfortune but claim that he became that way on purpose.
>
> ἔπειτα ποιοῦσι παραπλήσιον ὥσπερ ἂν εἴ τις ἀνδρόγυνος ἢ εὐνοῦχος μὴ τὴν ἀσθένειαν τοῦ σώματος μηδὲ τὴν τύχην αἰτιῷτο, προνοίᾳ δὲ φάσκοι γενέσθαι τοιοῦτος.
>
> (Aristides, *Oration* 34.48 Keil)

Aristides spent six months in the capital in 144 CE when he was twenty-six years old, some years after Favorinus' period of greatest celebrity at Rome under Hadrian, but not too late to have witnessed the eunuch sophist in action towards the end of his career. Gleason tantalizingly speculates that Favorinus could even have been the unnamed singing orator whose public embarrassment Aristides claims to have witnessed when the crowd, carried away by his monotonous repetition of the same prose rhythm, began chanting his clausulae in anticipation of their delivery (Aristides, *Oration* 34.47 Keil).[101] Philostratus says that Favorinus 'was born hybrid and intersex' (διφυὴς δὲ ἐτέχθη καὶ ἀνδρόθηλυς),[102] so that

Aristides could very well have had him in mind with both tenor and vehicle of the simile, the brazenly effeminate orator likened to a natural hermaphrodite boastfully calling himself a self-made eunuch.[103]

Conclusion

The many centuries that separate Favorinus from Menander complicate attempts to determine immediate models and sources of inspiration, and among the abundant literary parallels here surveyed it is often impossible in individual cases of eunuch adultery to distinguish Menandrean allusion and reminiscence from the mediating influences of other authors and works and even more general cultural stereotypes. It is clear enough, however, that Menander introduced eunuch and transvestite disguise into the comic adultery plot, so that direct and indirect reflexes of the motif alike, even if they are filtered through Terence, Cicero, Juvenal, and others, illuminate the afterlife and reception of Athenian comedy in the Roman Empire. With his paradoxes, Favorinus fashioned a public image at the intersection of discourses on three major themes of the Second Sophistic: Through his mastery of *paideia*, he was a Gaul who lived as a Greek; he confounded simplistic notions of gender by openly presenting himself as a eunuch who was charged with adultery; and by manipulating power dynamics he quarreled with the emperor yet survived. In each case Favorinus presented himself as triumphing from the disadvantaged position through self-empowerment. The mixture of self-deprecating irony (εἰρωνεία) and boastful imposture (ἀλαζονεία) expressed in the paradoxes presents Favorinus as the picaresque hero of his own comic life story. This strategy is of course reminiscent of Old Comedy and Aristophanes.[104] In the figure of the eunuch adulterer, however, Favorinus' enemies channeled a variant on the transvestite adultery plot traceable ultimately to Menander. That Cicero had done as much to Clodius in the *Bona Dea* affair shows that as a rhetorical strategy this use of comic abuse in oratory was nothing new. Favorinus' innovation was the re-appropriation from his detractors of this comic character for his own positive self-definition as a real man beneath his smooth exterior.

Notes

1 Philostratus, *Lives of the Sophists* 489; Lucian, *Eunuchus* 10; cf. [Dio Chrysostom], *Or.* 37.33–35. Polemo calls Favorinus lecherous in the extreme (*De physiognomonia*

1.160–2). For Plutarch and comedy, see Marshall, chapter 7 in this volume. For Dio Chrysostom, see Hawkins, chapter 4 in this volume.
2 'Although he was a Gaul, he lived as a Greek; although he was a eunuch, he was tried for adultery; he quarreled with an emperor and survived' (*Lives of the Sophists* 489: Γαλάτης ὢν ἑλληνίζειν, εὐνοῦχος ὢν μοιχείας κρίνεσθαι, βασιλεῖ διαφέρεσθαι καὶ ζῆν).
3 Philostratus, *Lives of the Sophists* 489: ambiguous genitalia at birth, effeminate voice, beardlessness; Polemo, *De physiognomonia* 1.160–2 Förster: congenital anorchism or cryptorchism, effeminate voice, beardlessness; Lucian, *Demonax* 12–13, *Eunuchus* 6–9, 12–13: effeminate voice, congenital anorchism or cryptorchism, beardlessness; Mason 1979: 2; Whitmarsh 2001: 114–15.
4 Mason 1979; Greaves 2012; cf. Graumann 2013: 182–4 with skepticism. Reifenstein's syndrome is a variety of Partial Androgen Insensitivity Syndrome (PAIS), a congenital resistance to male hormones in boys that inhibits growth of male secondary sexual characteristics at puberty and allows development of female ones. The Philostratean description of Favorinus as a hermaphrodite alongside Favorinus' self-identification as a eunuch in the same text (*Lives of the Sophists* 489) could be explained by a range of external genital abnormalities potentially associated with PAIS (perineoscrotal hypospadias, micropenis, clitoromegaly, bifid scrotum, and undescended testes); see Hughes and Deeb 2012: 582; cf. Mason 1979: 8. Some adult male PAIS patients report engaging in penile-vaginal intercourse, but it should be noted that recent evidence indicates serious impairment of sexual function in this population (Bouvattier, Mignot, Lefevre *et al.* 2006). Modern treatments, moreover, such as hormone replacement therapy and genitoplasty complicate the transferability of studies of intersex disorders including PAIS to ancient contexts. In this paper, however, my concern is not so much what Favorinus was as what others said about him and, more interestingly, what he said about himself.
5 On the relative chronology see Webster 1974: 3–5.
6 On transvestism and eunuchism as variations on the same New Comedy plot see Heslin 2005: 260–1. There is an extensive bibliography on Terentian modifications to the Menandrean original, focusing primarily on the question of *contaminatio*; see Barsby 1993 with earlier scholarship.
7 Athenaeus (469e–f = Diphilus T6 K-A) attests to *Eunouchos* as an alternate title of a reworking (διασκευή) of Diphilus' *Hairēsiteikhēs* ('The Wall-Breacher').
8 In Theopompus' *Stratiōtides* ('Soldierettes', 55–8 K-A) women apparently donned men's armor, possibly in response to a rash of draft-dodging among Athenian men during the Peloponnesian War; see Christ 2004: 34–5.
9 See Storey 2003: 37–9, 94–111; cf. Juvenal 2.91–2; Lucian, *Adversus indoctum* 27. Choruses of effeminate males and possibly transvestism figured in Cratinus' *Drapetides* ('Lady Runaways', 53–64 K-A) and *Malthakoi* ('Effeminates', 103–8 K-A); see Bakola 2010: 141–58.

10 The role of transvestism in Dionysiac ritual and the androgynous representation of Dionysus in art, literature, and cult are well known; see e.g. Delcourt 1961: 10–11, 24–7 with ancient sources and Miller 1999: 233–4 with more recent scholarship; on *Bacchae* and comic and comedic elements in the cross-dressing scene (912–70) see Seidensticker 1982: 123–9.
11 Whitehorne 2000: 311.
12 Christ 2004: 45; it is often remarked that Terence's *Eunuchus* is the only play in the extant tradition of New Comedy in which the rape occurs during rather than preceding the action.
13 Draft-dodging may also have motivated male-to-female transvestism in Eupolis' comedy *Astrateutoi* ('Draft-Dodgers') or *Androgynoi* ('Men-Women', 35–46 K-A); cf. the previously mentioned female-to-male transvestism in Theopompus' *Stratiōtides* ('Soldierettes', 55–8 K-A); Brisson 2002: 61–4; Storey 2003: 74–81; a comedy entitled *Stratiōtai* ('Soldiers') or *Stratiōtides* ('Soldierettes') is also attributed to Hermippus (51–8 K-A).
14 In Aristophanes' *Acharnians* the protagonist Dicaeopolis claims that the two eunuchs attendant upon the Persian ambassador are really the beardless effeminates Cleisthenes and Strato in disguise (117–22), but comparison with similar jibes at the same individuals in the other Aristophanic plays and fragments indicates that the lines simply constituted a throwaway joke at their expense and were probably not accompanied in the staging by an actual unmasking; on this scene see Chiasson 1984; cf. *Knights* 1373–4, *Clouds* 355, *Wasps* 1187, *Birds* 831, *Lysistrata* 621, 1090–92, *Thesmophoriazusae* 235, 574–6, 582–3, *Frogs* 48, 57, 422–4, *Holkades* ('Merchant Ships') fragment 422 K-A; Pherecrates 143 K-A; Cratinus 208 K-A; 1963: 144–5; only in *Thesmophoriazusae* 574–654 does Cleisthenes appear as a character onstage, whereas elsewhere as here his name serves merely as a punchline.
15 On Arjuna undercover among women as a eunuch in the *Mahābhārata* see O'Flaherty 1980: 297–9 and Pelissero 2002; additional Sanskrit examples of transvestite and eunuch disguise in Artola 1975.
16 Parthenius (15.2–3) and Pausanias (8.20.2) attribute the myth in this form to the elegist Diodorus of Elaea (date unknown, but probably Hellenistic) and the historian and mythographer Phylarchus (third century BCE).
17 As far as historiographical and ethnographical traditions are concerned, Llewellyn-Jones (2002: 38–9) notes that any hint of eunuch sex within the harem is absent from the extant sources on the Achaemenid court, where Greeks of the archaic and classical periods first encountered the institution of court eunuchs. Philostratus' report (*Life of Apollonius of Tyana* 1.34–7) of a eunuch seducing a woman within the Persian king's harem is a late fiction that participates in the same discourse of eunuch adultery of which the contemporary biographical tradition of Favorinus is itself a part.
18 Maaß 1925 with terms and ancient sources; more concisely Guyot 1980: 20–4; see also Ringrose 2003: 13–14.

19 Philostratus on Favorinus (*Lives of the Sophists* 489) is another example of the term εὐνοῦχος denoting a congenital condition; the jurist Ulpian (*Digest* 50.16.128) classes all types under the umbrella term *spado* (Greek σπάδων, from the verb σπάω, 'I pull [off or out]'); Cyril of Alexandria distinguishes 'natural eunuchs, who have the parts for lechery [i.e. genitalia] in some measure', from 'full eunuchs and castrates' (*Adversus eunuchos* = *Patrologia Graeca* 77.1109a–b οἱ σπάδοντες καὶ τὰ μόρια τῆς αἰσχρουργίας ποσῶς ἔχοντες … οἱ τέλεον ἀπόκοποι καὶ ἐκτετμημένοι); on *spadones* as 'natural eunuchs' (cryptorchid or otherwise hypogonadic adult males) in the Byzantine period see Ringrose 2003: 15, 63.

20 Paul of Aegina 6.88 Heiberg; *Hippiatrica* 20. Certain terms denoting non-congenital eunuchism are verbal nouns and participles that reflect the procedures through which it was acquired: ἐκτομίας, ἐκτετμημένος (from ἐκτέμνω, 'I cut out, excise'); ἀπόκοπος (from ἀποκόπτω, 'I cut off'); θλιβίας (Latin *thlibias*), ἐκτεθλιμμένος (from θλίβω, 'I press'); θλαδίας (Latin *thludius* or *thlasias* at *Digest* 50.16.128), τεθλασμένος (from θλάω, 'I crush'); ancient references at Guyot 1980: 22–3.

21 Whether the evangelist spoke literally of elective castration with respect to the third type, the self-made eunuch, or figuratively of ascetic devotion to the celibate life was the subject of exegetical controversy in antiquity; on castration among early Christians see Caner 1997.

22 Guyot 1980: 16–17 n. 5.

23 Bullough 2002: 4; Burke 2013: 96–7. For the traditional etymology of εὐνοῦχος from ὁ εὐνὴν ἔχων ('guardian of the bedchamber, chamberlain') see Maaß 1925: 437–8 and Guyot 1980: 20 n. 14.

24 The extravagant Callias has a eunuch doorkeeper in Plato's *Protagoras* (314c–d).

25 Terence, *Eunuchus* 665–6; Guyot 1980: 16–17 n. 5–6; Stevenson 1995: 499–504; Kuefler 2001: 97–9; Parker 2007: 290–1 n. 26; Burke 2013: 111 n. 96; cf. Lucian, *De Syria dea* 22; Dio Chrysostom 4.35–6; Heliodorus, *Aethiopica* 9.25.5; [Alexander of Aphrodisias], *Problemata* 1.9; Jerome, *Epistulae* 107.11 = *Patrologia Latina* 22.876.

26 Hippocrates, *De semine* 2 Littré; [Aristotle], *Problemata* 876b24–32; cf. Galen, *De semine* 4.472 Kühn.

27 'For example, Aristophanes, *Acharnians* 117–22; cf. [Aristotle], *Problemata* 879a36–880a5.'

28 For example, Aristophanes, *Frogs* 422–4; Athenaeus 13.564f–565f with Alexis 266 K-A; Seneca, *Epistulae* 47.7, 95.24, 122.7; Juvenal 2.11–13; Gleason 1995: 74–6.

29 For example, Nero's beloved Sporus: Suetonius, *Nero* 28; Cassius Dio, *Historia Romana* 62.28.2–3; Juvenal 10.306–9; Dio Chrysostom 21.4–7; Domitian's favorite Earinus: Cassius Dio, *Historia Romana* 67.2.3; Statius, *Silvae* 3.4.65–82; practice outlawed by Domitian: Suetonius, *Domitian* 7.1; Martial 9.5, 9.7; Statius, *Silvae* 4.33.13–15; see also *Digest* 48.8.3.4; Seneca, *Controversiae* 10.4.17; Seneca, *De providentia* 3.13, *De ira* 1.21.3, *Epistulae* 66.53; Petronius, *Satirica* 119.1.20–2; Pliny, *Naturalis Historia* 7.129; Quintilian, *De institutione oratoria* 5.12.17–21; Dio

Chrysostom 77/78.36; [Lucian], *Amores* 21; Claudian, *In Eutropium* 1.342–8; *Anthologia Latina* 97–8 SB; Cyril of Alexandria, *Adversus eunuchos* = *Patrologia Graeca* 77.1108c; Guyot 1978: 59–63; Brower 1996: 176–8; Burke 2013: 84–5, 112. These same youthful qualities of eunuchs were thought to appeal to women as well: Juvenal 6.366–7; Tertullian, *Ad uxorem* 2.8.4 = *Patrologia Latina* 1.1301b; Jerome, *Epistulae* 130.13 = *Patrologia Latina* 22.1117; *Anthologia Latina* 97.5–6 SB.

30 Guyot 1978: 63–6; Stevenson 1995: 499–509; Parker 2007: 290–1; Burke 2013: 112–13.

31 Guyot 1980: 16–17n. 5; Rousselle 1988: 122–8; Stevenson 1995: 497–8; Kuefler 2001: 33–5; Ringrose 2003: 15–16, 19–21, 57–64, 78, 122; Tougher 2008: 32–4; Burke 2013: 108–9.

32 Ringrose (2003: 57–9) infers this principle from Theophilus Protospatharius, *De corporis humani fabrica libri quinque* 4.29 (eunuchs castrated before fourteen years of age do not grow wisdom teeth, thought to be missing in women; cf. Aristotle, *Historia Animalium* 501b.19–21) and 5.35 (some eunuchs ejaculate sterile semen; children do not ejaculate because their seminal ducts are narrow and blocked): therefore some eunuchs have the larger seminal ducts of adults, because they have passed through puberty, considered to occur at fourteen years of age; cf. 5.28.

33 Juvenal 6.366–78; Martial 6.67; Jerome, *Adversus Iovinianum* 1.47 = *Patrologia Latina* 23.277b (for bibliography challenging Jerome's ascription of the *ecloga Theophrasti* to Theophrastus see Clark 2005: 158); Basil of Ancyra, *De virginitate* 46 = *Patrologia Graeca* 30.796c; cf. *Epistulae* 115 = *Patrologia Graeca* 30.532a; Isidore, *Etymologies* 10.93.

34 Juvenal 6.366–73b; Basil of Ancyra, *De virginitate* 44–5 = *Patrologia Graeca* 30.796a; John Chrysostom, *Homiliae in Epistulam ad Titum* 5.2 = *Patrologia Graeca* 62.690.

35 Cf. Juvenal 6.O31–2 (= 6.347–8) *sed quis custodiet ipsos custodes?* ('But who will supervise the actual supervisors?'); cf. Cyril of Alexandria, *Adversus eunuchos* = *Patrologia Graeca* 77.1108c μετὰ γυναικῶν δὲ ὡς φύλακες ἅμα καὶ σωφροσύνης δῆθεν ἰνδάλματα καθεύδοντες, ἀναισχύντως καὶ ἀπηρυθριωμένως αἰσχροπραγοῦσι ('And sleeping with women like their guardians and the very pictures of chastity, they shamelessly and impudently indulge their lust').

36 Modern evidence from studies of these populations shows that sexual drive and function are greatly reduced by castration and, if not eliminated, tend to decrease over time; results, however, vary among individuals, and the adrenal glands produce androgens in addition to the testes, so that sex is possible after castration, but nowhere near to the degree that the generalizations, exaggerations, and distortions of ancient satire and theological polemic would suggest; on the biology and modern evidence see Ågmo 2007: 191–206, 221–30.

37 Cf. Hippocrates, *De natura pueri* 20 Littré; Aristotle, *Historia animalium* 518a30–3, 631b32–632a4, *De generatione animalium* 784a4–10 (prepubertal castrates do not

grow androgenic hair; postpubertal castrates lose all androgenic hair except for pubic hair but do not go bald, and in this respect they become like women); *De generatione animalium* 746b21–4 ('natural' eunuchs). For Paul of Aegina the important distinction is not the age of the patient but the manner of castration: Eunuchs castrated by crushing (κατὰ θλάσιν) experience sexual desire, while those who were castrated by excision (κατὰ ἐκτομήν) do not (Περὶ εὐνουχισμοῦ 6.68 Heiberg).

38 Artemidorus, *Oneirocritica* 2.69 on dreams of beggars, actors, sophists, *galli*, and eunuchs as omens of deceptive expectations; cf. Lucian, *Pseudologista* 17, *Eunuchus* 6; *Historia Augusta*, Severus Alexander 23.7.

39 See Gleason 1995: 55–81.

40 For example, Martial 3.81 (cunnilingus), 6.2, 6.39.20–1, 6.67, 10.91, 11.81 (impotent); Juvenal 1.22 (a marriage between a eunuch and a Roman matron, presumably to avoid liability to prosecution for adultery; see Guyot 1978: 64), 6.O1–378; Claudian, *In Eutropium* 1.101–3, 1.128–30.

41 Edwards 1993: 81–4; cf. Foucault 1985: 84–6.

42 See especially Gleason 1995.

43 On the adultery mime see Reynolds 1946 and Kehoe 1984; on transvestism and *galli* with ancient literary and material evidence see Mignona 1996; Jory 2002: 240, 249. On the feminine dress of *galli* see Lucian, *De Syria dea* 27 and Graillot 1912: 298 with additional citations.

44 For example, Tibullus 1.4.67–70; cf. Catullus 63.63 with Skinner 1993: 112–14; additional references at Graillot 1912: 318n. 3; Roller 1999: 227–34. Passivity remained the default sexuality of the literary *gallus* in the imperial period: Juvenal 2.111–16; Apuleius, *Metamorphoses* 8.26; [Lucian], *Asinus* 35–6.

45 For example, Martial 3.81, 10.91, 11.81; Lucian, *De Syria dea* 22. Lucian's ethnographic pastiche of Herodotean narrative, historical method, and style is of limited evidentiary value for actual cultic practice; see Lightfoot 2003: 184–208 on the controversy over the question of Lucianic authorship. Rousselle 1988: 122–5 on the mad emperor Elagabalus gives the *Scriptores Historiae Augustae* excessive credence as a historical source.

46 Parsons 1971: 61; Parsons 1974: 35 n. 1; Heslin 2005: 261.

47 Jones 2012: 238–45

48 Heslin 2005: 257–61.

49 Hallett 1989 with Phaedrus, *Fabulae* 4.16, Martial 1.90, 7.67, and 7.70, and Seneca, *Controversiae* 1.2.23, to which may be added [Lucian], *Amores* 28.

50 See Brisson 2002: 68–70.

51 *Scholia in Lucianum* 275 Rabe.

52 Karavas and Vix 2014: 189.

53 Aristophanes in Plato's *Symposium* (191e) uses the term to refer to the split halves of the formerly female-female beings in his creation myth about the origin of love.

54 For a deeper, more theoretical consideration of the complex sexual dynamics and gender identities presented in this dialogue than the scope of the present discussion allows, see Gilhuly 2006.
55 Cf. Seneca, *Controversiae* 1.pr.10; Juvenal 6.O27–8; *Dialogi Meretricii* 5.3, quoted above.
56 Lucian, *Eunuchus* 10 = Solon, fragment 28c Ruschenbusch μοιχὸς ἑάλω ποτέ, ὡς ὁ ἄξων φησίν, ἄρθρα ἐν ἄρθροις ἔχων ('He was caught once in the act of adultery, "with genitals in genitals" as the code says'). Although Lucian appears to be quoting a Solonian statute, Favorinus' adultery was alleged to have been committed in Rome ([Dio Chrysostom], *Or.* 37.34), and he would have been tried under the terms of the *lex Iulia de adulteriis coercendis*, enacted by Augustus in 18 BCE and revived by Domitian (Martial 5.75, 6.2, 6.4, 6.7, 6.22, 6.45, 6.91, 9.6; Juvenal 2.29–37; Statius, *Silvae* 5.2.99–110); Pliny describes a trial under Trajan in which the convicted adulterer was punished with exile (*Epistulae* 6.31.4–6).
57 Choricius of Gaza, *Apologia mimorum* 30–5, 54–5 Förster-Richsteig; Reynolds 1946: 80; Kehoe 1994: 97. Marcus Aurelius considers mime the generic successor of New Comedy (11.6.2).
58 Anderson (1976a: 79n. 111) compares the exposé of the false philosopher Proteus Peregrinus (*De morte Peregrini* 7–31) as a similar instance of Lucian attributing his own mockery to an anonymous bystander. For Lucian, see also Storey, chapter 9 in this volume.
59 Anderson 1976a: 62–3, Anderson 1976c: 108.
60 Hermogenes, *On Issues* (Περὶ στάσεων) 4; Guyot 1980: 65; Russell 1983: 52n. 42; Gleason 1995: 134n. 15; Holford-Strevens 1997: 192n. 20; Heath 1994.
61 Russell 1983: 51.
62 Porter 2007 illustrates the adherence of Lysias 1 to the generic expectations of the conventional adultery plot, concluding that it was a skillfully executed fiction composed and circulated in order to advertise the logographer's professional skills to prospective clients.
63 Heath (1994: 114n2) notes that the identical question is at issue in the elder Seneca's case of the phallic tribad (*Controversiae* 1.2.23), cited earlier in the discussion of Lucian's Megilla (*Dialogi meretricii* 5).
64 Guyot 1980: 65 n. 108; Russell 1983: 52.
65 Lucian, *Eunuchus* 10; Guyot 1978: 65n. 108. Cf. *Adversus indoctum* 19, where a eunuch's concubine is included in a catalogue of useless possessions; Anderson 1976a: 123.
66 Geffcken 1973: 82–8.
67 In addition to Geffcken cf. most recently Harries 2007; Wright 1931 assembles all Ciceronian references to drama.
68 It is Cicero's practice not to display his Greek learning too ostentatiously in his political speeches, so as not to alienate his Roman audience, so any direct allusions or quotations would most likely have evoked Caecilius' *Androgynus* or Terence's

Eunuchus rather than their Menandrean models; cf. the references to Caecilius' *Hypobolimaeus* at *Pro Roscio Amerino* 46 and Terence's *Adelphoe* (also from a Menandrean original) at *Pro Caelio* 37–9; in the philosophical works too Cicero quotes Terence's *Eunuchus* (46–8 at *De natura deorum* 3.72 and 59–63 at *Tusculanae disputationes* 4.76); Cicero elsewhere (*De finibus bonorum et malorum* 1.4) speaks disparagingly of Romans who disdain to read Latin adaptations instead of Menandrean originals, but the very existence of a choice also shows that Menander's plays were known and accessible to educated Romans of his day.

69 Cf. Juvenal 6.335–45.
70 The ancient definitions of *ethopoeia* are collected in Ventrella 2005; see also Hagen 1966.
71 For the distinction between ethical declamation in the character of general types and the historical variety in the persona of named individuals from the Greek and Roman past, including myth, see Russell 1983: 87–128.
72 Philostratus, *Lives of the Sophists* 481; Lucian, *De saltatione* 65; Hermogenes, *On Types of Style* (Περὶ ἰδεῶν) 321; Quintilian, *De institutione oratoria* 3.8.49–51, 6.2.17; Hagen 1966: 81–2. See also Nervegna 2013: 213–14 on Menandrean fragments illustrating the rich/poor theme that were anthologized for school use. On the Latin side Terence's *Eunuchus* had a long life as a school text, starting in grammar school: Augustine, *Confessions* 1.16.26 with *Eunuchus* 584–91; Jerome *Commentarius in Ecclesiasten* 1.9 = *Patrologia Latina* 23.1019a with *Eunuchus* 41; Sidonius Apollinaris, *Epistulae* 2.2.2 with *Eunuchus* 107. The opening scene of Terence's *Eunuchus*, cited by Quintilian as an exemplar of theatrical delivery (*De institutione oratoria* 11.3.182 with *Eunuchus* 46–8) made a particular impression: Cicero, *De natura deorum* 3.72; Horace, *Satires* 2.3.260–71; Persius 5.161–74, using the Menandrean rather than the Terentian names for the characters; see Fantham 1984: 301.
73 See Amato 2005: 148 for bibliography on the genre and additional citations.
74 Cf. Goldhill 1995: 13 on *Daphnis and Chloe* 1.13–14 (Chloe's monologue on the symptoms of lovesickness).
75 Plutarch, *Moralia* 853c15–853f10; Quintilian, *De institutione oratoria* 10.1.69–72; Dio Chrysostom 18.7; Hermogenes, Περὶ ἰδεῶν 323–4; Nervegna 2013: 211–20, 223–34.
76 For example Cicero, *Orator* 70, *De officiis* 1.93–9; [Hermogenes], *Preliminary Exercises* (Προγυμνάσματα) 9; cf. Aristotle, *Rhetoric* 1408a10–32.
77 [Libanius], *Ethopoeiae* 26 Förster.
78 Amato 2005: 149; Amato 2006a; Amato 2006b; Amato 2007; Amato 2009; Amato 2010: 389.
79 Amato (2005: 149) also compares Fortunatianus, *Rhetorica* 1.21 Montefusco.
80 Philostratus, *Lives of the Sophists* 489 θερμὸς ... τὰ ἐρωτικά ('passionate in love affairs'); Polemo, *De physiognomonia* 1.160–2 Förster *libidinosus et dissolutus supra omnem modum* ("debauched and depraved out of all proportion").
81 Cf. Goldhill 1995: 13 on *Daphnis and Chloe* 1.13–14 with additional citations.

82 Cf. Lucian, *De Syria dea* 22; Dio Chrysostom 4.35–6.
83 Cf. Legré 1900: 14.
84 Legré 1900: 82–5.
85 Philostratus, *Lives of the Sophists* 489; Polemo, *De physiognomonia* 1.160–2 Förster; Lucian, *Eunuchus* 6–9, 11–13.
86 Bowersock 2002; Barigazzi 1966: 170; Amato 2010: 93–6; cf. Lucian, *Eunuchus* 8–9; *Dialogi mortuorum* 10.7–10, 20.5–6, *Timon* 54–5; Dio Chrysostom 33.53–4; Athenaeus 13.563d–565f; Juvenal 2.1–35; Martial 1.24, 1.96, 7.58.6–10; Aulus Gellius, *Noctes Atticae* 9.2.
87 In Quintilian's Latin, *opinio decipitur . . . ex contrario* ('expectation is frustrated by its opposite'); cf. [Hermogenes,] *On the Method of Forcefulness* (Περὶ μεθόδου δεινότητος) 34; Anonymous, *Tractatus Coislinianus* 6 Janko.
88 On this speech see Swain 1989: 54–5 and Gleason 1995: 3–20.
89 Gleason 1995: 13–16.
90 Swain 1989: 154 ('Like an adulterer Favorinus denies everything').
91 For example, Pindar, fragment 122 Snell; Gleason 1995: 17 ('Favorinus is slyly calling the kettle black').
92 Amato 2001.
93 Cf. Martial 3.81 (a cunnilingual *gallus*); *Anthologia Palatina* 12.236 (a pederastic eunuch).
94 Cf. Aulus Gellius, *Noctes Atticae* 16.3.1.
95 I thank Tom Hawkins for suggesting this parallel; cf. also *Lives of the Sophists* 589 (Hadrian of Tyre).
96 For the phrase τὰ Ἑλλήνων as παιδεία (Greek education and culture) in this passage see Whitmarsh 1998: 208–9; cf. Philostratus, *Life of Apollonius of Tyana* 2.31, 3.31, 5.8, 5.36, 7.42, *Lives of the Sophists* 536, 589; Trajan understood the Greek language (Cassius Dio 68.3.4).
97 Quintilian, *De institutione oratoria* 5.12.17–21, 11.3.19; Lucian, *Demonax* 12 (Favorinus); Dio Chrysostom 33.38–9 (eunuchs), 33.64 (hermaphrodites); Philostratus (*Lives of the Sophists* 492); on Dio's gendered invective in the *First Tarsian* (*Discourse* 33) see Hawkins 2014: 206–15.
98 E.g. Artemidorus, *Oneirocritica* 2.69.
99 Moles 1983 argues for a date early in the reign of Trajan, who assumed the principate in 98 CE, when Favorinus would have been in his late teens.
100 Cf. Dio Chrysostom 32.68 against singing oratory.
101 Gleason 1995: 125. Tom Hawkins suggests to me the parallel with Aristophanes, *Frogs* 1206–49 (Aeschylus repeatedly capping Euripidean prologues with the metrical phrase ληκύθιον ἀπώλεσεν, ('lost his little oil flask')).
102 The emphasis on Favorinus' gender status at birth (ἐτέχθη) shows that Philostratus has a biological rather than behavioral characteristics in mind with his description

here; Mason 1979: 3; cf. Polemo, *De physiognomonia* Förster, quoted and discussed earlier, with its repeated emphasis on Favorinus' birth 'without testicles' (*De physiognomonia* 1.162.21–164.8 Förster *sine testiculis natus*); *Suda* s.v. Φαβορῖνος (Phi 4 Adler) γεγονὼς ... τὴν τοῦ σώματος ἕξιν ἀνδρόγυνος (ὅν φασιν ἑρμαφρόδιτον) ('physically male and female at birth [what they call a hermaphrodite]'). The adjectives διφυής and ἀνδρόθηλυς are postclassical Greek synonyms respectively of δίμορφος and ἀνδρόγυνος, which are used regularly of hermaphroditism; Mason 1979: 2; Graumann 2013: 188–90; cf. ἀρρενόθηλυς (variant spelling ἀρσενόθηλυς), used, for example of a prodigious birth (a hermaphroditic lamb) at Cassius Dio 17.60.
103 Barigazzi 1966: 91; Gleason 1995: 124–5.
104 See Whitman 1964.

6

Comedies and Comic Actors in the Greek East: An Epigraphical Perspective

Fritz Graf

I.

In 124 CE, a wealthy citizen of the small city of Oenoanda in Northern Lycia founded a large public festival, a panegyris, that had to have his name, Demosthenia.[1] To classicists, Oenoanda is known (if at all) as the city in which another wealthy citizen, one Diogenes, inscribed – perhaps at about the same time – long excerpts from the books of Epicurus on a wall in the market place, to educate his fellow citizens to lasting happiness. Our founder, C. Iulius Demosthenes, belonged to a family whose wealth and influence had lasted at least from the early days of the imperial age when Caesar or Octavian had given Roman citizenship to an ancestor, and they must have been prominent as benefactors and cultivated their relationship with the Roman authorities; accordingly, the emperor was included in the celebrations of the new panegyris. The details of the new festival and its foundation are preserved on a large slab of local lime-stone that contained five documents out of a larger file, as cross-references show: the short confirmation of the foundation by Hadrian; the long document in which the founder gives all necessary details, from the ritual to the finances; the minutes of the local assembly that deliberated on the foundation and detailed additional processions and sacrifices; a decree of the council of the Termessians to which Oenoanda belonged; and an excerpt from a letter of the Roman governor who confirmed the tax privileges during the festival and the personal privileges of the organizer (*agōnothetēs*). It is from a number of such lengthy and detailed documents – all from the second and third centuries CE, but usually much worse preserved than the Oenoanda document – that we can piece together the way comedy was living and thriving in the cities of Asia Minor in the imperial age.

The core of the Demosthenia, that the founder called a πανήγυρις θυμελική, a 'theatrical festival', the emperor with more precision an ἀγὼν μουσικός, 'a contest in the arts of the Muses', consisted of eleven days of musical and literary performances. It opened on the provincial New Year's day, Augustus' birthday on September 23, when the ruling emperor received a public sacrifice; continued with interruptions by political assembly days, a market day, and two sacrifices to the city god Apollo; and ended with the grand finale on Artemision 20. But this was not the end: two days of non-competitive performances by hired mimes and other stage artists and a day of athletic contests among young citizens – with among other events a torch race – concluded a festival period that, with all additions and interruptions, lasted almost the entire first month of the local calendar.

The program has a clear progression. Heralds and trumpets mark the opening on New Year's day, and they go together with a procession into the theater and a sacrifice that the *agōnothetēs* offers for the emperor and the city gods. A day of praise orations and one of praise poems follow, moving from prose to poetry. Their topic is not stated. In the Mousea of Thespiae, there have to be ἔπαινοι in prose and poetry for the emperor and for the Muses; in Oenoanda, one imagines the praises of the emperor or the generous founder, but not necessarily the city god.[2] Two days of *chorauloi* – chorus performances with a flute player – transition to the dramatic performances that are the heart of the festival: first there are two days of comedy, then two days of tragedy; all this is then topped by the most noble and ancient art of the *kitharōidos*, the very traditional combination of singing and kithara playing. It is Apollo's favorite art and fits a festival where two days of sacrifices to the god are central. The grand finale puts the victors in the single disciplines against each other: it is specific for artistic festivals and is called the 'Over All (Contest)', διὰ πάντων, and defines the first, second and third overall prize.[3]

The progression is also a progression in value, as the prize money demonstrates. Trumpeters and heralds receive a first prize only, each of 50 denarii; the encomiasts get 75 denarii in each sub-category. After this, there is more money for each prize, and a second prize as well: 125 and 75 respectively for the *chorauloi* (that is the flutist; the chorus does not get a special prize), 200 and 100 respectively for the best two comic actors, 250 and 125 for the best two tragic actors, and 300 and 150 respectively for the *kitharōidoi*. In the final contest, there are three prizes but of less value, 150, 100 and 50 denarii each. The prize reflects the literary values of their society: a prose orator has much less prestige than a comic or a tragic actor, and even less than the *kitharōidos* with his old and high style art.

Other inscriptions from contemporary festival centers (such as Aphrodisias in Caria or Thespiae in Boeotia)[4] demonstrate that both the progression and the evaluation are common and traditional, with certain variations. There can be additional artistic disciplines, other instrumental soloists, but also – perhaps less expected – other traditional genres: the satyr play and the armed dance (the *pyrrhichē*). The sequence of the dramatic disciplines is more or less constant, from comedy to tragedy and then, in two instances, to the satyr play, with the *pyrrhichē* in one instance preceding, in another replacing the satyr play.[5] It is obvious how these programs of imperial time play with the elements of tragic performance in Athens, bringing comedy and tragedy in a clear relationship of rising value, and isolating the satyr play as a possible sub-discipline that concentrated on dancing and as such was comparable to or even exchangeable with the *pyrrhichē*.[6]

II.

In Oenoanda, the contests are named after the performers: ἀγὼν κωμῳδῶν, τραγῳδῶν, 'contest of actors in comedies' and 'tragedies'; the actors receive the first and second prize, and are set against all other victors in the grand finale. This wording could equally well mean a contest of recitation of selected excerpts from classical plays or the performance of entire plays.[7] But the fact that four days are set aside for comedy and tragedy contests argues for the latter: each day has at least its own play, if not several.

Other inscriptions confirm that it was entire plays to be staged and incidentally also answer another question. What does comedy (and tragedy and even satyr play) mean at this period? Are there new plays written, or were the classical plays, especially Menander and Euripides, performed over and over?[8]

The best evidence to answer both questions comes again from Aphrodisias. An agonistic foundation made by a certain Flavius Lysimachus and dated by the letter forms of its inscription to the late second or early third century offers more than just a contest of comic and tragic actors. The list of the prizes contains 'general comic or tragic actors' (κοινῇ κωμῳδῶν, κοινῇ τραγῳδῶν), new and old comedy (καινῇ κωμῳδία, παλαιᾷ κωμῳδία) and new and old tragedy (καινῇ τραγῳδία, παλαιᾷ τραγῳδία). Two similar lists from the Mousea in Thespiae, written in the second half of the second century CE, show that the juxtaposition of old and new comedy and tragedy in musical contests on the imperial stage is the norm, not the exception: they list victors in acting in old and new comedy and tragedy, and in writing new comedies and tragedies (ὑποκριτὴς or κωμῳδὸς παλαιᾶς/καινῆς κωμῳδίας, '(comic) actor of an old /new comedy', τραγῳδὸς παλαιᾶς/καινῆς τραγῳδίας, 'tragic actor of an old/new tragedy'; ποιητὴς καινῆς κωμῳδίας/τραγῳδίας, 'poet of an new comedy/tragedy')[9]. The parallelism between tragedy and comedy shows that new (καινή) tragedy and comedy must mean contemporary plays, whereas old (παλαιά) tragedy and comedy are the classical plays. On the side of comedy, it must mean Menander or Diphilus rather than Aristophanes or Cratinus: the papyri and mosaics demonstrate how New Comedy still had its audience and readership among the educated classes of the imperial age, whereas Old Comedy was read in school for the sake of Attic but needed too much explanation to gain a wider audience: the scholia and lexica demonstrate the need for intensive teaching help.[10] Thus, there were texts of comedies and tragedies written in the late second century CE and put on stage for the first time. In both the Mousea on Thespiae and the foundation of Lysimachos in Aphrodisias, in the category of classical plays only the actors won a prize, whereas in the category of contemporary plays both poet and actor could win: the great poets of the past had their prizes centuries ago, but the contemporary poets could emulate them. In Thespiae, there was also a winning σατυρογράφος, a writer of satyr plays, but no prize was given for an actor in satyr plays: satyrs danced as a chorus and were not differentiated according to virtuosity.[11] This is different from Hellenistic contests where prizes were awarded to 'actors in Satyr plays', the actors who played the heroic characters, and might reflect the evolution of the 'new' satyr play towards an almost pure dance performance, despite the topic still taken from myth; but one has to bear in mind that already on the Pronomos vase in about 400 BCE, the satyrs' chorus seems very important.[12]

Several lists from late Hellenistic Magnesia on the Maeander present the victors in the musical contests of their Rhomaia, founded at some point in the second century CE to celebrate the new lords of the East and presumably sponsored by a powerful local with ties to Rome, as for example in the Rhomaia in Chios, founded in the early second century.[13] They list victors in tragedy (τραγωιδιῶν), comedy (κωμῳδιῶν) and satyr plays (σατύρων); in the categories tragedy and comedy they give the name of the winning poet with the title of his play and of the winning actor, in the category satyr play only the poet and the title: again, satyr plays did not allow for the identification of an outstanding actor. The titles look conventional – mythology for tragedy (Hermione), contemporary life for comedy ('Ἐφεσία or 'The Girl from Ephesus', Ὅμοιοι or 'The Same'), fun with mythology in the satyr plays (Protesilaos, Aias, presumably also in 'The Sacrificer'[14]): 'Ephesia' resonates with Menander's 'Samia' or Terence's 'Andria' (after a lost play of Menander); we can project this onto the imperial evidence. Some poets and actors are also defined by their foreign citizenship, from Miletus, Ephesus, Tralles, or even Tarsus in far-away Cilicia.[15] The names without this indication thus belonged to locals: the contests in late Hellenistic Magnesia stimulated an intensive dramatic production for its musical contests among its own citizens, but also attracted artists from the wider region and beyond.

Why write new plays, given the power and renown of the old ones? Another inscription from Aphrodisias provides an answer. It is a file on the tragic poet C. Iulius Longianus from Aphrodisias and contains, after a very fragmentary honorary decree by an unknown city, a second decree by the city of Halicarnassus, and the honors that in 127 CE the association of Dionysiac artists conferred upon him: it thus is concerned with contemporary tragedies, but it seems equally valid for comedy. The Halicarnassians praise the poet because 'he honored and adorned us, and gave demonstrations of poems of every kind, by which he both delighted the older and improved the younger'; to express their gratitude for this delight (ἡσθείς), the city decided to exhibit his books in the library and put his bronze statue in the ephebic gymnasium, 'next to the old Herodotus': the renown of the contemporary poet reaches the glory of the great writer of the past.[16] Poetry's function is to please and to teach, and Longinus'\ poems did this in an outstanding way. Horace's *aut prodesse aut delectare*, taken over from Hellenistic poetics, has become common knowledge among the educated elite of the second century and resonates almost verbatim in the verbs εὔφρανεν καὶ ... ὠφέλησεν, (the founder) 'provided delight and ... help' to his community.[17]

But how do we understand the majority of the inscriptions that only list comic and tragic actors but not poets, like in the text of Demosthenes of Oenoanda? The Lysimachus list that has, among others, 'generally comic/tragic actors' (κοινῇ κωμῳδῶν, κοινῇ τραγῳδῶν) might hint at an answer. The program could contain both classical and modern plays, but the contemporary plays were not written for their first performance at this contest, but for an earlier event and simply put on stage again; this is why no poet gets a prize. An honorary decree for an elite woman in Aphrodisias, Tatas daughter of Diodorus, from the late second century praises her because when she was *stephanophoros* (mayor of her city), she sacrificed for the emperors and 'she herself got the best performances in Asia in the theatrical and scenic contests and showed them to her city' (ἔν τε τοῖς θυμελικοῖς καὶ σκηνικοῖς ἀγῶσιν τὰ πρωτεύοντα ἐν τῇ Ἀσίᾳ ἀκροάματα αὐτὴν πρώτως ἀγαγοῦσαν καὶ δείξασαν τῇ πατρίδι).[18] If we take this statement seriously it means that she attracted actors and musicians of high renown who had already made an impact elsewhere and who brought their repertoire with them; nothing prevents the assumption that it included not just performers but also contemporary plays that had been a hit elsewhere.

III.

This brings us to the performers, the actors, and musicians. The victor lists show that many of them came from elsewhere, cities in the region as well as places far away: they were travelling professionals. We saw that in Hellenistic Magnesia, most artists were locals or came from the region, but one, a poet, from far-away Tarsus. Three lists from Thespiae, drawn up not long after 150 CE, give a comparable picture: of thirty-eight performers whose origins are known, ten came from Thespiae or other Boeotian cities (Tanagra and Thebes), sixteen from other cities on the Greek mainland, with Corinth and Athens leading by far; two came from the islands Chios and Cos; the other twelve from Asia Minor, with a spread from the West Coast (Ephesus, Pergamum, Miletus) to the South (Aspendus) and North (Nicomedia). Again, we see that these contests stimulated the local art production, but also attracted a large number of travelling specialists; some had to travel considerably.[19]

These specialists were organized in the Guild of Dionysiac Artists, an organization that is in various forms attested from its foundation in the early third century BCE until the late third century CE.[20] Its history in the imperial epoch still remains to be written, and the relationship of local or regional associations to the overarching 'global' association remains unclear. Several papyri from Oxyrrhynchus present a collection of documents that demonstrates the continuity of the institution between Augustus and Aurelian and allows some tantalizing glimpses into the history of the world organization.[21] The earliest document, a letter written by Claudius in 47 CE, shows that Augustus conferred unspecified privileges on the association. Claudius addresses them as 'the victorious artists in sacred and classical [lit. 'crowned'[22]] contests around Dionysus from the entire world, and their fellow-contestants' and thus shows that the association was empire-wide,[23] and he allows them to put up images of himself. Both – the globalization and the connection with the ruler worship – might go back to Augustus: in Hellenistic times there were four regional associations, and the tight control of imperial cult was important for the first emperor.[24]

The papyrus file contains next an excerpt from a letter by Hadrian that lists all the privileges the members of the Association could count upon, from the freedom from taxes and liturgies in their own cities to inviolability, a crucial privilege for people who travelled professionally.[25] Other documents show even better how vital Hadrian was to the development and influence of the association. An inscription from Alexandria in the Troad, published in 2006, highlights the extent of this protection. It is a file with three letters from the Emperor Hadrian that react to a meeting with exponents of the Association in Naples, presumably in the summer of 133 CE, and concern mainly financial and organizational matters, among which two stand out.[26] The first letter contains mainly the emperor's reaction to the complaint that many cities under financial pressure cancelled a contest at the last minute to use the funds for more urgent matters, with serious consequences for travelling artists who lost time and income: the emperor prohibited the cancellation of contests and the use of dedicated funds for other purposes, and told some cities to pay the lost monies to the association. The second letter proposes a binding calendar of festivals and their dates, to make the travels of the artists easier, and rules that the prize money should be exhibited in the theater and handed over to the victors 'immediately under the eyes of the spectators': obviously, some organizers made the victors fight for their money, or did not pay it at all. The third letter confirms that artists should receive public meals – but only where this had already been granted: 'I am not used to imposing additional costs upon the cities'.

The letters show how deeply an emperor like Hadrian could engage with the Association, and how he could by his measures shape the performances in single cities. Comic actors and, in his time, also comic poets were members of the Association, and profited from it. In fact, the honors that the association under Trajan conferred upon the tragic poet C. Iulius Longianus were proposed by the comic actor Tryphon, son of Eubiotos, of Laodicea, and seconded by the comic actor Eutyches, son of Eutyches, of Hierapolis. A year later, two other comic actors proposed and seconded the honors for a local *agonothetes* in Ancyra (Anakara): one wonders whether comic actors had better person-skills than the haughty citharoedes or gloomy tragic actors that could help them to gain political influence.[27]

Under Hadrian, the Association could have the lengthy title of 'sacred association of the artists, victors in sacred and classical contests that follow Dionysus and our Lord the emperor Nerva Traianus Caesar Augustus Germanicus Dacicus, new Dionysus, and their fellow-contestants'[28]: the emperor was not only the main protector and sponsor of the Association and the contests in which the members performed, but also together with Dionysus the object of their worship. As the *Historia Augusta* tells us, the emperor himself was a great fan of dramatic poetry who staged various dramas in Rome and had dramatic poetry read during his banquets; the biographer does not specify whether he preferred Greek over Latin drama.[29] Later emperors followed suit as patrons of the Association, as later titles show, down to the 'Diocletianic Association' attested in one Oxyrhynchus document: Roman emperors felt always responsible for the happiness of the people in the empire, and the Association saw this as their main aim.[30] Accordingly, many old and new contests were extended to the emperor and the title Caesarea or Sebasteia was added to some of them, such as the Caesarea Sebasteia Mousea[31] or even the Traianeia Hadrianeia Sebasteia Mousea[32] in Thespiae.

Local patrons who founded new contests added ruler worship to their programs. C. Iulius Demosthenes in Oenoanda began his Demostheneia with a sacrifice to the emperor, as we saw. Another patron whose foundation we know in all details – in this case a series of dazzling processions without a contest (C. Vibius Salutaris in Ephesus) – had the gilded images of Trajan and the Empress Plotina carried in the procession from the Artemisium to the theater, together with statues of Artemis and personifications of Ephesian and Roman institutions.[33] They did this not just to sway the emperor who had to confirm any new contest, but they tried to connect their own city with the political center in Rome: as Roman citizens and members of the provincial elite, they were at home in both worlds, and had a vital interest in tying them together. The file of Salutaris' foundation in Ephesus that did not need an imperial permission for his foundation, nevertheless contains a letter from the proconsul who commends 'my dearest friend' to the Ephesian authorities for his initiative.[34] This, despite the fact that Ephesus, the provincial capital, had other events that made it highly visible, especially its Artemisia, that were well-known for their musical contest and that in about 163 CE was reformed and extended into a month-long event;[35] a small city like Oenoanda, that lacked other attractions, was literally put on the map by the musical and dramatic contests of the Demosthenia and the itinerant artists that visited it.

IV.

If they did not have important functions in their Association, comic actors remain almost invisible to us. One victor list of the Mousea of Thespiae of about 160 CE gives a brief glimpse of one Antiphon of Athens who won a victory not just as actor in a contemporary comedy, but also as its author and as performer of the *prosodion*, the song that opened the festival – a multi-talented artist with a fittingly classical name.[36] Another contemporary list shows one L. Marius Antiochus of Corinth who not only won as actor of a contemporary tragedy but also wrote the winning contemporary comedy and the winning satyr play: he was obviously a talented stage practitioner.[37] In the same contest, the winning comic actor, Claudius Apollonius of Miletus, also won the 'Over All', outshining all other winners in the various disciplines. A century later, under Maximinus Thrax, the Ephesians honored a comic actor who won in the Artemisia.[38] In late-second-century Side, one M. Aurelius Philoxenus was honored as herald and 'outstanding comic actor and winner in sacred contests' (ἱερονείκην παράδοξον), with victories in Side, Hermupolis in Egypt, and Antioch and Damascus in Syria that document the steep travel agenda of a leading performer.[39] It makes some sense, in terms of talent and income, that a comic actor also would use his voice at the contest of heralds. Another performer was even more versatile: in contemporary Didyma near Miletus, the Didymaean organizers dedicated the statue of one Bassus who won as comic actor at the Artemisia in Ephesus, as tragic actor at the Didymea and the Nea Caesarea in Didyma, and as citharode at the Greater Didymeia in Miletus.[40] Compared to other artists of the time, the number of multi-talented artists among comic actors is surprisingly high.

But not only adults performed in comedies on the imperial stage. A long text from third century Ephesus praises a παῖς κωμῳδός, a boy actor, Titus Flavius Sarpedon of Acmonia and Ephesus, victor in the Artemisia, 'for his excellence, moderate life style and his skilled delivery' (ἀρετῆς ἕνεκα καὶ σώφρονος ἀσκήσεως καὶ τῆς περὶ τὴν ὑπόκρισιν ἐμπειρίασας): despite his professional excellence, the moral taint that attached itself to actors at the time did not touch him, and his excellence must have moved the Ephesians to convey citizenship on him.[41] This is not a boy playing children's roles – of which I could not name one in existing comedy that would not be mute – but an actor in the specific discipline of 'Comedy for Boys', παῖδες κωμῳδοί: the discipline is attested in a Hadrianic victor list from Corinth, together with the 'Boys Singing to the Cithara', παῖδες κιθαρῳδοί.[42] From contemporary Corinth, we have a statue base in memory of L. Vibius Florus, a highly-accomplished boy comedian from Patrae and Corinth: he won the Heraea and the final prize (the διὰ πάντων) in Argos, twice the Caesarea and the final prize in Corinth and once in Sicyon, and the Asclepiea and the final price in Epidaurus. Born in Patrae and honored with the citizenship of Corinth, where he died at a young age, he competed regionally, but with high success, and the council of Corinth permitted his father to put up the image in the theater.[43] We cannot know whether these παῖδες κωμῳδοί played in their own plays or in the classical or contemporary comedies written for adults, or whether they were performing virtuoso extracts. The praise of the ὑπόκρισις of Titus Flavius Sarpedon suggests emphasis on the oral delivery more than on what we mean by acting: given the importance of song in Plautine comedy, comparable to the modern operetta or musical, and assuming that this describes also later comedy and is also suggested by the case of Bassus who was successful as a comic and tragic actor and as singer to the cithara, we can assume that the singing of these boys was as highly valued as their play-acting. That one of them won in all the final contests against the victors in all other disciplines, the other got a public honorary decree that must have come with an image, and that they both received honorary citizenships shows that their audiences adored them, as if they were gifted performers, perhaps as gifted as in another century and culture young Wolfgang Amadeus or Shirley Temple were.

V.

Inscriptions are the result of two things, the epigraphical habit and the chance of finding them; the more widespread the habit is – as it was in the second and third centuries of the imperial epoch – the more texts we have. But even so it is striking that we have few texts from the first century BCE and none from the first century CE: thus, we gain a blurry image only for the second and third century. Comedy lived and thrived – both the old texts and the new texts written by acclaimed or less famous local poets – exclusively in the milieu of the contests with which Greek cities and their elite sponsors tried to gain regional and international fame. The contests and the performers were unified and protected by their trade union, the Guild of Dionysiac Artists; culturally engaged emperors – especially but not exclusively the Hellenophile Hadrian – protected the Guild and encouraged the international contest circuit. Comedy, like tragedy and all the other 'musical' disciplines of the ἀγὼν μουσικός, thus were thriving in the shadow of the emperors and the imperial cult that was often connected with the great international games, and innovations such as the Boys' Comedy were due to the dynamics and interests of show business. But even so, the contemporaries saw more than just entertainment behind these performances: they understood them also as the modern tools and circuits that connected these later centuries with the great past of fifth and fourth century Greece.

Epigraphical publications

I. Aphrodisias Joyce Reynolds, Charlotte Roueché, Gabriel Bodard, eds., *Inscriptions of Aphrodisias 2007*, http://insaph.kcl.ac.uk/iaph2007

BE *Bulletin épigraphique*

CIG	Corpus Inscriptionum Graecarum
Corinth	Corinth. Results of Excavations Conducted by the American School of Classical Studies at Athens
I. Didyma	Richard Harder, ed., *Didyma. Teil 2: Die Inschriften* (Berlin: Mann, 1958)
I. Ephesos	Hermann Wankel et al., *Die Inschriften von Ephesos. Inschriften griechischer Städte aus Kleinasien* (Bonn: Habelt, 1979–84)
I. Magnesia	Otto Kern, *Die Inschriften von Magnesia am Mäander* (Berlin: Mann, 1900)
I. Thespies	Paul Roesch, *Les inscriptions de Thespies*. IV: *Concours: Les Mouseia. Les Erotideia. Concours indéterminé. Dédicaces de vainqueurs*. Édition électronique (Lyon: Maison de l'Orient et de la Méditerranée Jean Pouilloux 2007–09); http://www.hisoma.mom.fr/thespies.html
I.Chios	Fritz Graf, *Nordionische Kulte* (Rome: Swiss Institute, 1984), 427–61
IG	Inscriptiones Graecae
MAMA	Monumenta Asiae Minoris Antiqua
Milet	Ergebnisse der Grabungen und Untersuchungen seit dem Jahre 1899
SIG3	*Sylloge Inscriptionum Graecarum*, ed. W. Dittenberger, 3rd edition (Leipzig: 1015–1924)

Notes

1 On this inscription, found in 1976, see Wörrle 1988 whose commentary is still fundamental for the festival culture of the Roman Empire. For an overview see Jones 1993 and on the Christianization of late antique theatrical culture, with some glances backwards, Barnes 1996.
2 *IG* 7.1773, second or early third century CE.
3 On this finale of artistic contests see Strasser 2006.
4 See also the very detailed evidence from Hellenistic Iasus, Crowther 2007.
5 In Aphrodisias, satyr play preceded by *pyrrhichē CIG* 2758; Roueché 1993: 168 no. 52; *I.Aphrodisias* 11. 305 no. IV ii 5 and no. V ii 5; *pyrrhichē* after comedy, without satyr play *MAMA* 8. 420 (Pickard-Cambridge 1968: 321, no. 16b; Roueché 1993:173 no. 53; *I. Aphrodisias* 11.21) iii 9; satyr play also in Thespiae, *IG* 7.1773.29, and in late Hellenistic Magnesia on the Maeander, *I.Magnesia* 88a iii 3 (167–100 BCE). 88d ii 3 and 88e.3 (first century BCE).
6 Compare the importance of dancing satyrs in Lucian's *On Dancing* who also includes the armed dances (*Salt.* 10 and 11) and comedy and tragedy (26).
7 See Nervegna 2007.
8 See the victory list of a travelling actor from Tegea, inscribed in his home town, perhaps in the late third century CE, *SIG*³ 1080 (see Pickard-Cambridge 1968: 286): of his seven victories, five were in plays of Euripides.

9 *IG* 7.1773, *I.Thespies* 177. The two contests recorded in these lists are not far apart, because the same performers carried the first prize in the disciplines 'trumpet' and 'herald'; the writing style puts them not long after the middle of the century.
10 On the reception of Menander and New Comedy see Nervegna 2013.
11 *IG* 7. 1773. 23 (date as in note 9).
12 On the evolution of satyr plays see Shaw 2014: 123–48, with a victorious Σατύρων ὑποκριτής in Hellenistic (?) Teus p. 144, not necessarily a 'new' satyr play, as Shaw claims (all his other instances concern poets, not actors) [I owe this reference to Tom Hawkins]. On the Pronomos vase see Taplin and Wyles 2010, with an important overview of satyric dancing by Bernd Seidensticker.
13 *I.Magnesia* 88a (167–100 BCE). Similar lists 88d, 88e and 88g (σατύρων ποιητής, 'writer of satyr plays'; all first century BCE). Rhomaia in Chios *I.Chios* 78.
14 The topic of the 'Persians' by one Anaxion who won the first prize 'of satyrs' in Hellenistic Teus (Shaw 2014: 144) must remain opaque; this and 'The Sacrificer' are the only titles in the long list of Shaw 2014: 144–5.
15 Comic poet from Ephesus *I.Magnesia* 88d i 4; comic actor from Miletus 88a ii 5, from Tralles 88d i 7; writer of satyr play from Ephesus 88d ii 4, from Tarsus 88e 3.
16 *MAMA* 8, no. 418c; Roueché 1993: 223 no. 88; *I. Aphrodisias* 12.17, col. ii. On the status of poets in imperial Achaia, see Bowie 1989 (202 on Longinus); on the pride Halicarnassus felt about their Herodotus see also the Hellenistic inscription nicknamed 'The Pride of Halicarnassus', Isager and Pedersen 2004: 217–37; Gagné 2006.
17 Hor. *Ars*. 333; see Brink 1971 *ad loc*.
18 *CIG* 2820 ii; *MAMA* 8. 492; *I. Aphrodisias* 12.29.
19 *IG* 7.1773, 1776; *I.Thespies* 177.
20 On the history of the association still see Pickard-Cambridge 1968: 279–305, with an appendix of mostly epigraphical texts 306–32; documents in Stephanis 1988; a short summary in Roueché 1993: 50–2; for more recent data see Strasser 2010: 519, and for the Hellenistic period Ma 2007.
21 *P.Oxy*. 2476 and 2610; *BGU* 4.1073 and 1074; see Frisch 1986: nos. 1, 2, 3, 5.
22 An ἀγὼν στεφανίτης is a contest where the prize was a crown, after the model of the four main contests of the archaic age, Olympia, Pythia, Isthmia and Nemea; the crown remained the main prize in these contests and those that followed their model, even if later money prizes were added.
23 *P.Oxy*. 2476.2: τοῖς ἀπὸ τῆς οἰκουμένης περὶ τὸν Διόνυσον τεχνείταις, ἱερονείκαις στεφανίταις καὶ τοῖς τούτων συναγωνισταῖς, abbreviated in *BGU* 4.1073.1 and 1074.1; the rare term συναγωνισταί shows how much the victors mattered, compared to the other contestants who become mere *staffage*. A letter from Claudius in 48 CE, preserved in an inscription in Miletus (*Milet* 1:3.156) gives as address the much shorter τοῖς περὶ τὸν Διόνυσον ἱερονείκαις καὶ τεχνείταις. It remains unclear how these varying titles relate to each other. The Hadrianic file from Alexandreia Troas (Petzl and Schwertheim 2006) shows a similar fluctuation between συνόδῳ

θυμελικῇ περιπολιστικῇ τῶν περὶ τὸν Διόνυσον τεχνειτῶν ἱερονεικῶν στεφανειτῶν (letters 1 and 2, lines 5 and 58) and συνόδῳ θυμελικῇ τῶν περὶ τὸν Διόνυσον τεχνειτῶν (letter 3, line 86); other Hadrianic inscriptions have an even longer name. The shorter forms might simply be abbreviations either by the chancellery or the local secretary preparing the papyrus or epigraphical file.

24 On the problematic date of globalization see Pickard-Cambridge 1968: 297.
25 κεφάλαιον ἐκ διατάγματος θεοῦ Ἁδριανοῦ περὶ τῶν δοθεισῶν δωρεῶν τῇ συνόδῳ P.Oxy. 2476.4, BGU 4.173.3, 1074.3.
26 Petzl and Schwertheim 2006; see also Strasser 2010 and, for the date, Schmidt 2009.
27 Bosch 1967: 155 no. 128 (128/129 CE).
28 For example, Aphrodisias, *MAMA* 8, no. 418c
29 *Historia Augusta* 19.6 (in Rome) 'in the theatre he presented plays of all kinds in the ancient manner'; 26.4 'at his banquets he always furnished, according to the occasion, tragedies, comedies, Atellan farces'; the *Attellanae* are Latin, the other plays might be Latin or Greek. (Translation David Magie, Loeb edition.)
30 P.Oxy. 2476.13. On the emperor and *laetitia publica*, 'general happiness' see Belayche (2007): 144 and Graf (forthcoming).
31 *IG* 7.1774–6
32 *I.Thespies* no. 177.
33 *I.Ephesos* 27 (the file of the foundation); Rogers 1991.
34 *I.Ephesos* 27. 371–413.
35 *SIG*³ 867 = *I.Ephesos* 24 (a file that contained documents on this reform: A: a letter from the proconsul who confirmed the reform and commended the reformer, T. Aelius Marcianus Priscus; B: the reform decree of the city assembly; C: an honorary decree by the city for Marcianus Priscus).
36 *IG* 7.1773.
37 *I.Thespies* 177.
38 *I.Ephesos* 1147.
39 *Side Kitabeleri* 149.
40 *I. Didyma* 183.
41 *I. Ephesos* 1606.
42 Bears and Geagan 1970: 79 A 42.
43 *Corinth* VIII:3 no. 272, with the note *BE* 1971. 307; dated to the third century CE.

7

Plutarch, Epitomes, and Athenian Comedy

C.W. Marshall

The Comparison of Aristophanes and Menander (853a–854d) is a short work in Plutarch's *Moralia* that serves as a crucial touchstone in the reception of Athenian comedy among the educated Roman elite. In this chapter, I wish to suggest that a number of features of the *Comparison* are more unusual than is often recognized. This is not a detailed study of the work itself,[1] nor a survey of all of Plutarch's references to Old and New Comedy,[2] but an inquiry into how the modern understanding of the text in its current state reinforces certain prejudices of reading that have left us blind to the assumptions embedded within that reading practice, which in turn shapes our understanding of Athenian Comedy in the Roman Empire. By identifying those unspoken assumptions, and by situating the *Comparison* in the context of the knowledge of Old Comedy in the first and second centuries CE, I hope to suggest a wider scope for the original work than is often presumed, and point to a methodological problem that underlies any study of Athenian comedy in the Roman Empire.

The text that survives is doubly shortened, as a fragmentary epitome. While the authenticity of the work (perhaps surprisingly) is not in question, the shape of the surviving text does not originate with Plutarch. The work of the epitomator is explicit, since he distances himself from Plutarch four times with third-person singular verbs ('he says', and the like).[3] The fragmentary nature of the epitome is also self-evident: the text begins and ends with a lacuna, with a third lacuna near the beginning of §4, the final section that survives.[4] We therefore possess two passages from a longer work, the first of which is introduced by a series of distancing mechanisms. There is no means by which to tell how much is missing from any of the three gaps, but there is no particular reason to think that any of the gaps is small.

The first, longer part falls into three sections:

§1. The language of Aristophanes, including direct quotation of eight passages, five of which come from extant plays (*Acharnians, Knights*, and *Thesmophoriazusae*), but with no mention of Menander.

§2. The language of Menander, with no direct citation but with elaborate similes attesting to his virtuosity; but no reference to Aristophanes.

§3. A comparison of the two poets and their appeal, whether it is for the few or the many, with Aristophanes' poetry compared to a *hetaira*, but Menander's being all things to all men in all circumstances, apparently.

This is followed by §4, which begins with a sentence on actors of comedy, whereupon the text breaks off. When the text resumes, the second, shorter passage presents the respective qualities of the wit of each poet, where elaborate images are offered without recourse to citation (854c):

αἱ Μενάνδρου κωμῳδίαι ἀφθόνων ἁλῶν καὶ ἱερῶν μετέχουσιν, ὥσπερ ἐξ ἐκείνης γεγονότων τῆς θαλάττης, ἐξ ὧν Ἀφροδίτη γέγονεν.

Menander's comedies contain an abundance of salty wit and merriment, which seems like the salt derived from that sea out of which Aphroditē was born.[5]

This, the beginning of the second surviving passage from the fuller work, is 'as far as any ancient author goes in discussing humor in Menander'.[6] The fact that humour ('salt') emerges from romantic situations underlies the subsequent comparison with the birthplace of Aphrodite.

Taken together, the *Comparison* exhibits an inelegance that may point to greater corruption. While the practice of *synkrisis* between two individuals is characteristic of Plutarch, what is here does not reflect his usual literary habits. When Plutarch is comparing his *Lives*, both figures are regularly juxtaposed with each other. Here, §1–2 offer functionally independent summaries of the two playwrights. The prejudicial assessment in §3 is a *bon mot* that lacks the focused point Plutarch often exhibits, and again is not representative of Plutarch's syncretic activity. The transition to actors (whatever that discussion may have entailed before abridgement) is sudden and unmotivated. The praise of Menander in §4 is again independent of comparison with Aristophanes. As it stands, the work lacks identifying stylistic features evident in other Plutarchan comparisons.

We are not in a position to determine when the epitome was made, nor do we know when it became fragmentary, and whether it was a deliberate or an accidental abridgement. The presence of the title in the Lamprias Catalogue (no. 121) suggests but does not prove that the epitome had been made by the fourth century CE, when the catalogue was likely compiled. Whatever the case, the emphasis found in the extant text is not necessarily that of Plutarch. This invites the question, why should Plutarch compare Menander to Aristophanes in the first place? The question is easily answered for modern readers who possess Aristophanes as the sole extant representative of Old Comedy: for us today (and since late antiquity) each playwright is the primary representative of his period.

This comparison, however, would have been decidedly less natural in the second century, when plays of other Old Comic poets were in active circulation, including Eupolis and Cratinus (the works of whom share the linguistic and literary features that Plutarch censures).[7] As Ewan Bowie writes, 'educated Greeks … were aware what Old Comedy was, knew that Aristophanes, along with Cratinus and Eupolis, was one of its major exponents, and had read enough, whether in complete texts or in anthologies, to quote, to refer to, and to recognize the titles of plays and lines from all of them'.[8] Elsewhere, Plutarch cites all these poets, and if there are more passages of Aristophanes, part of the explanation must surely reside in our ability to detect indirect references to plays, which is more easily done when the plays to which comparison is made are extant. The triad of three poets of Old Comedy (a grouping built on analogy with the canon of three fifth-century tragic poets) is found in Horace, Persius, Quintilian, Dionysus of Halicarnassus, as well as in scholia and later sources such as Platonius and Diomedes the Grammarian. Within this canon it is not even clear that Aristophanes was primary – 'Everyone knows Eupolis', says Macrobius (*Sat.* 7.5.8 *notus est omnibus Eupolis*).

This is not to deny that Aristophanes could be presented as a representative comic playwright in the second century CE. He is typically cited more than his contemporaries, and the presentation of Socrates in *Clouds*, supported by the direct response to that presentation by Plato in *Symposium* and *Apology*, means that he could be presented as pre-eminent if the author so wished.[9] Indeed, if the passages cited in the *Comparison* were framed in these terms, it would be easier to read the short work as if it had been structured by Plutarch.[10]

Plutarch does know Aristophanes' work well. Elsewhere, he makes reference to all but one of the eleven extant plays (all except *Ecclesiazousae*), and he had access to more than that (several fragmentary plays are also cited). Plutarch is also able to cite Eupolis' *Demes* and Cratinus' *Dionysalexandros* and *Wine-Flask* and *Chirons*, as well as plays by Plato Comicus. The prominence of Aristophanes in the *Comparison*, without reference to Eupolis or Cratinus, is therefore exceptional. Though numerically there are more citations of Aristophanes than of these other poets, the degree to which that is true is reduced significantly once control factors are taken into account.¹¹ For example, eleven Aristophanic passages are cited in the *Comparison*. If we count the number of passages in the *Life of Pericles* (conscious that Eupolis' and Aristophanes' dramatic careers both essentially begin after his death), we discover four references from Aristophanes, one from Eupolis, and five from Cratinus – a reasonable distribution to suggest roughly equal familiarity given the small sample size.¹² In the *Life of Alcibiades*, there are two references from Aristophanes, one from Eupolis. That is to say, in biographical contexts Plutarch's use of all three comic poets remains comparable, even if in straight numbers Aristophanes is cited most often.¹³ While Plutarch does make more references to the plays of Aristophanes, it is not the case that he does not know Eupolis or Cratinus, and there is no particular reason that the *Comparison* should emblematize Aristophanes as the pre-eminent representative of the genre.

The unusual emphasis of the treatise is seen more clearly when Plutarch (c. 45–120 CE) is compared with the medical writer Galen (129–c. 200 or 216), writing up to a century later. We know of five lost works by Galen on Old Comedy (*On My Own Books* 19.48 K): *Ordinary Terms in Eupolis*, *Ordinary Terms in Cratinus*, *Ordinary Terms in Aristophanes*, *Examples of Words Specific to Comic Writers*, and *Whether Old Comedy is Useful Reading for Students*. Galen also praises Old Comedy's value for an Atticizing second-century author in *Avoiding Depression* 20–30, a work re-discovered only in 2005.¹⁴ Galen treats all the poets of the triad of Old Comedy, as indeed does Plutarch in his general habits of citation. Of course, there are different ways of appreciating Old Comedy, and Galen in seeking to describe Atticizing vocabulary is right to cast his net widely, even if he does limit himself to comic poets. But his wider pedagogical aim draws on all three as well.¹⁵ The *Comparison* appears therefore to be exceptional in its specific focus on Aristophanes.

In contrast, the prominence of Menander as a representative of New Comedy is not controversial at all: 'Ancient viewers everywhere thus saw Menander and his dramas in their daily surroundings. The iconographic tradition of Menander's comedy was longstanding, persistent, and trendsetting.'¹⁶ New Comedy was everywhere, as Plutarch attests in the *Comparison* (854a–b):

ὁ δὲ Μένανδρος μετὰ χαρίτων μάλιστα ἑαυτὸν αὐτάρκη παρέσχηκεν, ἐν θεάτροις ἐν διατριβαῖς ἐν συμποσίοις, ἀνάγνωσμα καὶ μάθημα καὶ ἀγώνισμα κοινότατον ὧν ἡ Ἑλλὰς ἐνήνοχε καλῶν παρέχων τὴν ποίησιν.

[Menander] has made his poetry, of all the beautiful works Greece has produced, the most generally accepted subject in theatres, in discussions, and at banquets, for readings, for instruction, and for dramatic competitions.¹⁷

Note the small ring-compositional form here, attesting in fact only to three contexts: dramatic competitions/in the theatres; instruction/in discussions; and readings/at banquets.[18] To these we can add a fourth context for encountering Menander in the second century, private reading. These vectors for exposure to Menander were not all shared by the Old Comic playwrights. Plutarch writes (854b):

τίνος γὰρ ἄξιον ἀληθῶς εἰς θέατρον ἐλθεῖν ἄνδρα πεπαιδευμένον ἢ Μενάνδρου ἕνεκα; πότε δὲ θέατρα πίμπλαται ἀνδρῶν φιλολόγων, κωμικοῦ προσώπου δειχθέντος;

For what reason, in fact, is it truly worth while for an educated man to go to the theatre, except to see Menander? And when else are theatres filled with men of learning, if a comic character has been brought upon the stage?[19]

In doing so, he is attesting to revivals of Menander, which inscriptions show took place in both the Greek East and Roman West until the mid-second century.[20]

We might even go further, and suggest that Aristophanes is not the best representative of the genre for Plutarch's purposes. The discussion in §1 about bad puns and variable linguistic tone and vocal register does recognize the poet's wit, by which measure Eupolis and Cratinus could have been used as less able examples, by these criteria; Hunter seems to recognize this when he alludes to 'the allegedly cruder style of the other poets of Old Comedy'.[21] When Plutarch maps his stylistic concerns about Aristophanes onto his own morality (as he surely does when he compares Aristophanes' plays to a *hetaira*), we can see that these concerns would fit more naturally onto the *hetairai* presented in Old Comedy, such as Cratinus' Wine-Flask herself and Mousike in Pherecrates' *Chiron*.[22] In the consideration of what sort of entertainment is most suitable with dinner (*Table-Talk* 7.8.3, *Mor.* 711f–712d), Old Comedy is seen as less desirable than New Comedy and Menander, and examples of comic targets come from Eupolis, Plato, and Cratinus. Aristophanes is only introduced as a counter-argument in the following paragraph (7.8.4, 712d), though no specifics are mentioned.[23]

By now I trust my contention is at least seen as plausible: that in this doubly shortened text, we may reasonably infer that when comparing Menander to the comic poets of the past, it would be more natural to refer to all the poets in the comic triad, and possibly others as well (Plato Comicus, Pherecrates), rather than simply to Aristophanes. It is not absurd to think that in its original form, the treatise may have been *On the Preeminence of Menander* (or something similar) rather than a direct *Comparison* with Aristophanes. A direct comparison between two playwrights is certainly not unthinkable. Aulus Gellius (*NA* 2.23) compares two passages from comedy (Menander's *Plokion* or *The Necklace* and its adaptation into Latin by Caecilius),[24] and the reader is invited to consider the two side-by-side. Instead, Plutarch's *Comparison* does not present the playwrights together until §3.

Another factor predisposes modern critics towards seeing the *Comparison* as legitimate: the modern reader knows that Plutarch did often compare two similar individuals in his biographical writing. This apparent parallel is misleading, however. No other biographical comparison existed independent of full lives (and no one proposes that there are lost Plutarchan biographies of the comic poets); other comparisons are juxtaposing individuals from separate cultures; finally, other comparisons attempt to draw together specific features, rather than the more patchwork back-and-forth that is evident here.[25] The use of *synkrisis* elsewhere in the Plutarchan corpus in fact cuts both ways: while it may be a feature of Plutarch's own literary design, it could equally be the result of a later hand shaping the essay into something that more closely matches other short works in the Plutarchan corpus.

There may be reasons why Plutarch would have singled out Aristophanes, but none proves determinative. Plutarch's Laconophile sympathies make Aristophanes a particularly likely target: that because of his interest in Sparta, he has spent particular time with comic texts that emphasize Sparta, and as a result it was to Aristophanes that the author turned when he imagined Old Comedy. If this were so, however, we would expect the evidence to favor plays such as *Lysistrata* (which has only two references) and not *Knights* (with its thirteen references outside of the *Comparison*). As Hunter describes, the language of Aristophanes reveals to Plutarch social aspects of literary criticism, raising concerns about playing to the mob,[26] which is one of the things the Old Oligarch disliked about Old Comedy as well (2.18). These sympathies, however, remain vague and under-supported, and are not connected in the surviving text with Sparta in any way. Another factor to consider might be Plutarch's Platonism. While this is not explicit in what survives of the *Comparison*, Plutarch is constrained in his opinions. It is possible he feels obliged to espouse Plato's suspicion of theatrical activity, but he must do so in a world that saw Menander as a paragon of the high culture and theatrical activity, despite its apparent hyperrealism ('O Menander, O Life ...', begins Aristophanes of Byzantium, on Syranius' *Hermogenes* 2.23). Plutarch is caught, because while Plato had the opportunity to be suspicious of Old Comedy, by the cruel linearity of time he could not equally suspect Menander and New Comedy. Plutarch can choose on a certain level to espouse Menander without compromising his commitment to Plato. In this context, we might note the prominence of *Clouds* with its presentation of Socrates in Plutarch's citations of Aristophanes, though there remain significantly more references to *Birds* and *Knights*. In the end, neither of these possibilities accounts for the shape of the text as we have it.

More probably, the focus on Aristophanes is not the emphasis given to the work originally, but emerged when Plutarch was being read later, after the other Old Comic poets fell out of circulation – when they were not in theatres, not in symposia, and not used for instruction. The Aristophanes-only emphasis would likely appear sensible to the epitomator, and then be reinforced when the epitomator's work was subsequently abridged. Even if this point cannot be proved conclusively, the example is important since it reminds us of the degree to which the way we frame discussions of the reception of comedy in antiquity is often shaped through the accidents of survival. Because *The Comparison of Aristophanes and Menander* seems so natural to modern readers, the true oddness of the comparison from the hand of Plutarch has gone unrecognized.

Notes

1   See the edition of Di Florio 2008, as well as Hunter 2000, Di Florio 2003, Bréchet 2005, Orfanos 2005, and Riu 2005. An early version of this chapter was presented at the *Plutarch Among the Barbarians* conference in Banff, Alberta, in March 2014. Thanks are due to Fran Titchener, Noreen Humble, Tom Hawkins, and Hallie Marshall.
2   For a survey of Aristophanes in Plutarch, see Di Floria 2004. For a survey of Menander in Plutarch, see Karavas and Vix 2014: 185–7 and Casanova 2005.
3   *Mor.* 853a ὑποκρίνει, 'he prefers'; προστίθησι, 'he adds'; 853b φησίν, 'he says', twice.
4   Lacuna at beginning: Bernardakis 1888–96 (Teubner). Lacuna at end: Fowler 1927: 461 ('even for a summary the end, as we have it, appears somewhat abrupt'). Lacuna in 854C, Wyttenbach 1797: 426 (*hoc loco Epitomator, nonnulla ad sententiam necessaria omisit*).
5   Tr. Fowler 1927: 471. I give Fowler's translation as a neutral witness for my purposes, but it seem more likely that the collocation of ἁλῶν καὶ ἱερῶν in fact is observing Menander's ability to juxtapose humor with seriousness.
6   Nervegna 2013c: 50. In contrast, 'For all of Aristophanes' claims to wit and refinement, in his comedies Plutarch can see only dirty and inappropriate jokes packed with malice and linguistic | chaos' (2013: 1–2).

7 The triad of Old Comic poets is found in Horace, Persius, Quintilian, Dion. Hal., and later Platonius, Diomedes the Grammarian (fourth century = T 82), and scholia (e.g. Aristophanes T 87 (K-A) = Schol. Thuc. 1.30.1; T 84 (= Schol. Dion. Thr.)). Tzetzes and anonymous (Koster III) know and perhaps have access to more than just three comic poets. There is no indication that Aristophanes was being isolated from his contemporaries in the second century.
8 Bowie 2007: 33. For Roman knowledge of Old Comedy, see Quadlbauer 1960.
9 Aristotle, *Poetics* 3, 1448a25–7, isolates Aristophanes as a representative playwright in his description of Sophocles, for example. Yet this passage demonstrates my larger methodological point, since in Aristotle's day it was Euripides' tragedies that were pre-eminent.
10 Aristophanes' prominence in Hellenistic scholarship can be overstated, but a gradual process whereby he emerged as first among the three can be discerned. In presenting this case, Nesselrath 2000 argues that Hellenistic scholarship saw a continuity between Aristophanes and Menander, a view that contrasts with the abrupt juxtaposition of the two found in Plutarch. The *Comparison* again stands in conflict with this scholarly tradition.
11 For this survey, I am simply using passages cited in Helmbold and O'Neil 1959, and have not sought to question or add to their attributions.
12 Xenophontos 2012: 616–18, and see Zanetto 2000.
13 Another factor to be controlled is the presence of references in spurious works, etc. In the *Life of Antiphon* (833b) for example there is reference to Cratinus' *Wine Flask*, but this is not a reference in Plutarch, who is not the author of the *Lives of the Ten Orators*. This work also holds two references from Aristophanes.
14 Boudon-Millot, Jouanna and Pietrobelli 2010 and Nutton 2013; and see Rosen 2010: 340–41 and von Staden 1998: 81–2.
15 Nutton 2009: 30 assumes that he possesses a personal copy of at least some of Plato Comicus. Galen can have a preference (31: 'When asked to recommend an ancient author to follow [for clear Attic style], Galen unhesitatingly plumps for Aristophanes'), while still recognizing the value of the wider range of poets.
16 Nervegna 2014: 718. Nevertheless, Plutarch's knowledge of Menander's contemporaries is apparently quite detailed: consider the use of Philippides in the life of Demetrius (Xenophontos 2012: 609–10).
17 Tr. Fowler 1927: 469.
18 See Nervegna 2013 and Hawkins and Marshall, chapter 1 in this volume.
19 Tr. Fowler 1927: 471.
20 Nervegna 2014: 724. These inscriptions confound our terminology, referring to 'new comedies' (those written by living playwrights – what Nervegna calls 'brand new comedies') and 'old comedies' by which the inscriptions mean the comedies of Menander; Aristophanes is not part of the performance tradition at this point.

21 Hunter 2009: 79.
22 Hunter 2009: 84.
23 Hunter 2014: 379–84.
24 Hunter 2009: 80–1.
25 For the use of comparison in Plutarch's *Lives*, see Pelling 1986 and 2005 and Boulogne 2000.
26 Hunter 2009: 85–7.

8

Lucian's Aristophanes: On Understanding Old Comedy in the Roman Imperial Period

Ralph M. Rosen*

Some time in the late second century CE, probably during the reign of Marcus Aurelius, Lucian wrote his satirical work *Against the Uneducated Book-collector*, in which he mocks an unnamed Syrian compatriot for his boorishness and pretension. This man had evidently amassed an enormous collection of books, but showed few signs of having read them properly or having understood them. The humor of the work derives from its portrait of extremes: a man with a huge library but without any genuine education, and so without any ability to appreciate what he is so proud to own. At one point in his diatribe, Lucian sarcastically asks the man about the authors he has been reading: '... have you plunged into, [ὑποδέδυκας] Aristophanes and Eupolis? Have you even read the *Baptai* [*Dippers*], the whole play? Did its content not have any effect on you, and did you not blush when you *understood* what it was about [γνωρίσας αὐτά]?' We have very little idea what Eupolis' fragmentary *Baptai* was about, except that it seems to have contained a comic attack on the Athenian general Alcibiades.[1] But Lucian's interaction with the boorish book-collector raises a larger question: how did people in the Roman imperial period read and understand the poets of Athenian Old Comedy, poets who had written and produced their plays more than five hundred years earlier for a specific festival occasion and a localized audience?

For Lucian, as this passage makes clear, it was one thing to read the plays (ἀναγιγνώσκω), but quite another to understand them (γνωρίζω). Not only was Old Comedy chronologically and culturally distant from the second century, but as a genre identified with aggressive political satire, freedom of speech and indecorous language, it was often out of step with contemporary notions of 'proper' comedy.[2] Less immediately accessible than Menander or other examples of Greek New Comedy,[3] Old Comedy took some effort by Lucian's time to extract actual meaning from its plays, and his question to the uneducated book-collector implies that reading the poets of Old Comedy was a specialized activity with the potential for significant personal impact on the reader. Why exactly Eupolis' play was supposed to have made the book-collector 'blush' is not clear – was it the indecent language, for example, or did it satirize someone as boorish as the book-collector? – but Lucian here implies that he, at least, understands what really goes on in an Old Comedy and that the genre offers a style that he endorses and finds meaningful.[4] Lucian also implies here that there is a correct way to read a play of Old Comedy which leads to a correct understanding of the play as it would have been intended by its author, or at least as Lucian would have imagined it was understood by an original audience in fifth-century Athens. This will likely seem a reasonable and uncontroversial starting point to most of us today interested in understanding an ancient literary text: even critics skeptical of recovering an author's intentions or unhappy with the very notion of a 'correct' reading of a text usually regard the historical and cultural background of a literary work as valuable for contemplating a work's meaning. But as we shall see in this chapter, Lucian's approach to Old Comedy – his interest in what such literature was actually *about* – was very unusual for his time, indeed virtually unique at least among the authors and texts available to us.

The questions I will address, then, concern not the extent to which plays of Old Comedy were being read or performed in the imperial period,[5] but *how* people were reading them, and more specifically, how sophisticated contemporary readers of Old Comedy were. By 'sophistication', I have in mind what Lucian seems to be driving at throughout his *Uneducated Book-collector*, namely that literary works become valued in a given era through a combination of learning (hence, the Book-collector's first sin is that he is *apaideutos*) and sensibility. 'Knowing about' what one is reading is as important as having a disposition receptive to understanding and interpreting it. To investigate the level of sophistication in imperial readers of Old Comedy, therefore, is another way of asking how self-conscious they were about large theoretical issues of genre, literary history, the appropriation of archaic texts and the nature of satire itself. What we will find is that despite the fact that certainly the most celebrated poets of Old Comedy (Aristophanes, Eupolis, and Cratinus), and many others as well,[6] were accessible and widely read, it is difficult for us to find readers in this period who showed an interest in understanding Old Comedy on its own terms, i.e., as a genre of satire in continual tension with a need to generate laughter and a pretense of seriousness and moral efficacy.[7] Certainly most critics of the time seemed insensitive to the literary subtleties we have come to associate with Old Comedy – irony, paradox or absurdity, for example – and remained content for the most part to conceptualize the genre as one of straightforward, uncomplicated mockery. The comic poet's targets were clear and his satirical goals, which were generally assumed to be malicious, self-evident. We see only rare glimpses in this period of any appreciation that the poets of Old Comedy had themselves any measure of literary sophistication; mostly these poets seem to have been appreciated as simple, often cautionary, examples of aggressive satire, or for their utility as models of classic Attic diction.[8]

We should not, perhaps, be too hard on the critics of the imperial period for missing so much of the richness and complexity of Old Comedy – the genre itself encouraged the idea that it was simple and accessible, and that its satire only targeted people whom any right-thinking person would agree deserved it. The paradoxical consequence is that this nuanced and complex genre entered the literary-critical tradition early on in a highly reductive, superficial way. As recent scholarship has shown,[9] Aristotle's narrative of the history of Greek comedy in the *Poetics* had an overpowering and ossifying influence on the way subsequent periods of antiquity thought about its development. Aristotle's well known discomfort with comic *aischrologia* and sustained verbal abuse allowed him to chart a teleology that began with a simplistic model of a primitivist mockery in Old Comedy moving towards the refined decorum and benign wit of fourth-century New Comedy. It is striking, as Csapo (2000) has shown in particular, how many avenues of understanding and interpretation were closed off for Old Comedy by Aristotle's authoritative taxonomies, and it is no wonder that the imperial period was left with only the most pedestrian, if not vacuous, conceptions of the genre.

The situation I have just described applies primarily to critics and commentators of the imperial period, who would have been educated in a conservative system shaped by a canon of influential classicized authors, Aristotle included. For them, by the second century CE, Old Comedy and its texts had become a remnant of a by-gone era, useful to resurrect for social or philosophical purposes,[10] but as Lucian shows, it was also possible to be a *practitioner* of Greek literary forms that were *doing* things that the poets of Old Comedy were doing.[11] Lucian was the great marvel of this period – an outlier, really – because his writing reveals an understanding of Old Comedy deeper and shrewder than the critics of his time seemed capable of, and an ability to exploit for his own literary purposes the various strategies that made Old Comedy so complex and dynamic. Lucian, as we will see, toyed with his audience's allegiances and affections as Aristophanes had, sometimes offering them laughter with a dose of truth, sometimes laughter at the expense of truth, but rarely truth at the expense of laughter.[12] Satire, after all, is really about the *problem* of laughter – who is supposed to be laughing at any given moment? At whom and at what, exactly? Lucian understood this perfectly, but for critics and philosophers of his time thinking about the satire of an Aristophanes, it was a problem primarily of content and morality. They were continually asking the question, 'what is the satirist trying to teach us?' usually ending with a further question, 'why did he have to be so malicious and aggressive?' or 'why did he have to use such bad language?' Indeed, Lucian seems to have crafted his own satire as a direct response to this mechanical and unnuanced understanding of Old Comedy.

Plutarch on Aristophanes

Plutarch offers several representative examples of this approach to Old Comedy. To put it simply, he was not a fan of the genre. Not only did he object to much of the language, but he was impatient with its topicality – the many references in a play of Old Comedy to historical people and events which had no meaning to an average reader more than half a millennium later. In *Sympotic Questions* 7.8.3 (711f–712a), which discusses the kind of entertainment most appropriate for a banquet, one of the interlocutors, Diogenianus, with whom Plutarch is clearly sympathetic,[13] objects to the recitation of Old Comedy for a variety of reasons, including tone, language and obscurity:

> As to comedy, the Old Comedy is, because of its unevenness of mood [διὰ τὴν ἀνωμαλίαν],[14] unsuitable for men who are drinking. For instance the so-called parabases are so serious and outspoken that they are too fiery and intense [παρρησία λίαν ἄκρατός ἐστι καὶ σύντονος]. Then too it has so little squeamishness in admitting jests and buffoonery that it is shockingly overloaded, nakedly indecent, and larded with words and phrases that are improper and obscene. What is more, just as a special waiter stands by each guest, at the banquets of the great, so everyone would need his own scholar to explain the allusions: who is Laespodias in Eupolis, and Cinesias in Plato, and Lampon in Cratinus, and so on with all the persons satirized in the plays. Our dinner party would turn into a schoolroom, or else the jokes would be without meaning or point [κωφὰ καὶ ἄσημα τὰ σκώμματα διαφέρεσθαι].

Diogenianus contrasts the unsuitability of Old Comedy with New Comedy:

> What objection, however, could anyone make to the New Comedy? It has become so completely a part of the symposium that we could chart our course more easily without wine than without Menander . . .

There follows a long eulogy of Menander (712b-d), who is praised, among other things, for his 'pleasant and simple style' (λέξις ἡδεῖα καὶ πεζή) and his 'blending of seriousness with the jocular' (ἥ τε τῆς σπουδῆς πρὸς τὴν παιδιὰν ἀνάκρασις). The passage culminates with the grand (and turgid) ethical claim that Menander's charm molds character and assimilates it to 'fair and humane things' (...πλάσιν τινὰ καὶ κατακόσμησιν ἐπιφέρει συνεξομοιοῦσαν τὰ ἤθη τοῖς ἐπιεικέσι καὶ φιλανθρώποις).

Diogenianus' concerns here are ostensibly limited to the question of entertainment only at symposia, and it is possible to imagine that he might feel differently about Old Comedy in a different setting. He objects, for example, that the parabases are too serious for a symposium and therefore inappropriate for an occasion that should be light and happy, but the rest of his objections seem to be general critiques of the genre which he would hold regardless of performance occasion. Most revealing is the critique of Old Comedy's topicality and his sarcastic comment that reciting such poetry at a banquet would turn the occasion into a 'schoolroom' (γραμματοδιδασκαλεῖον). These remarks show how distant and alien Old Comedy had become by this period, a world of texts that required study rather than poetry that could be meaningfully consumed by a contemporary audience. This was more the Old Comedy we find in such imperial authors as Didymus in his (lost) *Comic Expression* [Λέξις κωμική], Athenaeus in his *Deipnosophistae*, or Galen in his commentaries on the comic poets (above, n. 8), all of whom found the poets of Old Comedy 'useful' for a variety of purposes, especially historical lexicography, grammar, and diction, but showed virtually no interest in what we would call the comic poetics of fifth-century Athens. Menander, by contrast, also had his 'uses' in Diogenianus' eyes, but they are ethical rather than technical, and rely on the assumption that contemporary readers can take immediate aesthetic pleasure in a Menandrian play, unmediated by the necessity of any preliminary exegesis.

These polarities between Old and New Comedy are played out even more starkly in Plutarch's work *Comparison between Aristophanes and Menander*.[15] Although only an excerpt survives, his opinions about the two poets are unambiguous. As Nervegna has recently summed up: 'For Plutarch, Greek literature and Greeks in general could well do without Aristophanes. For all of Aristophanes' claims to wit and refinement, in his comedies Plutarch can see only dirty and inappropriate jokes packed with malice and linguistic chaos' (2013: 1). The treatise ends with a rhetorical flourish that further demonstrates Plutarch's complete lack of interest in attempting to understand Old Comedy on its own terms, or asking himself how it was that, according to his logic, every fifth-century Athenian who ever enjoyed an Aristophanic play must have been a disreputable person: 'For the man seems to have written his poetry not for any decent person, but he wrote the indecent and lewd parts for the licentious, the slanderous and bitter passages for the envious and malicious' (854d, Fowler 1936, mod.). Plutarch, in fact, cannot work out who Aristophanes' audiences could have been, since, as he says at 854c, he is '... neither pleasing to the many nor endurable to the thoughtful, but his poetry is like a harlot who has passed her prime and then takes up the role of a wife, whose presumption the many cannot endure and whose licentiousness and malice the dignified abominate' (tr. Fowler 1936). In other words, Aristophanic poetry was neither low-brow nor high-brow, and Plutarch cannot seem to find any space in between in which to situate him, nor can he conceive of any Aristophanic enthusiasts of whom he could approve.[16]

Not everyone in this period was as priggish about Aristophanes and Old Comedy as Plutarch, and plenty of others genuinely admired these playwrights, but, as we have seen, the evidence we have indicates that this admiration was more cultural and linguistic than literary.[17] It is unclear whether Old Comedy was ever actually staged during these centuries, though even allowing for an occasional re-performance as part of the prevailing cultural thirst for Attic authenticity, we have no access to how audiences would have responded to such events.[18] One suspects that a staged Aristophanic play, if there were any that attempted some measure of historical authenticity, would have had the feel of an amusing museum-piece, with audiences mystified by the localized names and political issues but delighting in the freewheeling mockery and slapstick. What would be most interesting to know in the case of a staged Old Comedy in this period is whether any audiences, or subsets of audiences, were capable of extracting from the topical details of the plots anything like the 'universals' that Menander seemed to offer its audiences, i.e., representations of characters types and human behavior that could transcend their fifth-century Greek particularity and speak to a contemporary audience. Would a staging of the *agon* of Aristophanes' *Frogs*, for example, end up a history lesson or a reflection on literary aesthetics for a second-century CE audience? More pointedly – since it was Old Comedy's abusiveness that most captured the imagination of this period – would the energetic invective exchanges between the Sausage-seller and Paphlagonian in a performance of *Knights* be amusing simply because of the spectacle of a bad politician being trounced by a self-righteous adversary, or would they also take note (for example) of the irony that both of those figures were *ponēroi*, and ponder the comic ironies of political culture in any age, especially their own?[19] Answers to such questions might be forthcoming if we had any idea what a production of Old Comedy might have looked like in this period, but unfortunately we do not (see n. 18). In the absence of any substantive testimony about reperformances of Old Comedy in this period from theater audiences, then, we can merely observe that anyone with a published and surviving opinion about Old Comedy at the time had only a limited, one-dimensional understanding of the genre.

The Dead Come to Life, or the Fisherman and Lucian's satiric program

In our search for someone in this period with a literary understanding of Old Comedy, we make more progress when we return to Lucian. Lucian's Aristophanic affiliations have long been observed in his dialogues, and he calls attention to this relationship more or less explicitly on a number of occasions.[20] Such programmatic passages, however, have not been analyzed as thoroughly as they should be, for, as we shall see, they not only confirm Lucian's appreciation of Old Comedy, but, more useful for our purposes, they have much to say about *how* he conceptualized the genre and understood its dynamics.

Lucian's *The Dead Come to Life, or the Fisherman* (= *Fisherman*) offers an oblique but unambiguous account of his conception of the poetics of Old Comedy. While the work is not specifically a treatise about Old Comedy, it presents a spirited and humorous defense of his own work, which was itself closely modeled on it. *Fisherman* presents itself as a response to criticism he received for his earlier work, *Sale of Lives* (*Vitarum Auctio*), in which he had mocked the various philosophical schools of the day. This conceit makes *Fisherman* similar to an Aristophanic parabasis in which the poet defends himself against detractors by accusing them of misunderstanding his intentions, not to mention how comedy is supposed to work.[21] As in an Aristophanic parabasis, as well, *Fisherman* also toys with its critics, one moment placating them, at another mocking them through a combination of irony and verbal dexterity.[22] The author in each case pretends, in short, to be on the defensive but sees to it that in the end he will always come out on top, uninterested in reforming his ways and ready to proceed with another satirical work in the same vein as the one that allegedly got him into trouble.

The Aristophanic provenance of *Fisherman* is evident in the opening lines:

βάλλε βάλλε τὸν κατάρατον ἀφθόνοις τοῖς λίθοις· ἐπίβαλλε τῶν βώλων· προσεπίβαλλε καὶ τῶν ὀστράκων· παῖε τοῖς ξύλοις τὸν ἀλιτήριον· ὅρα μὴ διαφύγῃ· καὶ σὺ βάλλε, ὦ Πλάτων· καὶ σύ, ὦ Χρύσιππε, καὶ σὺ δέ, καὶ πάντες ἅμα· συνασπίσωμεν ἐπ' αὐτόν.

Pelt, pelt the cursed wretch with tons of stones! Heap him with mud-clods! Heap broken dishes on top of that, too! Beat the scoundrel with your sticks! Watch out that he doesn't get away! Plato, hit him! You too, Chrysippus; and you too; everybody at once! Let's join forces to go after him!

The scene mimics any number of moments in an Aristophanic play when a character (or chorus) rushes on stage looking to attack an adversary,[23] and it seems likely enough that Lucian was thinking here specifically of *Acharnians* 280–3, where the chorus of Acharnians scramble to find Dicaeopolis in order to punish him for his peace treaty with Sparta:

οὗτος αὐτός ἐστιν, οὗτος·
βάλλε, βάλλε, βάλλε, βάλλε,
παῖε παῖε τὸν μιαρόν.
οὐ βαλεῖς, οὐ βαλεῖς;

That's the guy! That one!
Hit him, hit him, hit him, hit him!
Strike, strike the damned rogue!
Won't you hit him? Won't you hit him?

The rest of the opening scene of *Fisherman* continues in a style self-consciously Aristophanic: a group of philosophers resurrected from the dead swarm around a character called Parrhesiades (= 'Free Speech' or 'Frankness'), indignant at his treatment of individual philosophers, and of Philosophia herself, in his *Sale of Lives*. As the work opens, Parrhesiades tries to appease these indignant philosophers, ineffectively, by quoting from Homer and Euripides. For every quotation Parrhesiades offers, Plato counters with another in his attempt to trump Parrhesiades' defense. This repartee infused with poetic parody and 'capping' leaves little doubt that we are about to enter an Aristophanic world.[24]

Parrhesiades' is an obvious cipher for Lucian, and the name links him directly to Aristophanes as a champion of free and frank speech.[25] This is *comic* frankness, however, which professes a seriousness of purpose but never intends to deliver it in a straightforward or even coherent manner. With laughter the primary objective, the comic author must first curate this emotion in his audience before worrying about narrative or moral consistency. So in the case of *Fisherman*, the 'author' defends his earlier work by claiming that his intentions – sincere, serious, and didactic[26] – were misunderstood, but by the end of the work it is clear that his high-minded defense is disingenuous. If one compares what he says in *Fisherman* were his intentions in *Sale of Lives* to what he actually did in that work, not much holds up. In fact, the comic irony of *Fisherman* is that Lucian is able to satirize the philosophers in this work in just the same way as he had in *Sale of Lives*, even while claiming this was never his intention.

To drive this point home when it becomes clear that the debate between Parrhesiades cannot end amicably, Lucian, always with an eye to irony, brings on the figure of Philosophy, ostensibly to arbitrate, but in reality to advocate for Parrhesiades. In a crucial exchange at 14, Plato calls Parrhesiades (i.e., Lucian) the 'most impious of all profaners' (πάντων γε ἱεροσύλων ἀσεβέστατος) for having bad-mouthed (κακῶς ἀγορεύειν) both themselves and holy Philosophy herself. It is somewhat surprising, then, to find Lucian then presenting Philosophy as a character with a capacious and nuanced understanding of satirical poetics. Her attitude comes as a counter-intuitive surprise to the philosophers in the narrative and, presumably, to readers, since one assumes that any target of satire will be indignant at being mocked.[27] But Philosophia defends comic mockery of her by invoking the nature of 'Comedy' herself, here allegorized as a genre that means no harm, and in the end does some good:

> Then you were upset because someone was abusing you, though knowing that in spite of those things said about me by Comedy at the Dionysia, nevertheless I have thought of her as a friend [ὅμως φίλην τε αὐτὴν ἥγημαι], and never took her to court or approached her with blame. But I allowed her to play in ways that were proper and customary for the festival. For I know that nothing can become worse as a result of a joke [οἶδα γὰρ ὡς οὐκ ἄν τι ὑπὸ σκώμματος χεῖρον γένοιτο]. In fact, it's the opposite: whatever is fine glitters more brightly and becomes clearer, just like gold wiped clean when it is struck.

This passage is extraordinarily rich as a programmatic comment on Lucian's own comic *modus operandi*: not only is Philosophia tolerant of the abuse she has received from Comedy, but she presents herself as a 'friend' (φίλην) of Comedy. She berates the other philosophers for not having remembered (as they should have; εἰδότες) her amicable relationship with Comedy, and for objecting to Parrhesiades' mockery in the first place.

Lucian himself, of course, is masterminding this defense of satirical comedy, and we can distill from this passage some theoretical generalizations he seems concerned to make in it. First, satire is sanctioned by the fact that it occurs on a specific occasion that welcomes, even *requires*, mockery and abusive jesting (ἐφίημι δὲ παίζειν τὰ εἰκότα καὶ τὰ συνήθη τῇ ἑορτῇ). Philosophia has the Athenian festivals for Dionysus in mind here (ἐν Διονυσίοις) but her subsequent comments about joking become more general and less tied to that festival. Lucian leaves unanswered the question of what Philosophia might say about comedy and satire outside of a festival, but it is worth keeping in mind that Parrhesiades (i.e., Lucian) had not written *Lives for Sale* to be performed at an Athenian comic festival, so Philosophia's defense of that work cannot require that we imagine Lucianic satire to be sanctioned by a religious festival. Instead, we must think of Philosophia's 'religious ritual defense' as Lucian's reminder that satire is a literary genre, with cues and markers to its audience that help them distinguish it from the mockery of real life.[28]

Another programmatic trope that emerges from this passage is the classic alliance that satirists routinely claim with philosophical 'truth'.[29] Such an alliance is readily implied by Philosophia's friendship with Comedy, and at 17 Philosophia even brings Truth into the trial as a lawyer and arbitrator,[30] but her words in 14 say nothing, in fact, about the truth-value of *skommata*. Instead, using a numismatic metaphor, she states that a good/fine person should have no fear of satirical jokes, since being 'struck' (like a gold coin) wipes clean the surface to reveal that person's essential goodness. This is an arresting claim in itself: it holds for those who are regarded as already *kalos*, perhaps, but what about the fact that satirists typically claim to be interested in attacking only those who are 'bad', who *deserve* opprobrium? And what would be the point of a satirical joke against a philosopher who was 'fine'?[31] Are we really supposed to believe that Lucian's satire of philosophy in the *Sale of Lives* was intended to *burnish* philosophy's reputation as a fine (*kalon*) pursuit rather than to damage it? Presumably not, but Philosophia's case then becomes wildly disingenuous, and it is no wonder that the philosophers see right through it in the next section. Philosophia's insistence that she and Comedy are friends suggests, then, that there is no unilaterally correct way to understand, or – as a target – to endure, comic satire. Lucian is, rather, interested mainly in the risibility of philosophers, and any 'truths' that arise from satirizing them can not be uniform or consistent because what makes them risible to begin with takes many forms. Halliwell (2008: 435) aptly describes this scene as offering 'a slyly teasing self-image of Lucianic priorities', and notes the ultimate irony that the philosophers acquiesce to

Parrhesiades' case despite the fact that 'no distinction at all is drawn between old and new, or true and false, philosophers'. As the chorus of mystic initiates in Aristophanes' *Frogs* had warned in the parodos of that play, one needs to be prepared in a comic performance to encounter all manner of abuse; those who are easily offended have no business being there.[32]

A passage further on in *Fisherman* (25) shows the cynic philosopher Diogenes trying to counter Philosophia's defense of Comedy in an argument that reveals just how self-conscious Lucian was about the theory and practice of comic satire. In his litany of complaints against Parrhesiades, Diogenes particularly objects to the fact that Parrhesiades mocked philosophers (and philosophical 'seriousness') for no other reason than to get 'applause and praise' from an audience:

> And what's more, he has now made us hated in the eyes of the many, and you too, Philosophy, by calling your teachings nonsense and trash, and by reciting with continual mockery the most serious of the things you have taught us. He ends up with applause and praise from audiences, but we get revilement [ὥστε αὐτὸν μὲν κροτεῖσθαι καὶ ἐπαινεῖσθαι πρὸς τῶν θεατῶν, ἡμᾶς δὲ ὑβρίζεσθαι].

Diogenes then alludes with disdain to the argument that Philosophia had made about festival license, noting that for the 'popular mass' (ὁ πολὺς λεώς) it is natural to enjoy watching people mock and wrangle in a play (φύσει γὰρ τοιοῦτόν ἐστιν ὁ πολὺς λεώς, χαίρουσι τοῖς ἀποσκώπτουσιν καὶ λοιδορουμένοις), and to watch them deflate whatever is held to be solemn and serious (καὶ μάλισθ' ὅταν τὰ σεμνότατα εἶναι δοκοῦντα διασύρηται). Unlike Philosophia, Diogenes emphatically does not approve of the satirical procedures of Old Comedy, and adduces Aristophanes' and Eupolis' mockery of Socrates as his illustrative example.[33]

> ὥσπερ ἀμέλει καὶ πάλαι ἔχαιρον Ἀριστοφάνει καὶ Εὐπόλιδι Σωκράτη τουτονὶ ἐπὶ χλευασίᾳ παράγουσιν ἐπὶ τὴν σκηνὴν καὶ κωμῳδοῦσιν ἀλλοκότους τινὰς περὶ αὐτοῦ κωμῳδίας.
>
> And so, just as in a by-gone time they loved it when Aristophanes and Eupolis brought Socrates on the stage to mock him and made crazy comedies about him.

Philosophia had implied that truly 'good' targets, such as Socrates or herself, could withstand satirical jesting within a comedy and should not worry about any damage to their character. Reasonably enough, however, Diogenes only sees the criticism inherent in mockery, along with the pretense that such criticism is meant to be serious and efficiacious. He acknowledges, it seems, that an Aristophanes or Eupolis may not be concerned with the truth-value of their satirical criticism, but worries more about the effect such criticism can have on the opinion of the 'popular mass'. The festival occasion may allow the comic poets to behave this way, but, according to Diogenes, that does not mean it was a good practice even in fifth-century Athens. We might excuse Old Comedy for being a 'primitive' (note ἀμέλει καὶ πάλαι) form of literature, but that would not make it any less dangerous if adopted in Lucian's own time.

Old Comedy for Diogenes was bad enough, then, but Parrhesiades' practice (= Lucianic satire), he continues, is even more pernicious because it could not even claim festival license and so had no excuse for its unjustified mockery:

ὁ δὲ τοὺς ἀρίστους συγκαλῶν, ἐκ πολλοῦ φροντίσας καὶ παρασκευασάμενος καὶ βλασφημίας τινὰς εἰς παχὺ βιβλίον ἐγγράψας, μεγάλῃ τῇ φωνῇ ἀγορεύει κακῶς Πλάτωνα, Πυθαγόραν, Ἀριστοτέλη τοῦτον, Χρύσιππον ἐκεῖνον, ἐμὲ καὶ ὅλως ἅπαντας οὔτε ἑορτῆς ἐφιείσης οὔτε ἰδίᾳ τι πρὸς ἡμῶν παθών·

... but this man gathers the best people together, and after he's thought for a long time and prepared and written out some of his slanders in a thick book-roll, he openly maligns at the top of his voice Plato, Pythagoras, Aristotle right here, Chrysippus over there, myself, and in short, pretty much everyone, without a festival to permit it and without having suffered anything bad from us in private.

Diogenes' final complaint proposes a curious contrast between the poet of Old Comedy and the Lucianic satirist. Lucian's Diogenes imagines that Aristophanes or Eupolis were writing quickly or spontaneously, as opposed to Parrhesiades, who was deeply literary, 'thinking for a long time', 'preparing and writing out' all his slanders in a 'thick book-roll', until it all came out in full force against the philosophers. And Parrhesiades writes this way, he adds, outside any festival occasion and without any provocation from the philosophers themselves. This last point is particularly significant since it reflects an attitude typical of someone who has no understanding of satire as a literary form, and confuses literary satire with lived reality. Diogenes cannot understand, in other words, why someone would criticize another person – deliberately, with premeditation and without just cause – unless the critic were himself a bad, unworthy person to begin with, since that is how such a person would be regarded in the real world. Indeed, in the real world there are often laws and social sanctions against those perceived to be actual slanderers.[34] For Diogenes, to be a literary satirist, who actually plans to slander other people without provocation, is to be a slanderous person. In his view, in other words, one cannot separate the character of a writer of slander from the slander itself – no possibility, that is, to imagine a virtuous writer who just happens to write slanderous literature.

For Lucian, however, the case of Diogenes tells a cautionary, defensive tale about the ways in which satirical literature is perennially misunderstood. This trope of misunderstanding appears itself to be inherent in the logic of the genre, which thrives on the assumption that there will always be audiences somewhere, imagined or real, who will take offense at mockery whether or not it is directed at them. These are the audiences which Aristophanes' chorus in *Frogs* dismisses as unworthy to participate in the comic festivals, where mockery exists purely for the sake of laughter, even when it claims to be offering justified criticism of the world.[35] Parrhesiades eventually wins his case in *The Dead Come to Life* by convincing the philosophers that he only criticizes the corrupt and hypocritical among them. But Lucian knows that his self-righteousness is merely a ruse to get his comic hero off the hook, and give him the last laugh. The philosophers end up satirized in *The Dead Come to Life* as fully as they had been in *Sale of Lives*, and Lucian has explained how this can be through the debate about comic satire he has embedded in the work. As Lucian articulates through the characters in *The Dead Come to Life*, poets of Old Comedy laid down the principles of literary satire whose mockery worked in a volatile space between truth and fiction, relying on loops of irony and disingenuousness to please a discerning audience – an audience primed for laughter by the markers of the genre.

Lucian's *Double Indictment* (*Bis Accusatus*) and Old Comedy

Lucian's insight into the unstable and elusive space occupied by Old Comedy is also evident in one of his best known works, *Double Indictment*. It has long been observed that this work itself was modeled in large part on the *Pytinē*, by Aristophanes' older contemporary Cratinus.[36] The plot of *Pytinē*, which survives only in an ancient summary (a scholium to Aristoph. *Knights* 400 = Suda κ 2216), featured an allegorized character 'Comedy' complaining that her husband, the playwright Cratinus himself, had abandoned her for drink and young boys. In *Double Indictment* Lucian (here 'the Syrian') is accused of desertion by two companions (hence the 'double' indictment), first his wife, Rhetoric (*Rhetorikē*) and then, Dialogue (*Dialogos*). The final section where Rhetoric and Dialogue plead their cases before a court of law, with Justice and Hermes presiding, offer Lucian the opportunity once again to orchestrate a reflection on his own literary practices. The scenario he crafts for his (naturally) successful defense contains all the elements we would expect from a satirist who wanted to portray himself as attacked and cornered by his adversaries, but ultimately worthy of vindication. His case for vindication is also inscribed by the requirements of the genre: he is the enemy of all puffery and pretension, hypocrisy and sanctimony, and the champion of popular appeal and unconstrained laughter. As we will see, however, in comparison to the ordered and predictable practices of rhetoric and philosophy, Lucian's notions of satire and comedy, rooted as they are in Old Comedy, create more confusion than stability for his audiences.

The double court case against the Syrian at the end of *Double Indictment* offers a basic account of Lucian's literary career. Rhetoric describes how her marriage to Lucian made him rich and famous, as she accompanied him through all his travels around the Mediterranean. She complains (28), however, that he became infatuated with Dialogue, the literary form associated at the time with philosophy. Lucian's description of why he left Rhetoric for Dialogue at 31 implies that he is here charting a period of disillusionment in his own career with the rhetorical excesses of his day.[37] He describes, for example, how his 'wife', Rhetoric, began to put on too much make-up and wear her hair 'like a prostitute'. Soon there were lovers eager for her favors, and many opportunities for adultery and indecorous behavior. In contrast to this domestic situation, decamping for Dialogue's house seemed attractive, where the two of them (two males, it should be noted) could 'walk around in calm conversation, without any need of praise or clapping' (συμπεριπατεῖν ἠρέμα διαλεγομένους, τῶν ἐπαίνων καὶ κρότων οὐ δεομένους). But things soured quickly enough with Dialogue too, and it is his account of their falling-out that is particularly revealing for our purposes.

The problems in Lucian's 'relationship' with Dialogue arose from the fact that, although he was drawn to dialogue as a philosophical medium, Lucian was never really a philosopher, and, as we saw in *The Dead Come to Life*, he was mostly interested in exposing the absurdities of philosophers. As Dialogue puts it in 33, Lucian deflated him, dragging him down from the elevated heights of philosophical discourse to the pedestrian level of the common people (ἰσοδίαιτον τοῖς πολλοῖς ἐποίησεν). The details of his indignant speech deserve close analysis:

καὶ τὸ μὲν τραγικὸν ἐκεῖνο καὶ σωφρονικὸν προσωπεῖον ἀφεῖλέ μου, κωμικὸν δὲ καὶ σατυρικὸν ἄλλο ἐπέθηκέ μοι καὶ μικροῦ δεῖν γελοῖον. εἶτά μοι εἰς τὸ αὐτὸ φέρων συγκαθεῖρξεν τὸ σκῶμμα καὶ τὸν ἴαμβον καὶ κυνισμὸν καὶ τὸν Εὔπολιν καὶ τὸν Ἀριστοφάνη, δεινοὺς ἄνδρας ἐπικερτομῆσαι τὰ σεμνὰ καὶ χλευάσαι τὰ ὀρθῶς ἔχοντα. τελευταῖον δὲ καὶ Μένιππόν τινα τῶν παλαιῶν κυνῶν μάλα ὑλακτικὸν ὡς δοκεῖ καὶ κάρχαρον ἀνορύξας, καὶ τοῦτον ἐπεισήγαγεν μοι φοβερόν τινα ὡς ἀληθῶς κύνα καὶ τὸ δῆγμα λαθραῖον, ὅσῳ καὶ γελῶν ἅμα ἔδακνεν.

> And he took from me that tragic, temperate mask I had, and put another on me that was comic and satyr-like, practically ludicrous. Then he shut me up in one place with Jest, Iambos, Cynicism, Aristophanes and Eupolis, men who were terribly good at mocking holy things, and making fun of what is right. Finally, he even dug up one of those ancient dogs [= cynics], one Menippus, who barked loudly, as it seems, and had sharp teeth; and he directed that really terrifying dog against me, the dog with the unexpected bite because he laughs at the same time as he bites.

Dialogue complains first of all that he is at the mercy of the rigid categories that theatrical masks impose on a character: he wants to be serious like a tragic actor, but once the tragic mask, with all its connotations, is exchanged for a comic one, only the opposite is possible: he becomes irretrievably ridiculous, un-serious and incapable of ever escaping the comic world. The comic mask connotes a general performance context of non-seriousness and laughter, but the ensuing details specify a more precise literary amalgamation derived from the elements that made up Old Comedy – jesting, iambic invective, and pseudo-philosophical satire. Aristophanes and Eupolis are once again invoked as foundational figures in the history of this comedic style, and Dialogue's objections to them are similar to those we saw in *The Dead Come to Life*. The problem is not only the joking and irreverence characteristic of Old Comedy, but the accusation that these poets reveled in mocking inappropriate things, 'holy things' and 'what is right'. Finally, Dialogue regards the idea of the satirist who 'bites' with a smile as especially pernicious, because it confuses categories of behavior: the satirist's laughter leads his audience to expect goodwill and mirth, but instead we get what, for Dialogue, amounts to unexpected violence.

Whereas in *Fisherman*, however, the figure representing Lucian (Parrhesiades) tries to correct the charge against him by claiming that his Aristophanic mockery was directed only against those who deserved it, in *Double Indictment*, 'the Syrian' does nothing to challenge Dialogue's accusations of unjustified satire directed even against the good. Instead, in his reply to Dialogue at 34, the Syrian merely mocks Dialogue further for being too serious and sullen (σκυθρωπόν), and proceeds to describe his attempt to get Dialogue to lighten up, 'to walk like a normal human being on the ground… and to smile' (πρῶτον μὲν αὐτὸν ἐπὶ γῆς βαίνειν εἴθισα εἰς τὸν ἀνθρώπινον τοῦτον τρόπον... καὶ μειδιᾶν καταναγκάσας). As a final flourish, he 'teamed up' Dialogue with Comedy (ἐπὶ πᾶσι δὲ τὴν κωμῳδίαν αὐτῷ παρέζευξα), which won him the good favor of his audiences (κατὰ τοῦτο πολλήν οἱ μηχανώμενος τὴν εὔνοιαν παρὰ τῶν ἀκουόντων).[38]

As this passage makes clear, then, for Lucian his Old Comedy-inflected satire is not, in fact, predicated on righteous mockery – that turns out to be something of a pose – but rather on his ability to keep his audience laughing.[39] As the Syrian continues, this ability to make Dialogue smile and be appealing to audiences allowed them to overcome their fear of him: 'formerly, afraid of [Dialogue's] thorny spikes, they were wary of taking him in their hands as if he were a sea-urchin' (τὰς ἀκάνθας τὰς ἐν αὐτῷ δεδιότες ὥσπερ τὸν ἐχῖνον εἰς τὰς χεῖρας λαβεῖν αὐτὸν ἐφυλάττοντο). Lucian has ignored the question of whether turning Dialogue's serious, eristic philosophizing into comedy is a kind of dangerous deception. Will the audience eventually realize, for example, that they are holding a creature with spikes after all, and that these spikes are in fact painful? What, moreover, has become of Dialogue's philosophical seriousness as a consequence of her pairing with Comedy? Lucian does not answer any of these questions, and the programmatic moments we have examined suggest that there are no answers for this kind of comedy – at least no satisfying ones. Lucianic satire, with its provenance in 'jest, iambos, cynicism, Aristophanes and Eupolis' exists in a literary world of free-flowing irony and paradox which can only appeal to an audience prepared to revel in a jumble of mixed messages and disingenuous proclamations.

Concluding thoughts

Did such an audience actually exist in the imperial period – an audience, that is, for whom the adjective 'Aristophanic' or 'old comic' meant something more than simply 'vitriolic', 'obscene' or 'buffoonish', and implied instead a complex and sophisticated literary style that was still capable of evolving in the works of contemporary authors such as Lucian? To put this another way, when Lucian situates his own satiric enterprise within a distinctly Old Comedic tradition, were his audiences capable of conceptualizing Old Comedy with an accurate sense of literary history and generic understanding?

As we have seen, the burden of a literary-critical tradition that simplified and distilled Old Comedy into a monochromatic genre of uncivil and reckless abuse took its toll on readers and audiences of the period, but it is difficult to know how universal such attitudes were. Certainly for some members of the educated classes who were invested in Platonic and Aristotelian literary aesthetics, satirical comedy always seemed psychologically disruptive to the individual and socially disruptive to a community. Plutarch may offer an extreme example of this attitude in his *Comparatio*, but in its general outline, it seems to have been a common view. When Lucian defends his comic style, with its Aristophanic roots, in the passages we have examined, he seems to be pushing back against the shallowness of prevailing attitudes towards Old Comedy, which for the most part did not take the trouble to look much beyond its bad language and low-brow humor. Old Comedy may have been admired well enough as a model of Atticism among the *pepaideumenoi*, but as a model for contemporary literature it still remained something of a problem. The defensive postures in these scenes, fictionalized and ironized as they are, suggest that Lucian perceived a genuine need to open the eyes of at least some readers (especially, one assumes, elite, educated critics, who were potential taste-makers) to the dynamic, multifarious richness of Old Comedy. Lucian was himself popular enough in his own time, which suggests some popular appreciation of his Aristophanic roots at least at some level.[40] What was missing, however – and what Lucian seemed interested in promoting – was a properly theorized and historicized understanding of comic satire that abandoned the many anxieties about mockery and obscenity which had agglomerated over the preceding centuries.

Notes

* I thank the editors of this volume for their shrewd and helpful comments on an earlier draft of this chapter.
1 See Storey 2003: 94–11, esp. 103–5. Storey urges caution on Alcibiades' role in the play: 'I would not assume without question either that Alkibiades' role in *Baptai* was a major one, or that Eupolis was necessarily engaged in a play-length crusade' (104).
2 For a survey of Greek views of comic poets across antiquity, see Quadlbauer 1960, with 52–70 for the imperial period. See also Nervegna 2013: 49–54, Bowie 2007, Hunter 2014: 379–84.
3 On Menander's afterlife in the imperial period, see Nervegna 2013, *passim*, esp. 201–51.
4 In the opening sentences of 27 that lead into his mention of Aristophanes and Eupolis, Lucian seems to have satirical literature on his mind. He begins by asking what the book-collector has read, but his queries about specific authors are quite idiosyncratic – from philosophical authors (Plato and Antisthenes), he moves abruptly to authors famous for their invective (Archilochus and Hipponax, in poetry; Aeschines and Timarchus in prose). Lucian says sarcastically, 'surely you know all that stuff [i.e.,

Aeschines and Timarchus] and you understand [*gnorizeis*] everything about it ...', and at this point asks if he 'plunged into Aristophanes and Eupolis'. Lucian implies here that these poets of Old Comedy are particularly complex and require more skill and experience to understand than the other authors he has just mentioned.

5 This topic has been well documented; see, e.g., Ledegerber 1905, Householder 1941, and Bowie 2007.
6 See Sidwell 2000, esp. his useful appendix listing all the fifth-century Athenian comic poets mentioned in Athenaeus and Lucian, pp. 142–52.
7 See Rosen 2007: 3–42 for further discussion of satirical theory ('The Dynamics of Ancient Satirical Poetry'), esp. 16–22. For circumscribing satire specifically in Lucian, see Hall 1981: 393–4 and Camerotto 2014: 15–17.
8 See the following section on Plutarch's distaste for the aggressive satire of Aristophanes, Hunter 2009: 78–89, along with Marshall, chapter 7 in this volume. The second-century medical writer, Galen, wrote whole treatises on Aristophanes, Cratinus and Eupolis (all now lost) for what appear to be largely lexicographical reasons. Galen alludes to these works, including a work entitled *Whether Old Comedy is Useful Reading for Students*, in his *On my Own Books*, under a heading of 'topics common to grammarians and rhetoricians' (Ch. 20, Boudon-Millot 2007: 173). See also Galen's remarks in his recently recovered work, *De Indolentia*, about the scrolls of treatises on Old Comedy that he lost in the fire at Rome in 192 CE. At ch. 20 he mentions the 'fate of my work on words in Attic Greek and everyday language [part of which was] drawn from Old Comedy'. (tr. Nutton in Singer 2013: 84; Greek text in Boudon-Millot, Jouanna and Pietrobelli 2010: 8).
9 See, e.g., Csapo 2000.
10 See Cribiore 2001: 238–44, and Nervegna 2013: 202 (in the context of imperial-period reception of Menander): 'The end-product of the *enkyklios paideia*, what the Greeks called the *pepaideumenos*, was an "all-round", thoroughly prepared individual repeatedly exposed to the same material and authors'.
11 On characterizing a satirical genre according to the particular kind of work it is trying to do, its *telos*, see Rosen 2013: 90–6.
12 See Branham 1989: 11–63 (with n.79 for further bibliography on Lucian's 'theory of laughter' for the complex, elusive interaction between the 'serious' and 'comic' in Lucian). From the many traditions and theoretical strands that make up Lucianic humor, Branham (56) 'abstract[s] a central feature: a serio-comic text or performance works by revealing to the audience as problematic the appropriateness of laughter or seriousness in a given context'.
13 See Ruffy 2011: 135–6.
14 ἀνωμαλία is a difficult term. Hunter (2000: 271) translates as 'lack of uniformity', which he takes to evoke the comic language that 'evoke[d] ... the unpredictable and unordered rabble of the radical democracy of Aristophanes' own day'.

15 For a different approach to Plutarch on comedy, see Marshall, chapter 7 in this volume. Marshall finds the emphasis on Aristophanes (i.e., to the exclusion of other poets of Old Comedy) in the surviving epitome unusual, and suggests it may not be original to Plutarch.
16 It is curious that Plutarch seems more optimistic in his *How a Young Man Should Study Poetry* that one can avoid the bad influence of potentially pernicious literature (i.e., ambiguous literature that can be interpreted in good or bad ways), if one has a proper education. See, for example, 25e–28, with Hunter and Russell 2011: 145–57.
17 Citations and allusions to Old Comedy in literary texts were on the rise, as Bowie notes (2007: 33), attributable, no doubt, to the increasing interest in promoting the Attic diction of the Classical period, but New Comedy seemed the preferred mode for actual comic performances (see next note).
18 On the difficult question of reperformances of Greek 'old drama' in the Roman period, see Gentili 1979, Jones 1993, Nervegna 2007, Bowie 2007: 33, and Peterson in this volume. The evidence for genuine reperformances of Old Comedy in this period is sparse and ambiguous, and complicated by the fact that none of our sources ever distinguishes clearly between contemporary comic performances (i.e., new plays) that are modeled on Old Comedy and actual revivals which were historically authentic and not re-made in some fashion. Dio Chrys. *Orat.* 19.5, is often invoked as evidence for reperformances of Old Comedy in the late first century CE, but his phrasing is oblique and unhelpful. There he praises the performances of citharodists and actors (in preference to those of sophists and orators), and notes that most of their repertoire is 'archaic' [καὶ τά γε πολλὰ αὐτῶν ἀρχαῖά ἐστι]. The key phrase that follows, however, is enigmatic: 'as for the material of comedy, everything is left in, but with tragedy only the strong parts, it seems ...' [καὶ πολὺ σοφωτέρων ἀνδρῶν ἢ τῶν νῦν. τὰ μὲν τῆς κωμῳδίας ἅπαντα, τῆς δὲ τραγῳδίας τὰ μὲν ἰσχυρά, ὡς ἔοικε, μένει·]. The term ἅπαντα ['everything'] is too laconic for us to draw any certain conclusions about exactly what kinds of contemporary performances Dio had in mind. See further, Hall 2002: 17–18, Nervegna 2007: 39. Nervegna's conclusion that this passage 'attests that contemporary reperformances of old comedy and tragedy were not reduced to select excerpts' is unobjectionable, but it is not even clear whether Dio is referring to fully staged performances of 'archaic' comedy, or simply performances that allowed for the display of all the features one associated with Old Comedy (e.g., aischrologic invective, parabases, choral passages, etc.). Peterson's discussion of Aristides' speech *On the Banning of Comedy* (Or. 29), chapter 10 in this volume, leaves her more sanguine about the likelihood of *bona fide* reperformances of Old Comedy in this period.
19 Such questions are not limited to the second century, of course, and constitute a subset of a larger set of literary-philosophical conundra well articulated in Silk 2007, who discusses the 'historicist' problem that underlies all attempts of later ages to

reperform, translate or transpose a work of the distant past. The dilemma is well illustrated by juxtaposing two of Silk's remarks. On the one hand, 'Modern performances of Aristophanic drama seeks, should seek, to transpose a notional past to an immediate presence, and to conquer the cultural distance by whatever equivalence and transposition is judged necessary and appropriate' (293). On the other, 'If one is to have an equivalent, *any* equivalent, to Aristophanes, it does of course help to decide what Aristophanes is like in the first place' (294). In our own era we have become used to balancing diachronic/historicist and synchronic/ahistoricist approaches to contemporary reperformances of Classical drama, but most productions will begin, as Silk implies, with at least some conception of what Aristophanes was 'like' performed in its original setting. *Satirical* comedy, with its focus on *ad hominem* mockery and highly specific prosopographical and political detail, presents its own set of challenges, as Plutarch's Diogenianus pointed out (see above, p. 144). On this tension between diachrony and synchrony in satire, see Rosen 2014a and forthcoming 2015a.

20 For Lucian, see Storey, chapter 9 in this volume, and for the prominence of the parabasis as a point of reference in the second century CE, see Hawkins, chapter 4 in this volume.

21 The opening lines of the parabasis of Aristophanes' *Clouds*, 518–26, offer a classic example; see Hubbard 1991: 88–112 ('Misunderstood Intellectuals and Misunderstood Poets').

22 See Wright 2012: 52–60, with a useful discussion of Eupolis fr. 392 K-A (though his suggestion that there is more seriousness than irony is such passages seems somewhat forced).

23 As, e.g., at Aristophanes, *Lys.* 350–86.

24 On iambographic and symposiastic capping, see Collins 2004, Hawkins 2007, and Rosen, forthcoming 2015c. For Aristophanic capping, see, e.g., *Knights* 273–96 or *Frogs* 1200–42 (with Collins 2004: 30–43).

25 The name Parrhesiades is presumably one of Schwyzer's 'sprechenden Namen' (1939: 509) which uses a suffix otherwise associated with patronymics. Given the usual noun for 'free speech' (*parrhēsia*), a contemporary reader may well have understood the name at first as a patronymic, 'Son of Free speech', possibly even with a distinctly epic flavor (as in, e.g., the Homeric *Priamidēs*, 'son of Priam', *Il.* 3.356, for Paris). As a feminine noun, *parrhesia* would have been a less convincing allegorized cipher for Lucian himself, which may well account for the suffix we see in the form Parrhesiades. It does not seem impossible, however, to imagine Lucian also hinting at a patronymic in order to signal his literary lineage in invective comedy, from Aristophanes to himself (where 'Child of Free speech' suggests 'descendent of Aristophanes'). On grammatical gender in allegorized comic characters, see also Rosen 1998. Note that at 19, Parrhesiades does give his full patronymic, with 'speaking names' further

strengthening his descent from Old Comedy: 'Parrhesiades Son of Truthful, the son of Famous Critic' [Παρρησιάδης Ἀληθίωνος τοῦ Ἐλεγξικλέους].

26 See, e.g., *Fisherman* 5: 'Truly, gentlemen, you will put to death, you may depend upon it, the one man in the world whom you ought to commend as your friend, well-wisher, comrade in thought, and, if it be not in bad taste to say so, the defender of your teachings, if you put me to death after I have laboured so earnestly in your behalf' (tr. Harmon 1921).

27 More precisely, the conceit of a satirical work is that the effects will harm a target, and the content of the satire is constructed accordingly. Targets may well remain utterly unaffected by a satirist and even embrace the aggressive jesting with good humor and even friendship, as Philosophia does here, but the work itself needs to pretend it will always be dangerous. See further in Rosen 2007: 43–66.

28 See Halliwell 2008: 434. Aristophanes himself had made a similar defense for his comedy in the parodos of *Frogs* 354–72, where the chorus of mystic initiates proclaims that anyone who does not understand the mockery of their festival, should stay away. On the programmatic nature of this passage for Aristophanic poetics, see Rosen forthcoming 2015b.

29 See Halliwell 2008: 434–5, with specific reference to *Fisherman*.

30 Truth's role is essentially to vouch, at 38, for the truth of Parrhesiades' defense speech (29–37). After the speech Truth affirms that Parrhesiades' portrait of corrupt philosophers in *Sale of Lives* was clear 'as if in a painting' and realistic in all respects (ἔδειξε τοὺς ἄνδρας ἐναργῶς καθάπερ ἐπί τινος γραφῆς τὰ πάντα προσεοικότας . . .).

31 Parrhesiades makes the claim himself at 20: 'My own makeup, however, is such as to hate rogues and to praise and love good/honest men', τὸ μέντοι ἐμὸν τοιοῦτόν ἐστιν, οἷον τοὺς μὲν πονηροὺς μισεῖν, ἐπαινεῖν δὲ τοὺς χρηστοὺς καὶ φιλεῖν. This is a familiar trope from Roman satire as well, esp. Horace; cf., e.g., Hor. *Serm.* 2.1.39–46.

32 Aristoph. *Frogs* 354–72. The coryphaeus here debars from the festivities anyone who has 'no experience in this kind of [=comic] discourse' (355: ἄπειρος τοιῶνδε λόγων), does not enjoy buffoonish poetry (358: μηδὲ . . . βωμολόχοις ἔπεσιν χαίρει), behaves in ways dangerous to the city, or, when serving in office, cuts back on poetic awards because he is irritated at being satirized by comedians in the festivals (368: κωμῳδηθεὶς ἐν ταῖς πατρίοις τελεταῖς ταῖς τοῦ Διονύσου).

33 This is, in fact, the only explicit claim we have that Eupolis mocked Socrates in his comedies. Eupolis is also linked with Aristophanes in *Bis Accusatus* 33, without a mention of Socrates. For a detailed discussion see Patzer 1994: 68–75 and Storey 2003: 321–7. Storey is more cautious than Patzer with the fragmentary evidence and is aporetic about the role Socrates might or might not have played in Eupolis' comedies.

34 Horace is again (cf. above, n. 31) a useful comparative parallel for this trope as well; see *Serm.* 2.1.79–86.

35 See above, n. 32.
36 On Cratinus' *Pytinē*, see Bakola 2010: 59–64, with 60, n. 143 for further bibliography. On *Pytinē* in *Double Indictment*, see Sidwell 2009: 110–12.
37 There is no need, of course, for us to assume he is here recounting veridical autobiographical truth, especially given the fact that his narrative was modeled on the plot of Cratinus' *Pytinē*.
38 The Syrian's narrative of how he tried to get Dialogue to change is reminiscent of Euripides' description of his (successful) efforts to change Tragedy in Aristoph. *Frogs* 937–40. Just as the Syrian hopes to bring Dialogue down to earth so she would 'walk like a normal human being on the ground', so Euripides reduces the bombast of Aeschylean tragedy, slimming her down (941), and making her more intelligible (974–5). He famously describes the whole process at 952 as *demokratikon*.
39 See also Halliwell 208: 433, who discusses the importance of laughter as a theme in this scene ('an ambiguous, shifting force ...').
40 Sidwell 2009 argues that Lucian would have expected his audience of *pepaideumenoi* to have a good knowledge of the ancient scholarship on Old Comedy (his citation, p. 13, of *True Histories* 1.2 supports this well), and, specifically, that they would have understood from the scholarship that fictional characters could sometimes stand in for the comic author (in other words, that they would have had some sensitivity to the more subtle literary dynamics of Old Comedy). I have little doubt that this could be said of at least some of his élite and educated audience, but Lucian's defensiveness elsewhere about his Aristophanic roots seems directed at a larger constituency. Kuin (2015) argues that Lucian's works were likely performed in front of diverse popular audiences, not limited to the élite, which would make his programmatic defenses perhaps all the more useful as 'program notes' of a sort.

9
Exposing Frauds: Lucian and Comedy

Ian C. Storey*

If we seek a writer from the Roman period who had more than a little knowledge of Attic Comedy and who exploited that familiarity in his own fictions, we will find Lucian (career: *c*.120-*c*.180 CE) at the top of our short list. In his works he mentions by name the following comic poets:

- Aristophanes (*True History* 1.29; *Fisherman* 25, *Twice Accused* 33, *Against the Ignorant Book-Buyer* 27);
- Eupolis (*Fisherman* 25; *Twice Accused* 33, *Against the Ignorant Book-Buyer* 27);
- Kratinos (twice in *Long Lives* 25);
- Epicharmos (*Long Lives* 25);
- Alexis (*An Error in Greeting* 6);
- Philemon (*Long Lives* 25, *An Error in Greeting* 6);
- Menander (*Alexander* 33, *Pseudo-Critic* 4).

By author he cites Alexis F 299 and Philemon F 150 (both at *An Error in Greeting* 6), and Menander F 507 (at *Pseudo-Critic* 4). On several occasions Lucian attributes a quotation to 'the comic poet' (ὁ κωμικός) or as 'that line from comedy' (τὸ κωμικόν). It is often assumed that in ancient sources 'the comic poet' denotes Aristophanes,[1] but in Lucian 'the comic poet' can be identified as Menander (F 179K, cited at *Tragic Zeus* 53) and perhaps also at *How to Write History* 41, if Meineke is correct in relating the quotation cited therein to the prologue in a play by Menander spoken by Elenchos (F 507 cited above). The reference at *Teacher of Rhetoric* 12 to 'Thaïs of comedy' must be to Menander's comedy of that title (*PCG* VI.2 163-9). At *Nigrinos* 7 Lucian attributes to 'the comic poet' a well-known line from Eupolis' *Demes* (F 102.5) and a later line (F 102.7) is called 'that line from comedy' (*Demonax*) 10. Both the quotations from *Demes* are reasonably faithful to the original text: ἐγκατέλιπέν τι κέντρον τοῖς ἀκούουσιν (Lucian) ~ τὸ κέντρον ἐγκατέλειπε τοῖς ἀκροωμένοις (Eupolis), τὴν πειθὼ τοῖς χείλεσιν αὐτοῦ ἐπικαθῆσθαι (Lucian) ~ πειθώ τις ἐπεκάθιζεν ἐπὶ τοῖς χείλεσιν (Eupolis).

For some citations it is not immediately clear whether Lucian is quoting Old or New Comedy, apart from the reference to Kleon as 'a Prometheus after the fact' at *You are Prometheus* 2 (*PCG* VIII 461), which must come from a comic poet of the 5th century BC.[2] The line attributed to 'the comic poet' at *Fly* 11 about the well-known Athenian *hetaira* named Muia ('the Fly'), 'Muia has stung me all the way to my heart' (*PCG* VIII 459), could belong to any period of comedy. The same may be said of the 'certain comic iambics' cited at *Herakles* 5, 'the tongue of every talkative man is pierced at the tip' (*PCG* VIII 457), and of the request 'according to the comic poet' cited at *Tragic Zeus* 38, 'this is rather unpleasant, suggest something else to me' (*PCG* VIII 38).

At *You are Prometheus* 6 Lucian in his own person summarises the early comic scene at *Clouds* 133-221 where Strepsiades encounters the pupil of Sokrates, while the narrator at *True History* 1.25 defends Aristophanes for his account of Cloudcuckooland as 'wise and truthful and unfairly disbelieved for what he had written', obviously alluding to Aristophanes' *Birds* and expecting his reader to know the reference. At *Against the Ignorant Book-Buyer* 27 Lucian asks if the book-buyer has actually got into Aristophanes and Eupolis, whether he has read the whole of *Dyers* (*Baptai*), and if what he read there has actually gotten through to him. He twice mentions Kratinos ('the comic poet') in *Long Lives* 25, for his great age rather than for his comedy, but does cite *Wine-Flask* by name as Kratinos' last play before he died.

Lucian does not appear to employ the stereotypical divisions of Old and Middle and New Comedy. He does use the term *archaia komōidia* once (*An Error in Greeting* 6), but without naming any poet and the context is that of the use of the verb ὑγιαίνειν. At *Slander* 6, borrowing a distinction made at Herodotos 7.10, he defines the three persons involved in making a slander, the speaker, the person slandered, and the audience, adding 'just as in comedy'. The verb used for 'slander' (*diaballein*) is a favourite one in Aristophanes, and Old Comedy was stereotyped by the ancient critics for such abusive personal humour. Elsewhere Lucian calls comedy καλή , 'fine' (*Lexiphanes* 22) and φαιδροτάτη , 'brilliant' (*Dance* 2), comments on the treatment of bad actors in tragedy and comedy (*Nigrinos* 8) and on the gods behaving like extras in comedy (*Ikaromenippos* 9), describes the *kordax* as the typical dance of comedy (*Dance* 26), and refers to comedy's distinctive masks and costumes (*Dance* 29; *Anacharsis* 23, 32; *Saturnalia* 24). For Lucian comedy is linked with the 'laughable' (*geloia*) and the 'satyric', as at *Dionysos* 5, *Twice Accused* 33, *Dance* 68. On several occasions he presents the familiar antithetical pairing of tragedy and comedy (*On Salaried Posts* 30; *Anacharsis* 22, 32; *Dance* 26, *Lexiphanes* 22).

In three important passages Lucian outlines the extent to which comedy has influenced his work, keeping in mind that as with a comic poet we should be careful of taking whatever Lucian says at face value. In *You are Prometheus*, he writes in his own person, while in *Twice Accused* he slightly disguises himself as 'the Syrian' and in *Fisherman* as the 'son of free speech' (Parrhesiades).³ In the first crucial dialogue, *Fisherman*, a 'chorus' of famous philosophers has returned from Hades to take issue with Parrhesiades for his recent work *Lives for Sale*. They summon Philosophy to hear their complaint, who replies (14):

> So you are angry when someone says nasty things about you? Even though you know that despite what Comedy says about me at the Dionysia, I still consider her a friend, and that I have never taken her to court or come up to her and complained? I just let her make her usual jokes that are all part of the festival. For I know that no harm can come from a joke, but just the opposite that anything attractive shines more brightly and appears more brilliant, just like gold by being stamped and coined. I don't see why you lot have become so angry and irritated.

Later Diogenes, speaking for all the philosophers, claims that Parrhesiades has been appealing to the worst instincts of people in his attacks on philosophers (25):

> That's so typical of the general public. They really like those who make jokes and say rude things about people, especially when what is considered very serious [τὰ σεμνότατα] is being made fun of. It's just like long ago when they enjoyed Aristophanes and Eupolis dragging Sokrates here to be insulted on stage and writing some outlandish comedies about him. However, they launched those attacks against just one man and did so with the sanction at the sanctuary of Dionysos [ἐν Διονύσου ἐφιεμένον]. The joke just seemed to be part of the festival, as if 'the god being fond of laughter perhaps enjoyed a joke'.

The reference in both passages to the freedom of the festival makes it clear that Lucian sees his own caricature of current philosophers as belonging to the personally abusive tradition of Old Comedy. Parrhesiades will go on to maintain that, while he has indeed ridiculed contemporary philosophers, what he has said about them is the truth, that they are not worthy of the respect accorded to the great figures of the past standing before him. When he calls these modern degenerates *alazonas* (29), he speaks in the same voice as Dikaiopolis in *Acharnians* or Bdelykleon in *Wasps*.

Strictly speaking, comedy did not confine its philosophic attacks to 'just one man', since Protagoras was very likely a character in Eupolis' *Spongers* (421-D), the chorus of Ameipsias' *Konnos* (423-D) was made up of *phrontistai*, Plato is the most frequent target of fourth-century comedy, Gorgias is mentioned on a couple of occasions (*Wasps* 421, *Birds* 1701), and a character in Eupolis' *Goats* was a sophist named Prodamos. But Sokrates will have attracted most attention through Aristophanes' *Clouds* and the hagiographic writings of Plato, Xenophon, and others. Plato's *Apology* and *Symposium* would have been required reading for any student of philosophy. I have suggested elsewhere that the mentions in both works of Aristophanes' caricature of Sokrates in *Clouds* (*Apology* 18–19, 23; *Symposium* 221b) may explain why later antiquity came to regard Aristophanes as the prime poet of Old Comedy, and not because of an impressive victory-total, which he seems not to have had.[4] The inclusion of Eupolis here is supported by a comment by the scholiast to *Clouds* 96, 'Even if Eupolis mentioned Sokrates only on a few occasions, he still went after him more than Aristophanes in the whole of *Clouds*'. We cannot identify these 'few occasions', but Sokrates would not be out of place in *Spongers*, where Protagoras was a character, or in *Goats*, with its fictional sophist Prodamos, or even *Demes* (as the antagonist of Solon whom antiquity regarded as a 'wise man' as well as a poet and a lawgiver).

In the second crucial work, *Twice Accused*, Lucian, calling himself 'the Syrian', is the defendant in two lawsuits presided over by Justice. In the first the prosecutor is Oratory (*Rhetorikē*) and the charge phrased in terms of a lawful wife deserted by her husband for someone else – see below for the parallels with Kratinos' *Wine-Flask*. The second charge is put in the mouth of Dialogue, the 'someone else' of the first accusation, and has more to do with Lucian's literary offences. Dialogue complains that before he met the Syrian he was 'serious' (*semnon*, the same word used at *Fisherman* 25) and:

> I contemplated the gods and nature and the whole cycle of existence, treading the air high above the clouds, where great Zeus in heaven travels driving his winged chariot. But as I was wheeling above the vault and rising up over the back of heaven, this fellow yanked me down, broke my wings, and placed me on the same footing as everybody else. He snatched away my decent tragic mask and placed another one on me, a comic one, satyr-like, nothing short of ridiculous. Then he took and locked me up with Jest and Iambic and Cynicism, with Aristophanes and Eupolis, terribly clever people at making fun of what is serious and jeering at what is right. Finally he dug up and shoved Menippos in there with me, one of those old dogs, a howler, it seems,

with sharp teeth, a really frightening hound who bites you when you least expect it, because he grins at the same time as he bites. How have I not been horribly abused, since I no longer play my usual part, but act like a comedian or a clown and perform all sorts of strange roles for him?

When Dialogue claims to have been 'treading the air high above the clouds', he is of course alluding to Sokrates' appearance at *Clouds* 225, and it is typical of Lucian's excellent irony to turn Aristophanes' mockery into a more serious claim, combining it with two citations from Plato's *Phaedrus* (246–7).

The influence of Menippos upon Lucian is impossible to assess since we lack any extensive fragments of Menippos and must depend on seven titles cited by Diogenes Laertius (6.29, 99–101), plus two more mentioned by Athenaeus (629f, 664e), as well as the appearance of Menippos in certain of Lucian's dialogue, almost as an alter-ego for Lucian. Helm (1906) argued strongly that Lucian was only a derivative plagiarist of Menippos' satirical sketches and that we can thus use Lucian to recreate the Menippean originals. This view has been thoroughly demolished by McCarthy (1934) and Hall (1981: 64–150), and while he may have taken the combative personality of Menippos and some of his imaginative ideas, Lucian must be seen as a creator of fantasy in his own right. For example, Diogenes Laertius (6.29) records that Menippos wrote a *Sale of Diogenes* in which the philosopher was captured and sold at auction. The reader of Lucian's *Lives for Sale* will readily see how Lucian has taken Menippos' description of a single event and expanded it into a sale of all sorts of philosophers. McCarthy (1934: 55) sums up the case well: 'Lucian is not a revised Menippus. We have every reason to believe his own admission that he did something novel and original when he yoked Dialogue to Comedy'.

The third crucial passage comes from a short essay of self-examination *You are a Literary Prometheus*, where Lucian speaks in his own person to an admirer who has compared him to Prometheus, presumably as a result of his *Prometheus*. After shaking off the possible implications of such a compliment with a good dose of ironic self-mockery, he claims (5–6) that his work is comprised of 'two excellent things, Dialogue and Comedy':

> Certainly Dialogue and Comedy were not at first comfortable companions, since one of them [Dialogue] would pass his time at home by himself or walking with a few others in the covered walkways, while the other [Comedy] gave herself over to Dionysos and would spend her time in the theatre, fooling around, cracking jokes and making fun of people. She would process in rhythmically, sometimes with the *aulos*, ride in on anapaests, and insult

the companions of Dialogue by calling them 'thinksters' and 'airheads' and such like. She had made it her firm conviction to poke fun at them and to drench them with the freedom of the Dionysia, depicting them as walkers on air, hanging out with clouds, measuring the jumps of fleas, and talking in detail about airy affairs.[5]

The absence of Menippos here suggests that while Lucian could and did claim Menippos as an influence, he regarded his real models as (Platonic) dialogue and (Aristophanic) comedy. Lucian wonders if by merging Comedy with Dialogue he has created something monstrous, a *hippokentauros* in fact, and whether he has been deceiving his readers by placing before them 'bones covered in fat', that is comic laughter beneath the seriousness of philosophy.[6]

Whenever Eupolis is mentioned, he is paired with Aristophanes. These two are clearly linked in Lucian's mind as the exponents of Old Comedy, and here Lucian is adopting the familiar stereotype of Old Comedy as essentially a genre of personal abuse. The absence of Kratinos is curious since he was also one of the canonical Three, noted for personal attack in his comedy as well (*Knights* 527, Persius 1.123, Platonios 2). If the only comedies that Lucian knew were *Wine-Flask* and perhaps *Dionysalexandros* (see below), these may not have suggested the same sort of comedy as that of Aristophanes and Eupolis. For Lucian the special targets of Old Comedy were not so much politicians such as Perikles, Kleon, and Hyperbolos, but philosophers, and it is in this aspect that he regards Old Comedy as an important influence on his own work. If Lucian knew about other sorts of Old Comedy, such as the less abusive and more domestic plays of Krates and Pherekrates, he gives no hint in his writings.

In *Anacharsis* 22 Solon explains rather anachronistically and condescendingly the role of drama at Athens:

> When we gather people in the theatre, we teach them publicly through comedy and tragedy by showing them the virtues and failings of people of old, so that they may avoid the latter and turn to the former. We allow the comic poets to engage in insults and poke fun at any of the citizens whom they detect behaving shamefully and unworthily of the city, not just for the sake of the offenders themselves, since they are improved by being reproached, but for the sake of the many so that they may avoid being chastised for behaving the same way.

This last sounds rather like the famous defense of Old Comedy made in the opening lines of Horace's fourth satire (*si quis erat dignus describi . . . multa cum libertate notabant*, 'if anyone deserved to be singled out . . . they pointed him out with great freedom') and Cicero's grudging admission of the value of Greek comedy (*On the Republic* 4.10. F 11):

> Whom did it not touch, rather whom did it not assail? Admittedly it did attack villainous rabble-rousers, who were stirring up trouble in the state, like Kleon or Kleophon or Hyperbolos. Now we might allow that, even though citizens of that sort are better singled out by a censor than by a poet.

Anacharsis is one of Lucian's less engaging works as it maintains a steady course with Anacharsis as the curious stranger and Solon the condescending spokesman, intent on defending the enthusiasm of Athens (indeed of all Greek states) for athletics. It is left to Anacharsis to present a view of drama from the eyes of a stranger (23): it features large and clumsy shoes, ludicrous headpieces (both tragic and comic), loud shouting performers, and a sombre response from the spectators of tragedy.

Lucian's treatment of a classical source is not what we would understand by 'parody' or paratragedy, the careful and systematic use of an original by Aristophanes (*Acharnians* with Euripides' *Telephos*, Kinesias' song at *Birds* 1373–1400 with Bacchylides 5) or Strattis (with Euripides' *Phoenician Women*). In Lucian's *Prometheus*, one of the few places when we may compare Lucian with an extant original, the basic premise is taken from the drama attributed to Aeschylus, but from the outset Lucian makes major changes to the story. For example, the entry party comprises Hephaistos and Prometheus (as in the original), but Hermes from the epilogue of the tragedy replaces Kratos, and Hephaistos, an unwilling participant in the original, is only too happy to find a suitable place to impale the Titan. There are no obvious borrowings in language between the opening scene of the play and Lucian's first chapter, and Prometheus, silent in the original opening scene, engages at once in debate with Hermes and Hephaistos. Zeus' anger for the trick played on him by Prometheus with the sacrifice at Methone (Hesiod *Theogony* 541), not in the tragic version, is here added to the story (3) together with the theft of fire. This allows Lucian to create a two-pronged accusation, very much like that in *Twice Accused*, with Hephaistos accusing Prometheus for stealing fire and Hermes for the deceptive sacrifice and the creation of humanity. Prometheus' lengthy defence (7–19) does borrow from Prometheus' speech to the chorus at lines 436–506, but on the whole Lucian has taken an idea from a well-known classical play, moved the characters around, inserted a lengthy trial scene (5–19), made an allusion to the secret that he keeps (21) for which Zeus will owe him a favor, and then comically bursts the bubble in response to Hermes' question 'what favor?' by saying 'You know Thetis, don't you, Hermes? But I must say no more'.

Accordingly when we suspect the influence of a comedy on one of Lucian's fictions, we should not expect a close adherence to an original, but rather an idea that he has found in comedy and expanded for his own humorous purposes. Lucian is especially fond of scenes of verbal exchange, with ideas and arguments developed, accusations made and defenses offered, and often a formal trial in which issues are debated and resolved. All the passages cited above, where Lucian outlines his debt to comedy and dialogue, are set in the context of a debate or trial. Thus when we examine a possible link between a dialogue by Lucian and a classical comedy, we should be on the lookout for places where Lucian has expanded the original idea and added scenes of debate or exposition. Furthermore, it will be dangerous to assume from what Lucian has created in his fictional adaptation that there was something similar in the original comic text or that we can use Lucian to reconstruct confidently a lost play by Eupolis or a lost dialogue by Menippos.

In *Twice Accused* Lucian (calling himself 'the Syrian, a *logographos*') is defending himself against two prosecutions, the first by Oratory (*Rhetorikē*) presenting herself (27–9) as a wronged wife who has been responsible for the success of her husband's career. The Syrian, she alleges, has conceived a strong passion (ὑπεραγαπήσας μάλα ἐρωτικῶς) for an older man, Dialogue the alleged son of Philosophy. Scholars have long recognized that behind this scene lies Kratinos' comedy *Wine-Flask* (423-D),[7] in which Kratinos responded to the caricature of him by Aristophanes at *Knights* 526–36 (424-L) that Kratinos, formerly a brilliant writer of comedy, has now succumbed to the effects of senility and drink and is thus past his comic prime. In *Wine-Flask* Kratinos made himself his own main character, married to Comedy whom he has abandoned for a mistress, Methe (Drunkenness). We have twenty-three fragments (around thirty-five lines) and a partial summary at Σ *Knights* 400:

> He wrote a play, *Wine-Flask*, against himself and Drunkenness with the following plot. Kratinos portrayed Comedy as his wife, that she wished to stop living with him and accordingly launched a lawsuit against him for abusive treatment (*kakōsis*). Friends of Kratinos happened by and asking the cause of her enmity begged her not to do anything rash. She blamed him because he no longer wrote comedy, but spent his time with Drunkenness.

The parallels between *Wine-Flask* and chapters 27–9 are clear: a literary genre personified as the rejected wife (Comedy, Oratory), the central figure appearing in a first-person role (Kratinos, 'the Syrian'), a romantic triangle in which the central figure abandons his wife for a third person, a charge of abuse (*kakōsis*) brought by the wife, and a defense by the central character of himself and his art.[8]

But Lucian makes substantial changes to Kratinos' comedy. It is very likely that Methe appeared as a character in the comedy, probably as a non-speaking one.[9] If so, she would have resembled one of those attractive women who appear in Aristophanes as objects of male excitement: Diallage in *Lysistrata*, Opora and Theoria in *Peace*. She would have been younger than Kratinos and sexually appealing. Dialogue on the other hand is clearly described as bearded and soberly dressed, and above all an older male.[10] Lucian will thus have made a nice switch by making the Syrian the younger partner in male-male relationship.[11] Kratinos' life with Methe is clearly one of licentious abandon; the Syrian's new life is anything but. But the Syrian in his speeches of defense points out that Oratory was anything but a sober and dignified wife; she was in fact besieged by drunken lovers seeking her favors. Furthermore, he alleges, Dialogue has only been improved by his association with the Syrian. Associating with Jest and Iambus and comic poets and Menippos has made him easier to live with. *Wine-Flask* may have provided Lucian with his inspiration, but he has taken considerable liberties with his original.

What has not been noticed is that material from *Wine-Flask* occurs in an earlier scene of the dialogue, specifically in the accusation for kidnapping (*andrapodismos*) (13–18) launched by Drunkenness (Methe) against the Academy (Akadameia). Since several recent studies have shown that *Knights* 526–36, *Wine-Flask*, and *Wasps* are part of an ongoing intertextual and metatheatrical exchange between Kratinos and Aristophanes,[12] especially over the theme of drunken behavior and quality of poetry, Lucian's comparing the would-be prosecutors to a swarm of wasps (13) may be pointing his reader to a comic source. When Methe is invited to give the speech for the prosecution but cannot proceed, Justice asks Hermes to ascertain the cause of her silence.[13] Apparently the effects of drink have affected her tongue and her ability to stand upright, but she asks Academy to speak both the case for the prosecution and that for the defence. This reminds one of *Wasps* 944–9 where the defendant Laches cannot speak and Bdelykleon must speak in his place.[14]

This lawsuit concerns the Athenian philosopher Polemon (*PAA* 776720 – head of the Academy, 315–270), who used to consort with Methe, but who through association with the Academy has become a totally different person. The description of the old Polemon (16), 'who every day would revel in the centre of the *agora*, with a dancing-girl and singing from dawn to dusk, always drunk and headachy, with flowers in his hair', fits well with Kratinos in the grip of Methe and with the behavior of Philokleon in the closing scenes of *Wasps*. In chapter 16 'drinking water' as something pejorative picks up the theme of F 203 ('no-one can accomplish anything great by drinking water'), a sentiment assigned to Kratinos at Horace *Epistles* 19.1–3. Points of contact between chapter 16 and the comic description of Kratinos at *Knights* 526–36 include garlands – *Knights* 534; thirst – *Knights* 534; 'having forgotten all his songs' – 'losing the strings of his lyre' at Knights 533; and the verb ληρεῖν at *Knights* 536. More than one recent critic has concluded that the second part of *Wine-Flask*, as in Lucian probably a formal trial-scene, will have not contained a recantation by Kratinos of his association with Methe, but a justification that wine is essential for poetic success (F 203).[15] We can perhaps see in Methe's arguments as delivered by Academy hints of that defense. The choice of Polemon is an interesting one, for Diogenes Laertius (4.16–20), citing *Lives* by Antigonos of Karystos, describes his youthful dissolution, complete with garlands, and his drunken entry into the Academy, where he meets Xenokrates and undergoes a life-changing conversion to philosophy. Antigonos adds significantly that Polemon in his younger days had been sued by his wife for *kakōsis*.

Lucian then has taken from *Wine-Flask* a romantic triangle involving a first-person character and two rivals for his affection, and used them in two different contexts in *Twice Accused*. The second (26–9) gives itself away by the obvious wife-husband-lover relationship, but the attentive readers who know their Old Comedy will, I suggest, recognize the allusions to *Wasps*, *Knights*, and *Wine-Flask* (especially with the revealing name, Methe) and be pleasantly surprised when the material recurs later in the dialogue. We also see how inventive Lucian can be, turning the third party into an older male, replacing Kratinos with the later philosopher Polemon, undercutting the character of Oratory, and having the Academy speak for both the prosecution and the defense. But as Rosen (2000: 35) observes, what remains is the frequent theme of the poet as the underdog who pleads what some might see as a losing case and yet triumphs in the end.

In light of this example from *Twice Accused*, we may turn to some other dialogues where a possible Old Comic source has been or may be suspected. We are not looking for a close intertextual relationship, but for places where a comic original may have been adopted and adapted for use by Lucian. A first example will be *Fisherman*, which begins by mixing quotations from comedy, epic, and tragedy.[16] The opening words seem straight out of an Aristophanic comedy[17]:

> Stone him, stone the damned fellow with lots and lots of rocks. Throw on some clods of earth as well and add some broken pottery also. Beat the cursed man with your sticks. Make sure that he doesn't get away.

Acharnians 4.16–20 is perhaps the closest example here, since the 'cursed man', Lucian as Parrhesiades, will demand and receive a hearing from the hostile chorus of dead philosophers, although *Wasps* and *Birds* also feature the same confrontation of character and chorus.[18] The philosophers have obtained a leave of absence from the Underworld for one day to deal with Parrhesiades' comments about them, most notably in his recent work, *Lives for Sale*, in which he has depicted an auction of various philosophic lives. Comedy, satyr-play, and tragedy were all fond of using scenes either going to the world of the dead or coming from there.[19] *Demes* would certainly be one's first choice,[20] although in that comedy only four political figures came back from the dead to right affairs at Athens, and we do not know whether they came of their own initiative or were summoned (or fetched) by a live Athenian who needed their help. Sidwell points out that the word used at *Fisherman* 30 *nomothetas* is that used in Platonios 2 to describe the four returned leaders.[21] Other visitors from Hades in Lucian are Menippos in the dialogue of that title, who went down as a younger man and has now returned, and Charon, who like the philosophers has obtained a day-pass from the Underworld.

As noted above, Philosophy compares Lucian's attacks on contemporary philosophers to the caricatures in Comedy at the Dionysia (14), and 'Diogenes' (25) includes Parrhesiades in the company of Aristophanes and Eupolis for their making fun of Sokrates. Like Philosophy he has to admit that this joking was part of the festival tradition. Finally Parrhesiades insists that he is not attacking 'true philosophers' (37), but only those pretenders (*alazonas*) who are hated by the gods. These he will not stop refuting (*dielengchōn*) and making fun of (*komōidōn*).[22] Anderson argues that several of Lucian's works (*Fisherman, Timon, Cock, Symposium, Ikaromenippos*) are based structurally on plays of Old Comedy.[23] He divides these dialogues into Introduction (– prologue), Central Debate (three phases each followed by an interlude – the actual *agon* being the third phase), and a series of scenes exposing imposters or intruders, usually four in number. On the likely assumption that each of the Four in *Demes* had a scene with an appropriate adversary – we have that between Aristeides and a *sykophantes* at Eupolis F 99.78–120 – this was a comedy with four impostors exposed. The dismissal of the philosophers after a successful mission by Philosophy (52) does resemble the honoring of the Four in *Demes* (F 131).

In chapter 44 Philosophy proposes to put all the sham philosophers on trial, to be judged by her along with Virtue and Truth. When at this point all the charlatans flee the Acropolis in fear, Parrhesiades devises a plan, certainly in the style of Old Comedy, to lure them back. He borrows a fishing-rod and line from a nearby shrine, baits the hook with figs and gold, and casts out from the Acropolis. He manages to hook and land four sorts of philosophers, each with an appropriate fish connection: *kyon* (dog-fish) for the Cynics, a *hypoplatys* (flat-fish) for the Platonists, a fish with golden stripes for the decorated dress of the Peripatetics, and spiny sea-urchins for the Stoics. The use of puns and the personification of fish immediately suggests Archippos' *Fishes* as a source,[24] also the fact that the three fish mentioned at the start of chapter 48 can be found in the fragments of *Fishes*: *labrax* – F 23, *chrysophrys* – F 18, *galeos* – F 15, 23. The chorus in *Birds* makes much of their physical mistreatment by humans (333–5, 369–70, 1072–87), and we know that a later scene in *Fishes* featured as part of the new pact between humans and fishes the handing over of the glutton Melanthios to be eaten by the latter. Can we imagine an early fishing scene in *Fishes* that might be the original of Lucian's scene here? Alternatively we do not know how the return of the Four was staged in *Demes*. Some have suggested a debate scene in the Underworld, others a necromancy. Keeping in mind the offering of blood in *Odyssey* 11 to draw up the spirits of the dead, I wonder if some enticement was offered to draw up the Four, perhaps by casting through the open door in the *skēnē* front.[25]

Lucian is at his best with his lighter sketches about gods behaving badly, such as *Dialogues of the Gods* and *Judgement of the Goddesses*. The latter retells as a dramatic dialogue the famous Judgement of Paris involving a golden apple and three goddesses (Hera, Athena, Aphrodite), each set on winning that prize for beauty. Lucian's sketch begins with Zeus commissioning Hermes to take the goddesses to Paris, an attractive Trojan shepherd-prince with a reputation for being 'well-versed about sex', continues with some by-play during the aerial descent into Mount Ida, and then the actual judgement itself, the prize awarded as in the traditional myth to Aphrodite. The story of the Judgement goes back to the *Cypria* and was a mainstay of both classical myth and art. But engaged as we are on a search for comic influences upon Lucian, we wonder if he knew and used one of the best-known (to us) of all the lost plays of Old Comedy, Kratinos' *Dionysalexandros*, of which *P. Oxy.* 661 presents a good portion of the plot-summary, including this early section of the drama:

> ...judgement, Hermes leaves, while they [the chorus of satyrs] say some things to the spectators about the poets. They joke and make fun of Dionysus when he appears. When [the goddesses and Hermes arrive] and [make promises] to him: from Hera unshaken tyranny, from Athena success in war, and Aphrodite that he be as beautiful and sexually attractive as possible, he judges her [Aphrodite] to be the winner.

The thirteen fragments of the comedy provide about only fifteen lines of text, and nothing in these resonates with Lucian's narration, except for the word *boukoloi* in F 49 (– chapters 1, 7) and the presence of Hermes.[26] But Paris' request to see them all in the nude could certainly come from a comedy, perhaps Hermes' incentive or Dionysos' own libidinous nature showing through (cf. *Frogs* 53–4, 413–15, 740). Certainly attractive and naked female figures can be found throughout Old Comedy. But without any substantial remains of Kratinos' comic scene, we can say only that if Lucian knew Kratinos' comedy – he did know *Wine-Flask* – it would have made an attractive and obvious source.[27]

The final dialogue that I wish to consider is the difficult and sometimes impenetrable *Lexiphanes*, in which Lucian presents himself in the dialogue under his most common pseudonym, Lykinos.[28] The title character, bearing a *nom parlant* worthy of Old Comedy, is a sophist afflicted with verbal edema (17) and a desire to outdo the proponents of the Attic revival in speech and vocabulary – cf. chapter 25 'in your desire to be hyperattic you have honed your speech to a most old-fashioned point'. Lexiphanes admits in the opening chapter that he has created an 'anti-Symposium', clearly having Plato's landmark dialogue in mind.[29] What we get in his recitation (chapters 2–15) is a mixture of difficult and at times artificial vocabulary, some terms being now obsolete and forgotten, others Lexiphanes' own inventions, and others that can be misunderstood with humorous results. In a couple of places we get a cluster of words that are either solely or mostly comic, as in the gastronomic delights of chapter 6: ὀκλαδίαι καὶ ἀσκάνται ('folding-stools and pallets'), σχελίδες καὶ ἠτριαία ('sides of beef and tripe'), ἐκ ταγήνου ('from the saucepan'), μυττωτός καὶ ἀβυρτάκη ('savoury and sour sauce'), σελάχια ('fish without scales'), a foretaste of what Athenaeus would do in the next century with his *Deipnosophistai*.[30] Also the opening of chapter 12 contains a piece of invective that does credit to Aristophanes and his fellow poets of Old Comedy:

> 'Μῶν ἐκεῖνον', ἦν δ' ἐγώ, 'φὴς Δίωνα τὸν καταπύγονα καὶ λακκοσχέαν, τὸν μύρτωνα καὶ σχινοτρώκταν νεανίσκον, ἀναφλῶντα καὶ βλιμάζοντα, ἤν τινα πεώδη καὶ πόσθωνα αἴσθηται; μίνθων ἐκεῖνός γε καὶ λαικαλέος'.

> I said, 'Do you perhaps mean Dion the arse-bandit with the sack-sized scrotum, the toothpick-chewing young sex fiend, who jerks off and squeezes himself, when he sees a penis or a prick? There's a really active fucker for you'.

Two other references in chapter 8 might direct the reader's attention to comedy. The participle ὑπερπαφλάζων, meaning 'seethe over' should also recall Paphlagon-Kleon at *Knights* 919, and the verb εἰσεκύκλησε which describes the entry of the female entertainers the practice of wheeling dramatic characters on stage. The last part of *Lexiphanes* features a scene with the title character vomiting up his outlandish vocabulary, and here we might wonder about a connection with *Acharnians* with the reference to Kleon vomiting up the five talents (*Ach.* 5–6) and Dikaiopolis' pretending to spew at the fearsome sight of Lamachos (*Ach.* 585–6). The unusual word in chapter 24 *thymalōps* ('charcoal ember') is known principally in comedy (*Ach.* 321, *Thesm.* 729, Strattis F 58).

At the start of chapter 16 an exasperated Lykinos interrupts the flow of verbiage and in good dramatic fashion calls attention to the approach of Sopolis the doctor. Sopolis effects a humorous purge of Lexiphanes' verbal excesses in a scene which could have come from Old Comedy. We know that the cook would become a stereotypical character in Greek comedy, e.g. Sikon in Menander's *Dyskolos* and *Samia*, and Lamachos in *Acharnians* is already the braggart soldier of later comedy. There are mentions of the contemporary doctor Pittalos at *Acharnians* 1032, 1222 and *Wasps* 1432, and experts of all sorts can enter for their brief scene in the surviving comedies (poets such as Agathon and Kinesias, musicians like Chairis and Phrynis, the city-planner Meton, Hierokles the oracle-monger). It is not a long step to imagine a humorous comic episode with a doctor, either an *alazon* himself or a straight-man entering to cure someone on stage. Anderson has pointed out that Lexiphanes is vomiting up odd and curious expressions, identified by Lykinos much like Elenchos in *Fisherman* as Parrhesiades reels in the philosopher-fishes.[31] If I am right that this latter scene is based on a lost comedy, the same might be said for the equivalent scene in *Lexiphanes*.

Some have tried to find real contemporaries beneath the comic characters of Lexiphanes and Sopolis, Baldwin proposing to identify Sopolis in this dialogue as Galen.[32] But I would look in another direction. The name 'Sopolis' sounds suggestively like that of Eupolis' father, Sosipolis (*Suda* ε 3657) and I propose that Lucian is directing the careful reader's attention to this comic poet as his source.[33] So we are looking for a comedy by Eupolis with a scene, probably in the latter part of the play, involving a doctor inducing a character to vomit. The comic text may not have had that character vomiting up words or phrases, although we do find in comedy the dismissive comments on the language of youthful would-be *rhetores* at *Knights* 1375–81 and a similar passage at F 205 (*Banqueters*). Lucian is perfectly capable of taking a scene with a doctor inducing a character to vomit and turning it into the cure for Lexiphanes' swollen and abstruse vocabulary. We know that in *Demes* the four returned leaders (Solon, Miltiades, Aristeides, Perikles) put things right at Athens, but it is hard to see how any of these scenes would have required a doctor's expertise. If we want a comedy with a philosophic theme, then *Spongers* with Protagoras and perhaps Sokrates as characters might suggest itself. But I wonder if Lucian has left a clue earlier in *Lexiphanes*. In chapter 4 the speaker Philinos urges haste in going to the baths καὶ δέος μὴ ἐν λουτρίῳ ἀπολουσώμεθα κατόπιν τῶν Καριμάντων μετὰ τοῦ σύρφακος βύζην ὠστιζόμενοι ('and there is the danger that at the baths we may be bathing after the Karimantians, jostled along by a crowd of riff-raff'). For the otherwise unknown Karimantians, Meineke suggested the reading Γαριμάντων, but MacLeod prefers Μαρικάντων, based on the entry in Hesychios (μ 283) that 'Marikas' is a foreign nickname for a male child and is synonymous with *kinaidos* ('faggot', though no English term fits the semantic range of the Greek word). Reading 'after the *marikantes*' makes good sense of the context of the bathhouse and perhaps points us in the direction of Eupolis' *Marikas*. With the aid of a fragmentary commentary (F 192) we can reconstruct a fair bit of the first part of that comedy (a double chorus of rich men and poor men, at least one combat between Marikas-Hyperbolos and an adversary from the rich and famous, and the presence of a master to adjudicate), but the latter part is wide open and could have had a scene with a doctor attending to Hyperbolos or his mother. There are hints that Marikas-Hyperbolos came to a bad end in the comedy (F 209).[34] We know also from F 192.135–6 that Kleon was mentioned in *Marikas* with the participle παφλάζων – see my remarks above. If this reconstruction is right, then we have another instance where Lucian takes a memorable scene from a comedy and adapts it for his purpose.

In his study of Lucian's knowledge and citation of classical authors, Anderson comes to the aggressive conclusion that 'as far as learning is concerned he travelled light'; he points out that many of the allusions to older works 'are suspiciously near the beginning of their respective texts', the implications being first that the first part of a scroll is easier to unroll and second that Lucian did not bother to read any further.[35] In his opinion many of the quotations are due to 'double-borrowings' (e.g. his references to Stesichoros' *Palinode* at *Apology* 1 and *Images* 15 are essentially what Plato says at *Phaidros* 243–4), to collections of tags and familiar quotations, and to material gathered in learned handbooks. As for drama Anderson admits that Lucian may have read the standard plays of Aristophanes, but 'it is not safe to assume that . . . Lucian was widely read in lost Comedy and Tragedy' (66). In Anderson's view Lucian's knowledge of Eupolis was not first-hand and suspects Lucian of saying 'Aristophanes and Eupolis' when he means 'Aristophanes' (64). He knew from popular knowledge that *Demes* featured the return of well-known Athenians from the dead, and his citation of F 102 is due to its becoming 'a tag', at least the line about Persuasion sitting on a speaker's lips. Anderson is on weaker ground with the reference to *Dyers* (*Baptai*) at *Against the Ignorant Book Collector* 27, for this play was known for the presence of a wild goddess Kotyto, a chorus of effeminate worshippers, and something that offended Alkibiades. When Lucian asks if the collector has read right through to the end and 'did nothing of what you read there get through to you?' this suggests first-hand acquaintance rather than a scholar's crib-sheet. In *Birds* the name and description of Cloudcuckooland, mentioned at *True History* 1.29, do not occur until the second half of the comedy. Unless we want to assume that Lucian was basing his description on received knowledge and the significance of the name, Lucian must have read well into this comedy.

Anderson does well to prune the over-optimistic lists of Lucian's citations by Householder (1941) and Bompaire (1958). But he assumes the minimum position, that someone who quotes 'something is rotten in the state of Denmark' (*Hamlet* I.4) did not go on to read the whole play or was using the ancient equivalent of *The Oxford Dictionary of Quotations*. The instances that I have outlined above suggest rather that Lucian had read certain of the lost plays. Unless he had access only to the sources that produced Σ *Knights* 400, he knows what went on in Kratinos' *Wine-Flask* well enough to mine that comedy in two scenes of *Twice Accused*. The use of *Demes* in *Fisherman* is less obvious,[36] but *Demes* was probably the best-known comedy after the extant plays of Aristophanes and the sort of play to have attracted readers. Both Plutarch and Aelius Aristeides know and cite details from it. Its inclusion on the Cairo Papyrus (F 99) shows that scribes were still copying *Demes* at the very end of the classical age. If I am right in proposing that the original of the scene with Doctor Sopolis comes from Eupolis' *Marikas*, then Lucian knew that play well enough to make an allusion to *marikantes* as *kinaidoi* (6), to lay down a reference to Kleon-Paphlagon (8), and to extract the doctor's scene at the end. *Marikas* would also have been an accessible comedy. F 192 reveals the existence of an ancient commentary to the play, and the accusation by a supposedly aggrieved Aristophanes at *Clouds* 553 that *Marikas* was plagiarised from *Knights* would have made it the sort of comedy that devotees of Aristophanes would go on to read. Anderson does admit that Lucian did know the standard works of Aristophanes – I can detect allusions to and borrowings from *Acharnians, Clouds, Wasps, Birds,* and *Wealth* (this last in *Timon*).[37] To these I would add a direct knowledge of Kratinos' *Wine-Flask*, and *Marikas, Dyers,* and *Demes* by Eupolis.

It is true, however, that Lucian does not quote or parody his sources, but adapts them often significantly to create his satirical fictions. We cannot use Lucian to say with confidence what was in a lost comedy. We should expect variation and expansion rather than parody, and this is especially true in terms of Lucian's favorite themes of rhetorical flourish and philosophic debate. He has taken the serious form of the Platonic dialogue, added in the Cynical bite of

Menippos, and made good use of the freedom and imagination of Old Comedy. Sokrates, Aristophanes, and Menippos had one thing in common with Lucian – they all sought the truth, hated frauds, and liked nothing better than exposing these impostors.

Notes

1 Mitscherling 2003 examines Plato's use of 'the comic poet' and concludes that at *Apology* 18d 'the comic poet' is probably Aristophanes, but at *Phaedo* 70b–c and 91c it is more likely to be Eupolis.
2 Bergk ap. Edmonds 1957: 44-7, Gargiulo 1992, and Sidwell 2005: 3-4 favour Eupolis' *Golden Race* as the source. Edmonds and *PCG* VIII 461 rightly include it among the *adespota*.
3 Several critics associate *parrhēsia* with the freedom afforded the comic poets, but the word in Old Comedy occurs only at *Thesm.* 541, of the freedom to speak in an assembly, which is its usual association in fifth-century texts. It was also a key term of the Cynics – see Diogenes Laertius 6.69, who quotes Diogenes that the finest thing for men is *parrhēsia*. For Lucian's concept of *parrhēsia* see Branham 1989: 32–4, 229 n. 47.
4 Storey 2003: 3–4.
5 Hopkinson 2008: 116 finds a number of sexual innuendoes in this picture of Comedy. She is not the good wife of Kratinos' *Wine-Flask*, but more like Music in Pherekrates F 155 (*Chiron*), the *hetaira* with exponents of the New Music as her lovers.
6 On the *hippokentauros* as a repeated metaphor for Lucian's work see Hopkinson 2008: 110–11.
7 Hirzel 1896: 302–3, Kaibel ap. *PCG* IV p. 219, also Sidwell 2014: 268–9.
8 Marshall 2012 argues that the triangular relationship between Kratinos, Comedy, and Drunkenness in *Wine-Flask* lies behind the Daphne Mosaic (AD 250–270), where Menander is portrayed with Comedy and his mistress Glykera.
9 On this issue see Bakola 2010: 281–5.
10 Lucian may have taken up an idea in *Wine-Flask* as scholars have concluded from the masculine forms in F 195 that Kratinos' new life also involved attractive younger boys.
11 The appearance of Alkibiades in Plato's *Symposium* as unfulfilled lover of the older Sokrates could well have been the model here.
12 See especially Sidwell 1995, Rosen 2000, Biles 2009: 134–66, and Bakola 2010: 59–64.
13 Comic parallels here would include Hermes speaking for Peace at *Peace* 665–725 and for the goddesses in Kratinos' *Dionysalexandros*.
14 The three allowed actors are already taking the roles of Philokleon, Bdelykleon, and Kyon.

15 Norwood 1931: 116–18, Rosen 2000: 32–5, Biles 2009: 146–54, and Bakola 2010: 284–5.
16 A similar combination occurs at the opening of *Tragic Zeus*, where Hermes quotes comedy, Athena epic, and Hera refuses to take the third role, that of tragedy.
17 At *Dyskolos* 83–5 and 110–11 Pyrrhias describes being pelted with stones and clods of earth, but the action occurs off-stage and he is not interacting with a hostile chorus. For this reason Lucian's 'source' is more likely to be Old Comedy.
18 Both Hall 1981: 156 and Branham 1989: 33 accept *Acharnians* as Lucian's source. See also Helm 1906: 299.
19 Going: Aristophanes' *Frogs*, *Gerytades*; Pherekrates' *Tiddlers*, *Miners*. Coming: Eupolis' *Demes*, Kratinos' *Chirons*, perhaps Phormion in Eupolis' *Officers*; Aeschylus' *Persians*, Euripides' *Hecuba*.
20 So accepted by Hall 1981: 143, MacLeod 1991: 259, and Sidwell 2009. Helm 1906: 297 sees *Demes* as providing the impetus for Lucian's *Charon*.
21 Sidwell 2009: 112.
22 The verb *elenchein* is a crucial one for Lucian. It appears in the title *Zeus Confronted* (*Elenchomenos*) and Elenchos personified is an investigator at the end of *Fisherman*.
23 Anderson 1976a: 141–9.
24 For this comedy see Storey 2012.
25 Helm 1906: 304–5 finds other references to fish-as-men at *Knights* 313, Pherekrates F 117, and in certain of *Lampoons* (*Silloi*) by Timon of Phlius, satirical sketches of various philosophers (F 30, 32, 52).
26 In the opening scene of *Tragic Zeus* Hermes is associated specifically with Comedy.
27 Recent studies include Storey 2006, Wright 2007, and Bakola 2010: 82–102, 181–208, 272–94.
28 The only major study of *Lexiphanes* is that of Hall 1981: 279–91.
29 Lucian's own *Symposium*, also based on Plato's work, is a dystopian presentation of how men without manners and graces would behave at a supposedly elegant gathering.
30 On this passage see Baldwin 1973: 50–2.
31 Anderson 1976a: 107.
32 Baldwin 1973: 36–40. MacLeod 1991: 10 leans to supporting this identification. See also the comments of Anderson 1976a: 41–2 and Hall 1981: 543 n. 44.
33 Sosipolis ('City-Saver') may have been the real name of Eupolis' father or at some point in his plays Eupolis claimed to be 'the son of City-Saver'. Saving the city was a repeated claim by the poets in Old Comedy – see Storey 2011.
34 Sonnino 1997 argues that no one dies in Old Comedy and that Marikas-Hyperbolos may have been badly treated (or so threatened) but not killed.
35 Anderson 1976b: 66 and 59.
36 Sidwell 2009 makes the strongest case.
37 For the direct influence of *Wealth* upon Lucian's *Timon* see Hopkinson: 161–2, who argues that Lucian's Timon owes much to Menander's Knemon in *Dyskolos*.

10

Revoking Comic License: Aristides' *Or.* 29 and the Performance of Comedy

Anna Peterson

The Second Sophistic (*c.*100–230 CE) witnessed a revival of interest in the tradition of Greek comedy both in its own right and as a contested genre.[1] In literary circles, the educated elite debated the superiority of Aristophanes and Menander, with the latter drawing particular praise for his educational value and suitability for sympotic recitation.[2] Plutarch, for example, considers Menander the only comic poet worth watching and as important to a symposium as wine itself (*Moralia* 854b and 712b). In comparison, Aristophanes attracted his own fans, most notably Lucian, who makes the comic poet's free speech a significant component of his own biting satire.[3] Archaeological evidence adds to this picture by suggesting that comedy was not only studied and recited, but also written and performed.[4] Although often opaque, this evidence runs the gambit from possible admission tokens to inscriptions recording victories of revived comedies and new plays.[5] Imperial audiences, as Bowie hypothesizes, likely preferred the comedic style of Menander, while Aristophanes' popularity was restricted to the writings of the Atticizing literati.[6] Yet from this intriguing collection of evidence a curious pattern emerges: although both Aristophanes and Menander had their proponents in educated circles, this range of comedic preferences seems not to have fully translated to the actual stage.[7]

In this chapter, I explore a single piece of this puzzle that approaches comedy and the question of its performance from a surprisingly negative perspective, namely Aristides' call to ban the genre in *Or.* 29.[8] Delivered at Smyrna sometime between 157 and 165 CE, *Or.* 29 demands the removal of comic performances from the city's Dionysia on the grounds that their slanderous humor, once a hallmark of Old Comedy, defames religious worship and damages the reputation of the city.[9] Aristides, as it appears, attacks Smyrna's comic poets for reverting to that theatrical practice, suggesting a similarity between past and present comedic styles. In the first section, I examine two inscriptions that hint at a performance tradition of re-staging plays of Old Comedy and composing new ones in its mold. This evidence, although admittedly scant, raises the possibility that the influence of Old Comedy extended beyond the writings of the literary elite. Moreover, it provokes a rethinking of *Or.* 29 as an argument directed at actual comic practices of second-century Smyrna and their debt to Old Comedy's slanderous style of humor.

Aristides further corroborates a connection between Smyrna's plays and Old Comedy by attacking them through the revival of traditional arguments made against the genre, notably those expressed by Plato in the *Republic* and *Laws*. In the second section, I examine how Aristides' reworking of Platonic arguments complements larger rhetorical trends within his corpus, a feature of the speech that has thus far been overlooked. As the oration makes clear, Aristides directs his concerns not to the entire populace of Smyrna, but specifically to the city's *pepaideumenoi* or educated elite. I argue that Aristides capitalizes on Smyrna's comic stage as a point of entry to a larger rhetorical goal: to unite *logos* and the art of oratory with religious concerns and, therefore, to imbue the *pepaideumenoi* with a new, religious significance.[10]

Aristides' concern in *Or.* 29 with unchecked comic ridicule invites direct comparison with Old Comedy and challenges modern assumptions about what may or may not have been on the imperial stage. Scholars have generally resisted this comparison, with Nervegna rejecting outright the idea that Aristides has in mind plays from his own time.[11] Others have offered alternate interpretations for the performances described in this speech. Behr, for example, posits that they represent a 'general form of public satire', while Jones raises the possibility that Aristides decries comedies akin to the pseudo-Lucianic *Gout* and *Swift-of-Foot*.[12] These readings, however, overlook the formal performance context described by Aristides and the slanderous humor that comes to define Smyrna's comedies in *Or.* 29.[13] This chapter argues that the comparison to Old Comedy is central to the rhetorical aim of this speech and that it need not be read as a declamation, replaying a debate from the distant past, for this to be the case. Contemporary comic performances become for Aristides a vehicle for considering the broader question of what proper religious practice means for the educated elite. Through its attempts to refashion the audience as proper religious devotees, *Or.* 29 bears a closer relationship to the broader theme of religiosity that pervades Aristides' corpus than has previously been recognized.

I. Performance

Aristides likens Smyrna's comedies to those of Old Comedy through their performance context, use of choruses, and, most significantly, *ad hominem* style of humor. These comedies, as Aristides tells us, are performed as part of a theatrical competition (29.13 ἀγών) during Smyrna's Dionysia, which Behr interprets to be the equivalent of the Anthesteria in Athens.[14] Although Aristides records no specifics about plots or characters, he does indicate that these plays included choruses, whose songs, to his great displeasure, continue to be sung by women and slaves in the baths, streets and marketplaces (29.30). Furthermore, he repeatedly decries the slander (κακηγορία), personal abuse (λοιδορία) and blasphemy (βλασφημία) of these plays, common terminology for the *aischrologia* or aischrology associated with Old Comedy.[15] By singling out the tendency of Smyrna's comic poets to shame through laughter, Aristides situates himself within the broader anxiety found in Greek culture over this kind of humor.[16] It is this feature of Smyrna's comedies that poses the greatest threat to the city. A city, as Aristides contends, is only as good as its private citizens and the public mocking of them endangers that city's reputation. While Athens is honored for nearly all the literature it produced, comedy alone continues to provide opportunities for its detractors to attack it (29.27). Aristides here equates the two comic periods specifically in terms of the threat they pose to the cities that produced them.

That the anxiety *Or.* 29 expresses is anything more than a pretext for an academic argument has been called into question based on the presumption that New Comedy remained the prevalent comic model of the time. According to this reading of the speech, *Or.* 29 is a declamation, depicting a fanciful perspective of a bygone age, similar to that found in Aristides' Sicilian and Leuctran orations.[17] As models for Aristides' declamations, the Leuctran and Sicilian orations are 'elaborate historical' pieces.[18] In the Leuctran orations (*Or.* 11–15), for example, Aristides re-imagines the debate in 370 BCE between the supporters of Thebes, those of Sparta and those arguing for maintaining Athens' neutrality. Similarly, the Sicilian orations (*Or.* 5–6) replay the debate held by the Athenian assembly in 414 BCE regarding Nicias' request either for reinforcements or the recall of the Sicilian expedition. If we take these speeches as models, *Or.* 29 differs from them in two important respects. First, it is a single speech and therefore offers only one point of view on the question of comedy. In comparison, the Leuctran and Sicilian orations offer competing arguments in five and two speeches respectively. Second, and more significantly, *Or.* 29 does not maintain a fiction of being set in the past, which is a general trait of Aristides' declamations, a group that also includes the *Embassy to Achilles* (*Or.* 16). Instead, Aristides' evocation of Old Comedy in *Or.* 29 makes a clear distinction between the earlier comedic style and that of the present.

Given the fact that *Or.* 29's contemporary focus would seem to preclude classifying the speech as a declamation, there remains the question of whether the plays described by Aristides imitated to some degree the model of Old Comedy. Aristides, in fact, signals only one difference between contemporary comedies and their Old Comic predecessors: the absence of a parabasis (29.28). Although Old Comedy may endanger Athens' reputation, Aristides nevertheless lauds its parabases for the 'admonition and education' (29.28 νουθεσία καὶ παίδευσις) they offered the city, notably a view of the parabasis that equates it to the purpose of Aristides' own speech.[19] In contrast, he labels Smyrna's comedies as 'counterfeits' (29.28 κιβδηλίας). Despite the fact that Aristophanes' own *Ecclesiazusae* and *Wealth* lack a parabasis (in the versions that are preserved), Jones cites the stress Aristides places on its absence from Smyrna's plays as evidence against a comparison with Old Comedy.[20] This reading, however, misses the direct comparison that this statement invites. Aristides' point here is not that Smyrna's plays are a completely different form of comedy, which would render Aristides' complaint about the parabasis' absence redundant, but that Smyrna's comedies masquerade themselves as poor imitations of the original. Instead of discounting a connection to Old Comedy, Aristides' complaint in fact emphasizes one. If Aristides is describing actual performances, and I suggest he is, then the comparison he draws to Old Comedy presents an alternate perspective to the domination of the imperial comic stage by New Comedy. To support my suggestion, I want to examine two inscriptions that provide a glimpse into a much less attested practice of re-staging Old Comedy and modeling new plays on it.

The performance of new comedies alongside previously performed plays would not have been a novel phenomenon in the imperial period. Catalogues recording the winners of dramatic festivals from other cities provide glimpses into what appears to have been a widespread tradition of staging comedies. These inscriptions attest to the re-staging of old plays as well as the performance of entirely new ones. In the case of reprised plays, the most famous of these inscriptions are those from Athens. Ranging from the early fifth century BCE to the second century CE, they record the year 339 BCE as the first time the Great Dionysia included a previously performed comedy.[21] This trend increases in regularity after 311 BCE.[22] By the Hellenistic and Roman periods, specific competitive categories dedicated solely to these reprised comedies appear outside of Athens.²³ This practice continued into the imperial period, possibly as a result of later archaizing tastes. For example, the Museia, a festival celebrated in Thespiae, attracted participants and audiences well into the third century CE with its staging of old plays alongside new ones.²⁴

These records distinguish previously staged plays from new productions with the respective labels of παλαιά and καινή. One catalogue from the Museia, for example, records the victory of a certain Claudius Apollonius in a revived comedy as 'a comic actor of a reprised comedy' (κωμωιδὸς παλαιᾶς κωμωιδίας).²⁵ In this context, παλαιά marks the comedy as a revival and does not denote a specific subgenre of comedy. While the breadth of evidence for the performance of Menander's plays has led to the interpretation of παλαιά as referencing revivals of New Comedy, there is nothing inherent in the term itself to signal this.²⁶ In contrast to this convention, we possess an inscription contemporary with Aristides from the Lysimacheia in Aphrodias in Caria that possibly suggests a more varied revival tradition. Unlike the long-established Museia, the Lysimacheia was a relatively new festival most likely established in 181 CE by Flavius Lysimachus.²⁷ Included among its schedule of prizes, alongside newly composed comedies, is the remarkable category of 'Old Comedy' (ἀρχαίᾳ κωμῳδίᾳ).²⁸ As a category marker in a dramatic competition, the adjective ἀρχαία is not attested anywhere else in the surviving record and could be merely a synonym for παλαιά. Jones, however, has posited that the Lysimacheia may have revived plays exclusively from Old Comedy.²⁹ If this is the case, then this inscription not only reflects the increase in popularity that Aristophanes and his contemporaries experienced in the second and third centuries CE, it also suggests that his popularity extended occasionally to the stage.³⁰

If the Lysimacheia raises the possibility that plays from Old Comedy were revived, an inscription from Cos offers a possible example of its use as a model for new plays. Dating to the first century CE, this inscription records the honor bestowed by the city of Cos on 'a female poet of Old Comedy' for her victories at the 'holy Olympics and the Koinon of Asia in Pergamum' (*SEG* 54:787 lines 3–5 ποιήτριαν κω[μῳδίας] / ἀρχαίας νεικάσασαν τὰ [— — — Σε]- / βαστὰ Ὀλύμπια καὶ τὸν ἐν [Περγά]- / μῳ κοινὸν Ἀσίας).³¹ Although Plutarch records that a certain Aristomache dedicated a golden book for a victory at the Isthmian games, it would be a mistake to assume that female poets competing in dramatic festivals is anything but a rare phenomenon.³² Added to the uniqueness of this inscription is the use of the label of ἀρχαία to describe her poetry.³³ Given the fact that the role of poet and producer had been separate from one another since

380 BCE, her title of 'poetess' (ποιήτριαν) suggests that her victories were for new compositions and not revivals as in the case of the Lysimacheia.[34] The phrase ἀρχαία κωμῳδία in a literary context is the term commonly used to denote Aristophanes' style of comedy beginning in the Hellenistic period and would seem to signal Old Comedy here. Bosnakis, however, resists this reading in his commentary on this inscription, questioning whether the adjective ἀρχαία follows this Hellenistic practice.[35] Left unanswered by his rejection of ἀρχαία as alluding to Old Comedy is the question of how a recently composed play might be considered old. One possible solution to the problem of ἀρχαία is that her plays followed to some degree previously established comedic styles. In this reading of the adjective, it is conceivable that her work borrowed enough elements from Old Comedy to be considered as an example of that genre.[36]

The inscriptions from the Lysimacheia and Cos raise the possibility that Old Comedy's popularity extended to the imperial stage. Two inscriptions do not, of course, constitute evidence for a widespread trend, but they do provide important comparanda for attempts to understand what form Smyrna's comedies may have taken. If, as these two inscriptions suggest, plays of Old Comedy at least occasionally appeared on the imperial stage in revivals or more indirectly through new imitations of the genre, the anxiety expressed by Aristides regarding Smyrna's contemporary comedies is no mere rhetorical exercise whose topic belongs in the distant past. Although Aristides does not classify Smyrna's comedies as ἀρχαῖαι, he does invite comparison between past and present comedic genres through their performance context, style of humor and, as we will see, his criticism of that humor. For this comparison to be successful, the comedies performed in Smyrna must have at least resembled Old Comedy in these features, if not more. Aristides consequently bears witness in *Or.* 29 to a non-uniform comic scene and, as I will suggest, capitalizes on it to establish a contest for authority between comedy, rhetoric, and, in particular, Platonic philosophy.

II. Aristides on comedy

Or. 29's emphasis on the festival context of Smyrna's comedies allows us to consider its role in Aristides' larger program of combining the art of oratory with religious practice. Aristides' critique of contemporary comic performances directly challenges comedy's traditional place in celebrations of Dionysus and redefines what proper religious observance means for Smyrna's *pepaideumenoi*.

Often overlooked in discussions of this speech, this theme of proper religious observance requires contextualization within the broader category of Aristides' religious writings. Such works, in particular the prose hymns and *Sacred Tales* (*Or.* 47–52), engage in a larger imperial debate about what proper religious practice means for members of the social and intellectual elite.[37] While his contemporary Lucian tackles this question through ridicule and satire, Aristides approaches it unequivocally from an elite perspective that privileges rhetoric as the medium for interaction with the divine.[38] The prose hymns in particular illustrate this agenda by supplanting poetry as the vehicle for divine praise with rhetorical *logos*.[39] This connection between human and divine *logos* is amplified in the *Sacred Tales* where the god Asclepius oversees the recovery of Aristides' health and oratorical career. Written towards the end of his life in 171 CE, the *Sacred Tales* underscore Aristides' close connection to the divine and establish Asclepius as the source of Aristides' rhetorical success.[40] Once read as the private writings of a 'neurotic, deeply superstitious, and vainglorious man', the *Sacred Tales* have recently begun to be rehabilitated as an important component of Aristides' rhetorical program.[41] Petsalis-Diomidis has notably argued that the *Sacred Tales* shapes a new model for the *pepaideumenos,* one that places religion at its core.[42]

Although *Or.* 29 cannot be definitively dated in relation to the publication of the *Sacred Tales,* it bears witness to this larger rhetorical project through its critique of contemporary comic performances specifically in a religious setting. I argue that Aristides directs his anxiety over religiously-sanctioned performances of comedy to Smyrna's elite but redefines inclusion in that group as contingent upon their rejection of comedy. His arguments against maintaining comedy's traditional place in festivals of Dionysus draw heavily on philosophical arguments against comic license, notably those first expressed by Plato in the *Republic* and *Laws*. Aristides' adaptation of these arguments casts Smyrna's *pepaideumenoi* in the new role of guardians, to borrow a Platonic term, over the religious festivals.

References to Platonic arguments in defining a religious role for Smyrna's *pepaideumenoi* are a significant aspect of Aristides' overall concern in *Or.* 29 to imbue Smyrna's educated elite with a new religious purpose. From the outset of *Or.* 29, Aristides establishes requirements that make membership in the city's *pepaideumenoi* contingent upon the *pepaideumenos'* achieving a new understanding of pleasure, one that eschews the ribald and abuse-filled laughter that had once defined Old Comedy. On the surface, this represents Aristides' approach to making the audience more amenable to the idea of banning comic performances, but it has the added purpose of proposing a new, religious understanding of social and intellectual elite status for which Aristides is the model. Aristides enacts this at the beginning of the speech by demarcating the audience from the rest of Smyrnan society as elite based on their reaction to his advice.[43] As he acknowledges, it is a big advantage to a speaker to deliver 'speeches that bring his audience pleasure' (29.1 τὸ πρὸς ἡδονὴν εἶναι τοὺς λόγους τοῖς ἀκούουσιν). This is because most people do not usually agree with a speaker who 'rebukes' them (29.1 νουθετεῖν). Aristides' acknowledgment that some people may not enjoy criticism lays the groundwork for a distinction between an elite perspective and that of everyone else, which pervades this speech. According to the framework that this dichotomy establishes, his audience's intellectual and social status should produce a positive reaction to the concern he is about to voice regarding comedy. While most people dislike being criticized and 'behave like boors' (29.2 ἀγροικίζεσθαι), Aristides boasts that his audience possesses superior intelligence and education (29.2 συνέσει καὶ τῷ πεπαιδεῦσθαι). By praising his audience's refined behavior, Aristides defines inclusion among the *pepaideumenoi* as contingent upon their overall reaction to his advice.

The opening of *Or.* 29 sets his audience's reaction to his advice as a litmus test of their social status. While others behave rudely under these circumstances, Aristides characterizes his audience as well-disposed to listening and grateful for any advice offered them (29.2). This would be particularly important if Aristides were going to propose a laborious task and not the pleasant suggestion he has in mind, namely that they 'neither speak nor hear anything unpleasant' (29.3 μήτε λέγειν μήτ' ἀκούειν δυσχερὲς μηδέν). The main objective of this opening is to revise traditional notions of pleasure. For Aristides, an educated person can enjoy a festival only when what he regards as a traditional impediment to pleasure, namely comedy, is removed. By arguing that comic outlandishness is at odds with religious practice, Aristides rejects the view that comedy can serve serious religious ends and instead contends that its lack of seriousness threatens the city's wellbeing.[44] Since Aristides has already underscored the fact that his audience's elite status is contingent on their agreement with him, he now begins to redirect their notion of *paideia* to center on religious practice.

In the religiously motivated perspective that Aristides imparts to his audience, watching performances of comedy becomes antithetical to their social and intellectual status (29.4):

ἄρξομαι δὲ ὅθεν καὶ ὑμεῖς ἄριστ' ἂν ἀκολουθήσαιτε καὶ ἀπὸ τῆς ἐμαυτοῦ συνηθείας. φημὶ δὴ χρῆναι τῷ μὲν Διονύσῳ τὴν ἑορτὴν ποιεῖν καὶ νὴ Δία τῇ γε Ἀφροδίτῃ καὶ τοῖς ἄλλοις ἅπασι θεοῖς, σπένδοντας καὶ θύοντας καὶ παιωνίζοντας καὶ στεφανηφοροῦντας καὶ τῶν εἰς εὐσέβειαν μηδὲν ἐλλείποντας. ἐν δὲ τούτοις ὃ πρόσεστι τοῖς μὲν πολλοῖς ἐπιεικῶς κεχαρισμένον, τοῖς δ' ἐπιεικέσι πάντων ἀνιαρότατον, τοῦτ' ἐκποδὼν ἀνελεῖν, λέγω τὰς βλασφημίας καὶ τοὺς κώμους τουτουσὶ τοὺς μεθημερινούς, καὶ νὴ Δία ἔγωγε τοὺς ἐπὶ ταῖς παννυχίσιν, καὶ μήτε ποιητὰς εἶναι τούτων μήτε ἀγωνιστάς, μηδὲ παίζειν ἃ μὴ βέλτιον. ὡς ἔχει γε οὕτως, κακηγορίας ἄκοντας μὲν ἀκούειν οὐ τερπνόν, ἑκόντας δὲ ἀνέχεσθαι μελέτη κακοηθίας.

I shall begin at a point where you would best follow me and with my own practice. I say that it is fitting to celebrate a feast for Dionysus, and by Zeus, for Aphrodite, and all the other gods, with libations, sacrifices, paeans, the wearing of crowns, and with the omission of no pious act. But there is one more practice associated with festivals that, although it is generally pleasing to the common people, it is most distressing to people who are educated. This is what I ask you to remove; I mean the blasphemy in these daytime revels and by Zeus, those at night time festivals as well, and I ask that there be neither poets nor actors, and no jokes which were better not made. This is just how it is: it is not pleasant to listen to slander unwillingly, but to endure it willingly is practice for a malicious character.

Aristides once again returns to the dichotomy between the educated and uneducated, but here offers up himself as the model for proper piety and reverence. The theme of displaying appropriate forms of reverence recurs numerous times with particular emphasis on the use of auspicious language (29.7 εὐφημίαν).[45] Pious language is a requirement of proper religious observance both in terms of what is said as the rites are performed and what the participants say to each other. Festivals in this context become for Aristides 'tokens of friendship' (29.7 φιλίας συνθήματα) not only among the participants but also with the gods. In order for this friendship to persist, comic abuse must be avoided, even if it is justified (29.8). According to this framework, the removal of comedy from the festival has the potential to cement the relationship between the human and the divine that Aristides is so concerned to achieve elsewhere in his corpus.[46] Banning comedy becomes a community-building tool both within Smyrna and with the gods.

Aristides' treatment of comic performances is closely intertwined with his view of the *pepaideumenoi*. His audience can claim this status if and only if they accept his revision of pleasure and enjoyment, the embodiment of which is Aristides himself. The slander staged by the comic poets is established as antithetical to the celebration of the gods and the religious rhetorical model that Aristides offers his audience. Although Aristides' new model attacks comedy's traditional place in festivals to Dionysus, it is itself grounded in the Platonic anxiety about the public performance of religiously sanctioned laughter.[47] Socrates voices this view in Book 3 of the *Republic* when, in the course of establishing the unsuitability of dramatic performances for the young members of the guardian class, he calls into question the imitation of 'bad men ... who are cowards and are doing the opposite of what we just spoke about, both slandering and making a mockery of each other, and using shameful language while drunk or sober' (395e–396a Οὐδέ γε ἄνδρας κακούς, ὡς ἔοικεν, δειλούς τε καὶ τὰ ἐναντία πράττοντας ὧν νυνδὴ εἴπομε κακηγοροῦντάς τε καὶ κωμῳδοῦντας ἀλλήλους καὶ αἰσχρολογοῦντας, μεθύοντας ἢ καὶ νήφοντας).[48] Socrates' use of κακηγοροῦντάς and κωμῳδοῦντας signals comedy as the object of his criticism. It is worth noting here that Socrates does not condemn comedy outright but only as prospective forms of entertainment for the youth of the guardian class. In addressing the societal function of comedy, Socrates concentrates on the generalized language found in comedy, forbidding the youth to act out comic roles because of the negative effects that such parts have on both the character of the youth themselves and the audience that watches them.[49]

Aristides' own concerns about the shameful language of Smyrna's comedies likewise center on the education of the city's youth. Reiterating the common association between comedy and inebriation exemplified in Socrates' discussion of the genre, Aristides challenges whether intoxication and therefore comedy can influence people 'to live good lives' (29.17 ὅπως εἰς κάλλος βιώσονται). Always the elitist, Aristides contends that it cannot in the case of the majority of people because 'an education is not within the capacity of the masses, any more than legislation, and making proposals in the assembly' (29.17 μὲν οὐ πολλῶν τὰ τοιαῦτα παιδεύειν, οὐ μᾶλλόν γε ἢ νόμους τιθέναι καὶ γνώμας ἐν δήμῳ λέγειν). In this case, the initial dichotomy between the elite perspective and that of the masses established at the start of the speech becomes a rallying cry for his audience to protect the city's youth from comedy. Having already defined his audience as a community of *pepaideumenoi*, Aristides invokes the masses' incapacity for education and consequentially their immunity from experiencing the dangers of comic slander to emphasize the elite's youth capacity for both.

Socrates proscribes the imitation of shameful acts for his guardians on the grounds that it might produce in them the desire to behave badly. Aristides takes this argument a step further with the supposition that Smyrna's comic poets are themselves potential teachers and should not be allowed to instruct the city's youth (29.20–1):

> ὥστε πῶς εἰκὸς ἐν ᾧ τῶν ὄντων διδασκάλων τοὺς παῖδας ἀφίεμεν, ἐν τούτῳ τοὺς μηδὲν προσήκοντας καὶ τοὺς ἑαυτοὺς εἰσποιοῦντας ἐφιστάναι, καὶ μηδὲ παρ' αὐτοῦ τοῦ τόπου δύνασθαι μαθεῖν ὅτι ἄλογος ἡ προσποίησις. δεῖ γὰρ τόν γε διδάσκαλον οὐκ εἰς τὰ θέατρα βαδίζειν κἀκεῖ νουθετεῖν· ταῦτα μὲν γὰρ ταῖς ἡδοναῖς καὶ ταῖς ψυχαγωγίαις ἀνάκειται·

> How is it reasonable at the time when we give our children a vacation from their real teachers, to put men in charge of them who are unsuitable and who impose themselves, and to be unable to learn from the place itself that the pretense is absurd? A teacher ought not to go to the theaters and chastise there. Theaters are reserved for pleasure and enjoyment.

The theater, for Aristides, should be a place of pleasure if and only if it is the kind of pleasure free from unpleasant slander. That is, a pleasure devoid of comedy. Personal abuse becomes paradigmatic of Smyrna's comedies, yet Aristides refuses to acknowledge any value to it on the grounds that it is indiscriminate. Comic poets can, as he implies, be easily bought off with the result that those deserving of chastisement go unpunished, while the innocent have comedies written about them (29.24 κωμῳδοῦνται). The apparent moral corruption of comedy renders the genre a dangerous teacher of the city's youth and leads Aristides to state definitively that 'comedy must be stopped' (29.25 τούτου γε παυστέον τοῦ κωμῳδεῖν). From the outset of this speech, Aristides establishes himself as a moral paradigm for his audience. The problem with comedy is ultimately a Platonic one: the presence of comic abuse has the potential to corrupt the city's youth through its promotion of unjust behavior. In contrast, Aristides' form of entertainment, namely rhetoric, is just because it inspires its audience to do just things and this is itself a form of pleasure preferable to that on offer from comedy. Aristides' answer to the problem of comedy is, not surprisingly, his own rhetorical project.[50] This substitute of rhetoric for comedy becomes all the more powerful if comedy is actually being performed because it establishes a direct contest between the comic poets and the rhetorical entertainment offered by Aristides.

Genres duking it out for popularity and supremacy is not new. Both Aristophanes and Plato, for example, challenge the status of tragedy through the adoption of tragic language, scenarios and, in the case of Plato, the banishment of the genre from the ideal city of the *Republic*.[51] Plato likewise considers comedy's status as a subversive genre in the *Laws*. There, he allows for the genre but only under extreme restrictions that include the prevention of citizens performing in the genre and a ban on personal ridicule.[52] Comedies that involve abuse (935c λοιδορίαις) and the mockery of citizens, even if it is done 'without anger' (935d ἄνευ θυμοῦ) must be banned. Those devoid of such traits are allowed. In order to judge the suitability of an individual comedy for performance, the Athenian stranger gives the final say to 'the person who is to care for the entire education of the youth' (936a τούτου δὴ διάγνωσις ἐπιτετράφθω τῷ τῆς παιδεύσεως ὅλης ἐπιμελητῇ τῶν νέων·). For Aristides, Smyrna's comic poets represent a dangerous breed of teachers whose place in the city must be removed. He replaces the pleasure of laughing at a comedy with a revised pleasure that combines proper religious practice with a rhetorical education. The figures established as responsible for promoting this educational model, I would argue, are by the end of the speech Aristides' elite audience. Aristides casts them in the role of teacher but with a new broader purpose: care for the entire city by preventing the performance of comedy and preserving both the religious and educational standards of the community. This enjoinment combines a traditional concern regarding education with a newfound one for proper religious observance.

Where does this discussion leave us in terms of this speech's ambiguous status as a witness to imperial comic performances? I suggest that it furthers the possibility that Aristides is addressing actual performances of comedies and that these performances were not modeled on New Comedy. Discussions of problematic genres, like that of comedy, become vehicles to define the ideal citizen in terms of the genres being performed.[53] In the *Laws*, this works by restricting the performance of comedy to slaves and non-citizens and using comedy to stipulate that certain behaviors, namely defaming others through comic abuse, not be accepted in the city. Aristides' own discussion of comedy functions on much the same level, but the distinction is no longer between citizen and noncitizen. Instead, Aristides rewrites it to be one between those who possess *paideia* and those who do not. The ideal citizen for him is a member of the social elite, possesses a rhetorical education, and displays proper religious reverence. Despite his fear that comic poets educate and corrupt the youth, Aristides in fact uses comedy to instruct his audience and reshape their understanding of what it means to be a *pepaideumenos*. *Or.* 29 seeks to fashion its audience into ideal citizens at the same time as it tasks that audience with ensuring the creation of new ones. Yet this rhetorical move makes little sense if Aristides is not describing actual performances of new plays in Smyrna, performances that are almost unilaterally defined by the paradigmatic speech of Old Comedy. As the epigraphic record hints, Smyrna would not have been unique for staging such comedies. *Or.* 29 consequently capitalizes on the opportunity of such performances to promote the deep religiosity that runs throughout his corpus and becomes the lens through which all else, including the present problem posed by comedy and the traditional criticism of it, is viewed and understood.[54]

Notes

1 For an overview of comedy in the imperial period, see May 2014: 753–4, Green 1994: 142–71 and Jones 1993.
2 For a discussion of the imperial reception of Aristophanes, see Bowie 2007. For Menander, see Nervegna 2007 and 2013.
3 Branham 1989: 14–5, 32–4. Marcus Aurelius also lauds the free speech of Old Comedy in comparison to the imitative art of New Comedy (11.2).
4 For evaluations of this evidence, see Nervegna 2013: 63–119. When it comes to performance, the evidence is not always clear whether a given staging was in a public or private context. See Jones 1993: 40–1 and Friedländer 1919–21: appendix 14.
5 May 2014: 753. Arnott 1997: 51–2.
6 Bowie 2007: 43–9 includes a useful catalogue of references to Aristophanes in the works of Dio, Plutarch, Aristides, Lucian, Pausanias, Maximus of Tyre and Athenaeus.
7 For views against the performance of Aristophanes, see Nervegna 2013: 117–19 and Bowie 2007: 33.
8 Aristides' works are cited from Lenz and Behr 1976 for Orations 1–16 and Keil 1898 for the rest. All translations of Aristides are adapted from Behr 1981 and 1986.
9 Halliwell 1991: 48. For a discussion of the role of Old Comedy in Aristides' corpus, see Berardi 2014. Behr 1968: 91–96 dates the speech to the years 157–165 CE based on the presumption that it would have been covered in the lost sixth book of the *Sacred Tales*. While Behr's work remains an invaluable resource, the precision with which he dates many of the orations can be misleading. Jones 2007: 55–63 offers a chronology of the datable speeches.
10 A good point of comparison for *Or.* 29 is *Or.* 34, 'Against Those Who Burlesque the Mysteries' (*Or.* 34). Aristides' use of religious language to describe the art of oratory is well established. Behr 1994: 1164. Petsalis-Diomidis 2010: 123–32. Swain 1996: 255 n. 5 notes that this trope is itself borrowed from contemporary Platonic philosophy.
11 Nervegna 2013: 119.
12 Behr 1981: 388. Jones 1993: 41. Berardi 2014: 202–3.
13 The formal performance context described by Aristides is discussed in section I of this chapter.

14 Behr 1981: 388 n.1. Behr bases this connection on references in Aristides' first and second *Smyrnaean Oration* to 'jests from the wagons' (17.6, 21.4 τὰ ἐκ τῶν ἁμαξῶν). For the debate about the presence of full-fledged comic performances in the Athenian Anthesteria, see Csapo 2012: 27 and Wilson 2000: 32. The festival seems to have taken on a slightly different form in the imperial period. Csapo 2012: 28–9.
15 Halliwell 2004: 115 and 1991: 48.
16 Halliwell 2004: 115 notes that aischrology 'is a locus of educational, psychological, ethical, political and religious concern throughout the whole of Greek antiquity'.
17 Nervegna 2013: 119. Behr 1981: 388 also doubts the veracity of the speech.
18 Russell 1983: 4.
19 See Berardi 2014 for Aristides' broader imitation of the parabasis' form and function.
20 Jones 1993: 41.
21 *IG* II^2 2318.201–3. See Nervegna 2013: 65, Jones 1993: 43 and Mette 1977: 125. All translations of the epigraphic evidence are my own.
22 *IG* II^2 2318.316–18. Axandrides' *Thesaurus* is the first restaged comedy on record in 311 BCE. *IG* II^2 2323a.39–40. See Nervegna 2013: 65.
23 Nervegna 2007: 40. Jones 1993: 43–4.
24 For a catalogue and discussion of Boeotian festivals, see Manieri 2009.
25 *IThesp* 172.35–42. As Nervegna 2013: 40 notes, the Museia's victor lists represent 'our latest secure epigraphic evidence' for the performance of revived comedies and tragedies in a public theater with the last catalogue dating to after 212 CE.
26 This interpretation stems from the inclusion of titles in Hellenistic catalogues and the depiction of scenes from Menander's plays in imperial mosaics and wall paintings. Jones 1993: 43. It is unlikely, however, that there was standardization of terminology across all festivals. Csapo 1995: 188.
27 For 181 CE as the first year the Lysimacheia was founded, see Roueché 1993: 168.
28 *MAMA* VIII 420. Csapo 1995: 191–2, no.159B. It also lists a highly unusual 'joint' (κοινῇ) contest of comedy, which Csapo 1995: 191–2, no. 159B interprets as open to all categories of comic performance. Roueché 1993: 173–4, no. 53.
29 Jones 1993: 4 posits that 'either the adjective is being used loosely or in this contest only revivals of Old Comedy were allowed'. See also Csapo and Slater 1995: 188.
30 Nervegna 2013: 101.
31 *SEG* 54:787: ὁ [δ]ᾶμος ἐτείμασε [τὴν δεῖνα] / Ἀπολλωνίου Ἀλεξαν[δρίδα] / καὶ Κώιαν, ποιήτριαν κω[μῳδίας] / ἀρχαίας, νεικάσασαν τὰ [— — — Σε]- / βαστὰ Ὀλύμπια καὶ τὸν ἐν [Περγά]- / μωι κοινὸν Ἀσίας καὶ ἄλλους ἱ[ε]- / ροὺς ἀγῶνας, ἀρετᾶς ἕνεκα κ[αὶ] / εὐνοίας τᾶς εἰς αὐτάν· / ἁ εἰκὼν Δελφίδος τᾶς Πραξαγόρα Κώιας ἐλεγειογρά- / φου. ('The people honor such a woman, Alexandria daughter of Apollonius, from Cos, a poetess of old comedy, who won at the games of holy Olympia and the one in Pergamum shared by Asia and other holy contests, because

of her virtue and the good will towards her'). Bosnakis 2004: 103 deduces that her Olympic victory likely occurred at the Olympics held in Damascus.
32 Plutarch, *Table Talk*, 675b.
33 For a discussion of this reconstruction, see Bosnakis 2004: 102.
34 Bosnakis 2004: 102. For the funding of entertainment at Aphrodisias, see Rouché 1993: 7–11.
35 Bosnakis 2004: 102–3.
36 A point of comparison to this might be Pliny's *Epistle* 6.21, in which he lavishes praise on the comic poet Vergilius Romanus for a new play composed in the style of 'Old Comedy' (*comoediam ad exemplar veteris comoediae scriptam*). It is likely, based on Pliny's list of Vergilius' earlier comic models of *mimiambi* and the plays of Menander, that Vergilius is an imitator of past styles and that *veteris* denotes Old Comedy here. See Hawkins and Marshall in this volume.
37 For a discussion of the *Sacred Tales*' relationship to the rest of the corpus, see Downie 2008 and Petsalis-Diomidis 2008.
38 See Petsalis-Diomidis 2010: 129, and Storey in this volume.
39 Downie 2013: 128.
40 Although there is no indication that they were delivered publically, there is evidence that they were published with ten other orations (37–46) under the title of *Manteutoi* or 'Speeches Prescribed by the Oracle'. Behr 1981: 223 n.1. Petsalis-Diomidis 2010: 138.
41 Behr 1981: 425. For a discussion of the relationship between Aristides' body and literary project, see Holmes 2008.
42 Petasalis-Diomidis 2010: 129.
43 We unfortunately lack any information about where this speech was delivered. A theater or an odeion are both possible venues, but the latter is probably the more likely setting.
44 For the serious religious function of comedy, see the story of the introduction of Dionysus Eleutherius into Athens preserved in the *scholion* to Aristophanes' *Acharnians*, 243.
45 See also 29.12–15.
46 Petsalis-Diomidis 2008: 142 aptly describes this as 'his ever repeated desire for union with the divine, which is occasionally but never fundamentally satisfied'.
47 It is ambiguous whether Old Comedy should fall under the heading of ritual laughter or whether it developed out of it. See Halliwell 2008: 206–14, 225.
48 Translations of Plato are my own.
49 Halliwell 2008: 226.
50 This challenge becomes more literal if this speech was performed in a theater.
51 For this practice in Old Comedy, see Platter 2007 and Rosen 2006. For Plato's challenge of other genres, in particular tragedy and comedy, see Clay 1975 and Nightingale 2000.

52 See *Laws* 816d and 935d–936a.
53 Folch 2013: 340–1.
54 I first presented this work in a session, 'Greek Comedy in the Roman Empire', at the 2014 meeting of the American Philological Association in Chicago, Illinois. I would like to thank the organizers of that panel and this volume, Tom Hawkins and C. W. Marshall, for their very helpful comments during the APA session and since, as I revised and expanded my argument into this paper.

11

Aelian and Comedy: Four Studies

C.W. Marshall

I. Socrates goes to the theatre

In a showcase passage in his *Historical Miscellany*, second-century CE sophist Claudius Aelianus describes the relationship between Aristophanes and Socrates (*VH* 2.13).[1] Drawing on the language of *Clouds* and Plato's *Apology*, Aelian describes how Aristophanes was persuaded by Anytus (one of the prosecutors of Socrates in 399 BCE) to attack Socrates to win popular approval in the theatre from cheering audiences and judges:

> ... [Anytus and his associates] persuaded the comic poet Aristophanes, who was – and aimed to be – a vulgar and ridiculous humorist, to lampoon Socrates, making of course the well-known charges against him, that he was a windbag [ἀδολέσχης[2]], that when he talked he would make the weaker argument seem superior, that he introduced foreign deities, was an atheist and did not honour the gods; that he taught his associates these same doctrines and persuaded them to believe accordingly. Aristophanes applied himself to the task with great energy, adding a little humour to it and some metrical versatility, and making the best man in Greece his theme. His play was not aimed at Cleon; it was not a satire on the Spartans, the Thebans, or Pericles himself, but on a man loved by the gods as a whole and especially Apollo. Since Socrates was an unusual subject, an odd figure on the stage in a comedy, the play at first [πρῶτον] astounded the Athenians by its unexpected theme. Later [εἶτα], as they had a natural tendency to jealousy and made a habit of criticizing the best people, not only those in political life and officeholders, but to an even greater degree men famous for their literary accomplishments or honourable behaviour, this play, *The Clouds*, was thought to be a very agreeable entertainment, and they applauded the poet.
>
> (tr. Wilson)

The passage is central to the understanding of Socrates in the second century CE, even though it is filled with chronological compressions and implausibilities (Anytus, for example, is not known to be active as early as 423). As the passage continues, Aelian seems to be unaware of the critical failure that *Clouds* received in its original performance:

> They [the spectators] shouted that he should win the prize, and told the judges to put Aristophanes, and no one else, at the top of their list [ἄνωθεν³]. That is the story of the play.
>
> (tr. Wilson)

The play's third-place finish is a fact well represented in our extant partially revised text (e.g. *Clouds* 518–62⁴), and the relationship between *Clouds* and the historical Socrates was important throughout the Second Sophistic. Unless we imagine a lacuna in the above passage or an elaborate compression of thought ('... nevertheless, the play failed as we all know, demonstrating the sense of the masses against the foolishness of the judges', *vel sim.*), we must concede that Aelian appears indifferent to the actual placement of the play in the competition, and that he deliberately, even aggressively, suppresses it with the insistent final sentence.⁵

The discussion of Socrates continues however, with two further anecdotes, ascribing to Socrates a fondness for Euripides but only a single visit ever to a comedy:

> But Socrates did not often go to the theatre. However, if the tragic poet Euripides was entering the competition with new plays, then he would go. If Euripides was competing at the Piraeus, he would even go down there, since he enjoyed his work, obviously because of its wisdom and poetic quality. Alcibiades son of Clinias and Critias son of Callaeschrus once teased him and cajoled him into going to the theatre to see comedies as well. He did not get any pleasure from them and, being a man of sound judgment, just, good, and in addition sagacious, was severe in his contempt for men who dealt in insults and abuse and had nothing sensible to say. These men annoyed him greatly.

This is also the only indication that Euripides competed at a Piraeus festival, and if accurate this constitutes important evidence for participation of major playwrights at supposedly minor festivals.⁶ Following this digression, Aelian returns to the main focus of the story, which is Socrates attending comedy. There are no indications at this point in the narrative which comedies Socrates is supposed to have watched (or which year), but the passage does seem to presuppose that all the comedies of a given competition could be viewed on a single day.⁷

Aelian has reversed cause and effect in his imaginative reconstruction of events, as it is suggested that the prosecutors from 399 are actively warring against Socrates a quarter century earlier. This is evident as Aelian continues his short essay, alleging a kind of corruption in the comic competition:

> These facts were the germ of the comedy written against him; it was not just the issues known to have been raised by Anytus and Meletus. Probably Aristophanes made money out of this; given that they wished, indeed were making every effort to bring malicious charges against Socrates, while the poet was both a poor man and morally depraved, is it implausible that he should have accepted money for an immoral purpose? About this he alone knows the truth. But his play was famous. In fact, if ever the remark of Cratinus [fr. 395 K-A] was a reality, it was then: the theatre audience lost its wits.
>
> (tr. Wilson)

We do not know the source of the Cratinus fragment (or even if it is being cited verbatim), but it shows Aelian drawing on his wider knowledge of comedy to explicate the particular events that interest him.⁸ The narrative returns to Socrates appearing on stage:

> Since the Dionysia were being celebrated, a very large number of Greeks came out of interest to watch. When [the character of] Socrates was moving around on the stage and referred to frequently (and I should not be surprised if he was also recognizable among the figures on stage, for it is clear that the makers of the masks [οἱ σκευοποιοί] had portrayed him with an excellent likeness) the foreigners, who did not know the person being satirised, began to murmur and ask who this man Socrates was. When he heard that – he was in fact present, not as a result of luck or chance, but because he knew that he was the subject of a play, and he sat in a prominent position in the theatre – at any rate, in order to put an end to the foreigners' ignorance, he stood up and remained standing in full view throughout the play as the actors performed it [ἐξαναστὰς παρ' ὅλον τὸ δρᾶμα ἀγωνιζομένων τῶν ὑποκριτῶν ἑστὼς ἐβλέπετο]. So great was Socrates' contempt for comedy and the Athenians.
>
> (tr. Wilson)

In these lines, the richness of Aelian's understanding of the play emerges. He rightly knows that *Clouds* is a Dionysia play, and that the Dionysia is likely to have more non-Athenian spectators (compare *Acharnians* 504–8, about the privacy of the Lenaia). Earlier in *VH* 2.13 the reader was told that Socrates only attended comedies once, and so if these anecdotes are to be made consistent with each other (though it's not certain that they are), then we must conclude that Aelian believes Alcibiades and Critias brought Socrates to the theatre to see *Clouds* in 423. If correct, this would mean that Socrates also saw Cratinus' *Pytinē*[9] and Ameipsias' *Connus*, another play with Socrates as a character. Aelian seems not to know the content of *Connus* (he assumes there is only a single play with Socrates), and so it is not right to imagine that the portrait mask and the silent, standing figure of Socrates refer to that play. It does follow, however, that if these historical details are accurate (as they are typically taken to be), then *Clouds* will have preceded *Connus* in the sequence of production.

The standing Socrates invites direct comparison between himself standing in the audience and his stage representation. Aelian's assumption that portrait masks were employed fits into a larger tradition that supposes the existence of portraits of famous Athenians, though I believe that there is no reason to assume that such portraits were verisimilitudinous. Rather, it is more plausible for the mask employed for Socrates to be the standard mask employed in satyr drama for papposilenus.[10] That is, it was not a lifelike representation of Socrates, but a distorted caricature that proved so resonant that in the fourth-century both Plato and Xenophon accepted the characterization as meaningful, even if its effect is turned into self-deprecating acceptance (Plato, *Symposium* 215b, *Theaetetus* 143e; Xenophon, *Symposium* 4.19, 5.7). It is to this satyric representation, apparently, that the Socrates is inviting comparison in this anecdote. This gesture is also instructive, however, since it demonstrates that in the open-air daylight theatre audience members are understood to be visible and can be indentified as individuals.

The relationship between Socrates and Aristophanes was the subject of much speculation in subsequent centuries, with a presumptive hostility often presenting Socrates as victim.[11] We might even hypothesize that Socrates' allegiance with Euripides may have emerged in the biographical tradition due to their shared position as comic victims of Aristophanes. Regardless, Aelian's depiction in *VH* 2.13 invites associations with other second-century descriptions of Socrates that seem to engage with the afterlife of *Clouds*. We might imagine that Aelian had access to the first *Clouds* but not the extant, partially re-written, version, but such a scenario is improbable. Nor is it likely that he knows of *Clouds* only indirectly: otherwise unattested details, such as Euripides competing at the Piraeus and Socrates' fondness for him, the portrait masks, and Socrates standing up to invite direct comparison between the stage figure and himself, are too vivid and plausible for them to be accidental or felicitous inventions. While Aelian does not actually say that the play did win, the emphasis on the appeal to the judges and the omission of their action seems designed to evoke a specific, non-historical conclusion, because it fits the agenda of the narrative he is telling. Further, the anecdote presents additional evidence against the reduction of comedies during the Peloponnesian War. Aelian knows *Clouds*, and appears unconcerned about subordinating the history he knows (and which some of his readers must know as well) to the elegant artifice of the situation he presents.[12]

II. Plays Aelian knows

Aelian's *VH* is an anthology that leaps between subjects and teases the reader to seek connections of thought that often remain elusive. His literary practice at times seems to draw upon or epitomize earlier authors, and yet he can also offer strikingly new insights into familiar figures, often with an idiosyncratic spin that is at odds with the larger tradition. Not all of this can be ascribed to lost sources. Aelian emerges as a literary artist, operating within a literary aesthetic that prizes variation and erudition alongside a disarming plain-spokenness. A survey of Aelian's *VH* and *On the Characteristics of Animals* (*NA*) reveals some direct knowledge to specific plays of Aristophanes and Eupolis, and indirect knowledge of many others. As has been just demonstrated with *Clouds*, Aelian's concern is not to summarize comic plots but to engage with them creatively, which means that positive conclusions about lost plays are not easily extracted by modern authors.

Three passages in Aelian appear to show knowledge of Aristophanes' *Birds*. *Birds* 1179–82 is cited in a discussion of hawks at *NA* 12.4, and lines 471–5 on larks at *NA* 16.5.[13] The verbatim citation demonstrates a kind of scholarly professionalism, but it is possible that the passages come to him not directly, but already excerpted, perhaps in an ornithological or zoological compilation, such as Callimachus' *On Birds*.[14] Such an argument from silence is unable to be pushed very far. Discussion of the francolin at *NA* 4.42 notes that Aristophanes mentions the bird, but without the citation. Aelian does possess other ornithological sources, as in *NA* 12.9 when he cites Aristophanes fr. 29 K-A (*Amphiaraus*), fr. 147 K-A (*Geras*), and Autocrates fr. 1 K-A (*Tympanistae*). Taken together, it seems likely that Aelian did have access to *Birds*, and drew upon it as it occurred to him to do so. He also makes reference to *Geras* (*Old Age*) at *NA* 6.51, when he describes the Dipsas serpent, sloughing off old age (*geras*; i.e. shedding its skin), mythically tied to Prometheus and drawing on Sophocles (*TrGF* fr. 362, *The Silent Satyrs*), Apollophanes (fr. 9 K-A), and Aristias (*TrGF* 9 fr. 8).[15]

These citations fall short of the sense of encyclopedic completeness that is central to the literary impression conveyed by Athenaeus. Aelian wears his learning more lightly, drawing on examples with less precision and without forcing the identification, but occasionally leaving clues to be discovered only by the careful reader. Unspecified comic poets (*adespota* 72 K-A) are a source for a story about folly at *VH* 13.15.[16] Specific ichthyological knowledge is mentioned only in *NA* 13.4, on the stargazer fish:[17] this same passage preserves two fragments of New Comedy, from Menander's *Messenian Woman* (fr. 231 K-A) and Anaxippus' *Epidicazomenus* (fr. 2 K-A), and mentions the mid-fourth-century playwright Mnesimachus (fr. 5 K-A). A more general ichthyological point is made at *NA* 9.7, where the comic parasite is equated to parasitic fish such as the lamprey, citing the example of Theron in Menander's *Sicyonioi* (fr. 13 b), though not mentioning the play's name. Not every Aelianic passage is so artistic. *NA* 12.10 gives the proverb κατὰ μυὸς ὄλεθρον ('like a mouse's death', found at Menander fr. 166 K-A), to describe a gradual dissipation.[18] This is followed by a variety of comic passages, not all of which are relevant: Menander, *Plocion* fr. 309 K-A mentions turtle-doves, as does Demetrius I in *Sicelia* (fr. 4 K-A); the sex drive of mice is mentioned in Cratinus, *Drapetides* (fr. 58 K-A), Epicrates, *Chorus* (fr. 8 K-A), and Philemon *Paroinos* (fr. 65 K-A). Similarly, when Aelian *NA* 7.19 compares the sex lives of baboons (who supposedly rape human *parthenoi*, virgins) with the young men in Menander at all night festivals, the allusion is likely generalizing and not a specific evocation of a lost play called *Pannuchis* ('All-Night').[19]

The selectivity of what has survived to the present day stilts how we understand Aelian's kowledge. At *VH* 1.18, readers are told in passing τῶν δὲ Ἀττικῶν γυναικῶν τὴν τρυφὴν Ἀριστοφάνης λεγέτω ('and concerning the women of Attica, let Aristophanes describe their luxuriousness'). This has been understood to refer to an extant passage from Aristophanes' second *Thesmophoriazusae* (fr. 332 K-A), a lost rewrite to the extant play and a play that Galen could cite.[20] Yet this association is in no way inevitable, and Aelian's comment could equally be referring to a lost passage or even to Aristophanes generally. The reader is supposed to connect the comment with something, certainly, but we cannot be confident that this passage is evoking any specific comment concerning the luxuriousness or wantonness (τὴν τρυφήν could mean either) of Athenian women. Other passages in Aelian suggest the existence of an intermediate anthology on passages describing luxury, as when Menander (fr 66 K-A) is used to corroborate the fragmentary historian

Damon (*FGrH* 389 F1) that the city of Byzantium turns merchants into drunkards (*VH* 3.14). That is a possible source here.

Aelian appears to have had direct access to at least two plays of Eupolis, *Maricas* and *Autolycus*. *VH* 12.30 makes reference by name to *Maricas*, citing an observation that men of Cyrene wear valuable rings (fr. 202 K-A). Normally, this would be unexceptional, were it not for the case that the same detail is preserved in Plutarch (*Mor.* 779d, *ad Princ. inerud.*), but without the attribution to Eupolis. While we cannot discern between three possible explanations for this sequence (Plutarch suppressing Eupolis in a story from an earlier source shared with Aelian; an intermediate source adding Eupolis and Aelian drawing on it and not Plutarch; and Aelian adding the information himself), the last of these is the most straightforward. And yet the possibility of the source being no more than an anthology of passages on luxury, as proposed above, means that we can't be certain even of this. At *NA* 10.41, a story about Eupolis and a Molossian puppy is plausibly associated with the first *Autolycus*. In section IV of this chapter I trace some of the ways that this anecdote can reveal certain literary features of Eupolis' play, but for now it is enough to note that a comic plot appears to have been appropriated as an example of canine fidelity, something that would seem to require access to a complete play (not even the fullest hypothesis that survives to us, *P. Oxy.* 663 to Cratinus' *Dionysalexandros*,[21] possesses the level of narrative detail evoked here.)

In other cases, we simply do not know enough about lost comedy to be able to determine with precision how much Aelian actually knew. This is our limitation, however, and not his. For example, *VH* 10.6 cites the early fourth-century poet Alexis (fr. 148 K-A) amidst discussion of Athenians who are identified as comically thin, a passage which is perhaps an abridgement of Athenaeus 551B–552D.[22] A similar passage can be found amidst the Aelianic fragments: fr. 99 Herscher (*Suda* θ 171) provides a testimonium for the comic playwright Theopompus, whose career seems to have spanned from *c.* 410 to the 370s.[23] Though the passage seeks to explain visual elements on a dedicatory plaque that had been dedicated to Asclepius, the antecedent story features Theopompus emaciated before being healed by the god, at which point he returned to staging comedies. It is possible this anecdote seeks to explain a gap in the production career of the poet.

Aelian's engagement with Athenian comedy in *VH* and *NA* appears to show direct knowledge of Aristophanes' *Clouds* and *Birds* and of Eupolis' first *Autolycus* and possibly *Maricas*. In no case, I believe, is knowledge of these texts required by the reader, but those who do know the plays would better perceive Aelian's cavalier approach to his source material, subordinating it to his deliberate purpose. His works additionally preserve tidbits from many other comedies, but his knowledge of them does not appear to be direct and could easily come from a wide range of intermediary texts. Epigrams that have been ascribed to Aelian demonstrate a similar fondness for Menander, though no specifics about plays are given.[24] *Rustic Letters* evinces a similar ambivalence, but in that text direct knowledge of Menander's *Dyscolus* does enhance reader appreciation.

III. The structure of *Rustic Letters*

The most sustained engagement with comedy by Aelian comes in *Rustic Letters*, a collection of twenty short epistles. Scholarship has begun to assert the literary virtues of Aelian's collection, which exemplifies qualities of simplicity or plainness (*apheleia*) and variation (*poikilia*) through the process of character presentation in miniature (*ethopoeia*).[25] This revival has reoriented the understanding of these texts so that supposed faults identified in previous generations are understood positively. In particular, the dependence on previous authors, including comic poets, can now be seen, rightly, as an evocation of a particular world for specific literary effects.[26] My contribution to this discussion will offer a new description of the overall structure of the letters as a book, and will use that framework to examine the four letters between Callipides and Cnemon, who are characters in Menander's *Dyscolus*.

Aelian's rustics (*agroikoi*) are manual laborers: that they are literate and able to evoke the classics is explained only in the final sentence of the collection, where it is announced explicitly that they are 'Athenian farmers' (*Ep.* 20: Ἀθηναῖοι γεωργοί).[27]

Their personalities differ, but they brush against the expectations of the Athenian farmer in an idyllic age known to the Roman readers only through literature. These men (and two women, Opora in *Ep.* 8 and Tryphe in *Ep.* 12) are distinct from the Hellenistic shepherd: it is not simply life in the countryside that is being created, but a rural ideal of society distinct from the pastoral; a life of community and hard work, not one of idleness and song. As Smith notes, this 'rustic subjectivity' finds a touchstone in an Athenian comedy, Aristophanes' *Clouds* 41–52.[28] It is an ideal shared with Alciphron, who also wrote books of literary epistles, including one book by farmers.[29] The interpretative challenge offered by Aelian's book emerges from its deceptive simplicity. It appears so ordinary and plain that it suggests an unpracticed artlessness, and generalizations can lead to unhelpful oversimplification (as generalizations always do). A typical summary from a sympathetic scholar summarizes the relationship to comedy thus: 'Aelian's letters are, after all, firmly rooted in the traditions of Attic New Comedy and the plays of Menander'.[30] Given the explicit associations of four of the letters with *Dyscolus*, this is true, at least to a point.

There is an elaborateness and intricacy in the overall structure of the work that has not been fully appreciated. We can start with the most obvious elements of patterning: 'Aelian constructs his collection around two pairs of letters (*Letters* 7–8, 11–12) and one group of four (*Letters* 13–16), while the rest of the individual letters offer variations on country themes ... Aelian's work gains additional coherence through brief reappearances of characters: thus the name Mania appears in *Letters* 1 and 2 and the farmer Anthemion who writes *Letter* 4 becomes the addressee of *Letter* 5 ... Aelian postpones his most programmatic piece until the end of the book (*Letter* 20)'.[31] Further, the collection as it survives purports to be excerpts from a larger collection (its title is ἐκ τῶν Αἰλιανοῦ ἀγροικικῶν ἐπιστολῶν, 'From the *Rustic Letters* of Aelian'), which points to the existence of an editor, either a real person giving shape to Aelian's collection after the fact, or a fictional construct of the author himself, adding an extra interpretative layer for those who wish to perceive it.[32] In either case, the patterned structure of the book as a collection of letters is foregrounded for the reader.

I believe the structure of *Rustic Letters* is more elaborate than the above summary suggests. One of the features that distinguishes epistolary correspondence is the sense of exchange, the ask and the answer. It need not be this, but just as every letter has a writer and a receiver, so the tangible presence of a letter in one's hands seems to demand a reply. The structure of Aelian's collection is built around pairs. They are playfully presented so that this pattern emerges subtly, and it is possible to read the letters for pleasure without discerning it. But Aelian (or his editor) seems keen to play with the doubleness (and duplicity?) of epistolography. Athenian comedy is important to this structure, but it is not the entirety of it, and consequently there is a risk that the comedic elements that help pattern the sequence of letters can be overstated.

Ep. 1–2 demonstrate many of the typical characteristics associated with Aelian.[33] Letters generate a sequence, while at the same time they mark absences: they are an alternative to face-to-face conversation, allowing communication when the recipient is displaced in space and inevitably occupies a future time.[34] They invite speculation about the events they purport to describe, while at the same time they may enjoin the sharing of personal information and even secrecy (*Ep.* 1: τοῦτά σοι πρὸς τοῦ Πανὸς μυστήρια τὰ μεγάλα ἔστω, 'May these things, by Pan, be like the Great Mysteries for you'). In these initial letters, the writer and recipient are different, and the four men are linked only through their mutual acquaintance with Mania. Strangely enough, the explicit sex in *Ep.* 1, as Euthycomides describes his relationship with Mania, likely marks the narrative as not dependent on a comedy: τὰς μὲν ῥᾶγας εἴασα, ἐφερπυσας δὲ καὶ μάλα ἀσμένως τὴν ὥρας ἐτρύγησα – 'I dropped my grapes and very happily reaped her harvest'. The combination of titillation and humorous euphemism shares more features with mime, a suspicion reinforced when Mania re-appears in *Ep.* 2 as the wife of the recipient Dropides, revealing the sexual encounter as adulterous. This detail also explains the need for secrecy stressed in *Ep.* 1, and the voyeuristic nature of the description. Aelian is not unaware of comedy, however, and the mime-plot is bolstered with explicit allusions to Old and New Comedy, but these comic tags (*Ep.* 1 cites Aristophanes and Eupolis; *Ep.* 2 cites Menander's *Georgos* 46–52 and closes with a joke familiar from Aristophanes' *Plutus* 1103–6) exist as literary flourishes on a mime plot.[35]

Ep. 3–6 offer a pair of pairs, interwoven in a straightforward chiastic structure (*abba*). The outer pair form a frame that draw explicitly on crimes prefigured in Athenian oratory, *Ep.* 3 on Isaios, *Ep.* 6 on Demosthenes,[36] as Aelian's rustics deal with the realities of theft and property damage. These serve as a frame to a pair of letters involving three men, Anthemion to Draces boasting about the work he has accomplished (modeled on Aristophanes, *Acharnians* 995–8[37]), followed by Baeton to Anthemion concerned about his abandoned beehives. These letters generate a creative engagement with the possibilities of epistolary fiction, as a third voice is interjected into the presumptive intimacy of a letter exchange. The intended contrast pertains to work on the farm, and the pathetic appeal from Baeton for his bees is both touching and revelatory. Aelian knows a lot about bees,[38] and here reveals the trauma and loss felt by Baeton, his loss magnified in contrast with the recipient Anthemion's overall abundance known from the previous letter. Though many of the names emerge from known comedies (and perhaps contain small ironies, as the bee-less Baeton complains to Mr. Bloom), the emphasis in this cluster is on kinds of loss, from criminal activity or mysterious nature.

Ep. 7–10 constitute another pair of letter pairs, loosely linked, and 'all concern young men and sex'.[39] *Ep.* 7 and 8 appear to draw on Alexis' *Opora* (*Autumn*),[40] a lost play, but the nature of a personified Autumn – or the Ripeness associated with harvest-time – is also found in Aristophanes' *Peace*, when she becomes the bride of Trygaeus.[41] They are the first pair to constitute an exchange between only two individuals, and *Ep.* 8 is the only letter in the first half of Aelian's book purporting to be written by a woman. The comic connection seems immediately comparable to the exchange between Menander and Glycera in Alciphron, *Ep.* 4.18–19 (positioned in a prominent place at the end of that collection).[42] Dercyllus celebrates the richness of Opora's name (the fading of summer, and the ripeness of the fruit picked then), and we learn from her response that his letter accompanied gifts. Dercyllus' fruit and wine were meant to compliment the etymology of Opora's name, but she sees nothing but inexpensive offerings. Opora is a prostitute (*hetaira*), and the harvest she seeks from her clientele (which includes Dercyllus) must keep her in her old age, since ἑταίρας δὲ ὀπώρα μία ('There is single harvest for a *hetaira*'). The inevitable winter of her old age means that she, like a good farmer, must maximize her yield, as Aelian reverses the more usual association of the female body as earth-to-be-plowed (see, e.g., Sophocles, *Trach.* 31–3).

Ep. 9 'is almost a New Comic plot in one page'.[43] Rooted in comedy of Menander, from which Aelian cites invective, the story closely reflects the plot of Terence's *Eunuchus*, and the names cited as Chremes writes to Parmenon are those of Terence. While it is possible that Aelian's source is Menander's play and the substitution is accidental,[44] more likely we have an indication that Aelian's sources could include Latin comedy as well, as would be natural for a Roman from Praeneste. Chremes is a character-name Terence uses frequently: in *Andria*, he is an Athenian citizen, father to Philumena; he is main character in *Heauton Timoroumenos*, 'a man presented from the start as a pompous and self-satisfied busybody, ever ready to tell others how to organize their lives but blithely unaware of what is going on in his own household';[45] in *Phormio* he is the elder brother of Demipho, father of Phaedria; only in *Eunuchus* is he young, as here. The letter's association with *Eunuchus* determines which Chremes is intended. In *Eunuchus*, the slave Parmeno warns his master Phaedria to avoid prostitutes (*Eun.* 59–63), and yet in Aelian thanks for a warning heeded comes instead from Chremes. Throughout, the reader benefits from knowing the Terentian plot: the reader is invited to integrate the interpersonal relationships of the letter into what is known of the plot. Does Chremes perhaps misconstrue his rival's name (as Terence's Thraso becomes Thrasyleon)? More probable is that we are to imagine a parallel situation as Chremes avoids the rape narrative of Terence's play, with his Thebaïs and Thrasyleon replacing Thaïs and Thraso. We don't need an answer to this, or to why Chremes is writing to another man's slave, because consistency isn't expected. The letter's enjoyment comes from contemplating the differences between the situation here and that necessarily familiar to the reader in Terence's play.

It seems likely that associations with *Eunuchus* carry into *Ep.* 10, which also seems to present a generic rape plot that could derive from New Comedy (so many plays are lost that we today cannot determine every literary reference made).[46] *Ep.* 10, with its humorous suggestion that the rustic father geld his son to curb his sexual proclivities, adds an ironic inversion of the pseudo-*Eunuch* situation evoked in the previous letter, and invites reading the pair together in their manipulation of emasculatory themes. Unfortunately, not enough is known about Menander's play of that name (fr. 137–49 K-A) to know if it is being adapted to a greater degree in these letters. In a collection this small, other associations suggest themselves even without precise verbal echoes: talk of gelding may evoke in some readers the swollen groin described in the passage adapted from Menander's *Georgos* in *Ep.* 2.

The five pairs of letters that form the first half of Aelian's collection demonstrate an elaborate and rich variation (*poikilia*) offering an intricate interweaving of themes that have been dominated by the influence of Old and New Comedy. The pattern presented – a pair, four tightly integrated letters, then four loosely integrated ones – will be repeated in the collection's second half, as the first ten letters are answered by the second ten. This is not accident: the chiastic pattern of *Ep.* 3–6 will be answered by the longest sequence in the collection, *Ep.* 13–16, the four letters drawing on Menander's *Dyscolus*. Further, as will emerge below, correspondences between *Ep.* 8 and *Ep.* 18 also create a bond between the two halves of the collection.

As the second half of the collection begins, *Ep.* 11 and 12 appear to be another proper exchange between a man and a woman, thereby recalling *Ep.* 7 and 8. Lamprias and his sister Tryphe write each other, and again the letters accompany a gift, this time of a rabbit skin. Part of the scene may draw on Xenophon's *On Hunting with Hounds* [*Cynegeticus*],[47] reminding readers (as seen with *Ep.* 3 and 6) that Aelian has not chosen to model his letters on comedy exclusively. The chaste exchange here offers an implicit contrast not only with *Ep.* 7 and 8 but also the adulterous situation described in *Ep.* 1 and 2 which occupy the corresponding place in the structure of the first half of the collection.

Ep. 13–16, between Callipides and Cnemon, are discussed in detail below. Structurally, they correspond to the chiastic structure seen in *Ep.* 3–6, reinforcing the parallel development of the two halves of the collection.

Ep. 17 and 18 bring together two apparently different themes, but, as Hodkinson has observed, they form a pair that ruminates on how morality and financial well-being may coincide for a farmer.[48] *Ep.* 17 begins by imagining Plutus, the god of wealth, has regained his sight. This premise is most familiar from Aristophanes' *Plutus*.[49] The letter ends wishing that a rustic's heart would not be consumed with greed. Similarly, *Ep.* 18 ends with the relativistic observation that though farmers work hard and yield little, the predictability of rustic life is preferable to seafaring. The prominence of the sea in *Ep.* 18 is striking: as the writer Demylus fantasizes about travelling by sea, he offers a vision of life that contrasts with the countryside that has been Aelian's focus. It may be significant that this letter occurs at a point that corresponds to Opora's letter (*Ep.* 8) in the first half of the collection: while it would go too far to posit an allusion to Alciphron's books of letters of fishermen and of courtesans, this pair does remove Aelian's readers from the agrarian world he is creating and comparison can helpfully be made to Alciphron *Ep.* 2.4, where a farmer considers a life at sea.

The final pair is only loosely connected, as if Aelian is rejecting the doubling structure that has been so carefully pursued throughout the collection. *Ep.* 19 is written to Chremes, who was the Terentian writer of *Ep.* 9, at the corresponding point in the first half. In *Ep.* 9, Chremes was thanking Parmenon for advice on fleeing courtesans. In *Ep.* 19, Mormias describes his son's actions bringing home a freed *hetaira* as his bride. This situation, which shares many narrative elements found in New Comedy (though no specific play can be identified), also sews together many other elements in the collection. The reference to a Phrygian maid recalls Opora's Phrygian maid in *Ep.* 8 who alone was fit to drink the poor offerings from Dercyllus. And *Ep.* 9 also evoked the situation in *Ep.* 2, and so forth.

Ep. 20 also serves an integrative function. Praising nature and the country life, it elevates the rustic life above other pursuits. The temperance espoused here contrasts with the sexual wantonness (*akolasia*) at the conclusion of the first half (*Ep.* 10).[50] Certainly, it does so with some knowing irony. Yet the moral elevation of the simple life coincides with the literary virtues of simplicity (*apheleia*) and variation (*poikilia*) that Aelian most values: ἔστι γάρ τις καὶ ἐνταῦθα σοφία, φλώττῃ μὲν οὐ πεποικιλμένη οὐδὲ καλλωπιζομένη λόγων δυνάμει, σιγῶσα δὲ εὖ μάλα καὶ δι' αὐτοῦ τοῦ βίου τὴν ἀρετὴν ὁμολογοῦσα ('for there is a wisdom [*sophia*] even there, not dazzling with words nor beautified by the power of argument, but holding very well in silence and conveying its virtue through life itself'). *Ep.* 20, which programmatically presents a *raison d'être* for the collection, at the same time shows its debts to its classical sources and comedy in particular, by proclaiming its authors as specifically Athenian farmers. This conclusion seems addressed more to the reader of the collection than the ostensible addressee Sthenon, praising a rustic sense of temperance and justice.

This is not the only way to make sense of the structure of *Rustic Letters*, but I hope to have shown that there does exist a structure, and that it is much more elaborate than has previously been suggested. It is not simply that 'Aelian is concerned with the careful arrangement of *Rustic Letters*'[51] – though that is true. A quite rigorous parallelism between the two halves structures the entire collection, and can be set out diagrammatically (see fig. 1). In the doubled structured pairing of letters, some of the ways that the letters connect to each other may appear baroque (or Hellenistic). Knowledge of classical sources, and of certain plays of Aristophanes and Menander in particular seems to be presumed, but clearly Aelian is drawing on a much broader range of material. Further, he seems to be doing so based on his own reading of earlier literature, and not simply taking choice phrases from, e.g., Alciphron.[52] That some readers will recognize the passage from *Georgos* lurking barely beneath the surface of *Ep.* 2 offers one approach to that initial pair, but it is not exclusive, and others will pursue half-remembered mime performances and assume that they are primary. If there is any text that Aelian does presume his audience knows, however, it is Menander's *Dyscolus*.

Central to Aelian's *Rustic Letters* is the four-letter exchange between Callipides and Cnemon (*Ep.* 13–16).[53] The association with *Dyscolus* is apparent to us now, but it was not always so. As a result, early assumptions about the debt to the story of the misanthrope Timon are no longer persuasive.[54] This is the only exchange between correspondents in Aelian's book that go beyond a single pair, and as a result, the reader is invited into the day-to-day world of these two older men. The

Ep. 1 – Mania	*Ep.* 11 – Lamprias-Tryphe
Ep. 2 – Mania	*Ep.* 12 – Tryphe-Lamprias
Ep. 3 (a) – *oratory*	*Ep.* 13 (a) – Callipides-Cnemon
Ep. 4 (b) – Anthemion	*Ep.* 14 (b) – Cnemon-Callipides
Ep. 5 (b) – Anthemion	*Ep.* 15 (a) – Callipides-Cnemon
Ep. 6 (a) – *oratory*	*Ep.* 16 (b) – Cnemon-Callipides
Ep. 7 – Dercyllus-Opora	*Ep.* 17 – *morality and finances*
Ep. 8 – Opora-Dercyllus (prostitute) <—>	*Ep.* 18 – *morality and finances* (sailor)
Ep. 9 – *eunuch* (Chremes, prostitute) <—>	*Ep.* 19 – *bride* (Chremes, *prostitute*)
Ep. 10 – *eunuch* (wantonness) <—>	*Ep.* 20 – *sphragis* (*temperance*)

Fig. 1. Diagrammatic structure of Aelian's *Rustic Letters*.

[Linked themes in *italics*; echoes of other half of the collection in (round brackets).]

letters reflect two conflicting perceptions of rustic life and sets them against one another.[55] The resolution of this tension is central to an appreciation of *Rustic Letters*. Cnemon, the ill-tempered man referred to in the title of Menander's *Dyscolus*, is the play's principle blocking figure and appears in four of the five acts, opposing the marriage of young Sostratus to his daughter. On the other hand Callipides, the father of Sostratus, only appears in act V (onstage from 784–860 or 865). Though he too is a blocking figure, his opposition to the marriage of his daughter is overcome easily. It is possible to extrapolate these contrasting perspectives to philosophical schools generally (Thyresson associates Cnemon with the Cynics and Callipides with the Cyrenaics),[56] but this is, I believe, not the primary purpose of the letters.

Ep. 13 has Callipides offering friendly advice to Cnemon on how to live in the country well (for example, he counsels against throwing rocks to attack one's neighbours). Cnemon's indignant response in *Ep.* 14 includes the wish to be like Perseus, to fly away and to turn people into stone. Comparison with the text of *Dyscolus* reveals both situational parallels and many extensive precise verbal echoes of act I, and particular of Cnemon's entrance monologue (*Dysc.* 153–9).[57] One way to read these letters is as an epistolary summary of the play's first act. Readers familiar with the play appreciate the redeployment of familiar phrases as material is recombined into brief compass. Additionally, the conversation exists in parallel with the play's action. Callipides and Cnemon never meet on stage (though as the play ends with them about to become in-laws, this will change), but the reader is presented with their letters that must precede their imagined first encounter.

Aelian exploits the narrative opportunities of the letter, allowing a conversation between two men of different attitudes and values to take place. Each can set out his perspective, and the reader familiar with Menander can smile at the misanthrope being lured into dialogue almost against his will. The letter speaks for him, allowing him to maintain distance, but indirectly it integrates Cnemon into a larger place in society, making him say much more than he otherwise would. For some readers, additionally, the imagined timing of this exchange is raised: since Callipides' slave Pyrrhias is only assaulted with rocks immediately before his entrance at line 81, the exchange would seem to take place during the interval between acts I and II (lines 232/3). This recognition adds humorous elements to the characterization of Cnemon: what had been an empassioned diatribe at line 153 becomes something different in the act-dividing interval: we can imagine Cnemon feeling self-satisfied with his earlier outburst, receiving a letter, and being lured into conversation with a stranger; we can laugh at him redeploying his earlier bilious outburst and committing it to writing (an act that requires time, care, and intention). The epistolary form is seen to be both amenable to the misanthrope, but also a means to integrate him into his community and to mollify his fury, even as he attempts to replicate it through the written word.

Ep. 15 and 16 continue the conversation: the fact of the extended correspondence demonstrates the inherent superiority of Callipides' position, supporting the social world of rustic society (and, by extension, affirming the moral virtues of Aelian's collection). Indeed, these are the longest letters of the entire collection: Cnemon is both socialized and domesticated through the letter. Again, close verbal parallels demonstrate a deep familiarity with the Menandrean play;[58] in *Ep.* 15 it is also possible to identify allusions to fragments of Cratinus (fr. 301 K-A) and Eupolis (fr. 332 K-A). This suggests that there are many more comic fragments present throughout *Rustic Letters* that remain inaccessible to us simply due to our ignorance of the larger comic tradition.

Central to Callipides' second letter is the request that Cnemon integrate himself into the community, and particularly into the worship life of the rural area. A shrine of Pan occupies the central door on Menander's stage, and consequently the example Callipides gives (*Ep.* 15: θύω τοίνυν τῷ Πανί, 'And so I sacrifice to Pan') is hardly accidental: in the light of the play it is understood as a means of integrating Cnemon into his immediate community. In his response, Cnemon avows, τοὺς δὲ θεοὺς τούς τε ἄλλους καὶ τὸν Πᾶνα ἀσπάζομαί τε καὶ προσαγορεύω παριὼν μόνον, θύω δὲ οὐδέν (*Ep.* 16: 'As for the gods, both Pan and the others, I address and greet them on my own as I am passing by, and I sacrifice nothing'). I think it is natural to imagine this takes place before the events of act V, when Callipides appears on stage having learned of his son's engagement and when Cnemon in fact does go to a public sacrifice at Pan's cave (his last exit form the stage at line 858 is into the shrine). The act break between act IV and V (lines 783/4) seems to provide an opportunity for the second exchange of letters to take place.

Appreciation of the four-letter sequence between Callipides and Cnemon is enhanced for any reader who knows Menander's *Dyscolus*. While not necessary knowledge for the reader, knowledge of the comedy invites rich associations between specific moments of the play and the text of *Rustic Letters*, again with a specificity that would seem to belie the apparent simplicity of Aelian's text. Aelian loves comedy, and it seems that he makes no distinction between that of the fifth and fourth centuries. Drawing broadly on comedy and including Latin works, mime, and other genres, he demonstrates arguably the broadest appreciations of

Greek humor that we find in any Roman author (matched perhaps only by Lucian). Drawing on a variety of works to different degrees, he can pull together literary threads that replicate the feel of the classical Athenian farmer with a nuanced comedic sensibility and he can present it with a novel elegance that displays variation, wit, charm, and a deep understanding of human nature.

IV. Eupolis and his puppy.

A final Aelianic passage may give insight into a lost play of Eupolis. Aelian, *NA* 10.41, includes a story of Eupolis receiving a Molossian puppy, whom he named Augeas after the man who gave it to him.[59] When a 'fellow slave' (ὁμόδουλος) named Ephialtes was stealing some of Eupolis' plays, the dog killed him.[60] Later, when Eupolis died at Aegina, the dog lamented its master before expiring on its tomb, giving the place the name *Kunos Threnos* 'The Dog's Lament'. This is a curious story and the network of associations points to the plot of a lost Eupolidean comedy, which Storey has identified tentatively as the first *Autolycus*.[61] In this final section, I support Storey's argument, introducing additional elements that appear to be operating, which thereby supplements what can be said about *Autolycus*.

Eupolis was not himself a slave, and the story of him being a slave with 'Ephialtes', who attempted to steal his plays, is obviously fictionalized: rivalry between two slaves is at the center of the plot of Aristophanes' *Knights* (424 BCE), where an allegorical household of Demos (the People) is served by two slaves, identified implicitly with the historical figures of the generals Nicias and Demosthenes. The Aristophanic household is disrupted by a Paphlagonian slave, a coded Cleon, from whom the slaves steal some oracles, and this leads to the introduction of a Sausage-seller named Agoracritus who challenges and defeats the Cleon figure. The similarities between *Knights* and the anecdote are significant, particularly since there are sufficient narrative differences that details are not simply transferred directly from it to Aelian: an intermediary source, such as a lost play riffing on the pattern found in *Knights*, seems likely.[62] This is where the proposed *Autolycus* fits: like *Knights*, it would seem to have a pair of slaves representing real individuals, interacting with a Cleon-figure in a plot involving the stealing of some written text. That the Molossian hound is to be seen as a Cleon-figure is evident from Aristophanes' *Wasps* (422 BCE), where one of the many Cleon doublets is one of the witnesses in the domestic trial, the dog (*kuōn*, for *Kleōn*, both of which are from the deme of Cydathenaeum, the same deme to which Aristophanes belonged).

There were two versions of Eupolis' *Autolycus*, with the first performed in 420 BCE.[63] Storey speculates on the plot, asking 'Can we imagine a pair of comic poets, portrayed as slaves, competing for the tutorship of the young [athlete] Autolycus?' (Autolycus is historically attested), adding, 'The obvious person to lurk beneath "Ephialtes" is, of course, Aristophanes'.[64] The reason this is obvious is because of the deep and sustained mutual engagement between comic poets in the late 420s. Only a brief overview is possible here.[65] Eupolis fr. 89 (from *Baptae*, c. 416) claims some sort of authorial collaboration between Eupolis and Aristophanes in *Knights* (424).[66] The year following this play, in *Pytinē*, Cratinus innovates by presenting himself as a dramatic character, seemingly in response to the characterization of him by Aristophanes at *Knights* 526–36. In that play, Cratinus accused Aristophanes of using Eupolis' material (Cratinus fr. 213 K-A, and see Eupolis fr. 89 K-A). Eupolis' *Maricas* (421) mocked the demagogue Hyperbolus in a way reminiscent of the treatment of Cleon in *Knights* (so *Clouds* 553–6).[67] Now in 420, it would seem that Eupolis makes an accusation of someone stealing his plays (as Aristophanes did in *Knights*) while presenting himself as a character (as Cratinus did in *Pytinē*) but coding his rival in a way that was transparently interpretable even if it was not explicit (as he had done in *Maricas* and Aristophanes had done in *Knights* and *Wasps*). Further connections with one of Euripides' *Autolycus* plays are also possible: fr. 282 disparages athletes and could be either a source for Eupolis or a response to him.

Many puzzles remain. The Molossian hound in the story, biting 'Ephialtes' to death, likely represents some real individual lies behind the coded representations. Cleon had died in 422, but another demagogue is possibly intended. Possibly the name Ephialtes represents Aristophanes, but it need not do so (or, that need not be the totality of the character's meaning). The name Ephialtes is attested in later fifth century Athens. Its most famous Athenian possessor was the radical democrat apparently assassinated in 461 (*PAA* 452930 = *LGPN* ii, s.v. 1), following his reactionary reforms of the Areopagus court (Plutarch, *Cimon* 15.2).[68] The name was used in the later fifth century: the father of Philocrates, mentioned in Demosthenes 23.116–17 and Xenophon *Hell.* 4.8.24 (*PAA* 452935 = *LGPN* ii, s.v. 3), must have been alive around this time (*PAA* gives c. 420/19 as a date), and someone with that name is possibly on the casualty list of 411 (*PAA* [452920] = *LGPN* ii, s.v. 2). We should therefore be cautious about denying any historical reality to the supposed thief mauled by Eupolis' dog. Perhaps we are even to discern canine urinary behavior in fr. 57 from this play (Photius (b, z) α 1797): ἀνεκάς τ' ἐπαίρω καὶ βδελυρὸς σὺ τὸ σκέλος ('You raised your leg upwards, you disgusting man').[69]

The situation is further complicated by the comic playwright Phrynichus and the tragic playwright Sophocles. A lost play by Phrynichus called *Ephialtes* (or possibly *Epialtes*, 'Nightmare')[70] suggests another possible antecedent source for the content of the proposed Eupolidean *Autolycus*. Both forms of the title are preserved. Phrynichus fr. 1 (Σ Aristophanes *Wasps* 1348a) contains a pun on the name Ephialtes, demonstrating that even if the play was called *Nightmare*, some association with a known Ephialtes was operating. Reference to the play is also made in fr. 4 (b) (Σ Lucian *Tragic Zeus* 48). Speculation can easily run beyond the evidence, but for various reasons the issue of authorial collaboration is again introduced, between Phrynichus and Eupolis and Phrhynichus and Ameipsias.[71] Similarly, in his life of Polemon (head of the Academy for almost forty-five years until his death in 270/69), Diogenes Laertius describes Polemon's particular fondness for Sophoclean passages in which κύων τις ἐδόκει συμποεῖν Μολοττικός (D. L. 4.20, = Aristophanes fr. 958 K-A, = Sophocles T 144a Radt: 'it seemed a Molossian hound was the co-author'). The passage is attributed by Diogenes to 'the comic poet' (κατὰ τὸν κωμικόν), which Bergk associated with Aristophanes, and this brings to mind the similar accusations about Euripides and his slave Cephisophon (Aristophanes fr. 596 K-A, Euripides T 52–4 Kannicht).[72]

It is not possible to disentangle all of these alleged authorial collaborations, or to understand exactly what they mean in terms of the comic competition in the late 420s, but clearly there is some comic currency between these events, and they appear to cluster around the details contained in the story of Eupolis and his Molossian dog. What it means for Sophocles to have been assisted by a Molossian dog as a playwright is not at all clear, but the accusation for literary interdependence, among comic and tragic playwrights, demonstrates that an allegorical understanding of the Eupolidean anecdote in these terms is immediately interpretable by an audience in 420.

Through it is not known how Eupolis died, the anecdote in Aelian is the only one that associates his death with Aegina; the more accepted story suggest that he died in a shipwreck c. 411 BCE: καὶ ἀπέθανε ναυαγήσας κατὰ τὸν Ἑλλήσποντον ἐν τῷ πρὸς Λακεδαιμονίους πολέμῳ (*Suda* ε 3657: 'He died in a shipwreck in the Hellespont during the Peloponnesian War').[73] The story of the faithful hound lamenting its master evokes shades of Odysseus' Argos (Homer, *Od.* 17.290–327), but more resonant perhaps is the aitiological explanation of Κυνὸς Θρῆνος ('the lament of the dog'), which I believe is meant to evoke Κυνὸς σῆμα (Cynossema, 'the sign of the dog'), the place name given at Euripides' *Hecuba* 1273 for the marker of Hecuba's death after she is metamorphosed, in a play dating *c.* 421 BCE.[74] For the line in Hecuba to be meaningful, Cynossema must be a recognizable place name at this time. The sentence in Euripides is part of a prediction of Hecuba's fate, and the syntax is divided across two lines because of stichomythia: τύμβῳ δ'ὄνομα σῷ κεκλήσεται ... κυνὸς ταλαίνης σῆμα, ναυτίλοις τέκμαρ (1271 and 1273: 'The name for your tomb will be Cyno-bloody-sema, a marker for sailors'). Additionally, the lexical infixation, inserting ταλαίνης within the place-name, presumes audience familiarity. Later, the promontory off the Thracian Chersonese would be the site of a naval battle in 411 (Thuc. 8.104–7; Diod. Sic. 13.40.6). Was there an actual place at Aegina named Cunosthrenos? We do not know, but even without an actual place, the connection with the climactic prophecy in *Hecuba* would be resonant for an audience in 420.

There is also something suspicious about the name of the giver of the dog, Augeas of Eleusis. The mythical Augeas was from Elis, and was renowned for the number of his cattle (remember the fifth Labour of Heracles and the Augean stables). Augeas from Eleusis (*Eleusinios*, not *Ēleiakos* or *Ēliakos*) is otherwise unknown, but his name surely would evoke Elis at this time, *c.* 420. Following the Peace of Nicias, Elis in 421 had renounced allegiance to Sparta and formed a league with Argos, Corinth, and Mantinea (Thuc. 5.31); arising from this, at the Olympics in 420 Sparta was excluded (Thuc. 5.49–50). Just as the name Autolycus necessarily evokes the mythical figure of that name (known from Euripides' satyr play or plays, if they predate this), so Augeas here evokes his mythical namesake, which is associated with Elis at a time it is most relevant to the Athenian war effort, while still keeping the action of the purported play localized in Attica.

If the anecdote of Eupolis' Molossian puppy in Aelian does derive, directly or indirectly, from Eupolis' *Autolycus*, then various threads knot together that are particularly relevant for Athenians in 420: there are associations with *Knights* (424) and *Wasps* (422); there are associations with Euripides' *Hecuba* (*c.* 421) and arguably with *Autolycus* fr. 282 (of uncertain date); there are possible associations with a historical Ephialtes and a play by the comic playwright Phrynichus; and there are associations with Elis, which achieved a new political relevance in 421. Into this network additionally may be placed accusations of Sophocles co-authoring plays with a Molossian hound. Since each of these associations is independent of the others (and each is outside of the content of Aelian's narrative), the resulting network of associations supports the connection with *Autolycus* in 420 as envisaged by Storey.

Notes

1. Extant works of Aelian are abbreviated using short forms of the Latin titles as follows. *VH* = *Historical Miscellany* [*Varia Historia*] (text and translation by Wilson 1997). *NA* = *On the Characteristics of Animals* [*de Natura Animalium*] (text and translation Scholfield 1958–59). *Ep.* = *Rustic Letters* [*Epistulae*] (text and translation Benner and Fobes 1949, and see Leone 1974). For an overview see Kindstrand 1998. I would like to thank Tom Hawkins, Ian Storey, and Melissa Funke for valuable feedback.
2. The word is used in *Clouds* 1485, Aristophanes fr. 506 K-A (of Prodicus), and Eupolis fr. 386 K-A (of Socrates).
3. N. Wilson's translation is kept here, but I prefer to understand ἄνωθεν as indicating the front-row seats of the judges (the shouts come 'from above [and behind]'), following P. Wilson 2000: 347 n. 230 (and see Marshall and van Willigenburg 2004: 92–3).
4. Testimonia for the first production of *Clouds* and fragments 392–401 are collected with translations at Henderson 2007: 294–305, with indirect reference also at *Wasps* 1045–50.
5. Similarly, it would be wrong to conclude from this passage that Aelian has knowledge of a second performance of *Clouds*. Though πρῶτον ... εἶτα may refer to two separate events, the conclusion is not inevitable, and this more likely describes the changing sense of the play in its single performance.
6. Socrates' purported interest in Euripides also is seen in a story about the initial performance of *Orestes* in 408 BCE, when Socrates stood and called for the first three lines to be spoken again (Cicero, *Tusc.* 4.29.33). Euripides competing at the Piraeus remains an interpretative challenge. I find the detail of a major playwright competing at regional festivals credible, and such festivals ought not to be thought of as testing-grounds for subsequent (major) productions. Plays were conceived of as sets – a tetralogy at the City Dionysia, a dilogy at the Lenaia – and the idea of field-testing would remove this component from the artistic structure of the production. That said, there remains room for doubt, and Socrates on the road from Athens to the Piraeus does seem to evoke the context of Plato's *Republic*, and consequently the association may deserve future consideration. Note also the reference to 'new plays', framing the anecdote in terms of later competitive practice.
7. Since Luppe 1972, it has generally been accepted that all comedies at the Dionysia and Lenaia were staged on the same day, though it can still be argued that a reduction of comedies in certain years during the Peloponnesian War resulted in one comedy being staged after each tragic tetralogy at the Dionysia (see Storey 2002, and Hartwig 2010 for redating Plato Comicus' *Rhabdouchoi* [*Staff-bearers*] to 421, which challenges the reduction of comedies only during the Peace of Nicias); a good summary against a reduction can be found at Hartwig 2012: 195–7.

8 Aulus Gellius 17.4 similarly implies that Philemon beat Menander only through corruption; and that in tragedy Euripides himself was often defeated by inferior poets. Such biographical anecdotes, I suggest, emerge naturally from the judging system in which not every vote is read and it is possible to win having received fewer than half the votes cast (see Marshall and van Willigenburg 2004: 100–1).
9 It does not however follow that Cratinus fr. 395 K-A comes from *Pytinē*. We do not know to what or whom the phrase referred or in what context it was used in its original play.
10 Marshall 1999: 194 and 201–2 n. 56. Socrates was in his late 40s when *Clouds* was presented, and could have been presented with the white hair of papposilenus as part of the larger characterization, or he could have been given a mask that merely evoked papposilenus.
11 On Aristophanes and *Clouds* see, for example, Maximus of Tyre *Or*. 3.3: 'This man [Socrates] first of all flew into a rage with Aristophanes, took his stand in the midst of the Athenians and satirized him in return, at the Dionysia before a jury of drunkards' (Trapp 1997: 27). This conflicts with Maximus' comment at 12.8 that 'Socrates refused to grow angry with Aristophanes . . .' (1997: 113), but the passages agree on the close association between the two men. A similar passage in Plutarch can be found at *Mor*. 10c (*de Lib. Educ.*). On Socrates' supposed contempt of the Athenians in Aelian, see *VH* 2.1 and 2.6.
12 I am not arguing that Aelian is deceiving his readers, or attempting to mask the play's original lack of success. Rather, because the biographical tradition (before Aelian, presumably) has insinuated Socrates' prosecutors into his earlier life, the *Clouds* result can be reinterpreted as the 'right' response to an initial mean-spirited attack, before the opinion of the Athenian populace is subsequently turned against Socrates.
13 Smith 2014: 176.
14 Athenaeus cites this lost work and Aristophanes within close proximity to each other at 388 D and 395 E-F.
15 Aelian considers Aristias a comic poet, either through carelessness or because of his reputation as a writer of satyr-plays. This passage also mentions Dionolochus, a Sicilian comedy writer (fr. 8 K-A; compare the mention of Sophron in *NA* 15.6). *NA* 6.51 is discussed at Davies 1987: 69–75.
16 Marcovich 1976.
17 Thompson 1947: 98–9.
18 A different comic association for mice is found at Epicrates, *Chorus* fr. 8 K-A (Foka 2013: 66–8).
19 There were however plays called *Pannuchis* by Eubulus, Hipparchus, Pherecrates, and Alexis (Hunter 1983b: 175, and see 175–7).
20 Nutton 2009: 31.
21 See Storey 2011: 1.284–91.

22 Wilson 1997: 318.
23 The early date is suggested by the apparent appearance of his name four places before Ameipsias on the sequential list of Lenaea victors, *IG* ii² 2325.116–38 (see Storey 2011: 1.36–41). Ameipsias was competing in 423 BCE, coming second ahead of *Clouds*, but there are many victors listed before him before the known figures from the 420s. The late date is supported by Theopompus fr. 31 K-A.
24 Six epigrams survive on herms of Menander and Homer found in Rome, which may come from a suburban villa of Aelian (*IG* 14.1168, 1183, esp. 1183.10–15 [= Ar. Byz. T9 Slater]): though one of them uses the name, there were many Aeliani and the connection cannot be proved (Bowie 1989: 244–47). The association is not implausible, and it may be that Aelian is to be seen as a key witness for the perception that Menander was second only to Homer among Greek poets.
25 See esp. Rosenmeyer 2001: 308–21, Hodkinson 2013, Smith 2014: 29–46, and (for Alciphron) see Anderson 1997: 2201.
26 Rosemeyer summarizes the approach by the Loeb editors Benner and Fobes: 'They criticize Aelian for his frequent use of clichés, his vulgarity, and his numerous echoes of classical authors . . . — all elements we have accepted in Alciphron as integral to his specific literary undertaking' (2001: 308).
27 There are comic opportunities that seem not to be pursued by Aelian, e.g. Alciphron's letters revel in so-called speaking names (*redende Namen*), a technique employed for the farmer-heroes of Aristophanes (e.g. Dicaeopolis, Philocleon, Trygaeus, Peisetairus); see Anderson 1997: 2201.
28 Anderson 1997: 2191 ('the deliberately unmissable starting-point') and Smith 2014: 33–4. For this passage and its relationship to Aristaenetus, see Barbiero, chapter 13 in this volume.
29 See Funke, chapter 12 in this volume. Determining the relative dates of Alciphron's and Aelian's letters (esp. in relation to Longus) is a mug's game (Bonner 1909a and b; Hunter 1983: 13–15, Anderson 1997: 2194, Kindstrand 1998: 2978–9). Reich 1894 asserted that Alciphron was earlier than Aelian, a conclusion challenged as soon as Bonner 1909a: 32–41 but repeated in Benner and Fobes 1949: 6–18 and often since.
30 Smith 2014: 32.
31 Rosenmeyer 2001: 309 and 310, and cf. Hodkinson 2013: 269–71, who underplays the literariness of the letters. For the programmatic nature of *Ep.* 20, see Benner and Fobes 1949: 345, Hodkinson 2013: 260 ('an authorial *sphragis* of sorts', and cf. 273–4).
32 Rosenmeyer 2001: 309: 'In the spirit of the fiction, we could ask ourselves who collected these letters, how they came into Aelian's hands, and why they are ordered the way they are.'
33 For *Ep.* 1–2, see Rosenmeyer 2001: 310–12, and see Hodkinson 2013: 302 and Smith 2014: 36–7.
34 Hodkinson 2013: 287–91.

35 Various lists of Aelian's literary (and especially comic) allusions exist: see Bonner 1909a: 42-44 and Kindstrand 1998: 2979–80. For *Ep.* 1–2, see Bonner 1909a: 42, Benner and Fobes 1949 *ad loc.*, Rosenmeyer 2001: 310–12, and Smith 2014: 36–7.
36 De Stefani 1912. Bonner 1909a: 37 also compares *Ep.* 2 with Alciphron 2.15 and Aristophanes, *Wealth* 1103–6. Comic influence is not primary, but it is not absent.
37 Bonner 1909a: 42.
38 See Scholfield 1958–9: 3.404 for apian passages in *NA*, none of which deal with the abandonment of a hive.
39 Hodkinson 2013: 302, and see 302–3.
40 Warnecke 1906, Rosenmeyer 2001: 318–20, and see Arnott 1996a: 496–501, esp. 498–501. There was also a comedy by Amphis with this name.
41 Opora is onstage at *Ach.* 520–728 (she and Dicaiopolis kiss at 710), 819–55, and 1329–59. Though she has no lines, she is a significant stage presence.
42 See Anderson 1997: 2202–3. Aristaenetus *Ep.* 2.1 uses Aelian *Ep.* 7–8 for a model; cf. also Alciphron *Ep.* 4.8–9 for an epistolary exchange on the fiscal demands of a *hetaira*.
43 Hodkinson 2013: 303, pointing to Leone 1974 *ad loc.* who cites Terence, *Eunuchus* 929–40 and Menander fr. 152 K-A (*The Ephesian*). See Smith 2014: 39–40.
44 As suggested by Steffen: 'The switch from the Greek to the Latin playwright may well be a mental lapse, as we find in Sigmund Freud, and is explainable as an example of linguistic interference' (1972a: 304).
45 Brown 2006: 96.
46 Smith 2014: 40–1
47 Viellefond 1929: 357.
48 Hodkinson 2013: 277–80, and see Rosenmeyer 2001: 320–1.
49 Leone 1974 *ad loc.* also suggests parallels with Plato, though Hodkinson 1013: 295 n. 75 expresses doubt.
50 Smith 2014: 41, and see 34–6.
51 Hodkinson 2013: 270, and cf. Smith 2014: 41 n. 31: 'Other combinations are of course possible.'
52 Thus already at Bonner 1909a: 44: 'When it is remembered that the resemblances ... have to do with rather unusual terms of expression, and that none of them is matched in Alciphron, it seems a justifiable conclusion that Aelian studied the comic poets independently; and in the light of this conclusion we should regard it as highly probable that the comic words and phrases ... were taken by Aelian directly from the Attic Comedy, and not through the medium of Alciphron's Letters.'
53 See Thyresson 1964, Rosenmeyer 2001: 315–17, Guida 2004 and 2007, Hodkinson 2013: 276–7, and Smith 2014: 41–5. Associations with Menander's play were first suggested with insight by Graux 1877: 228–9 n. 5, and see Ribbeck 1888: 11–15.

54 Reich 1894 had argued for the importance of Timon, but without access to *Dyskolos* which was only published in the 1950s. Bonner 1909a: 34 and Anderson 1997: 2194 rightfully discount the relevance of Timon.
55 Thyresson 1964: 10.
56 Thyresson 1964: 20–4.
57 Thyresson 1964: 10–15 traces these in detail.
58 Thyresson 1964: 15–20.
59 Storey 2011: 2.34–5 (= T xii).
60 Aristotle, *HA* 9.1 (608a 28–31) reports that Molossian sheep-dogs confront the attacks of wild animals with particular courage; Aristophanes *Thes*. 416–17 mentions that they keep adulteres away.
61 Storey 2003: 81–94, esp. 87–8, 2011: 2.68–79, and see Sidwell 2009: 113–14. Kyriakiki 2007: 137–49 doubts the association with *Autolycus*.
62 It is even possible that a more creative engagement with a completely unrelated story is possible. As Tom Hawkins points out to me, features of this dog story are shared with that of Maera, the hound in Eratosthenes' *Erigone*, in which a loyal dog identifies his master Icarius'\ killers and dies on his tomb, before being catasterized into the star Sirius (see Hyginus, *Fabulae* 130), though this is not a story known to have been treated in fifth-century tragedy.
63 Athenaeus 216d. Σ *Wasps* 1026 suggests Aristophanes is there criticizing Eupolis' *Autolycus*. This must be incorrect, reversing the chronological relationship. It is however relevant for this discussion because it rightly (in my view) implicates *Wasps* in the Autolycus story. These two plays of Eupolis also bore some relationship to the two lost plays of Euripides called *Autolycus* (see Collard and Cropp 2008: 278–87), which were probably satyr plays. Though their narrative content was different (Euripides focusing on Hermes' trickster son and Eupolis on a young Athenian athlete), there will have been associations between the plays made by the audience regardless. There are no good arguments for the dates of the Euripidean plays. The fact that both authors restaged versions of their plays with this title is seemingly an unusual coincidence.
64 Storey 2011: 2.69.
65 See Sidwell 1993, 1994, and Kyriakidi 2007.
66 A testimonium for *Baptae* (Σ (φ) *ad* Juv. 2.91–2 = T ii (d) in Storey 2011, 2.82–3) curiously claims *quo titulo Eupolis et Aristophanes comoediam scripserunt* ('Eupolis and Aristophanes wrote a comedy with this title'). Seemingly an error, this reproduces the claim made in fr. 89 about *Knights*.
67 See Sommerstein 2000 for the Hyperbolus comedies that followed.
68 Stockton 1982 has questioned whether in fact Ephialtes was murdered. Though his suggestion that a death of natural causes remains possible (even if it has not been widely accepted), what is important is that his death was seen to be suspicious

throughout the fifth century, and could be referred to as a murder at Antiphon 5.68 (415 BCE).
69 I owe this observation to Ryan Johnson.
70 Storey 2011: 3.48–53.
71 Storey 2011: 3.48–9 raises the possibility of the play at the Lenaia of 423 and connects the playwright with Eupolis; a later date in the 410s is also possible (3.38–9, which also discusses a possible connection with Ameipsias).
72 See Kovacs 1990.
73 Storey 2011: 2.28–9, and see Storey 2003: 56–60, 378–81. This narrative was later associated specifically with Alcibiades and Eupolis' *Baptae*. Referring to a casualty list that includes a 'Eupolis', Storey concludes, 'My own preference is to accept the story in the Suda of Eupolis' death at sea and to identify that battle with the combat at Kynos Sema in the summer of 411. I have no real problem with identifying the man on the casualty list (*IG* i³. 1190. 52) as the comic poet ...' (2003: 59). Note that this is the same casualty list that may list an Ephialtes at line 92, though that name is now restored as ΚΗΦΙΣ- (*PAA* 566970). Another weird coincidence.
74 For the date (rather than the more usual *c.* 424), see Marshall 2001: 228–9 n. 10. Though an earlier date remains possible, it does not change the point here, but only makes the referent less proximate to *Autolycus*.

12

The Menandrian World of Alciphron's *Letters*

Melissa Funke*

All four sets of letters in Alciphron's collection of epistolary fiction betray the influence of Menander and New Comedy.[1] Most of the letters share a domestic and quotidian emphasis with New Comedy, while all have a distinctly fourth-century Attic setting. All are written in the voices of and peopled by the standard stock characters found in Menandrian New Comedy, including young men and women with romantic problems, soldiers, parasites, difficult old men and courtesans.[2] Menander himself appears in the fourth book of the collection as a correspondent with his paramour, Glykera,[3] an indication that the playwright's work is the dominant influence on Alciphron's archaizing and Atticizing agenda.

Despite the overwhelming evidence of Menander's influence on his writing, reading through the entire collection reveals that Alciphron makes liberal use of several other genres from Classical literature, including pastoral poetry, Old Comedy, and possibly even elegiac poetry. The first two books of letters, grouped under the headings Ἐπιστολαὶ Ἁλιευτικαί ('Letters of Fishermen') and Ἐπιστολαὶ Ἄγροικαι ('Letters of Rustics'), seem in many ways to be more representative of the rural milieu of Theocritean pastoral than of Menander's urban settings, especially letters such as 2.9, with its *locus amoenus* and musical shepherd.[4] Old Comedy, specifically that of Aristophanes, turns up shortly after this in 2.11, which condenses the plot of *Clouds* into a short letter from a father to his son who has taken up with the philosophers at the Academy.[5] The *exclusus amator* of love elegy even makes an appearance in 4.8, Simalion's plea to the *hetaira* he offended.[6]

Rosenmeyer would have such letters (along with the rest of the collection) read as an intellectual exercise, in which the reader is invited to imagine a response to an unanswered letter; in her reading, they offer the 'intellectual delight of pretending to be back in the *locus classicus* of Menander's Athens'.[7] Anderson, in a slight variation from Rosenmeyer, sees the inclusion of pastoral and Old Comic motifs as presenting a 'Menander's-eye view' on other classical Greek authors,[8] and as portraying a world in which the rules of New Comedy, especially regarding the maintenance of an illusion of reality, must be followed.[9] While both of these models apply to Alciphron's work, I propose a third reading of Menander's influence on the *Letters* that addresses their epistolary format: Alciphron reorients and recreates the world of Menander's plays by presenting it from the perspectives of his secondary characters.

Through this process of reorientation, I argue that although Alciphron incorporates New Comic characters like young men with romantic troubles and boastful soldiers into the *Letters*, more often his own focus is the perspective of the secondary characters from Menander's plays, who, while integral to the plots of New Comedy, usually have little to do with driving them forward. These include the concubines and courtesans, parasites and servants who often accompany Menander's main characters, for the purpose of highlighting those figures' actions and words.[10] This *modus operandi* extends to the very periphery of Menander's plays, so that Alciphron often has his letter writers describe how actions by primary characters affect them, Menander's secondary or even tertiary characters, in the world of the letters. This reorienting of the plot effectively reverses the process that Goldberg identified, with Menander's primary characters now existing only within the experience of his secondary ones. In explaining how Alciphron remakes the world of Menander from these perspectives, I shall begin by outlining the links between what Menander depicts onstage and Alciphron's epistolary reconstruction of Hellenistic Athens before turning to the special case of the *Letters of Courtesans*. My conclusion considers the function of the epistolary format in redirecting the reader's attention to the secondary characters of Menander.

Tracing Menander in the *Letters*

There are two points worth addressing before I outline the correspondences between Menander and Alciphron. The first is that while I am most concerned with handling the specific influence of Menander's plays on Alciphron's writing, I cannot ignore the fact that Menander himself was heir to a set of conventions, however well-established (or not) they were by his time. Hunter, for example, points out that the soldiers and parasites of New Comedy have clear precedents in Old Comedy.[11] On the other hand, aspects of New Comedy such as the reduced role of the chorus, increased emphasis on realism and three-door set seem to have been somewhat in flux in early fourth-century comic productions and only became convention during Menander's time. The same is true regarding character-types, many of which were likely either introduced or expanded on in plays from the early fourth century.[12]

My second point, however, is that while Menander may have shared many of these conventions with his fellow New Comic poets, it is clear that when Alciphron draws on this genre, he looks to Menander's plays as an exemplar of New Comedy. The most obvious clue for this is Alciphron's inclusion of Menander as a letter-writer in his collection of letters between *hetairai* and their lovers. The correspondence between Menander and his paramour, Glykera, concerns an invitation from Ptolemy for Menander to join him in Egypt (letters 4.18 and 19).[13] In *Letter* 4.2, Glykera frets about sending Menander off to the Isthmian games with her alluring colleague Bacchis. The existence of the historical Glykera is a matter of some debate,[14] as this name is given to the title character of *Perikeiromenē*, there is a single fragment attributed to a play titled *Glykera* and there is no contemporary mention of the actual *hetaira*. But the reality of her existence is of little importance to her role in the *Letters* since her consistent association with Menander in post-Hellenistic times (as demonstrated by images depicting the poet and the courtesan together)[15] gives her a quasi-historical status which is then mirrored in her letters. The Glykera of the letters is a brilliant device that links setting, characters, and playwright in what amounts to the grand finale of the collection.[16]

Alciphron's mimicry of Menander operates at the basic level of language. In his study of Menander's vocabulary, Durham found that Alciphron used at least forty-one words with distinct Menandrian flavor (i.e. not from the Attic Greek employed by the orators, Plato, Thucydides, and Old Comic playwrights). Lucian, for the sake of comparison with another Atticist, uses seventy of these words spread over his far larger corpus. Longus, who makes liberal use of New Comic characters (e.g. Gnathon the parasite) in his novel that is comparable in length to the *Letters*, uses Menandrian vocabulary only seven times.[17] Clearly the epistolographer turned to the language of Menander more regularly than his peers. Alciphron even adapts well-known phrases from Menander's plays, as when Panope, beseeching her husband, the fisherman Euthybolus, not to waste all of their money on a *hetaira* from the Peiraeus, reminds him of the parameters of their marriage: οἵ με ἐγγυητὴν ἐπίκληρον ἐπὶ παίδων ἀρότῳ γνησίων συνῆψάν σοι γάμῳ, (1.6.1: '[My mother and father] joined me, a betrothed heiress, to you in marriage for the bearing [lit. plowing] of legitimate children').[18] The popularity of variations of this formula in New Comedy (versions appear in *Dyskolos*

842–4, *Perikeiromenē* 1013–14, and *Samia* 726–7) reinforces the specifically Athenian version of marriage around which Menander builds the majority of his plots.[19] Its reappearance in Alciphron is a reminder to the reader that Menander's play mediates the version of Athens in the *Letters*.

Beyond using the same vocabulary and phrasing, both authors have their characters speak (or write) a version of the Attic dialect that is not dependent on social status or education. While Menander's Attic is a product of his own time and place, Alciphron's use of this dialect anchors his work in the world that Menander created. Although Menander has the freedom to employ other dialects for comic effect (e.g. the use of Doric as part of a disguise in *Aspis*),[20] he does so very sparingly, so that even slaves who are obviously foreigners speak the same Greek that their masters do.[21] There is little to no distinction in register among the characters from varying social classes.[22] In his comparison of Aristophanes and Menander, Plutarch makes the following remark: ἀλλὰ Μένανδρος οὕτως ἔμιξε τὴν λέξιν, ὥστε πάσῃ καὶ φύσει καὶ διαθέσει καὶ ἡλικίᾳ σύμμετρον εἶναι, (*Moralia* 853: 'But Menander mixed his diction in such a way that it was appropriate to every nature, condition, and age'), i.e. Menander used high and low registers indiscriminately to create a consistent dialect for all of his characters. In Alciphron, we observe a similar phenomenon, with apparently rustic farmers and fishermen writing to each other using much the same language as 'Menander' does in his letter to Glykera.[23] This blurs the social distinctions between the groups of letter writers (the same effect that has slaves and masters speaking in the same dialect in Menander) but it also draws attention to the artificiality of the Athens in the *Letters*.[24] This version of Athens, while internally coherent as a replica of the world of New Comedy, should be read as divorced from historical reality, which Alciphron's use of language signposts. The way in which his characters use language thus draws the reader's attention to Alciphron's skill as a creator of a fictional world.

Menander's plots and characters strike a similarly delicate balance between realism and fantasy, creating a 'controlled tension between the familiar and unfamiliar, convention and reality, the typical and the exceptional'.[25] Alciphron also mirrors this carefully constructed pseudo-realism which is necessarily divorced from contemporary concerns, just as the politics of Menander's day never intrude on his plays. In the very few instances where Alciphron makes a reference to a specific historical event, he does so in such a way that while he asserts his Attic setting, a necessity for creating his Menandrian milieu,[26] he does not indicate anything other than a vaguely post-Classical timeframe.[27] Just as Menander's interest is in the complex nature of human relationships over the 'real' world,[28] Alciphron is sufficiently concerned with the historical to be compelling but not so much as to be unrecognizable to an ancient audience familiar with New Comedy.

Thus, when Alciphron appropriates plot elements from Menander, he adapts them so that they are easily identifiable but not exact replicas. In 2.35, for example, a letter-writer who tells of her own rape resulting in marriage is not a *parthenos* but rather a widow. Pointing to several of Menander's plays that resolve with a marriage (or two), Alciphron gives the new husband/assailant's name as Moschion (a character in *Kitharistēs, Perikeiromenē, Samia, Sikyonioi/Sikyonios* and up to three of the *Fabulae Incertae*).[29] In another letter, one parasite gossips to another about his mistress, who gave birth only five months after getting married and then exposed the child, placing recognition tokens with it (γνωρίσματα, 3.27.1), which is the plot of *Epitrepontes*. Here, though, the husband is unaware of his wife's actions.[30] In both letters, the action of these plots is mediated through the perspective of characters that would be either non-speaking or secondary (at most) in the plays.

Alciphron's choice of Menandrian supporting characters as his correspondents is a noteworthy reorientation of Menander's plays. Even the division of the letters and their writers into groups of fishermen, rustics, parasites and *hetairai* signals a focus on the periphery of society, and in the case of the fishermen and rustics, a move to the countryside of Attica.[31] Letter after letter from the fishermen and rustics emphasizes the difference between those correspondents and city-dwellers; writers wonder at the barefoot (ἀνυπόδητος) fellows wandering around the Stoa (1.3.2), fret at their wives mixing with indiscreet Athenian women (1.4.3),[32] and wonder at how people can live enclosed in city walls (2.28.1). Winking at his source of inspiration for the *Letters*, Alciphron even has one of his rustics visit the theatre in Athens, although in maintaining Alciphron's carefully constructed reality, he says that he cannot recall the shows he saw there (2.17.1–2: τὰς μὲν οὖν ἄλλας οὐ συνέχω τῇ μνήμῃ).[33] When urbanites come out to the countryside as in the boat-party of letter 1.15, the reader becomes a spectator alongside the fisherman writing the letter. In the urban books of letters, the Ἐπιστολαὶ Παρασίτων and Ἐπιστολαὶ Ἑταιρικαί, Alciphron underscores the economic reliance of these characters on their patrons, through constant references to hunger from the parasites (e.g. 3.1 and 39) and demands for payment by the *hetairai* (e.g. 4.9 and 15).

Identifying stock characters from Menander in the letters reveals that Alciphron not only modifies the playwright's plots but also applies this peripheral perspective to them. By examining how Alciphron works with two types of central characters, the soldiers and young men, we can see that he maintains their roles in Menander's plots while shaping their depictions through non-central viewpoints. Letter 2.13, for example, addressed to a young man from his mother, acts as a prequel of sorts for one of Menander's boastful soldiers. In it she warns of the dangers of the military life and accuses him of abandoning his responsibilities on the farm while loudly praising the triple-crested helmet and being in love with a shield instead (2.13.2: κράνους δὲ ἐπαινεῖς τριλοφίαν καὶ ἀσπίδος ἐρᾷς). The name of the future mercenary? Thrasonides, a name which appears only in Menander in other literature, where it is given to the soldier returned from Cyprus (see fr. 5) in *Misoumenos*. In letter 2.34, Alciphron brings the insufferability of Menander's soldiers to the forefront, with a farmer listing all the ways in which these characters are outrageous to those around them. In the case of this letter, the farmer describes how the soldier overuses military jargon (an ideal means for Alciphron to display his own knowledge of this) and brags of his successes. The rustic here expresses a sentiment similar to the feelings of the parasite toward his soldier-patron in *Kolax*. Plutarch quotes him as saying, οἶα τὰ σκώμαθ' τὰ σοφὰ καὶ σττρατηγικά,/ οἶος δ' ἀλαζών ἐστιν ἀλιτήριος, (fr. 8.2–3=*Mor.* 547e: 'What clever general's jokes! What an offensive braggart he is!'). The soldier of this letter also shows off his captive women and prisoners, an act which flattens out Menander's more nuanced and therefore sympathetic portrayal of soldier-characters (as with Polemon over the course of *Perikeiromenē*).[34] This is a product of the shifted perspective in Alciphron; looking at the soldier character from the farmer's point of view invites a comparison with the mundane life of the farmer, emphasizing the extreme nature of his actions.

This is not to say that Alciphron doesn't adopt at least some of Menander's nuance when making use of his soldier characters. Perspective, however, can account for much of the sympathy found in letter 3.22, from one parasite to another about the man they have been dining with. The writer chastises his fellow parasite for slandering their patron and defends the soldier on the grounds that he is in fact not jealous at all over prostitutes (3.22.1), which seems to be a reversal of the situation between Polemon and Glykera at the beginning of *Perikeiromenē*. Of course this writer, as a parasite, is heavily invested in maintaining a good relationship with the soldier, and so is compelled to portray him in a flattering, possibly insincere, manner.

When young men of the type who are central to Menander's plots appear in Alciphron's letters, they undergo a process of compression that is based on perspective similar to the one that we have already seen with Menander's soldier characters. In letter 1.15 (mentioned above), the nautical party of Pamphilus, his friends and a variety of paid female companions (a flute-girl, harpist and a cymbal-player) convinces Nausibius, who has rented out his fishing boat for the occasion, that the young men of Athens are overly-swayed by luxury to the point of effeminacy (he describes them as τρυφερός and ἁβρόβιος, 1.15.1). On the other hand, the parasite who writes letter 3.38 is certain that the young man in whom he had placed his hopes is living far too austerely, leaving him worried about his own prospects: εἰ γὰρ ὁ τρέφων δεῖται τοῦ θρέψοντος, τί ἂν εἴη ὁ τρέφεσθαι ὀφείλων; (3.38.3: 'If the one who provides the food needs someone who provides food, what of the one who needs food provided?'). The first case is reminiscent of the beginning of *Epitrepontes*, when Charisios has hired Habrotonon and been attending drinking parties after learning of his new wife's supposed infidelity, while the second reduces the dynamic between parasite and patron to feeder and fed. These letters, along with 2.13, 2.34, and 3.22 demonstrate Alciphron's realignment of Menander's characters and plots to emphasize the concerns of his secondary characters.

The special case of the Ἐπιστολαὶ Ἑταιρικαί

While this process of giving attention to secondary characters is very much at play in the Ἐπιστολαὶ Ἑταιρικαί, Alciphron ties these letters to a more specifically historical Athens than the version from his other three books and in doing so interweaves Menander's onstage version of Athens with the Athens inhabited by Menander. Almost every letter in the fourth book is peppered with references to Menander's cultural milieu while the *hetairai* themselves are our most 'realistic' correspondents of the four books.[35] *Letter* 4.1 describes Praxiteles' statues at Thespis, while 4.3, 4 and 5 touch on the famous trial of Phryne for impiety and her infamous defense by Hypereides.[36] The philosophers obliquely touched upon in 1.3 and 2.11 are characterized as the opponents of the courtesans in 4.7: ἐπεὶ σύγκρινον, εἰ βούλει, Ἀσπασίαν τὴν ἑταίραν καὶ Σωκράτην τὸν σοφιστήν, καὶ πότερος ἀμείνους αὐτῶν ἐπαίδευσεν ἄνδρας λόγισαι, (4.7.7: 'So judge, if you will, between Aspasia the *hetaira* and Socrates the sophist, and consider which of them educated better men').[37] Philosophers seem to be in for a particularly hard time from the *hetairai*, with Leontium bemoaning her lot as the mistress of the elderly Epicurus: ὄντως ἐπιπολιορκητὴν ἔχω τοιοῦτον, οὐχ οἷον σύ, Λάμια, Δημήτριον, (4.17.3: 'I really have quite the besieger, not like you have in Demetrios, Lamia').[38] The addressee of that letter, Lamia, writes her own letter to her lover, Demetrios Poliorketes ('The Besieger'), the Macedonian general with a reputation for licentiousness.[39]

But even with these references it is clear that what goes on in this version of Athens could still comfortably take place in the world of Menander's plays. (Even Lamia's letter, with its transparent historical connections, avoids any political commentary.) In *Letter* 4.6, Thaïs relates the abuse she faced from a rival while attending the all-night women's ritual known as a *pannuchis*. *Pannuchides* are of course characteristic of Menander's plots, as the setting in which young women get raped by their eventual husbands (cf. *Perikeiromenē* and *Samia*).[40] If the fisherman in 1.15 can be present at a party suggestive of the opening of *Perikeiromenē*, then surely Thaïs could attend the sort of *pannuchis* that precedes the action of that play. Her name itself points to the title character of the play *Thaïs*.[41] Although little is known about the content of this play, Traill has suggested that Menander's version of Thaïs may have been essential in establishing the stock role of the *hetaira* and become associated with this type of character even more than similar characters like Chrysis or Glykera.[42]

We can return to *Letter* 4.8, in which Simalion, the would-be lover of the *hetaira* Thettale, begs for her attention as he claims to be visiting her door over and over (4.8.1: τὸ πολλάκις ἡμᾶς ἐπὶ τὰς θύρας φοιτᾶν). I suggest that, like the party on the boat, the *pannuchis* and the other plot points borrowed from Menander, this is based on a New Comic trope. *Misoumenos* opens with Thrasonides shut out by his lover and *Fabula Incerta* 8 includes a variation on this type of scene where a young man laments that he is locked out from the house of the woman he loves (but whose face he hasn't actually seen) (fr. A.5–10).[43] This type of scene, known as a *paraclausithyron*, is not an entirely Menandrian innovation (Aristophanes, for example, parodies this type of scene at *Ecclesiazusae* 938–1111), and it may even have precedents in fifth-century Greek lyric.[44] Yet a scene in which a man has been shut out by an angry lover is especially suited to Menander's world, particularly if that lover is a *hetaira*. Petale's letter in response (4.9) is not only a nod to the epistolary format and a frustration of Simalion's hopes, but also a completion of the story: Simalion needs to pay up.[45]

Standing out from the rest of the letters in this book both in its detail and length, *Letter* 4.13 is the only one in the entire collection to approach the length of the correspondence between Menander and Glykera and describes a visit to the countryside by a group of *hetairai* and their patrons to visit a shrine to Pan and the Nymphs. In the first three books of letters, there are many examples of exchange and conflict between urban and rural, but this is the only example from the fourth book to include any such encounter and the only letter to narrate such a story from an urban point of view. Upon arrival at the shrine, guarded by images of its tutelary deities, the women in the party build a makeshift altar, make offerings to Pan and pray to the Nymphs (4.13.4–5). Deciding to have their dinner party in the grove, everyone sets about building cushions from foliage then drinking and eating (8–10). After some drinking and music and a particularly arousing performance by a woman named Plangon,[46] the couples slip off to a nearby thicket to consummate their desire.[47] Afterwards, they return to the grove for another meal, drink even more and the couples sleep together once more, so intoxicated that they no longer bother to hide their activities from one another (18 τῆς ἀφροδίτης παρακλέπτειν).

Since Menander's plays generally have very little of the risqué portrayed in them, particularly for a genre that consistently features sex-workers, what amounts to an orgy may seem shocking in a collection of letters that has reflected Menander's chastity thus far. I propose a Menandrian model for this most revealing of letters: the worshippers of Pan in *Dyskolos*. Pan in fact opens the play as the deity who delivers the prologue and mentions that part of the setting is his own shrine (1–2). The chorus of the play is composed of drunken worshippers of Pan (230 Πανισταί),[48] who become interwoven in the action of *Dyskolos*, through the proximity of the shrine and the sacrifice to Pan performed by Sostratos' mother. Sikon the cook recounts the group's activities and describes the drinking, toasts, and dancing of two young women (946–53), before leaving off as the play itself ends. Not only is the revel he describes a drunken escapade, it also lasts all night; the courtesans end their party when the neighbor's cock crows (4.13.18). Since this chorus stands out from all other choruses in Menander by its integration into the plot and setting,[49] it is fitting that Alciphron commemorate it in such a distinctive way. Alciphron's incorporation of this chorus in his letters from the *hetairai* in such a graphic manner confronts the chastity of Menander's plays. Although he populates his plays with prostitutes and their clients and centers his plots on erotic miscommunications, Menander cannot put sex center-stage. Alciphron, in contrast, can take these themes to their ultimate conclusion by virtue of his genre and foreground what Menander can only hint at.

Even if the ordering of the letters in the surviving manuscripts does not reflect Alciphron's arrangement of his work,[50] the letters between Menander and Glykera still tie a neat bow around Alciphron's entire enterprise.[51] If the Ἐπιστολαὶ Ἑταιρικαί combine the onstage world of Menander with a quasi-historical Athens, this pair of letters draws Menander into the world that he has created.[52]

In Glykera's response to her lover's news, she lists a set of plays which are most likely to entertain Ptolemy in Egypt and in doing so underscores the material from which Alciphron has created his letters (4.19.19).[53] She also winkingly suggests that he prepare the play in which she appears (likely *Perikeiromenē*, 20). I suspect that her list is not a perfect guide to Alciphron's allusions, but rather a list of Menander's greatest hits (or what was most popular in Alciphron's time) and so the reader cannot help but be reminded of the many plots and characters that are in the rest of the letters. At least two of these plays (*Epitrepontes* and *Misoumenos*) are depicted in mosaics from the 'House of Menander' at Mytilene and *Sikyonioi/Sikyonios* is shown in a wall painting from Ephesus,[54] so there is a possibility that Glykera's list could even nod to a set of visual depictions known only to the particularly *pepaideumenos*.

The epistolary Menander

So far I have only touched lightly upon Alciphron's epistolary format, yet this is truly the key to understanding how he adapts Menander's characters and plots. The popularity of collections of fictionalized letters written in Greek during the Roman Empire is well-documented.[55] Many of these contained (pseudo) biographical information about well-known historical individuals, a trend which Hodkinson and Rosenmeyer connect to the tradition of writing *bioi*, a means of discussing the private lives of public people.[56] This genre may also have grown out of *ethopoeia*, a common rhetorical exercise that asked what a person or character might do in a specific situation.[57] Letters as a medium for fiction give their authors several distinct advantages, the main one being a claim to (apparent) authenticity: they play at representing the writer's unmediated voice and therefore give the audience direct access to the perspective of the letter-writer, with no intervening narrator, as though by reading these letters, one is eavesdropping.[58]

Just as letters seem to represent an authentic point of view, they also have a flexibility that gives the author the ability to manipulate the narrative. There is great potential for persuasive writing, for saying what is difficult to express in person and saying it without interruption, as each writer alone controls the narrative within an individual letter, and the author can then use this to characterize the writer. Letters are also automatically understood to be a smaller piece of a larger dialogue, so the gaps and repetitions that are part of correspondence can be employed to augment an author's storyline. Part of this is the 'I-you' aspect of letters, with the 'I' (the writer) expecting a 'you' (the addressee), and both voices sharing a specific relationship; the writer is defined by the addressee.[59] The letter also implies the absence of the writer but the presence of the addressee.[60] The other important aspect of letters is what Altman terms 'temporal polyvalence'.[61] A letter implies multiple points in time: when it is written, when it is sent, and when it is read (by both its internal and external audiences). The author of a fictionalized letter can also use this quality of the letter to define the present of its actual composition against the present of its fictional composition.

Alciphron uses the epistolary format to mimic the advantages of drama, in which the audience hears the characters' words straight from their mouths and suspends disbelief. The letter itself acts as set, costume, and mask in encouraging the audience to forget the work of the author, and the degree to which this is accomplished can be considered a mark of both an author's or a playwright's talent. Much of Menander's comedy revolves around failed communications; Alciphron imitates this with his inconsistent inclusion of responses to requests or through an individual writer's mischaracterization of a situation.[62]

Perspective and temporality, however, are the two most integral aspects of the letter to Alciphron's collection in allowing him to transcend the limitations of the stage while maintaining a distinctly Menandrian world. Alciphron does this in part by representing the perspectives of Menander's secondary characters. If the *Letters* are read as a series of *ethopoeiae*, *qua* Rosenmeyer, they answer the question of how these characters would experience events from New Comedy while considering how they might interact with each other – something given little to no space on the stage. If they are to be read as 'miniatures', *qua* Anderson, they point outward in their limited compass and expand the possibilities of New Comedy. The epistolary format also gives Alciphron a flexibility with time that Athenian dramatic conventions did not grant to Menander. This gives his characters the opportunity to reflect on past events while freezing those same events in time, so that they are always happening in the world of the letters.

I would like to conclude by reflecting on the capacity of letters to preserve Menander's world and to draw Alciphron's audience into the time that his characters inhabit. As with all literary representations of the Classical and Hellenistic past from the imperial period, any image of authenticity or unity is carefully forged by its creator. Although the epistolary format elides this fact, it is also the means by which Alciphron is able to depict a convincing facsimile of Menander's world, one peopled with his characters. Menander originally created this version of Athens, and Alciphron re-made it in the image of Menander's plays. Indeed, as Glykera ponders her lover's departure, she asks, τί γὰρ Ἀθῆναι χωρὶς Μενάνδρου; τί δὲ Μένανδρος χωρὶς Γλυκέρας; (4.19.5 'For what is Athens without Menander? And what is Menander without Glykera?').

Notes

* I would like to express my gratitude to the editors of this volume, who have provided productive and enlightening comments on several drafts of this chapter. Any errors are my own.
1 Cf. Bowie 1970 on Atticism and the use of archaic language as a cultural phenomenon and Kim 2010 on the origins of this phenomenon. Since there seems to be no evidence of Alciphron's name in ancient Greek and Roman sources until the c. sixth-century CE epistolographer Aristaenetus (whose own identity and date are uncertain and assigned through internal indicators, cf. Bing and Höschele 2014: xii–xiii), scholars have typically assigned him to the late second/early third century CE based on correspondences between his writing and that of Lucian and Aelian (e.g. Bonner 1909a and b). See Anderson 1997: 2189-90 on potential connections between Alciphron the epistolographer and the philosopher of the same name mentioned by Marcus Aurelius (*Med.* 10.31).
2 The list I provide is not exhaustive in terms of either Menander's characters or their appearance in Alciphron, but a sampling from the broad categories outlined in Pollux's catalogue of masks (*Onomasticon* 4.143-54), as discussed by Wiles (1991: 74-80). The most thorough discussion of Pollux's catalogue, including Greek text for each character type is Webster 1995: 5-51.
3 Throughout this chapter, I refer to the character who purportedly writes each letter as a writer or a correspondent. The letter's intended recipient is referred to as the addressee. I use reader or audience to mean the external audience, i.e. Alciphron's reader. The author refers to Alciphron.
4 See Rosenmeyer 2001: 278-9 and Hodkinson 2012: 44-5 on this letter and others reflecting idyllic themes. The pastoral motif of the *locus amoenus* also appears in letter 4.13, in which it is thoroughly subverted as the venue for an orgy of prostitutes and their lovers. Morello and Robinson also suggest that Theoc. 11, 13, and 28 can be read as letters (2007: 4), which means that these letters could reflect Theocritus' form as well as his genre.
5 Anderson shows how Alciphron even takes language directly from his Aristophanic model (1997: 2191). As with his distortion of pastoral in 4.13, Alciphron also turns his Old Comic model on its head in his letters of *hetaerae*, when in 4.7, the courtesan Thaïs chastises her lover for abandoning her for the diversions of the Academy.
6 Fögen 2007: 195-6. As a potential response to Latin literature this letter is particularly intriguing, as Alciphron's program is clearly Hellenizing and in fact,

Atticizing. Menander and his characters, on the other hand, pop up in Latin elegy in Ovid's roll-call of famous poets in *Am.* 1.15: *dum fallax servus, durus pater, inproba lena/ vivent et meretrix blanda, Menandros erit*, (17–18 : 'While the deceitful slave, stern father, shameless procurer and the fawning whore live on, Menander will too'). For more on potential Greek models for this letter and the subsequent response to it, see below.

7   Rosenmeyer 2001: 280.
8   Anderson 1997: 2191.
9   Anderson 1997: 2197–8.
10 Goldberg 1980: 29–43.
11 Hunter 1985: 8–9.
12 Nesselrath 1990: 329–30.
13 Pliny also mentions the invitation at *NH* 8.30.31. It is not, therefore, a fiction invented by Alciphron.
14 Although Athenaeus and Diodorus Siculus say that she was the mistress of Harpalus, the Macedonian aristocrat (Ath. 13.586c and Diod. 17.180.6), both are writing late enough that much of the information available to them about the grand Athenian *hetairai* was likely a mixture of historical fact and fiction drawn from literary sources (cf. McClure 2003: 208 n. 35).
15 These include the Lateran-Menander relief (a copy of a Hellenistic original *c.* the first century CE, depicting Glykera, Menander, and a variety of masks) and the floor mosaic from Daphne in Antioch (*c.* 250–75 CE, depicting Komodia, Glykera and Menander, all of whom are labeled). For more on the Daphne mosaic and its connection of Menander and Cratinus, see Marshall 2012.
16 The MSS in Family 3, which is the only group containing the Ἐπιστολαὶ Ἑταιρικαί, have only a fragmentary letter lauding the beauty of Laïs after the pair of letters between Glykera and Menander. The length (in comparison to all the other letters) and topic (the departure of Menander) of these letters suggest that they were meant to cap off or even introduce the collection.
17 Durham 1913: 103. Originally published in 1913, Durham's study does not include *Dyscolos* and significant sections of *Samia, Aspis,* and *Dis Exapaton*. I suspect that an augmented study would only increase Durham's numbers for Alciphron's borrowings.
18 Text of Alciphron taken from the Teubner edition of Schepers (1905).
19 Scholars of both literature and social history have pointed out that Menander, as well as New Comedy more broadly, never portrays a violation of Athenian laws pertaining to citizenship and marriage, especially the Periclean version thereof in which both parents must be of Athenian birth to assure their children's rights in the city (e.g. Lape 2003: 68–109 and Ogden 1996: 174–80).
20 The fake doctor speaks using Doric forms for his entire time onstage (439–64).
21 Cf. Wiles's remarks on Daos the Phrygian slave character and his apparent lack of foreign accent/dialect (1991: 218).

22 That is, the type of language that the characters of both Menander and Alciphron use is determined by their shared situational framework (Willi 2010: 297) as opposed to class, ethnicity, or gender.
23 See my section on epistolarity for a discussion of the apparent paradox of characters who should be illiterate corresponding by letter.
24 Schmitz 2004: 98.
25 Arnott 1979: xxxii.
26 Cf. Treu 1973: 208 on the inconceivability of Menander without his Athenian settings.
27 For example, one of the fishermen discusses his friend's haul of Persian coins, likely from Salamis, and says that this battle happened 'during the time of our ancestors' (1.5.1: ἐπὶ τῶν προγόνων τῶν ἡμετέρων).
28 Walton and Arnott 1996b: 99.
29 Although this name appears on many Attic inscriptions from the Hellenistic period, Menander is our only literary source aside from Alciphron and Lucian (*Dialogues of Courtesans* 11) for the name Moschiōn, making Alciphron's use of this name rather pointed.
30 The husband from this letter is named Phaedrias, the same as the deceased husband from 2.35, which suggests that Alciphron may have distributed plot elements from *Epitrepontes* across multiple letters.
31 In the words of Rosenmeyer, the notable feature about most of these letters is 'the extreme ordinariness of their writers' lives' (2001: 266).
32 The threats that these temptations of the city pose to rural people are a constant theme in the first two books of letters, with women concerned about their husbands' behavior in the city at 1.6 and –21 and 2.18 and –22, another husband worried about his wife taking on urban ways at 2.8, and children enticed by the temptations of the city (both romantic and intellectual) at 1.11 and 12 (daughter to mother and the mother's response) as well as 2.11 and 38.
33 The entertainments are referred to as διαφόροις θεωρίαις (2.17.1: 'various shows'). Later in the letter, the writer describes shows including sleight-of-hand tricks, which suggests that the performances were mime.
34 Cf. MacCary 1972: 284 and 297.
35 Rosenmeyer 2001: 298.
36 Hypereides (or sometimes Phryne herself) is said to have torn open the *hetaira*'s clothing at a crucial moment in the trial, exposing her breasts and winning sympathy from the jury (Ath.13.590e–f). See Cooper 1995 on the sources for this trial and Hypereides' rhetoric.
37 Labelling Socrates a sophist is in accordance with this writer's task of winning her patron's attentions back from the philosophers and recalls the ridiculous depiction of the philosopher in *Clouds*. Aristaenetus also refers to this play and its lead character, Strepsiades, in his own collection of letters (2.3). See also Barbiero (ch. 13), in this volume.

38 Diogenes Laertius mentions Leontium as a lover, but more importantly, as a correspondent of Epicurus (*Vitae* 10.6–7). Lamia refers to the letters he writes to her and to his philosophical works in a merging of fictional correspondence and historical detail (cf. Gordon 2013: 151).
39 Both Plutarch and Athenaeus detail the relationship between Lamia and Demetrios (Plut. *Demetr.* 16.3–4 and 27.1ff and Ath.13.577c).
40 This is in turn drawn from a long tradition of *parthenoi* in literature being attacked at this type of celebration, especially as represented in the tragedies of Euripides, including *Ion*, *Alopē*, and *Augē*, which Menander points to as his source by quoting it in *Epitrepontes* (1123–6). See Furley 2009: 390–2 on the position of the *pannuchis* and similar festivals in New Comic plots and Traill 2008: 142–3 on the religious rituals in which the women of New Comedy participate. See Porter 1999–2000 on Menander's adaptation of Euripides' plot.
41 Athenaeus mentions a Thaïs who was a lover of Alexander the Great who later became the consort of Ptolemy Soter (13.576e). It is very unlikely that this woman would have been the inspiration for Menander's character.
42 Traill 2001: 292.
43 Both Plautus (*Curculio* and *Truculentus*) and Terence (*Eunuchus*) have similar scenes in their plays, strengthening the odds that this was a common scene in New Comedy.
44 Cummings 2001 investigates the likelihood of Gnesippus being the first to codify the *paraclausithyron* in Greek poetry. He claims that adultery or some kind of activity that could impugn a woman (as signified by Eupolis' use of μοιχοί in describing Gnesippus' poetic innovation in fr. 148) was an essential characteristic of this type of scene (2001: 48). Copley briefly addresses the Greek origins of the *paraclausithyron* in the introduction to his study of these scenes in Latin poetry but proposes, based on the opening scene of *Curculio*, that this is a native Italian motif (1956: 28). The existence of the Menandrian scenes mentioned above disputes this claim.
45 Cf. Rosenmeyer 2001: 284 on the destruction of the image of Simalion as *exclusus amator* from his own letter.
46 This name may appear in *Synaristoi* as the name of a young *hetaira*, based on evidence from a mosaic at Mytilene which labels two women seated with the *lena* Philainis. Henry suggests that in this play Plangon is character raised by a *hetaira* to be a *hetaira* (1988: 128).
47 In describing this consummation, Alciphron brilliantly uses the phrase παρεμπορεύομαι τῆς Ἀφροδίτης (4.13.16: 'to traffic in besides'). The financial sense which the verb usually carries alludes to the monetary basis of these relationships.
48 This is Lloyd-Jones' emendation from παιανιστάς in the MS, which is supported by the importance of Pan's shrine to the plot.
49 Lape 2006: 101.

50 The current order is more likely the result of various editors' choices than Alciphron's own (König 2007: 272).
51 Anderson calls them the '*sphragis*' of the entire collection (1997: 2202).
52 As Ozanam shows, this pair of letters is a tangled knot of mimesis, with Glykera an image of the 'real' Glykera who may have inspired a character in Menander's play; this Glykera is a character of Alciphron, who reproduces the art of Menander, who appears as a character in Alciphron's letters (1999: 31).
53 The plays she lists are *Thaïs, Misoumenos, Thrasyleon, Epitrepontes, Rapizomenē,* and *Sikyonioi/Sikyonios*.
54 For more on the visual tradition arising from Menander's plays, see Nervegna 2013: 137–8.
55 Cf. Hodkinson 2013b: 286. Examples of such collections include Aelian's *Letters of Farmers*, the love letters attributed to Philostratus and the epistolary novel attributed to Chion of Heraclea. There are also letters attributed to historical figures such as Euripides, which are also very likely to be products of the Second Sophistic.
56 Hodkinson and Rosenmeyer 2013: 7.
57 Rosenmeyer 2001: 260.
58 Hodkinson 2007: 298.
59 Altman 1982: 117.
60 Cf. Hodkinson 2007: 291.
61 Altman 1982: 118.
62 Cf. König 2007 on the patterns of request and unanswered refusals in Alciphron.

13

Two Clouded Marriages: Aristainetos' Allusions to Aristophanes' *Clouds* in *Letters* 2.3 and 2.12

Emilia A. Barbiero*

Comedy and letters go well together. Although no Greek comedies containing the epistolary motif have survived, the notice of several new comedies entitled Ἐπιστολή or Ἐπιστολαί[1] suggests that letters served as an important plot device in the genre. To be sure, in Plautus' Latin translations of Greek New Comedy missives figure prominently and are written, sent, and read onstage, the scheming *personae* capitalizing on the thorny conventions of the medium to advance the plot and enact deceit.[2] Likewise, the work of later epistolographers, in which the stock characters of Greek comedy are transformed into letter-writers, evinces this affiliation of the epistolary medium and the comic stage. The theatrical world of Hellenistic Athens is thus recreated in the four books of Second Sophistic author Alciphron. In a highly literary exercise of *ethopoeia*,[3] the author imagines the missives of mask types drawn directly from the plays of Menander and company – fishermen, farmers, parasites, and courtesans, marking the genre's passage 'from stage to page'.[4] So too does Aelian invoke New Comedy as his main model in twenty letters composed by Attic farmers. These vignettes, which feature storylines typical of comic plots, conjure up an idealized conception of fourth-century Athens populated by peasant letter-writers capable of sophisticated literary allusion.[5] Several centuries later, the late-antique epistolographer Aristainetos followed in these writers' footsteps. His set of fifty fictional love letters organized into two books are filled with *personae*, scenarios and even entire lines lifted from Greek comedies, among various other genres of literature.[6] A few clues allow us to date these letters to between 425 and 520 AD,[7] even if their author remains a mystery about whom we know virtually nothing[8] – not even his real name. Since the text's *editio princeps*,[9] editors have called him 'Aristainetos' after the title written by a copyist onto the first page of his work's sole witness,[10] a manuscript from the twelfth or thirteenth century discovered at Otranto in 1492. It seems, however, that this authorial attribution is derived from the name of the collection's first letter-writer,[11] a *sprechender Name* ('Praiser of the Best'[12]) like most of the names in the corpus.[13] 'Aristainetos', then, is almost certainly a stand-in for 'Anonymous'.

Whoever he was, Aristainetos has left us a series of epistolary mini-plots in which invented correspondents write to their addressees about erotic adventures and assorted vicissitudes of the heart including love triangles, illicit affairs and even a *ménage-à-trois* (1.2).[14] The letters are a mix of first-person and third-person accounts,[15] and none is accompanied by a direct reply.[16] Thus in every text the narrative is suspended, and we never do find out what becomes of the *hetaira* whose sister has been flirting with her lover (1.25), or the unfortunate man hopelessly in love with his mother-in-law (2.8). This interruption of the narrative arc in each missive is a result of and parallel to the incompleteness of the epistolary process within the premise of the collection, for as we have access to them, these letters exist as though undelivered, suspended in the journey between sender and recipient. That is in the perspective afforded to the reader by the author, these epistles are yet short of their destination, and just as the outcome of the tales they contain, we can only imagine the reaction and response elicited in the addressees. As if intercepting these letters in mid-voyage, we are allowed to 'eavesdrop' on only one side of some very private conversations.[17]

Aristainetos relies extensively upon the Greek literary tradition to compose his epistles, borrowing motifs, phrases and, often, entire passages *verbatim* from texts in both prose and verse. For this reason, earlier criticism dismissed the epistolographer as a literary thief, accusing him of pillaging classical works in order to 'trick out his own second-rate talents'.[18] Recent years, however, have seen a reevaluation of the merits of this late-antique oeuvre. In a 2012 article, Höschele reveals the text's metaliterary reflection on artistic imitation through a reading of epistles 1.1 and 2.10. Calling the collection a 'panopticum of Greek literature',[19] she demonstrates that Aristainetos' literary appropriation is, far from plagiarism, studied and self-conscious.[20] Much more, however, remains to be said about this long-neglected author and his creative use of a wide network of sources.

I propose to continue the investigation of Aristainetos' *mimēsis*,[21] contemplating his engagement with the Greek comic tradition by looking at epistles 2.3 and 2.12, two texts about unhappy marriages modeled, in part, upon the scenario in Aristophanes' *Clouds*. In this play, Strepsiades, son of an Attic farmer, has been driven to bankruptcy by the expensive tastes of his rich wife and their son, Pheidippides. The desperate father turns to Socrates' 'Reflectory' in the hopes that he might learn rhetorical techniques to escape his many creditors.

At the beginning of the play, Strepsiades expresses his marital sorrow in the following speech, a section of Aristophanes' text that is seminal for the two epistles to be examined in this paper. It is worth quoting in full:

> εἴθ' ὤφελ' ἡ προμνήστρι' ἀπολέσθαι κακῶς
> ἥτις με γῆμ' ἐπῆρε τὴν σὴν μητέρα.
> ἐμοὶ γὰρ ἦν ἄγροικος ἥδιστος βίος.
> εὐρωτιῶν, ἀκόρητος, εἰκῇ κείμενος,
> βρύων μελίτταις καὶ προβάτοις καὶ στεμφύλοις   45
> ἔπειτ' ἔγημα Μεγακλέους τοῦ Μεγακλέους
> ἀδελφιδῆν ἄγροικος ὢν ἐξ ἄστεως,
> σεμνήν, τρυφῶσαν, ἐγκεκοισυρωμένην.
> ταύτην ὅτ' ἐγάμουν, συγκατεκλινόμην ἐγὼ
> ὄζων τρυγός, τρασιᾶς, ἐρίων, περιουσίας,   50
> ἡ δ' αὖ μύρου, κρόκου, καταγλωττισμάτων,
> δαπάνης, λαφυγμοῦ, Κωλιάδος, Γενετυλλίδος.
> οὐ μὴν ἐρῶ γ' ὡς ἀργὸς ἦν, ἀλλ' ἐσπάθα,
> ἐγὼ δ' ἂν αὐτῇ θοἰμάτιον δεικνὺς τοδὶ
> πρόφασιν ἔφασκον· ὦ γύναι, λίαν σπαθᾷς.   55

> Would that the matchmaker perish wretchedly,
> the one who impelled me to marry your mother.
> For I had a rustic life – the sweetest there is:
> mouldy, undisturbed by bugs, lying about at will,
> filled with bees and sheep and pressed olives.   45
> And then I went and married the niece of Megacles, son of Megacles,
> I, a country-boy; she, a city-girl,
> classy, insolent, all Koisyra-like.
> When I married her I went to bed with her,
> redolent with unfermented wine, figs, wool, and plenty,   50
> she, on the other hand, with perfume, saffron, and French kisses,
> extravagance, gluttony, Kolian Aphrodite and Genetyllis.
> But I won't say that she was lazy: she did weave, packing the threads
>   close together.
> And I used to say to her, holding up my cloak like this as justification:
> 'O woman, you're laying it on too thick!'[22]   55

First, I will examine how Aristainetos uses this monologue from Aristophanes as a generative nucleus for letters 2.3 and 2.12. Based upon correspondences in motif and structure, I go on to suggest that these two missives form a thematic diptych and ought to be taken as a pair, manifesting an interplay of allusion both to *Clouds* and to another epistolary diptych in Aristainetos' collection. This sophisticated matrix of internal and external reference, which pivots upon Aristainetos' engagement with comedy, betrays the deliberately artful arrangement of his epistolary collection. Finally, I propose in a postscript that such a synoptic reading of the text not only yields greater insight into the method of this epistolographer's comic *mimēsis*, but may also produce evidence for a disputed reading of a line in *Clouds*.

A literary diptych

Epistle 2.12 presents the complaint of the author Euboulides about the imperiousness of his spendthrift spouse, Deinomache.[23] The miserable husband laments that although his wife's family was originally poor, she has now surpassed all other women in her extravagant tastes. The letter-writer resolves to kick Deinomache out of the house, lest she continue her reign of terror. Arnott has demonstrated the influence of New Comedy on this narrative about a husband and his bossy wife. Beyond the epistle's language, which he calls a 'medley of comic, often precisely Menandrian commonplaces', Arnott remarks upon the resemblance of Deinomache to New Comedy's *epiklēros* ('heiress') character or *uxor dotata* ('endowed wife'), though he attributes the novelty in making the letter-writer's overbearing spouse of impoverished lineage to 'some lost comedy'.[24] Euboulides' declaration to banish Deinomache from the house – καὶ πέρας ἓν μόνον ἐμοὶ τούτου δοκεῖ, τὴν βάρβαρον ἐς κόρακας ἐκπέμψασθαι τῆς οἰκίας[25] (2.12.23–5 'There seems to me to be only one end to this: to kick the barbarian the hell out of the house . . .') – has also been traced to New Comedy. Arnott sees a reference to the fragment of Menander's *Plokion* in which the husband yields to his wife's orders to kick their attractive slave girl out of the house (fr. 296.3–4 K-A),[26] whereas Magrini prefers to read a specific reference to *Samia* lines 352–4, when Demeas threatens to expel his mistress Chrysis in the belief that the baby she is breastfeeding is her own, raised despite his orders that any child was to be exposed.[27]

Epistle 2.12 is also indebted to Old Comedy, for these same lines (2.12.23–5) simultaneously recall a verse in Aristophanes' *Clouds*, as Magrini first recognized.[28] In fact, Aristainetos' beleaguered husband quotes directly from this play in his epistle, telling his addressee that he has reenacted Strepsiades' futile complaint from *Clouds* line 55 to his own intolerable wife[29]:

ἐγὼ δὲ θοἰμάτιον αὐτῇ δεικνύς, ὅπερ ἂν τύχω φορῶν, κωμικῶς τὴν ἄσωτον ὑπαινίττομαι φάσκον· "ὦ γύναι, λίαν σπαθᾷς."

'But I, holding up to her my cloak, which I happen to be wearing, comically allude to her profligacy, saying: "O woman, you're laying it on too thick!"'

2.12.18–20

Criticism has gone no further in investigating Aristainetos' engagement with *Clouds* in epistle 2.12. But not only does this text's scenario at once reflect and reverse the *euporos gametē* ('rich wife') *topos* of new comedies like Menander's *Plokion* and Plautus' *Aulularia*,[30] but it also recalls the scenario in Aristophanes' play, which likewise revolves around an unhappy marriage caused (according to the husband) by the wife's profligacy. What is more, Aristainetos' letter plays upon its relationship with *Clouds*, deliberately inverting its configuration of the marital motif. For whereas Aristophanes' beleaguered husband Strepsiades is a simple country boy lorded over by the rich girl from Athens he has married, in Aristainetos' epistle it is wealthy Euboulides who has come to be dominated by the originally poor Deinomache. The epistolographer, then, has kept the *Clouds'* tyrannical wife, but he has reversed the status of the spouses. By this rearrangement Aristainetos has made Deinomache twice as 'terrible' as her literary ancestress: both wives devour the family finances, though Strepsiades' wife depletes the money she herself brought to the marriage. Deinomache, on the other hand, is spending all of her husband's wealth, having (presumably) contributed nothing in view of her impoverished origins.

Aristainetos has added another funny detail to his adaptation of Aristophanes' comic scenario by making the letter's miserable husband a victim of his own caution gone awry. The hapless Euboulides tells his correspondent that he married Deinomache on purpose (ἐξεπίτηδες) precisely to escape his present predicament:

ἐγὼ γὰρ πενιχρὰν ἐξεπίτηδες ἠγαγόμην, ὅπως εὐπόρῳ γαμετῆς μηδὲν ὑποστήσωμαι σοβαρόν.

'For I married her, poor as she was, on purpose, lest I have to submit to the insolence of a rich wife.'

2.12.3–5

Alert to the suffering that comes along with a wealthy girl, Euboulides tried – albeit unsuccessfully – to dodge this fate by marrying poor. The unhappy spouse's 'speaking name', then, is ironic: prudent foresight has failed this 'son of good counsel'.[31] Foolishly, the wealthy Euboulides failed to realize that any girl he married would become just that – a rich wife. Further, we may read the name 'Euboulides' as an intertextual nod, implying the letter-writer's metaliterary knowledge of his comic antecedents, both old and new. The name of the unhappy husband tells the reader, as it were, that his character is acquainted with the havoc wrought by rich wives in the comedies that serve as Aristainetos' models. It is this literary self-consciousness explicitly demonstrated in the letter-writer's quotation of Strepsiades' line that informed Euboulides' wariness of an *euporos gametē*, precisely what he ends up with.

In the Aristophanic passage that Aristainetos' husband draws upon in his epistle, Strepsiades uses a metaphor to illustrate his wife's extravagance. He characterizes her spending as excessive, like the thickly packed threads that result from over-weaving: the verb in *Clouds* line 55, σπαθᾶν literally means to strike the woof with a wooden blade, the σπάθη. If, as τοδί ('this thing here') in line 54 suggests, the old man in Aristophanes' comedy holds up his ragged coat while speaking this verse, the joke in *Clouds* is that the woman's wasteful ways have had precisely the reverse effect of the image invoked by her spouse to symbolize it, resulting in a threadbare coat rather than the dense fabric of the analogy.[32] As Dover elucidates, 'the joke is that his wife's metaphorical λίαν σπαθᾶν ("excessive weaving") has had the opposite result from literal λίαν σπαθᾶν'.[33] Euboulides reports that he delivered the line while reenacting this very same motion, raising, as his comic predecessor before him, a tattered *himation* to demonstrate his own wife's wasteful spending by way of inversion: ἐγὼ δὲ θοἰμάτιον αὐτῇ δεικνύς, ὅπερ ἂν τύχω φορῶν (2.12.18–19 'But I, holding up to her my cloak, which I happen to be wearing …'). The wretched husband, then, portrays his literary quotation as explicitly theatrical, explaining that he performed it using both physical gesture and a prop. Such an embedded dramatic quotation entails a fascinating interweaving of media, for Strepsiades' words and gesture in *Clouds* have gone from text in the theatrical script, to speech in performance and back now into text again, filtered through Euboulides' re-enactment of the scene to his profligate wife. The letter-writer himself demonstrates awareness of this Aristophanic intertext, signaling his quotation as self-referential with the phrase κωμικῶς … ὑπαινίττομαι (2.12.19–20 'I comically allude'). This presentation leaves no doubt that the wretched spouse knows Aristophanes' comedy *qua* text. Like Aristainetos himself, then, Euboulides is portrayed as 'versed' in the genre that serves as his template. Amusingly, the author's literary memory has not kept him from becoming a comic victim, for Euboulides now suffers from a marriage as unhappy as that of Strepsiades in *Clouds*. Thus the epistolographer alludes to his reversal of Aristophanes and comments, tongue-in-cheek, on the relationship between literary prototype and imitation. The character patterned on Strepsiades cannot escape his fate as miserable husband, for it has already been enshrined in the literary tradition.

In letter 2.3, the *neonumphos* ('newlywed bride') Glykera writes to her matchmaking cousin, Philinna, bemoaning her new husband Strepsiades' obsession with rhetoric and law cases to the complete exclusion of sex.[34] The bride begs Philinna to rectify the situation; otherwise, she vows, she will leave Strepsiades and let another orator 'handle her case'.[35] Once again, Arnott has revealed this text's reliance on comedy, noting that the names of 2.3's author and addressee, Glykera and Philinna,[36] as well as the theme of the unhappy wife, are typical of New Comedy. He argues, however, that Aristainetos' principal model in this letter is Old Comedy, for the bridegroom's name, Strepsiades, and his intellectual fixation recall *Clouds*.[37] Further, Arnott observes that Aristainetos has copied the matchmaking motif from Aristophanes' text: Glykera's epistle is addressed to her matchmaker, imploring Philinna to fix the bad pairing she has made and thereby recalling Strepsiades' curse on the προμνήστρια ('matchmaker') who hooked him up with his 'awfully wedded' wife at *Clouds* lines 41–2.[38]

Just as epistle 2.12, the troublesome marriage of 2.3 invokes the unhappy union in Aristophanes' comedy as its model. In fact, both epistolary scenarios look specifically to Strepsiades' complaining speech about his wife at *Clouds* lines 41–55. This literary nucleus generates the speeches of Aristainetos' wife and husband, as the letters allude to the beginning and end of the Aristophanic passage.[39] I would submit, then, that Aristainetos has arranged letters 2.3 and 2.12 to invert *Clouds*. Both epistles reverse the Aristophanic constellation of roles relevant to the marital situation. *Letter* 2.3 contains a thematic rearrangement of Aristophanes in making the complainant of the awful marriage a female,[40] an inversion that parallels 2.12's switch of rich and poor spouse. At the same time, however, Euboulides' letter also returns to the original disposition of the model text, for 2.12's scenario restores the *Clouds*' alignment of gender and complainer disrupted by 2.3. Here is an illustration of this corresponding set of reversals and reinstatements:

Clouds	rich wife	poor, complaining, rhetorical husband
Epistle 2.3	complaining wife	rhetorical husband
Epistle 2.12	poor wife	rich, complaining husband who quotes rhetorical husband

Thus the constellation of status, gender, and role in the Aristophanic marital scenario criss-crosses between Aristainetos' two letters, embodying the epistolographer's technique of *imitatio cum variatione* ('imitation with variation')[41] within his own collection.

Aristainetos' inventive *mimēsis* does not stop there, for both letters 2.3 and 2.12 contain the leitmotif of leaving the family home. Glykera swears to walk out on Strepsiades should their sex life not improve, just as Euboulides resolves to expel Deinomache lest she reduce him to beggardom. The common *topos* is once again presented *vice versa* in the two letters. Both entail a wife's abandonment of the home; in 2.3 the bride proclaims that she will leave of her own accord, whereas in 2.12 it is the husband who demands her removal. This element can be traced back to comedy. Zanetto connects Glykera's vow to Menander, whose *Epitrepontes* and *Perikeiromenē* contain similar scenarios of spousal abandonment,[42] and, as mentioned above, Euboulides' resolution to kick Deinomache out has been linked to both the *Plokion* and the *Samia,* as well as to *Clouds*. In the old comedy, Strepsiades declares to Pheidippides that he will throw him out, angry that his son is refusing to attend the 'Reflectory': ἀλλ' ἐξελῶ σ'εἰς κόρακας ἐκ τῆς οἰκίας (123 'But I'll drive you the hell out of the house'). In defiance, however, the youth walks right back into the house at *Clouds* lines 124–5. Knowledge of the Aristophanic model once again adds a funny irony to this comic allusion, for the informed reader is thus led to suspect that Euboulides' resolve to expel Deinomache will have the same force as that of Strepsiades *vis-à-vis* his son – none at all!

Aristainetos, then, has replicated yet another motif from Aristophanes, which manifests itself in both epistles by way of inversion. This time, however, the epistolographer borrows an element from *Clouds* that occurs outside the marital scenario serving as his main template, transferring the expulsion *topos* in Aristophanes from the father-son relationship to that between husband and wife.[43] The motif has been displaced not only thematically, but also structurally, for Aristainetos has transferred it from its original position in the comic text to coincide with the allusions to Strepsiades' speech, which occurs seventy lines earlier in *Clouds*. What is more, the intertext increases the likelihood that the author is familiar with the Athenian comedy in its entirety, not just the protagonist's monologue at the beginning of the text. This is unsurprising given the popularity of *Clouds* in the Byzantine period and its inclusion in the so-called Byzantine triad of Aristophanes' works along with *Wealth* and *Frogs*.[44]

Each of Aristainetos' complaining letter-writers concludes by invoking a proverb comparing their spouse's behavior to that of an animal, cementing the parallels between the letters. The *neonumphos* of letter 2.3 proclaims the urgency in resolving her predicament before it escalates further by employing the following expression:

ἐγὼ γὰρ τὸν λύκον τῶν ὤτων ἔχω, ὃν οὔτε κατέχειν ἐπὶ πολὺ δυνατόν, οὔτε μὴν ἀκίνδυνον ἀφεῖναι, μή με δικορράφος ὢν ἀναίτιον αἰτιάσηται.[45]

'I have the wolf by his ears, but it is possible neither to hold on to him for long, nor to let him go without danger lest, innocent though I am, the legal eagle take me to court.'

2.3.21–4

Likewise, Euboulides ends his epistle illustrating his verdict on Deinomache thus:

κατάδηλος ἡ γυνή· ἄρκτου παρούσης, φασίν, οὐκ ἐπιζητήσω τὰ ἴχνη.[46]

'It's crystal-clear what the woman is: the bear, as they say, is in the room; I shall not look for its tracks.'

2.12.28–9

Although these are not the only such zoological proverbs in Aristainetos' collection,[47] the homologous endings of epistles 2.3 and 2.12 serve to underscore the letters' coincidences in source and theme. These parallels strongly suggest that Aristainetos composed Glykera and Euboulides' missives as a diptych to be read together, since both texts treat the same topic from two corresponding perspectives, forming a complete picture of unhappy marriage from the female and male points of view.

An epistolary quartet

This sophisticated technique of thematic pairing is not exclusive to Book Two of Aristainetos' collection. As Zanetto first argued,[48] Book One also contains a diptych: letters 1.5 and 1.22 likewise play upon their common comic source, flaunting literary self-consciousness and revealing their correlation through the identity of the epistolary correspondents, the second sophistic authors Alciphron and Lucian, who are writing to each other.[49] In this diptych, the letter-writers swap stories about women who succeed in recovering the affections of a man through a trick accomplished with the help of a female ally.[50] The epistles draw extensively from Menandrian comedy, both thematically and via verbal echoes.[51] Remarkably, the crafty girl in letter 1.22 is named Glykera,[52] after the protagonist of Menander's *Perikeiromenē*, and so shares a name with epistle 2.3's unhappy bride. In fact, the *neonumphos* may hint at the literary provenance of her name in *New* Comedy when she calls herself a young girl, κορή, in 2.3.7. This implicitly differentiates the newlywed from her mature literary model, the nameless wife of Aristophanes' *Clouds*, who is an adult woman – a γυνή – with an adolescent son. The tender age of 2.3's Glykera, one might then say, signals the origin of her name in the Greek New Comic tradition, although the situation involving her intolerably rhetorical husband is modeled on Old Comedy.[53]

This doubled Glykera character in letters 1.22 and 2.3 creates an onomastic link between the two texts,[54] calling the reader, I think, to search for other affinities between the pair of missives and 'sweet' girls. Their similarities are striking. In 1.22, Lucian recounts the plight of a *hetaira* named Glykera who wishes to increase her beloved's desire. The girl's procuress, Doris,[55] devises and executes a plan to trick the boy into thinking that he loves Glykera more than he is loved by her, curing him in this way of his arrogant indifference. Thus 1.22 also features a woman named Glykera suffering from unrequited affection, though the nature and social milieu of the amorous scenarios have been reversed, for the lopsided relationship between a *hetaira* and her client in 1.22 is transformed into 2.3's marriage of a 'skilled orator' (2.3.1 τῷ σοφῷ ῥήτορι[56]) and his bride. Accordingly, the status of the women that both Glykerai seek out for help is reversed – a madam in 1.22 and a matchmaker in 2.3. Both roles involve bringing men and women together, though to different ends! Moreover, epistle 1.22 might represent a possible solution to the conundrum presented in 2.3: by reading these related letters in reverse order, moving from 2.3 back to 1.22, we discover a response of sorts to the *neonumphos*' letter. Linked by theme and correspondent, Alciphron's epistle may provide an answer to Glykera's predicament by suggesting a clever strategy to be employed by Philinna as a cure for her cousin's marital woes. What has worked for one heartsick Glykera might well work for another! Thus the identical names of the letters' female protagonists provoke the attentive reader into a second reading of the text, prompting him to scroll back to discover 1.22 and 2.3's inverted sequentiality, a process that Herrnstein Smith has called 'retrospective patterning'.[57]

Letters 1.22 and 2.3, then, are closely connected – not only through their shared comic ancestry and theme of female deceit,[58] but also by way of correspondences and reversals in content and motif. Significantly, the two other components of Aristainetos' pair of thematic diptychs, epistles 1.5 and 2.12, are related in precisely the same way. In letter 1.5, Alciphron tells Lucian about the trick of an unnamed wife who accepts a dinner invitation from a womanizer only to unexpectedly find out that her elderly husband is also in attendance. Realizing that her spouse will surely recognize the robe she has left outside, the cunning woman contrives to sneak out of the party and secretly transfer the garment to her neighbor and ally. When her husband returns from the festivities fuming at his dishonest wife, the trickster's accomplice in deceit enters pretending to return the 'loaned' *himation,* even offering her 'lender' a taste of the leftovers from the party.[59] Scholars have, once again, perceived Aristainetos' reliance upon Menander in this letter, noting several verbal parallels with the *Samia*.[60] What is more, critics have remarked that the narrative's setting is implicitly theatrical, for, much as the day of a play's performance in the ancient world, the dinner party takes place during a public feast.[61] I would add that the crafty wife's solution to her predicament is also evocative of drama or perhaps mime: the adulteress stages a plot involving role-play, acting the part of faithful wife while her abettor pretends to be a partygoer. This skit even involves props to add verisimilitude to the performance when the swindler's fellow conspirator authenticates her story using the party's 'leftovers' and, crucially, the naughty wife's robe.[62]

The *himation,* which is transformed in 1.5 from evidence of the spouse's guilt into proof of her 'innocence', is recalled by Euboulides' tattered robe in 2.12, a garment that also serves as evidence of a wife's behaviour – Deinomache's reckless spending. The genders in the parallel scenarios have been reversed, as in its passage from Book One to Book Two of the corpus, the robe goes from the hands of a woman to that of a man. This gender inversion involving possession of the *himation* is mirrored in the perspective of the letters' narrative about the trials of married life, for epistle 1.5 recounts a wife's victory over her duped spouse from her own point of view, whereas in 2.12 the husband gives his side of the story about the couple's unhappy union.[63] In both letters the *himation* is used to create theatre. It is the lynchpin of letter 1.5's production, and, as I have argued above, Euboulides uses it to conjure up Strepsiades' comic persona in 2.12. Corresponding to the 'Glykera association' between epistles 1.22 and 2.3, then, is this 'material' link between letters 1.5 and 2.12, which are joined by the presence of a theatrical robe in both texts.[64]

In this way, the two thematic pairs of Aristainetos' epistolary collection, one in each book, are intertwined, creating a chiasm of comic reference that accentuates the author's engagement with drama and reveals the deliberate organization of his oeuvre. Here is an illustration of this configuration:

1.5 (theatrical robe) + 1.22 (Glykera's love woes)

2.3 (Glykera's love woes) + 2.12 (theatrical robe)

By picking up on these commonalities, we are invited not only to read each book's diptych together, but also to perceive the parallels and reversals that link the two sets as a quartet. Aristainetos' collection of narratives about love affairs are deliberately composed and arranged to highlight affinities among the epistles and showcase the author's creative use of his model material. A reading that not only looks at each letter in isolation, but that searches for meaningful thematic sequences within the oeuvre is crucial, then, to fully appreciating Aristainetos' artistry.[65] The epistolographer's technique of adaptation is a testament both to his literary *mimēsis*, and to the thriving *Nachleben* of Greek comedy in late antiquity, as the unfortunate marriage of Strepsiades in *Clouds* continued to live on long after the fifth century BC, generating a pair of dissatisfied spouses and two clouded marriages 1,000 years later.

Postscript: Clearing-up dirty joke in *Clouds*

Scholars have observed that the weaving metaphor used by Strepsiades in *Clouds* and, in turn, transcribed in Euboulides' letter, seems to contain a ribald inference to the woman's unrestrained sexual appetite in addition to a comment on her overspending.[66] *Clouds*' rich wife is wearing her husband down by sex, wanting to 'whack the woof' all too frequently.[67] Dover disagrees, arguing that if we take σπαθᾶν to mean sexual intercourse, the joke implicit in Strepsiades' threadbare coat is spoiled.[68] Drago has recently advocated Dover's position based on the apparent absence of a *double entendre* in letter 2.12.[69] A look back to the letter's companion piece, however, suggests otherwise. The epistolographer's dialogue with *Clouds* in letter 2.12 ought to be reevaluated in light of the text's relationship to epistle 2.3. In fact, a close reading of 1.5 and 1.22, Book One's epistolary diptych, will reveal that both Aristophanes and Aristainetos (as well as Alciphron, as we shall see) were being bawdy.

Glykera's erotic preoccupation in letter 2.3 may reflect Strepsiades' intimations of the same on the part of his spouse in *Clouds* lines 51–2, for the old man recalls his rich bride's 'scent' of French kissing (51 καταγλωτισμάτων), Kolian Aphrodite and of Genetyllis, a female goddess with erotic associations, on their first night together as newlyweds. An overly healthy libido is shared by both wives of Strepsiades, though the roles of dissatisfied spouse are again reversed. Aristophanes' husband complains of too much sex, whereas the *neonumphos* is frustrated by none at all. One might even say that Aristainetos has given the *Clouds*' silent wife a voice, for in epistle 2.3 she gets to tell her side of the story, finally able to express her sexual frustration. If we view epistles 2.3 and 2.12 as a thematic pair based on *Clouds*, the sexual motif of Glykera's letter may be associated with Euboulides' quotation from the same speech. That is the erotic meaning of σπαθᾶν in epistle 2.12 is furnished by letter 2.3. The wretched husband's reference to *Clouds* in letter 2.12, then, requires a double reading to be comprehended, for the comic quotation is brought into alignment with the sexual suggestion of the source text only when 2.12 is read together with 2.3.

There is one more text we might add to this discussion to bolster the idea that Aristophanes and Aristainetos use σπαθᾶν to 'say' sex. Alciphron, one of Aristainetos' models, invokes this very verb in his second book of epistles in a missive that seems to be engaging with *Clouds*.[70] In Alciphron, *Ep.* 2.32, the parasite Gnathon tells his addressee about the fate of his former patron, Timon:

> Τίμωνα οἶσθα, ὦ Καλλικωμίδη, τὸν Ἐχεκρατίδου τὸν Κολλυτέα, ὃς ἐκ πλουσίου, σπαθήσας τὴν οὐσίαν εἰς ἡμᾶς τοὺς παρασίτους καὶ τὰς ἑταίρας, εἰς ἀπορίαν συνηλάθη . . .[71]

> 'O Kallikomides, you know Timon, the son of Echecratides from the deme of Collytus. Well, from wealth he was reduced to poverty, having spent away his riches on us parasites and on prostitutes.'
>
> 2.32.1–4

Much as Strepsiades and Euboulides, Timon has been made penniless, although in an interesting twist he owes this state to his own profligacy and indulgent spending on parasites and women of the *demimonde* rather than the wastefulness of a wife.[72] Crucially, Alciphron uses the verb σπαθᾶν to describe the youth's impoverishment, which here, too, seems to have an erotic connotation,[73] for given what the youth has been indulging in (parasites[74] and prostitutes), we may perceive a racy innuendo of the text that is the corollary of its 'straight' reading; *viz.* 'Timon pumped away his money on parasites and call girls' / 'Timon "pumped" away his money on parasites and call girls'.[75] Alciphron also perceived some naughtiness in Strepsiades' line, cleverly reconfiguring the *double entendre* inherent in σπαθᾶν to fit the scenario of Gnathon's epistle. The metaphor at *Clouds* line 55 is, in fact, a dirty joke, and a highly successful one at that, for it has been woven into the subsequent literary tradition in the epistolary discourse of both Alciphron and Aristainetos.

Notes

* I am grateful to Peter Bing, Tom Hawkins, Regina Höschele, Toph Marshall and David Sansone for their comments and suggestions on this paper.
1 See Rosenmeyer 2001: 64 and n.11, and Jenkins 2005: 363.

2 There are eighteen letters referred to in nine out of Plautus' twenty-one surviving plays. In five of these comedies – *Trinummus, Bacchides, Persa, Curculio,* and *Pseudolus* – an epistle functions as an essential element of the plot; see Petrone 1983: 133–6, Jenkins 2005 and 2006: 101–7 and Barbiero 2014.
3 See Ureña Bracero 1993.
4 Thus Höschele 2014: 744. On Alciphron, see Anderson 1997, Rosenmeyer 2001: 255–307, Schmitz 2004, Hodkinson 2007, König 2007, and Funke in this volume. As Tom Hawkins has pointed out to me, the stock types of Greek New Comedy had already taken on literary form in Theophrastus' *Characters*, though this work transports only the masks themselves and not their comic universe.
5 On Aelian, see Rosenmeyer 2001: 308–21, Hodkinson 2007; 2013a, Drago 2014, and Marshall in this volume.
6 Unlike Alciphron and Aelian, whose primary model is Greek comedy, Aristainetos' source material runs the ancient literary gamut including authors as diverse as Hippocrates, Callimachus, Plato, and Menander.
7 On the date of Aristainetos, see Mazal 1977, Arnott 1982: 294–6, Burri 2004: 83–7, Drago 2007: 25–36 and Bing and Höschele 2014: xiii–xvi.
8 Burri (2004: 83): 'Über Aristainetos ... wissen wir so gut wie nichts mit Sicherheit, weder wann und wo er gelebt und geschrieben hat, noch wie er wirklich hieß'. Burri reviews the evidence for his identity on pp.88–91.
9 The corpus' *editio princeps* was published in 1566 by Johannes Sambucus. On the text's early editorial history, including Sambucus' edition, see Mazal 1968 and Drago 2007: 9–10.
10 There is, however, some disagreement over what, precisely, this title says; for a review of the scholarly debate, see Bing and Höschele 2014: xii n.5.
11 Mercier was the first to express suspicion about the name 'Aristainetos' in his 1595 edition of the text. Arnott (1982: 293–4) and Bing and Höschele (2014: xii–xiii) agree; *aliter* Zanetto (1987: 199), in whose view 'la collocazione dell'epistola di Ἀρισταίνετος posta all'inizio della raccolta ... ne costituisce una sorta di σφραγίς e contribuisce a enfatizzare la figura dello scrivente (e quindi dell'autore) rispetto agli altri scriventi'.
12 Thus do Bing and Höschele (2014: xiii) translate this compound speaking name based upon the content of epistle 1.1, a tribute to the beauty and charm of the author's beloved, Lais. Similarly, Zanetto (1987: 195) renders 'Aristainetos' as 'colui che sa ottimamente lodare'. *Aliter* Lesky (1951: 8), Arnott (1982: 293) and Drago (2007: 17), who translate the name passively, *viz.* 'Best Praiseworthy'.
13 On the names in Aristainetos' collection, see Arnott 1982: 291–4, 317.
14 The epistolographer, however, deliberately avoids explicit sexuality, stopping short of describing the deed he so beguilingly prefaces. On this tantalizing technique, see Arnott 1982: 310–15 and Bing and Höschele 2014: xvii–xviii.
15 For the mix of perspective in the collection, see Zanetto 1987: 196. Aristainetos' use of the third person is particularly interesting given that, as Zanetto notes, several

such letters (nine, to be exact), contain no reference to the author or recipient's personal experience, nor do they betray the relevance to either party of the events being narrated. In fact, although all of these texts are clearly epistles, prefaced as they are by the names of the author and addressee, the collection as a whole is largely devoid of the epistolary medium's usual characteristics, such as epistolary formulae and references to the letter's composition and delivery; see Höschele 2012: 160–4 and Bing and Höschele 2014: xvi. Höschele points out, however, that Aristainetos' choice of the epistolary medium is anything but haphazard (as Arnott 1982: 297 asserts); rather, she posits, the author uses the defining quality of letters as *sermo absentium* – conversions with an absent interlocutor – to 'communicate' with his models of the literary past: 'Could not the intervening distance between writer and addressee marking any epistolary communication reflect the temporal and cultural remoteness of earlier authors in relation to Aristainetos in a comparable manner?' (p.165; and see Bing and Höschele 2014: xxvi–xxvii). For the *topos* of *sermo absentium* in ancient epistolography, see Thraede 1970.

16 So too the letter collections of Aristainetos' second sophistic predecessors, Alciphron, Aelian and Philostratos, contain many unanswered letters and, therefore, unresolved situations; see Rosenmeyer 2001: 255. Bing and Höschele (2014: xxii), however, point out that Aristainetos' letters do feature epistolary dialogue, though it is of the intertextual kind: two of these authors, Alciphron and Lucian, appear as correspondents (1.5 and 1.22; see below), whereas both Aelian and Philostratus are letter-writers in the collection (1.11 and 2.1).

17 Of course, as Tom Hawkins reminds me, the expectation that a letter ought to be met by a reply may be conditioned by epistolary literature such as Cicero's letters or Ovid's *Heroides*, both very much concerned with reciprocity.

18 Arnott 1973: 197. To be sure, Arnott tempers this judgment in a 1982 article, stating that his use of the term plagiarism was 'excessively harsh and culturally unjustified' (p.304 n. 38).

19 Höschele 2012: 166.

20 To Höschele's 2012 article, we might add Drago's 2007 Italian translation and commentary on the letters, and the 2014 edition of Bing and Höschele, the first English translation of Aristainetos in 300 years.

21 *Mimēsis* is the term employed by Whitmarsh (2001) to define the imitation of classical literature so pervasive amongst imperial Greek authors. He argues thus: 'To engage in literary practice was necessarily to anchor the present in tradition and to reanimate the past. The dominant notion in the literary aesthetic of Roman Greece was *mimēsis*, a complex term that covers both "artistic representation" and "imitation" of predecessors ... *Mimēsis* marks not only the traditional temper of Roman Greek culture, but also its modernity: an "imitation" of a literary forebear is not simply a xerographic reproduction but also ... a transformation' (pp.26–7).

22 All translations are my own.
23 This hilariously appropriate name ('Terrible-in-Battle') for such an imperious wife is widely attested in the historical record. In fact, Alcibiades' mother was so called; see Drago 2007: 517.
24 Arnott 1973: 206–7; 1975: 27–8. Arnott suggests Menander's *Plokion* (known only from the excerpts quoted by Aulus Gellius at *NA* 2.23) as the epistle's main intertext which, he thinks, Aristainetos fused with material from other comedies, including verbal echoes of various comic fragments and the direct quotation of Aristophanes' *Clouds* in 2.12.18–20. His assertion that the innovation in the bossy wife's social background must have been anticipated in one of Aristainetos' models, however, is purely speculative.
25 The text of Aristainetos I cite throughout is that of Mazal 1971.
26 Arnott 1973: 206–7.
27 Magrini 1981: 156. In fact, Demeas repeats his command later in the same scene at line 382. The resemblance of Euboulides' declaration to these verses had already been noted by Arnott (1973: 206), who, however, sees the *Plokion* as Aristainetos' main intertext. For the phrase ἐς κόρακας ('go to hell'), which appears already in archaic lyric, see Drago 2007: 520–1.
28 ἀλλ' ἐξελῶ σ'εἰς κόρακας ἐκ τῆς οἰκίας (*Clouds*.123: 'But I'll drive you the hell out of the house'). Magrini 1981: 156; see my discussion of the expulsion motif below.
29 The quotation was first noticed by Mercier 1610: 285.
30 On the *euporos gametē topos* in comedy and throughout classical literature, see Drago 2007: 514–16.
31 Drago 2007: 515.
32 The weaving metaphor also seems to hint at the profligate wife's libido; see the final section below.
33 Dover 1968: 101.
34 As Drago (2007: 445–6) points out, Glykera's self-definition as a *neonumphos* in 2.3.10 underlines her 'interesse prevalentemente sessuale più che affettivo'.
35 I am borrowing this phrase from the translation of Bing and Höschele 2014: 71.
36 For the occurrence of these names in literature and the historical record, see Drago 2007: 443–4. See my comments on similarities between 2.3's newlywed bride and the corpus' other Glykera, a *hetaira* in epistle 1.22, below in the next section.
37 Arnott 1973: 203; 1975: 24–5; 1982: 306. In addition to this letter's comedic influence, Drago (2007: 443) observes affinities with the epigrams of Agathias and Paul the Silentiary, which are 'organizzati intorno al motivo degli affari forensi che distolgono dall'amore'.
38 Arnott (1973: 203; 1975: 25; 1982: 306) evinces the specific influence of *Clouds* in the letter by pointing out that at 2.3.19 the epistolographer uses the word for 'matchmaker' found at *Clouds*.41, προμνήστρια, a term he employs only here. As

Drago (2007: 448) perceives, elsewhere Aristainetos uses μαστροπός for 'matchmaker'. She adds that προμνήστρια might also evoke the words of Euripides' Hippolytus, who calls his nurse τῶν κακῶν προμνήστρια (*Hipp*.589 'the matchmaker of evils'). On 2.3's matchmaking motif, see further Zanetto 1987: 203.

39 While Glykera's letter picks up on the matchmaking motif from the monologue's start, Euboulides' re-performance of Strepsiades' line comes from its conclusion, an order of allusion that mirrors the letters' sequence in the epistolary collection as the *codex unicus* presents it. Although it is unknown whether this manuscript gives the authorial order of the text or that of a scribe, the configuration of reference to Aristophanes' comedy strongly suggests the former. The collection's subtle internal connections might, of course, represent the work of a clever editor, though this seems less likely. After all, an editor would have to first study the corpus to discover this complex of allusion to and inversion of *Clouds*, and only then position the texts accordingly, whereas the author could compose and order his compositions *ad libitum*.

40 Bing and Höschele 2014: 127.

41 This technique of appropriation with a twist is what Hutcheon (1985: 10) defines as 'parody' – imitation coupled with 'an ironic and critical dimension of distanciation'. Just as essentially auto-reflexive modern art involves, according to Hutcheon, 'an integrated structural remodeling process of revising, replaying, inverting and "trans-contextualizing" previous works of art', so too, it seems to me, does Aristainetos engage in ironic play with his model material, reversing and reorienting what he borrows from classical comic texts.

42 Zanetto 1987: 203. Zanetto notes that ἀποκοιτήσω ('I shall sleep out of the house') in 2.3.11 may signal Aristainetos' dependence on Menander, for this exceptional use of ἀποκοιτέω, a verb that usually designates the act of sleeping away from one's assigned post, appears at *Epitr*.136, ἀπόκοιτός ἐστι ('he is sleeping out'). Once again, as Zanetto observes, Aristainetos has inverted the gender of his model, for in Menander, the husband Charisios threatens to abandon his newly wedded wife, Pamphila.

43 Thus in Aristainetos' adaptation of the Aristophanic motif, one domestic relationship is switched for another: a situation between father and son becomes one between husband and wife. As Tom Hawkins has pointed out to me, the change might be dictated, at least in part, by genre, for whereas the relations between parents and children are an important preoccupation of drama, this focus on the family is out of place in the universe of Aristainetos' erotic epistles.

44 Likewise, Aristainetos demonstrates familiarity with other dramatic texts in their entirety such as Menander's *Dyskolos*, as shown by Arnott 1982: 308–9. On the epistolographer's thorough knowledge of his sources, see also Zanetto 1987: 202.

45 For this proverb's occurrence in both Greek and Latin literature, see Arnott 1975: 25 and Drago 2007: 449.

46 As Drago (2007: 521) discerns, this (apparent) adage appears only here, though the *topos* of avoiding a useless or even dangerous search is widespread in Greek literature.
47 There are four other proverbial expressions involving animals in the corpus (1.4.21–2, 1.17.18, 1.25.34–5, 2.20.26–7). The adage in epistle 1.25 also comes at the text's conclusion. On the frequent use of proverbs throughout Aristainetos' collection, see Tsirimbas 1950 and Arnott 1982: 301, who connects this tendency to the author's rhetorical education.
48 Zanetto 1987: 198.
49 On the affinities linking the two letters as a pair, see Zanetto 1987: 198–9, Höschele 2014: 748 and Bing and Höschele 2014: xxiiii–xxiv. As Bing and Höschele note, 1.5 and 1.22 are the only set of 'reciprocal' epistles in Aristainetos' corpus that are exchanged between the same two characters.
50 Despite their thematic similarities, these two texts do not correspond formally as one might expect of an epistolary exchange; that is Lucian's missive does not reply to Alciphron's by addressing the contents of his note or even by acknowledging its receipt. Nevertheless, Bing and Höschele (2014: xxiv) suggest that Lucian may be seen to 'answer' Alciphron's sexy tale with one of his own, an erotic exchange that might be an evocation of Lucian's association with the genre of dialogue through his *Dialogues of the Courtesans*.
51 See Arnott 1973: 205–6; 1975: 21 and Drago 1997: 178–86. Höschele (2014, 748) builds upon Drago's observations, noting that the epistolary scenario contains a clever inversion of the comic situation in Menander: whereas the *Perikeiromenē* features the jealous rage of Polemon, who shaves off his beloved Glykera's hair after having caught sight of her embracing another man (who is, in fact, Glykera's brother), jealousy is deliberately provoked by the Glykera of Aristainetos' letter, whose bawd Doris pretends that the girl is in love with a man named Polemon. *Aliter* Magrini (1981: 154–5), who sees Lucian's *Dialogues of the Courtesans* as the epistolographer's main model, with details added from the plays of Menander.
52 In Alciphron's epistolary collection, Menander is featured as corresponding with a *hetaira* named Glykera (4.18 and 19; Glykera writes to Bacchis about Menander in 4.2), hearkening back to the biographical tradition about the playwright's love affair with a girl of that name. On letters 4.18 and 4.19, see Bungarten 1967 and Rosenmeyer 2001: 301–6. Höschele (2012: 165–6) suggests that by including Menander as a letter-writer in the final book of an oeuvre replete with allusions to New Comedy, Alciphron 'absorbs' his literary model into his epistolary universe and prefigures his own inclusion as an author in Aristainetos' work.
53 I owe these reflections on Old *vs.* New Comedy to Regina Höschele.
54 Letter 1.19 also contains a reference to a girl named Glykera. There are other onomastic overlaps in the oeuvre: Pamphilos appears in 1.25, 2.16 and 2.18, Polykles in 1.13 and 2.7, Pythias in 1.12, 1.19 and 2.2 and Thelxinoe in 1.19, 1.25 and 2.18.

55 Doris is the name of Glykera's maid in the *Perikeiromene* as well.
56 As noted by Arnott (1973: 203); (1982: 306) this phrase alludes to *Clouds:* "μάκαρ ὦ Στρεψίαδες / αὐτός τ᾽ ἔφυς, ὡς σοφός, / χοῖον τὸω υἱὸν τρέφεις", / φήσουσι δή μ᾽οἱ φίλοι χοἰ δημόται / ζηλοῦντες ἡνίκ᾽ ἂν σὺ νι - / κᾷς λέγων τὰς δίκας (*Clouds*.1206–11 '"O lucky Strepsiades / how wise you are / and what a son you have", / so will they say – my friends and neighbours / envious as they are when, fighting, you win cases'). Drago (2007: 444) points out that the position of this allusion in the epistle's *incipit* emphasizes Aristainetos' reliance on the Aristophanic text.
57 Herrnstein Smith 1968: 119: '[C]onnections and similarities are illuminated, and the reader perceives that seemingly gratuitous or random events, details or juxtapositions have been selected in accord with certain principles'. For an exploration of these reading strategies in ancient literature, see Miller 1994: 52–77. On 'second readings', see Höschele 2010: 18–19.
58 For the theme of cunning in letters 1.5 and 1.22, see Grandolini 1978: 144–5, 151.
59 The letter's element of spousal misrecognition that pivots upon a robe may also be a Homeric intertext, suggestive of Odysseus' disguise upon his return to Ithaca. I am grateful to Tom Hawkins for this insight.
60 Arnott 1973: 203–4; 1975: 12, Drago 2007: 151–3, Höschele 2014: 748.
61 Bing and Höschele 2014: xxiii n. 44.
62 In fact, Bing and Höschele observe that the duped husband '. . . interprets the neighbor's sudden appearance as a kind of *deus ex machina*' (2014: 109), completing the theatrical performance, one might say. To my mind, the cunning wife's plan is particularly reminiscent of Plautine comedy, which features an explicitly theatrical deception devised and executed by the play's comic hero.
63 On the other hand, the narrative perspectives of letters 1.22 and 2.3 are parallel rather than reversed, for both are 'female' epistles written from the feminine point of view.
64 Many thanks to Regina Höschele for pointing out to me that 1.5 and 2.12 share a *himation*.
65 Although to compare his work with the subtly wrought *libelli* of Hellenistic and Roman poets would be going too far, nevertheless recent scholarship on ancient poetry books is useful for understanding Aristainetos' play upon links between single epistles, as well as for appreciating the meaning invested in the arrangement of his text. See Höschele (2010: 8–26) who observes the following of literary collections and their constituent parts: 'Das semantische Potential der separaten Elemente wird in dem Moment modifiziert, wo sie zueinander in Bezug treten. Wir können das Gedichtbuch *per se* als Makrotext charakterisieren, da es einerseits eine Vielzahl an autonom rezipierbaren Mikrotexten enthält und andererseits als – trotz seiner Heterogenität – einheitliches Ganzes funktioniert' (p.18).
66 Henderson (1991[2]: 172) explicates Strepsiades' *double entendre* as (1) 'Holding up my shirt, I took occasion to reprimand my wife on her spendthrift ways' and

(2) 'Holding up my nightshirt as a defense, I said, woman, you hit too hard [in coitus], or, you are squandering my reserve of sexual energy'. This reading is endorsed by Van Daele and Coulon (1948³: 166), Mastromarco (1983: 336 n.12), Degani (1990: 212) and Guidorizzi and Del Corno (1996: 193–4).

67 This pun was suggested to me *in litteris* by David Sansone.
68 Dover 1968: 101.
69 Drago 2007: 520.
70 See also Alciphron's letter 2.8, which, I propose, likewise engages with *Clouds*. In this epistle a farmer berates his wife who has abandoned her family for the glamour of Athens and now worships Kolian Aphrodite and Genetyllis, precisely the goddesses mentioned by Strepsiades as 'perfuming' his newlywed wife at *Clouds* 52.
71 The text is that of Benner and Fobes 1962².
72 Timon is an amalgam of Old and New Comedy. After evoking Strepsiades from *Clouds*, Timon (whose *persona* is modeled on the proverbial misanthrope, Timon of Athens) is transformed into Menander's Knemon, living in isolation and throwing clods of earth at passersby in 2.32.4–14; see *Dyskolos* lines 81–122.
73 *Aliter* Drago 2007: 519.
74 Although we have no evidence for an association between parasites and eroticism in Greek comedy, in the later classical literary tradition these *Fresser* are explicitly associated with sex; see Fontaine 2010: 223–48.
75 Thus Alciphron's letter also absorbs and inverts the element of excessive sexual appetite from *Clouds*, for it features the woes of an overly libidinous male.

Bibliography

1. Books and Articles

Abadie-Reynal, C. and J.-P. Darmon (2003), 'La Maison et la mosaïque des Synaristôsai: (Les Femmes au déjeuner de Ménandre)', in R. Early *et al.* (eds.) 2003, 79–99.

Adams, J.N. (1982), *The Latin Sexual Vocabulary* (London: Duckworth).

Ågmo, A. (2007), *Functional and Dysfunctional Sexual Behavior: A Synthesis of Neuroscience and Comparative Biology* (Amsterdam and New York: Elsevier Ltd.).

Altman, J. (1982), *Epistolarity: Approaches to a Form* (Columbus: Ohio State University Press).

Amato, E. (2001), 'Favorino nell' *Anthologia Palatina* (e un epigramma contestato a Meleagro)', *Scholia* 10, 92–104.

Amato, E. (2005–10), *Favorinos D'Arles: Oeuvres*. 2 vols. (Paris: Les Belles Lettres).

Amato, E. (2006a), 'L'autore dell'εὐνοῦχος ἐρῶν (Ps.-Lib. ethop. 26 Foerster) ed il più antico frammento in prosa di etopea d'autore', in E. Amato, A. Roduit, and M. Steinrück (eds.) 2006, 363–77.

Amato, E. (2006b), 'An Unpublished *Ethopoea* [sic] of Severus of Alexandria', *GRBS* 46, 63–72.

Amato, E. (2007), 'Éthopée et roman: le fragment probable d'un roman d'amour grec perdu', *Classica et Mediaevalia* 58, 193–207.

Amato, E. (2009), *Severus Sophista Alexandrinus: Progymnasmata quae exstant omnia* (Berlin and New York: Walter de Gruyter).

Amato, E. and J. Schamp, eds. (2005), 'ΗΘΟΠΟΙΙΑ: *La représentation de caractères entre fiction scolaire et réalité vivante à l'époque impériale et tardive* (Salerno: Helios).

Amato, E., A. Roduit, and M. Steinrück, eds. (2006), *Approches de la troisième sophistique: hommages à Jacques Schamp* (Brussels: Latomus).

Anderson, G. (1976a), *Lucian: Theme and Variation in the Second Sophistic. Mnemosyne* suppl. 41 (Leiden: Brill).

Anderson, G. (1976b), 'Lucian's Classics. Some short cuts to culture', *BICS* 23, 59–68.

Anderson, G. (1976c), *Studies in Lucian's Comic Fiction. Mnemosyne* suppl. 43 (Leiden: Brill).

Anderson, G. (1997), 'Alciphron's Miniatures', *ANRW* 2.34.3, 2188–2206.

Anderson, W.S. (1982), *Essays on Roman Satire* (Princeton: Princeton University Press).

Armstrong, D. (1989), *Horace* (New Haven: Yale University Press).

Arnim, H. von. (1898), *Leben und Werke des Dio von Prusa* (Berlin: Weidmann).

Arnott, W.G. (1973), 'Imitation, Variation, Exploitation: A Study in Aristaenetus', *GRBS* 14, 197–211.
Arnott, W.G. (1975), 'Annotations to Aristaenetus', *MPhL* 1, 9–31.
Arnott, W.G. (1979), *Menander Vol. I* (Cambridge, MA: Harvard University Press).
Arnott, W.G. (1982), 'Pastiche, Pleasantry, Prudish Eroticism: The Letters of "Aristaenetus"', *YCS* 27, 291–320.
Arnott, W.G. (1996a), *Alexis: The Fragments* (Cambridge: Cambridge University Press).
Arnott, W.G. (1996b), *Menander Vol. II* (Cambridge, MA: Harvard University Press).
Arnott, W.G. (2000), *Menander Vol. III* (Cambridge, MA: Harvard University Press).
Arnott, W.G. (2010), 'Middle Comedy', in G.W. Dobrov (ed.) 2010, 279–232.
Arnott, W.G. ed. and tr. (1979–2000), *Menander* (Cambridge, MA: Harvard University Press).
Artola, G.T. (1975), 'The Transvestite in Sanskrit Story and Drama', *Annals of Oriental Research of the University of Madras* 25, 57–68.
Arweiler, A. and M. Möller (2008), *Vom Selbst-Verständnis in Antike und Neuzeit / Notions of the Self in Antiquity and Beyond*. Transformationen der Antike, Bd. 8 (Berlin and New York: Walter de Gruyter).
Augoustakis, A. and A. Traill, eds. (2013), *A Companion to Terence* (Malden, MA: Wiley-Blackwell).
Axer, J. (1980), *The Style and the Composition of Cicero's Speech Pro Q. Roscio Comoedo: Origin and Function* (Warsaw: Wydawnictwa Uniwersytetu Warszawskiego).
Bakhtin, M. (1984 [1965]), *Rabelais and His World*, tr. H. Iswolsky (Bloomington: Indiana University Press).
Bakker, E.J., ed. (2010), *A Companion to the Ancient Greek Language* (West Sussex: Wiley-Blackwell).
Bakola, E. (2008), 'The Drunk, the Reformer and the Teacher: Agonistic Poetics and the Construction of Persona in the Comic Poets of the Fifth Century', *CCJ* 54, 1–29.
Bakola, E. (2010), *Cratinus and the Art of Comedy* (Oxford: Oxford University Press).
Bakola, E., L. Prauscello and M. Telò, eds. (2013), *Greek Comedy and the Discourse of Genres* (Cambridge: Cambridge University Press).
Baldwin, B. (1973), *Studies in Lucian* (Toronto: Hakkert).
Balty, J. (1995), *Mosaïques antiques du proche-orient: Chronologie, iconographie, interpretation* (Centre de Recherches d'Histoire Ancienne 140; Paris: Les Belles Lettres).
Balty, J. (2004), 'Les Mosaïques d'Antioche: Style et rayonnement', in B. Cabouret, P.-L. Gatier, and C. Saliou (eds.) 2014, 257–69.
Barbiero, E. (2014), 'Reading Between the Lines: Letters in Plautus' (PhD Diss.: University of Toronto).
Barchiesi, A. (1999), 'Traces of Greek Narrative and the Roman Novel', in S.J. Harrison (ed.) 1999, 124–41.
Barchiesi, A. (2009), 'Final Difficulties in an Iambic Poet's Career: *Epode* 17', in Lowrie (ed.) 2009, 232–46.

Barchiesi, A. and A. Cucchiarelli (2005), 'Satire and the Poet: The Body as Self-referential symbol', in K. Freudenburg (ed.) 2005, 207–23.

Barigazzi, A. (1966), *Favorino di Arelate: Opere* (Florence: Le Monnier).

Barry, W.D. (1993), 'Aristocrats, Orators, and the "Mob": Dio Chrysostom and the World of the Alexandrians', *Historia* 42, 82–103.

Barsby, J.A. (1993), 'Problems of Adaptation in the *Eunuchus* of Terence', in N.W. Slater and B. Zimmerman (eds.) 1993, 160–79.

Bartley, A., ed. (2009), *A Lucian for Our Times* (Newcastle: Cambridge Scholars Publishing).

Bartoletti, V. (1962), 'Noterelle papirologiche. 1.- Un rotolo illustrato di Menandro?', *SIFC* 34, 21–24 and plate I.

Barzilai, S. (1999), *Lacan and the Matter of Origins* (Stanford: Stanford University Press).

Bastianini, G. and A. Casanova, eds. (2004), *Menandro: cent'anni di papyri: atti del convegno internazionale di studi, Firenze, 12–13 giugno 2003* (Florence: Istituto papirologico G. Vitelli).

Bather, P. and C. Stocks, eds. (Forthcoming), *Ego primus iambos ostendi Latio: Re-evaluating Horace's Epodes* (Oxford: Oxford University Press).

Bathrellou, E. (2014), 'New Texts: Greek Comic Papyri 1973–2010', in M. Fontaine and A.C. Scafuro (eds.), 803–70.

Bean, G.E. (1965), *Side Kitabeleri* [*Inscriptions of Side*]. Yayinlarindan 5: 20 (Ankara: Türk Tarih Kurumu).

Beard, M. (2014), *Laughter in Ancient Rome: On Joking, Tickling, and Cracking Up* (Berkeley: University of California Press).

Beare, W. (1964), *The Roman Stage: A Short History of Latin Drama in the Time of the Republic*, 3rd ed. (London: Methuen).

Bears, W.J. and D.J. Geagan (1970), 'A New List of Victors in the Caesarea at Isthmia', *Hesperia* 39, 79–83.

Behr, C.A. (1968), *Aelius Aristides and the Sacred Tales* (Amsterdam: A. M. Hakkert).

Behr, C.A. (1994), 'Studies on the Biography of Aristides', *ANRW* 11.34.2, 1140–1233.

Behr, C.A. ed. and tr. (1981), *P. Aelius Aristides, the Complete Works*. vol. II, *Orationes* xvii–liii (Leiden: Brill).

Belayche, N. (2007), 'Des lieux pour le "profane" dans l'antiquité tardo-antique? Les fêtes entre *koinônia* sociale et espaces de rivalités religieuses', *Antiquité Tardive* 15, 35–46.

Benner, A.R. and E.H. Fobes, eds. (1962), *The Letters of Alciphron, Aelian and Philostratus* 2nd vol. (Cambridge, MA: Harvard University Press).

Berardi, E. (2014), 'Elio Aristide tra comici e commedia', in M. Reig and X. Riu (eds.) 2014, 207–20.

Berczelly, L. (1988), 'The Date and Significance of the Menander Mosaics at Mytilene', *BICS* 35: 119–26.

Berry, D.H. and A. Erskine, eds. (2010), *Form and Function in Roman Oratory* (Cambridge: Cambridge University Press).

Bieber, M. and G. Rodenwaldt (1911), 'Die Mosaiken des Dioskurides von Samos.' *JdI* 26: 1–22.

Bierl, A., P. von Möllendorff, S. Vogt, and H. Flashar, eds. (1994), *Orchestra: Drama, Mythos, Bühne* (Stuttgart: Teubner).

Biles, Z. (2006–7), 'Aeschylus' Afterlife: Reperformance by Decree in 5th c. Athens?', *ICS* 31–32, 206–42.

Biles, Z. (2011), *Aristophanes and the Poetics of Competition* (Cambridge: Cambridge University Press).

Biles, Z. (2014), 'The Rivals of Aristophanes and Menander', in M. Revermann (ed.) 2014, 43–59.

Bing, P., and Höschele, R., eds. (2014), *Aristaenetus, Erotic Letters* (Atlanta: Society of Biblical Literature).

Blum, R. (1991), *Kallimachos: The Alexandrian Library and the Origins of Bibliography*, tr. H.H. Wellisch (Madison: University of Wisconsin Press).

Blume, H.-D. (2010), 'Menander: The Text and its Restoration', in A.K. Petrides and S. Papioannou (eds.) 2010, 14–30.

Bompaire, J. (1958), *Lucian écrivain: imitation et creation* (Paris: E. de Boccard).

Bonfante, L. (2008), 'Freud and the Psychoanalytic Meaning of the Baubo Gesture in Ancient Art', *Notes in the History of Art* 27.2/3, 2–9.

Bonner, C. (1909a), 'On Certain Supposed Literary Relationships I', *CP* 4, 32–44.

Bonner, C. (1909b), 'On Certain Supposed Literary Relationships II', *CP* 4, 276–90.

Booth, J., ed. (2007), *Cicero on the Attack* (Swansea: Classical Press of Wales).

Borg, B. (2004), *Paideia: The World of the Second Sophistic* (Berlin: Walter de Gruyter).

Bosch, E. (1967), *Quellen zur Geschichte der Stadt Ankara im Altertum*. Yayinlarindan 7: 46 (Ankara: Türk Tarih Kurumu).

Bosher, K. (2012a), 'Hieron's Aeschylus', in K. Bosher (ed.) 2012b, 35–55.

Bosher, K., ed. (2012b), *Theater Outside Athens: Drama in Greek Sicily and South Italy* (Cambridge: Cambridge University Press).

Bosher, K. (2014), 'Epicharmus and Early Sicilian Comedy', in M. Revermann (ed.) 2014, 79–94.

Bosnakis, D. (2004), *The Hellenistic Polis of Kos: State, Economy and Culture: Proceedings of an International Seminar Organized by the Department of Archaeology and Ancient history, Uppsala University, 11–13 May, 2000,* (Uppsala: Uppsala Universitet).

Bost-Pouderon, C. (2006), *Dion Chrysostome: Trois discours aux villes (Orr. 33–35). Tôme 1: Prolégomènes, édition critique et traduction; Tôme 2: Commentaires, bibliographie et index. Cardo: Études et Textes pour l'Identité Culturelle de l'Antiquité Tardive, 4–5.* (Salerno: Helios Editrice).

Boudon-Millot, V. (2007), *Galien, Tome 1, Introduction générale. Sur l'ordre de ses propres livres. Sur ses propres livres. Que l'excellent médecin est aussi philosophe* (Paris: Budé).

Boudon-Millot, V., J. Jouanna, and A. Pietrobelli, eds. (2010), *Galien, Œuvres, Tome IV: 'Ne Pas se chagriner'* (Paris: Budé).

Boulogne, J. (2000), 'Les ΣΥΓΚΡΙΣΕΙΣ de Plutarque. Une rhétorique de la ΣΥΓΚΡΙΣΙΣ', in L. van der Stockt (ed.) 2000, 33–44.

Bouvattier, C., B. Mignot, H. Lefèvre, Y. Morel, and P. Bougnères (2006), 'Impaired Sexual Activity in Male Adults with Partial Androgen Insensitivity', *Journal of Clinical Endocrinology & Metabolism* 91, 3310–15

Bowersock, G. (2002), 'Philosophy in the Second Sophistic', in G. Clark and T. Rajak (eds.) 2002, 152–72.

Bowie, E. (2007), 'The Ups and Downs of Aristophanic Travel', in E. Hall and A. Wrigley (eds.) 2007, 32–51.

Bowie, E.L. (1970), 'Greeks and their past in the Second Sophistic', *Past and Present* 2, 3–41.

Bowie, E.L. (1989), 'Poetry and Poets in Achaia', in A.M. Cameron and S. Walker (eds.) 1989, 198–205.

Bowie, E.L. (1998), 'Greek Sophists and Greek Poetry in the Second Sophistic', *ANRW* II 33.1: 209–58.

Bramble, J.C. (1974), *Persius and the Programmatic Satire: A Study in Form and Imagery* (Cambridge: Cambridge University Press).

Brancacci, A. (2000), 'Dio, Socrates, and Cynicism', in S. Swain (ed.) 2000, 240–60.

Branham, B.R. (1989), *Unruly Eloquence: Lucian and the Comedy of Traditions* (Cambridge, MA: Harvard University Press).

Braund, D. and Wilkins, J., eds. (2000), *Athenaeus and his World: Reading Greek Culture in the Roman Empire* (Exeter: University of Exeter Press).

Braund, S. and J. Osgood, eds. (2012), *A Companion to Persius and Juvenal* (Malden, MA and Oxford: Wiley-Blackwell).

Braund, S.H, ed. (1989), *Satire and Society in Ancient Rome* (Exeter: Exeter University Press).

Braund, S.H. (1988), *Beyond Anger: A Study of Juvenal's Third Book of Satires* (Cambridge: Cambridge University Press).

Braund, S.M. (1996a), *Juvenal: Satires, Book 1* (Cambridge: Cambridge University Press).

Braund, S.M. (1996b), *The Roman Satirists and Their Masks* (Bristol: Bristol Classical Press).

Braund, S.M. (2004a), *Juvenal and Persius* (Cambridge, MA: Harvard University Press).

Braund, S.M. (2004b), 'Libertas or Licentia? Freedom and Criticism in Roman Satire', in I. Sluiter and R.M. Rosen (eds.) 2004, 409–28.

Bréchet, C. (2005), 'Aristophane chez Plutarque', *Pallas* 67, 11–23.

Bright, D.F. and E.S. Ramage, eds. (1984), *Classical Texts and their Traditions: Studies in Honor of C.R. Trahman* (Atlanta: Scholars Press).

Brisson, L. (2002), *Sexual Ambivalence: Androgyny and Hermaphroditism in Graeco-Roman Antiquity*, tr. J. Lloyd (Berkeley and Los Angeles: University of California Press).

Brower, G.R. (1996), 'Ambivalent Bodies: Making Christian Eunuchs' (Diss.: Duke University).

Brown, P. (1996), *Terence: The Comedies* (Oxford: Oxford University Press).
Brown, P. (2013), 'Terence and Greek New Comedy', in A. Augoustakis and A. Traill (eds.) 2013, 17–32.
Brown, P.G. McC. (1990), 'Plots and Prostitutes in Greek New Comedy', *Papers of the Leeds International Latin Seminar* 6, 241–66.
Bruneau, P. (1970), *L'Îlot de la Maison des Comédiens. Délos 27* (Paris: De Boccard).
Bruneau, P. (1972), *Les Mosaïques. Délos 29*. Paris: De Boccard.
Bruneau, P. (1984), 'Les mosaïstes antiques avaient-ils des cahiers de modèles?' *Revue Archéologique*, 241–72.
Bruneau, P. (1999), 'Le Répertoire mosaïstique et sa transmission', in D. Mulliez (ed.) 1999, 45–50.
Bruzzese, L. (2011), *Studi su Filemone comico* (Lecce: Iseo).
Bullough, V.L. (2002), 'Eunuchs in History and Society', in S. Tougher (ed.) 2002, 1–17.
Bungarten, J.J. (1967), 'Menanders und Glykeras Brief bei Alkiphron' (PhD Diss.: University of Bonn).
Burke, S.D. (2013), *Queering the Ethiopian Eunuch: Strategies of Ambiguity in Acts* (Minneapolis: Fortress Press).
Burri, R. (2004), 'Zur Datierung und Identität des Aristainetos', *MH* 61, 83–91.
Bushnell, R., ed. (2006), *The Blackwell Companion to Tragedy* (Oxford: Blackwell).
Cabouret, B., P.-L. Gatier, and C. Saliou, eds. (2004), *Antioche de Syrie: Histoire, images et traces de la ville antique*, (Lyon: Maison de l'Orient Méditerranéen–Jean Pouilloux).
Cairns, D.L. and R.A. Knox, eds. (2004), *Law, Rhetoric and Comedy in Classical Athens: Studies Presented to Douglas M. MacDowell* (London and Swansea: The Classical Press of Wales).
Cairns, F. (2005), 'Parabsis in Euripides and Sophocles (Pollux IV 111)?', *Aevum Antiquum* 5, 135–44.
Cameron, A.M. and S. Walker, eds. (1989), *The Greek Renaissance in the Roman Empire* (London: Institute for Classical Studies).
Campbell, S. (1988), *The Mosaics of Antioch* (Subsidia mediaevalia 15; Toronto: Pontifical Institute of Mediaeval Studies).
Campbell, S., R. Ergeç, and E. Csapo (1998), 'New Mosaics', in D. Kennedy (ed.), 1998, 109–28.
Campbell, W.A. and R. Stillwell (1941), 'Catalogue of Mosaics 1937–1939', in R. Stillwell (ed.) 1941, 171–219.
Caner, D.F. (1997), 'The Practice and Prohibition of Self-Castration in Early Christianity', *Vigiliae Christianae* 51, 396–415.
Carawan, E., ed. (2007), *Oxford Readings in the Attic Orators* (Oxford: Oxford University Press).
Carey, C. and L. Swift, eds. (Forthcoming), *Greek Iambos and Elegy: New Approaches* (Oxford: Oxford University Press).
Casanova, A. (2005). 'Plutarco e Menandro', in A. Casanova (ed.) 2005a, *Plutarco e l'età ellenistica*. Firenze. 105–118.

Casanova, A., ed. (2014), *Menandro e l'evoluzione della commedia greca* (Firenze: Firenze University Press).
Cazzato, V., D. Obbink and E. Prodi, eds. (Forthcoming), *The Cup of Song: Studies on Poetry and the Symposium* (Oxford: Oxford University Press).
Çelik, Ö. (2009), 'Yukarı Harbiye mozaik kurtarma kazısı (Perikeiromene, Philadelphoi, Syaristosai, Theophorosmene)', *17 Müze Çalışmaları ve Kurtarma Kazıları Sempozyumu (28 Nisan-1 Mayis 2008, Side)* (Ankara: Kültür ve Turizm Bakanlığı) 41–52.
Charitonidis, S., L. Kahil, and R. Ginouvès (1970), *Les mosaïques de la maison du Ménandre à Mytilène* (AntK-BH 6; Bern: Francke Verlag).
Chiasson, C. (1984), 'Pseudartabas and his Eunuchs: *Acharnians* 91–122', *CPh* 79, 131–6.
Christ, M.R. (2004), 'Draft Evasion Onstage and Offstage in Classical Athens', *CQ* 54, 33–57.
Clark, E.A. (2005), 'Dissuading from Marriage: Jerome and the Asceticization of Satire', in W.S. Smith (ed.) 2005, 154–81.
Clark, G. and T. Rajak, eds. (2002), *Philosophy and Power in the Graeco-Roman World: Essays in Honour of Miriam Griffin* (Oxford: Oxford University Press).
Clay, D. (1975), 'The Tragic and Comic Poet of the Symposium', *Arion* 2.2, 238–261.
Collard, C. and M. Cropp, ed. and tr. (2008), *Euripides: Fragments. Aegeus-Meleager* (Cambridge, MA: Loeb Classical Library).
Collins, D. (2005), *Master of the Game: Competition and Performance in Greek Poetry* (Cambridge, MA: Harvard University Press).
Colton, R.E. (1967), 'Juvenal and Propertius', *Traditio* 23, 442–61.
Connolly, J. (2007), *The State of Speech: Rhetoric and Political Thought in Ancient Rome* (Princeton: Princeton University Press).
Cooper, C. (1995), 'Hyperides and the Trial of Phryne', *Phoenix* 49, 303–18.
Copley, F.O. (1956), *Exclusus Amator: A study in Latin love poetry* (Madison: American Philological Association).
Courtney, E. (1980), *A Commentary on the Satires of Juvenal* (London: Athlone Press).
Cousland, J.R.C., and J.R. Hume, eds. (2009), *The Play of Texts and Fragments: Essays in Honour of Martin Cropp* (Leiden: Brill).
Cribiore, R. (2001), *Gymnastics of the Mind: Greek Education in Hellenistic and Roman Egypt* (Princeton: Princeton University Press).
Crowther, C. (2007), 'The Dionysia at Iasos: Its Artists, Patrons, and Audience', in P. Wilson (ed.) 2007, 294–334.
Cryle, P.M. (2001), 'Producing the Voice in Erotic Narrative', in B. Nelson, A. Freadman, and P. Anderson (eds.) 2001, 97–133.
Csapo, E. (1997a), 'Mise en scène théâtrale, scène de théâtre artisanale: Les mosaïques de Ménandre à Mytilène, leur contexte social et leur tradition iconographique', *Pallas* 47 (= *De la scène aux gradins: Théâtre et représentations dramatiques après Alexandre le Grand*, edited by B. Le Guen [Toulouse: Presses Universitaires du Mirail]), 165–82.

Csapo, E. (1997b), 'Riding the Phallus for Dionysus: Iconology, Ritual, and Gender-Role De/Construction', *Phoenix*. 51.3/4, 253–95.

Csapo, E. (1999), 'Performance and Iconographic Tradition in the Illustrations of Menander', *Syllecta Classica* 10, 154–88.

Csapo, E. (2000), 'From Aristophanes to Menander', in M. DePew and D. Obbink (eds.) 2000, 115–34.

Csapo, E. (2012), ' "Parade Abuse", "From the Wagons" ', in C.W. Marshall and G. Kovacs (eds.) 2012, 19–34.

Csapo, E. (2014), 'The Iconography of Comedy', in M. Revermann (ed.) 2014, 95–130.

Csapo, E. and N.W. Slater (1995), *The Context of Ancient Drama* (Ann Arbor: University of Michigan Press).

Csapo, E. and W. Slater, eds. (1995), *The Context of Ancient Drama* (Ann Arbor: University of Michigan Press).

Cucchiarelli, A. (2001), *La satira e il poeta: Orazio tra Epodi e Sermones* (Pisa: Giardini).

Cucchiarelli, A. (2012), '*venusina lucerna*: Horace, Callimachus, and Imperial Satire', in S. Braund and J. Osgood (eds.) 2012, 165–89.

Cummings, M.S. (2001), 'The Early Greek *Paraclausithyron* and Gnesippus', *Scholia: Studies in Classical Antiquity* 10, 38–53.

Damon, C. (1997), *The Mask of the Parasite: A Pathology of Roman Patronage* (Ann Arbor: University of Michigan Press).

Darmon, J.-P. (2004), 'Leçons des décors en mosaïque de Zeugma (Belkis, Turquie)', *Revue Archéologique*, 198–203.

Daviault, A. (1981), *Comoedia togata: Fragments* (Paris: Les Belles Lettres).

Davies, M. (1987), 'The Ancient Greeks on Why Mankind Does Not Live Forever', *MH* 44, 65–75.

De Stefani, E.L. (1912), 'La fonte delle epistole III e VI di Eliano', *SIFC* 19, 8–10.

Dedoussi, C. (1980), 'Fr 246 (PSI 847): An Illustrated Fragment of Menander's ΕΥΝΟΥΧΟΣ', *BICS* 27, 97–102.

Degani, E. (1990), 'Appunti per una traduzione delle "Nuvole" aristofanee', *Eikasmos* 1, 119–45.

Delcourt, M. (1961), *Hermaphrodite: Myths and Rites of the Bisexual Figure in Classical Antiquity*, tr. J. Nicholson (London: Studio Books).

Depew, M. and D. Obbink, eds. (2000), *Matrices of Genre: Authors, Canons, and Society* (Cambridge: Harvard University Press).

Deroux, C., ed. (1989), *Studies in Latin Literature and Roman History* 5 (Brussels: Latomus).

Desideri, P. and Francesca Fontanella, eds. (2007), *Elio Aristide e la legittimazione greca dell'impero di Roma* (Bologna: Il mulino).

Di Florio, M. (2003) 'L'estetica del comico e la *Aristophanis et Menandri Comparatio*', *Ploutarchos* 1, 21–34.

Di Florio, M. (2004), 'Presenze e valuatione di Aristophane nei *Moralia* di Plutarco', in S.M. Medaglia (ed.) 2004, 157–86.

Di Florio, M. (2008), *Plutarco: Il Confronto tra Aristofane e Menandro (compendio)* (Naples: M. D'Auria Editore).
Diels, H. (1907), 'Arcana cerealia', *Miscellanea di archeologia, storia, e filologia dedicate al Professore A. Salinas* (Palermo: Virzi), 3–14.
Diggle, J. (2004), *Theophrastus: Characters* (Cambridge: Cambridge University Press).
Dobrov, G., ed. (1995), *Beyond Aristophanes: Tradition and Diversity in Greek Comedy* (Atlanta: Scholars Press).
Dobrov, G., ed. (1998), *The City as Comedy: Fictions of the Polis on the Greek Comic Stage* (Chapel Hill: University of North Carolina Press).
Dobrov, G. (2001), *Figures of Play: Greek Drama an Metafictional Poetics* (Oxford: Oxford University Press).
Dobrov, G., ed. (2010), *Brill's Companion to the Study of Greek Comedy* (Leiden: Brill).
Dover, K. (1993), *Aristophanes: Frogs* (Oxford: Clarendon Press).
Dover, K.J. (1958), 'Aristophanic Studies', *CR* 8.3–4, 235–7.
Dover, K.J. (1968), *Aristophanes: Clouds* (Oxford: Oxford University Press).
Downie, J. (2008), 'Proper Pleasures: Bathing and Oratory in Aelius Aristides' *Hieros Logos I* and *Oration 33*', in W. Harris and B. Holmes (eds.) 2008, 115–30.
Downie, J. (2013), *At the Limits of Art: A Literary Study of Aelius Aristides'* Hieroi Logoi (Oxford: Oxford University Press).
Drago, A.T. (1992), 'Due esempi di intertestualità in Aristeneto', *Lexis* 15, 17–87.
Drago, A.T. (2007), *Aristeneto: Lettere d'amore. Introduzione, testo, traduzione e commento* (Lecce: Pensa Multimedia).
Drago, A.T. (2014), 'Menandro nell'epistolografia greca di età imperiale', in Casanova (ed.) 2014, 259–76.
Dunbabin, K. (2006), 'A Theatrical Device on the Late Roman Stage: The Relief of Flavius Valerianus', *JRA* 19, 191–212.
Dunbabin, K. (2007), 'Homer, Euripides, Menander and Vergil on Mosaics: The Reach of Mythology in the Mid- to Late Empire [review of *Darstellungen aus dem Epos und Drama auf kaiserzeitlichen und spätantiken Bodenmosaiken: Eine ikonographische und deutungsgeschichtliche Untersuchung*, by D. Stefanou]', *JRA* 20, 572–77.
Dunbabin, K. (2008), 'Domestic Dionysos? Telete in Mosaics from Zeugma and the Late Roman Near East', *JRA* 21, 193–224.
Dunbabin, K. (2010), 'The Pantomime Theonoe on a Mosaic from Zeugma', *JRA* 23, 413–26.
Durham, D.B. (1913), *The Vocabulary of Menander* (Amsterdam: Adolf M. Hakkert).
Dutsch, D., and A. Suter, eds. (Forthcoming), *Ancient Obscenities: Their Nature and Use in the Ancient Greek and Roman Worlds* (Ann Arbor: University of Michigan Press).
Dynes, W.R. and S. Donaldson, eds. (1992), *Homosexuality in the Ancient World* (London: Routledge).
Early, R. *et al.* (2003), *Zeugma: Interim Reports, Rescue Excavations (Packard Humanities Institute), Inscription of Antiochus I, Bronze Statue of Mars, House and Mosaic of the*

Synaristôsai, and Recent Work on the Roman Army at Zeugma (Portsmouth, RI: *JRA* Suppl. 51).

Easterling, P. and E. Hall, eds. (2002), *Greek and Roman Actors: Aspects of an Ancient Profession* (Cambridge: Cambridge University Press).

Edmonds, J.M. (1957), *The Fragments of Attic Comedy*, vol. 1 (Leiden: Brill).

Edwards, C. (1993), *The Politics of Immorality in Ancient Rome* (Cambridge: Cambridge University Press).

Fantham, E. (1984), 'Roman Experience of Menander in the Late Republic and Early Empire', *TAPA* 114, 299–309.

Fantham, E. (1988), 'Mime: The Missing Link in Roman Literary History', *CW* 82, 153–63.

Fantham, E. (2002), 'Orator and/et Actor', in P. Easterling and E. Hall (eds.) 2002, 362–76.

Faraone, C.A. and L.K. McClure, eds. (2006), *Prostitutes and Courtesans in the Ancient World* (Madison, WI: University of Wisconsin Press).

Feeney, D. (1992), '*Si licet et fas est*: Ovid's *Fasti* and the Problem of Free Speech Under the Principate', in A. Powell (ed.) 1992, 1–25.

Feeney, D. (2002), 'Una Cum Scriptore Meo: Poetry, Principate, and the Traditions of Literary History in the Epistle to Augustus', in T. Woodman and D. Feeney (eds.) 2002, 172–87.

Feeney, D. (2006), Review of Goldberg 2005, *BMCR* 2006.08.45.

Fendt, G. (2014), *Comic Cure for Delusional Democracy* (Lanham, MD: Lexington Books).

Ferrari, F. (2004), 'Papiri e mosaici: Tradizione testuale e iconografia in alcune scene di Menandro', in G. Bastianini and A. Casanova (eds.) 2004, 127–49.

Ferri, R. (2014), 'The Reception of Plautus in Antiquity', in M. Fontaine and A.C. Scafuro (eds.) 2014, 767–81.

Ferriss-Hill, J.L. (2015), *Roman Satire and the Old Comic Tradition* (Cambridge: Cambridge University Press).

Fiske, G. (1920), *Lucilius and Horace* (Madison: University of Wisconsin Press).

Fitzgerald, R. (1988), 'Power and Impotence in Horace's *Epodes*', *Ramus* 17, 176–91.

Fögen, T. (2007), '*Splendeurs et misères des courtisanes*: zur Charakterzeichnung in den Hetärenbriefen Alkiphrons', *WJA* 31, 181–205.

Foka, A. (2013), 'Beauty and the Beast: Feminity, Animals and Humour in Middle Comedy', *Classica et Mediaevalia* 62, 51–80.

Folch, M. (2013), 'Unideal Genres and the Ideal City', in A. Peponi (ed.) 2013, 339–70.

Fontaine, M. (2010), *Funny Words in Plautine Comedy* (Oxford: Oxford University Press).

Fontaine, M. (2014a), 'Dynamics of Appropriation in Roman Comedy: Menander's *Kolax* in Three Roman Receptions (Naevius, Plautus and Terence's *Eunuchus*)', in S.D. Olson (ed.) 2014, 180–202.

Fontaine, M. (2014b), 'The Reception of Greek Comedy in Rome', in M. Revermann (ed.) 2014, 404–23.

Fontaine, M. and A. Scafuro, eds. (2014), *The Oxford Handbook of Greek and Roman Comedy* (Oxford: Oxford University Press).
Fortenbaugh, W.W. (2003), *Theophrastean Studies* (Stuttgart: Franz Steiner Verlag).
Foucault, M. (1985), *The Use of Pleasure, Volume 2 of The History of Sexuality*, tr. R. Hurley (New York: Vintage Books).
Fowler, H.N. (1927), *Plutarch, Moralia X* (Cambridge, MA: Harvard University Press).
Fratantuono, L. and C. Stark, eds. (Forthcoming), *A Companion to Latin Epic, ca. 14–96 ce* (Malden, MA: Wiley-Blackwell).
Fredricks, S.C. (1973), 'The function of the Prologue (1–20) in the Organisation of Juvenal's Third Satire', *Phoenix* 27, 62–7.
Freud, S. (1963), 'Fetishism', in P. Rieff (ed.) 1963, 214–19.
Freudenberg, K. (1993), *The Walking Muse: Horace on the theory of satire* (Princeton: Princeton University Press).
Freudenburg, K. (2001), *Satires of Rome: Threatening Poses from Lucilius to Juvenal* (Cambridge: Cambridge University Press).
Freudenburg, K. (2005), *Cambridge Companion to Roman Satire* (Cambridge: Cambridge University Press).
Friedländer, L. (1919–21), *Darstellungen aus der Sittengeschichte Roms in der Zeit von Augustis bis zum Ausgang der Antonine.* Rev. ed. (Leipzig: S. Hirzel).
Friend, A.M. (1941), 'Menander and Glykera in the Mosaics of Antioch', in R. Stillwell (ed.) 1941, 248–51.
Frisch, P. (1986), *Zehn agonistische Papyri* (Opladen: Westdeutscher Verlag).
Furley, W.D. (2009), 'Drama at the Festival: A recurrent motif in Menander', in J.R.C. Cousland and J.R. Hume (eds.) 2009, 389–401.
Gagné, R. (2006), 'What is the Pride of Halicarnassus?' *Classical Antiquity* 25, 1–33.
Galán Vioque, G. (2002), *Martial, Book VII. A Commentary.* Tr. J.J. Zoltowski (Leiden: Brill).
Gallo, I. and C. Moreschini, eds. (2000), *I generi letterari in Plutarco* (Naples: M. D'Auria).
Garelli, M.-H. (2007), *Danser le Mythe: La pantomime et sa réception dans la culture antique* (Louvain: Peeters).
Gargiulo, T. (1992), 'Cleone, Prometeo e gil oracoli', *Eikasmos* 3, 153–64.
Garrigou-Kempton, E. (2010), 'If Your Vagina Could Speak, What Would it Say: Dangerous Femininity, Anxious Masculinity, and the Threat of Female Desire in the 1975 Pornographic Movie "The Sex that Speaks"', *Thinking Gender Papers*. UCLA Center for the Study of Women. <https://escholarship.org/uc/item/6br2j4v1>.
Geffcken, K.A. (1973), *Comedy in the Pro Caelio, with an Appendix on the* In Clodium et Curionem (Leiden: Brill).
Gentili, B. (1979). *Theatrical Performances in the Ancient World: Hellenistic and Early Roman Theatre* (Amsterdam: Brill).
Gilhuly, K. (2006), 'The Phallic Lesbian: Philosophy, Comedy, and Social Inversion in Lucian's Dialogues of the Courtesans', in C.A. Faraone and L.K. McClure (eds.) 2006, 274–91.

Gill, C., T. Whitmarsh, and J. Wilkins, eds. (2009), *Galen and the World of Knowledge* (Cambridge: Cambridge University Press).

Gleason, M.W. (1995), *Making Men: Sophists and Self-Presentation in Ancient Rome* (Princeton: Princeton University Press).

Gödde, S. and T. Heinze, eds. (2000), *Skenika: Beiträge zum antike Theater und seiner Rezeption* (Darmstadt: Wissenschaftliche Buchgesellschaft).

Goldberg, S.M. (1980), *The Making of Menander's Comedy* (London: The Athlone Press).

Goldberg, S.M. (2005), *Constructing Literature in the Roman Republic: Poetry and Its Reception* (Cambridge: Cambridge University Press).

Goldhill, S. (1995), *Foucault's Virginity: Ancient Erotic Fiction and the History of Sexuality* (Cambridge: Cambridge University Press).

Goldhill, S. and R. Osborne, eds. (1999), *Performance Culture and Athenian Democracy* (Cambridge: Cambridge University Press).

González, J., ed. (Forthcoming), *Diachrony: Diachronic Aspects of Ancient Greek Literature and Culture*. MythosEikonPoiesis (Berlin: Walter de Gruyter).

Gordon, P. (2013), 'Epistolary Epicureans', in O. Hodkinson and P. Rosenmeyer (eds.) 2013, 133–52

Görkay, K., P. Linant de Bellefonds, and É. Prioux (2006), 'Some Observations on the Theonoe Mosaic from Zeugma', *Anadolu* 31, 19–33.

Gowers, E. (1993), *The Loaded Table: Representations of Food in Roman Literature* (Oxford: Clarendon Press).

Gowers, E. (2002), 'Blind Eyes and Cut Throats: Amnesia and Silence in Horace "Satires" 1.7', *CPh* 97.2, 145–61.

Gowers, E. (2012), *Horace Satires Book 1* (Cambridge: Cambridge University Press).

Gowers, E. (Forthcoming), 'Girls Will be Boys and Boys Will be Girls: The Gender of Horace's *Epodes*', in P. Bather and C. Stocks (eds.) Forthcoming.

Gowing, A. (2005), *Empire and Memory: The Representation of the Roman Republic in Imperial Culture* (Cambridge: Cambridge University Press).

Graf, F. (2005), 'Satire in a Ritual Context', in K. Freudenburg (ed.) 2005, 192–206.

Graf, F. (Forthcoming), *Roman Festivals in the Greek East: From the Early Empire to the Middle Byzantine Era* (Cambridge: Cambridge University Press).

Graillot, H. (1912), *Le culte de Cybèle, mère des dieux, à Rome et dans l'Empire romain* (Paris: Fontemoing).

Grandolini, D. (1978), 'Osservazioni sul tema dell'astuzia nelle epistole di Aristeneto', *Materiali e contribute per la storia della narrativa greco-latina* 2, 143–153.

Graumann, L.A. (2013), 'Monstrous Births and Retrospective Diagnosis: The Case of Hermaphrodites in Antiquity', in C. Laes, C.F. Goodey, and M.L. Rose (eds.) 2013, 181–209.

Graux, C. (1877), 'Chorikios, Apologie des Mimes', *RPh* 1, 209–47.

Greaves, A.M. (2012), 'Partial Androgen Insensitivity Syndrome (Reifenstein's Syndrome) in the Roman World', *CQ* 62, 888–92.

Green, J.R. (1985), 'Drunk Again: A Study in the Iconography of the Comic Theatre', *AJA* 89: 465–72
Green, J.R. (1994), *Theatre in Ancient Greek Society* (London: Routledge).
Green, J.R. (Forthcoming), 'Additions and Alterations to *MNC*³', *BICS*.
Griffiths, A., ed. (1995), *Essays in Ancient Drama in honour of E.W. Handley*, BICS Supplement 66 (London: Institute of Classical Studies).
Grig, L., ed. (Forthcoming), *Locating Popular Culture in the Ancient World* (Cambridge: Cambridge University Press).
Guida, A. (2004), 'Convertire il dyskolos: da Manandro a Eliano (con un'appendice su Giuliano)', in G. Bastianini and A. Casanova (eds.) 2004, 165–84.
Guida, A. (2007), 'Da Menandro a Eliano attraverso Terenzio: personaggi comici fra corruttele e interferenze linguistiche', *Eikasmos* 18, 325–41.
Guidorizzi, G. and D. Del Corno, eds. (1996), *Aristofane: Le Nuvole* (Milano: Mondadori).
Gutzwiller, K. and O. Çelik (2012), 'New Menander Mosaics from Antioch', *AJA* 116, 573–623.
Guyot, P. (1980), *Eunuchen als Sklaven und Freigelassene in der griechisch-römischen Antike* (Stuttgart: Klett-Cotta).
Habinek, T. (2005), *Ancient Rhetoric and Oratory* (Malden, MA and Oxford: Wiley-Blackwell).
Hall, E. (2002), 'The Singing Actors of Antiquity', in *Greek and Roman Actors: Aspects for an Ancient Profession*, in P. Easterling and E. Hall (eds.) 2002, 3–38.
Hall, E. and R. Wiles, eds. (2008), *New Directions in Ancient Pantomime* (Oxford: Oxford University Press).
Hall, E. and A. Wrigley, eds. (2010), *Aristophanes in Performance: 421 bc–ad 2007: Peace, Birds and Frogs* (London: Legenda).
Hall, E. and S. Harrop, eds. (2010), *Theorizing Performance: Greek Drama, Cultural History, and Critical Practice* (London: Duckworth).
Hall, J. (1981), *Lucian's Satire* (New York: Arno Press).
Hallett, J.P. (1989), 'Female Homoeroticism and the Denial of Roman Reality in Latin Literature', *Yale Journal of Criticism* 3, 209–27.
Halliwell, S. (1991), 'Comic Satire and Freedom of Speech in Classical Athens', *JHS* 111, 48–70.
Halliwell, S. (2004), 'Aischrology, Shame, and Comedy', in I. Sluiter and R. Rosen (eds.) 2004, 115–44.
Halliwell, S. (2008), *Greek Laughter: A Study of Cultural Psychology from Homer to Early Christianity* (Cambridge: Cambridge University Press).
Halperin, D., J.J. Winkler, and F. Zeitlin, eds. (1991), *Before Sexuality: Constructions of Erotic Experience in the Ancient Greek World* (Princeton: Princeton University Press).
Handley, E.W. (2011), 'The Rediscovery of Menander', in D. Obbink and R. Rutherford (eds.) 2011, 138–59.

Hanses, M. (2014), 'Plautinisches im Ovid: The *Amphitruo* and the *Metamorphoses*', in I.N. Perysinakis and E. Karakasis (eds.) 2014, 225–58.

Hanses, M. (Forthcoming), '*Statius vortit barbare*: (A) Comedy in the *Achilleid*', in L. Fratantuono and C. Stark (eds.). Forthcoming.

Hardwick, L. (2003), *Reception Studies* (Cambridge: Cambridge University Press).

Harries, B. (2007), 'Acting the Part: Techniques of the Comedic Stage in Cicero's Early Speeches', in J. Booth (ed.) 2007, 134–6.

Harris, W. and B. Holmes (2008), *Aelius Aristides: Between Greece, Rome and the Gods* (Leiden: Brill).

Harrison, S.J., ed. (1999), *Oxford Readings in The Roman Novel* (Oxford: Oxford University Press).

Harrison, S.J. (2007), *Generic Enrichment in Vergil and Horace* (Oxford: Oxford University Press).

Hartwig, A. (2010), 'The Date of the *Rhabdouchoi* and the Early Career of Plato Comicus', *ZPE* 174, 19–31.

Hartwig, A. (2012), 'Comic Rivalry and the Number of Comic Poets at the Lenaia of 405 B.C.', *Philologus* 156, 195–206.

Harvey, D. and J. Wilkins, eds. (2000), *The Rivals of Aristophanes: Studies in Athenian Old Comedy* (London: Duckworth and the Classical Press of Wales).

Hawkins, T. (2007) 'Lycambes gets capped', in D. Katsonopoulou, l. Petropoulos and S. Katsarou (eds.) 2007, 49–63.

Hawkins, T. (2014), *Iambic Poetics in the Roman Empire* (Cambridge: Cambridge University Press).

Hawkins, T. (Forthcoming), 'Pollio's Paradox', in L. Grig (ed.) Forthcoming.

Heath, M. (1994), 'The Substructure of Stasis-Theory from Hermagoras to Hermogenes', *CQ* 44, 114–29.

Helm, R. (1906), *Lukian und Menipp* (Leipzig: Teubner).

Helmbold, W.C. and E.N. O'Neil, eds. (1959), *Plutarch's Quotations*. APA monographs 19 (Oxford: Blackwell).

Henderson, J. (1991), *The Maculate Muse: Obscene Language in Attic Comedy* (Oxford: Oxford University Press).

Henderson, J., ed. and tr. (2008), *Aristophanes: Fragments* (Cambridge, MA: Loeb Classical Library).

Henderson, J.G.W. (1987), 'Suck it and See (Horace, *Epode* 8)', in M. Whitby, P. Hardie, and M. Whitby (eds.) 1987, 105–18.

Henderson, J.G.W. (1995), 'Pump Up the Volume: Juvenal, *Satire* 1.1–21', *PCPhS* 41, 101–37.

Henderson, J.G.W. (1998), *Fighting for Rome: Poets and Caesars, History and Civil War* (Cambridge: Cambridge University Press).

Henderson, J.G.W. (2009), 'Horace Talks Rough and Dirty: No Comment (*Epodes* 8 and 12)', in M. Lowrie (ed.) 2009, 401–17.

Henry, M.M. (1988), *Menander's Courtesans and the Greek Comic Tradition* (Frankfurt: Verlag Peter Lang).
Hercher, R. (1854), 'Zu Aelians Briefen', *Philologus* 9, 756–58.
Herrmann, K. (2011), *Nunc levis est tractanda Venus: Form und Funktion der Komödienzitate in der römischen Liebeselegie* (Frankfurt a. M.: Lang).
Herrnstein Smith, B. (1968), *Poetic Closure: A Study of How Poems End* (Chicago: University of Chicago Press).
Hertz, N. (1983), 'Medusa's Head: Male Hysteria under Political Pressure' *Representations* 4, 161–93.
Hine, H.M. (2010), 'Form and Function of Speech in the Prose Works of the Younger Seneca', in D.H. Berry and A. Erskine (eds.) 2010, 208–24.
Hirzel, R. (1895), *Der Dialog: ein literarhistorischer Versuch* (Leipzig: S. Hirzel).
Hodkinson, O. (2007), 'Better Than Speech: Some Advantages of the Letter in the Second Sophistic', in R. Morello and A.D. Morrison (eds.) 2007, 283–300.
Hodkinson, O. (2012), 'Attic Idylls: Hierarchies of Herdsmen and Social Status in Alciphron and Longus', *JHS* 132, 41–53.
Hodkinson, O. (2013a), 'Aelian's Rustic Epistles in the Context of his Corpus: A Reassessment of Aelian's Literary Programme and Qualities', in Vox (ed.) 2013, 257–310.
Hodkinson, O. (2013b), 'Better Than Speech: Some Advantages of the Letter in the Second Sophistic', in O. Hodkinson and P. Rosenmeyer (eds.) 2013, 323–47.
Hodkinson, O. and P. Rosenmeyer, (2013a), 'Introduction', in O. Hodkinson and P. Rosenmeyer (eds.) 2013b, 1–37.
Hodkinson, O. and P. Rosenmeyer (2013b), *Epistolary Narratives in Ancient Greek Literature* (Leiden: Brill).
Holmes, B. (2008), 'Aelius Aristides' Illegible Body', in W. Harris and B. Holmes (eds.) 2008, 81–114.
Hopkinson, N. (2008), *Lucian. A Selection* (Cambridge: Cambridge University Press).
Horstmanshoff, M. and C. van Tilburg, eds. (2010), *Hippocrates and Medical Education* (Leiden and Boston: Brill).
Höschele, R. (2010), *Die blütenlesende Muse: Poetik und Textualität antiker Epigrammsammlungen* (Tübingen: Narr).
Höschele, R. (2012), 'From Hellas with Love: The Aesthetics of Imitation in Aristaenetus's Epistles', *TAPA* 142, 157–86.
Höschele, R. (2014), 'Greek Comedy, the Novel and Epistelography', in M. Fontaine and A.C. Scafuro (eds.) 2014, 735–52.
Householder, F. (1941), *Literary Quotation and Allusion in Lucian* (New York: King's Crown Press).
Hubbard, T.K. (1991), *The Mask of Comedy: Aristophanes and the Intertextual Parabasis* (Ithaca and London: Cornell University Press).
Hubbard, T.K., ed. (2013), *A Companion to Greek and Roman Sexualities* (Malden, MA and Oxford: Wiley-Blackwell).

Hudson, N.A. (1989), 'Food in Roman Satire', in S.H. Braund (ed.) 1989, 69–87.
Hughes, A. (2012), *Performing Greek Comedy* (Cambridge: Cambridge University Press).
Hughes, I.A., and A. Deeb (2006), 'Androgen Resistance', *Best Practice & Research Clinical Endocrinology & Metabolism* 20, 577–98.
Hunter, R. (2000), 'The Politics of Plutarch's Comparison of Aristophanes and Menander', in Gödde and Heinze (eds.) 2000: 267–76.
Hunter, R. (2009), *Critical Moments in Classical Literature* (Cambridge: Cambridge University Press).
Hunter, R. (2014), 'Attic Comedy in the Rhetorical and Moralising Traditions', in M. Revermann (ed.) 2014, 373–86.
Hunter, R. and D. Russell, eds. (2011), *Plutarch: How to Study Poetry* (Cambridge: Cambridge University Press).
Hunter, R.L. (1983a), *A Study of Daphnis and Chloe* (Cambridge: Cambridge University Press).
Hunter, R.L. (1983b), *Eubulus: The Fragments* (Cambridge: Cambridge University Press).
Hunter, R.L. (1985), *The New Comedy of Greece and Rome* (Cambridge: Cambridge University Press).
Hunter, R.L. (2000), 'The Politics of Plutarch's *Comparison of Aristophanes and Menander*' in S. Gödde and T. Heinze (eds.) 2000, 267–76.
Hutcheon, L. (1985), *A Theory of Parody: The Teachings of Twentieth-Century Art Forms* (New York: Methuen).
Isager, S. and P. Pedersen, eds. (2004), *The Salmakis Inscription and Hellenistic Halikarnassos* (Odense: University Press of Southern Denmark).
Janko, R. (1984), *Aristotle on Comedy: Towards a Reconstruction of Poetics II* (Berkeley: University of California Press).
Jenkins, T. (2005), 'At Play with Writing: Letters and Readers in Plautus', *TAPA* 135, 359–92.
Jenkins, T. (2006), *Intercepted Letters: Epistolarity and Narrative in Greek and Roman Literature* (Plymouth: Lexington).
Jocelyn, H.D. (1992), 'A Greek Indecency and its Students: λαικάζειν', in W.R. Dynes and S. Donaldson (eds.) 1992, 208–40.
Jocelyn, H.D. and H.V. Hurt, eds. (1993), *Tria Lustra: Essays and Notes Presented to John Pinsent* (Liverpool: LCM).
Jones, C.P. (1978), *The Roman World of Dio Chrysostom* (Cambridge, MA and London: Harvard University Press).
Jones, C.P. (1991), 'Dinner Theater', in W.J. Slater (ed.) 1991, 185–98.
Jones, C.P. (1993), 'Greek Drama in the Roman Empire', in R. Scodel (ed.) 1993, 39–52.
Jones, C.P. (2013), 'Elio Aristide e la legittimazione greca dell'impero di Roma', in P. Desideri, and F. Fontanella (eds.) 2007, 39–67.

Jones, F. (2001), 'Performance in Juvenal', *Latomus* 60, 124–34.
Jones, M. (2012), *Playing the Man: Performing Masculinities in the Ancient Greek Novel* (Oxford: Oxford University Press).
Jory, J. (2002), 'The Masks on the Propylon of the Sebasteion at Aphrodisias', in P. Easterling and E. Hall (eds.) 2002, 238–53.
Joyal, M., ed. (2001), *In Altum: Seventy Five Years of Classical Studies in Newfoundland* (St. John's: Memorial University of Newfoundland).
Jufresa, M., F. Mestre, P. Gómez, and P. Gilabert, eds. (2005), *Plutarc a la seva època: Paideia i societat* (Barcelona: Sociedad Española de Plutarquistas).
Kahil, L. (1970), 'Remarques sur l'iconographie des pieces de Ménandre', in *Ménandre: Sept exposés suivis de discussions* (Entretiens sur l'antiquité classique 16; Vandoeuvres-Geneva: Fondation Hardt) 229–54.
Kahn, C.H. (1983), 'Drama and Dialectic in Plato's Gorgias', *Oxford Studies in Ancient Philosophy* 1, 75–121.
Kahn, C.H. (1998), *Plato and the Socratic Dialogue* (Cambridge: Cambridge University Press).
Karamanou, I. (2006), *Euripides: Danae and Dictys* (Munich and Leipzig: K.G. Saur).
Karavas, O. and J.-L. Vix (2014), 'On the Reception of Menander in the Imperial Period', in A. Sommerstein (ed.) 2014, 183–98.
Kasprzyk, D. and C. Vendries (2012), *Spectacles et Désordre à Alexandrie: Dion de Pruse, Discours aux Alexandrins. Histoire. Série Histoire ancienne* (Rennes: Presses Universitaires de Rennes).
Katsonopoulou, D., I. Petropoulos and S. Katsarou, eds. (2007), *Archilochus and his Age* (Athens: The Paros and Cyclades Institute of Archaeology).
Kay, N.M. (1985), *Martial Book XI: A Commentary* (London: Duckworth).
Keane, C.C. (2003), 'Theatre, Spectacle, and the Satirist in Juvenal', *Phoenix* 57, 257–75.
Keane, C.C. (2006), *Figuring Genre in Roman Satire* (Oxford: Oxford University Press).
Kehoe, P.H. (1984), 'The Adultery Mime Reconsidered', in D.F. Bright and E.S. Ramage (eds.) 1984, 89–106.
Keil, B. (1958), *Aelii Aristidies Smyrnaei quae supersunt omni,* vol. II, *Orationes* XVII–LIII *Continens* (Berlin: Weidmann).
Kennedy, D. (1998), *The Twin Towns of Zeugma on the Euphrates: Rescue Work and Historical Studies* (Portsmouth, RI: *JRA* Suppl. 27).
Kenney, E.J. (2012), 'Satiric Textures: Style, Meter, and Rhetoric', in S. Braund and J. Osgood (eds.) 2012, 113–36.
Kernans, A. (1959), *The Cankered Muse* (New Haven: Yale University Press).
Kim, L. (2010), 'The Literary Heritage as Language: Atticism and the Second Sophistic', in E.J. Bakker (ed.) 2010, 468–82.
Kindstrand, J.F. (1998), 'Claudius Aelianus und sein Werk', *ANRW* 2.34.4, 2954–96.
King, H. (1998), *Hippocrates' Woman: Reading the Female Body in Ancient Greece* (London: Routledge).

Klotz, F., and K. Oikonomopoulou, eds. (2011), *The Philosopher's Banquet: Plutarch's Table Talk in the Intellectual Culture in the Intellectual Culture of the Roman Empire* (Oxford: Oxford University Press).

Kokkinia, C. (2007), 'A Rhetorical Riddle: The Subject of Dio Chrysostom's *First Tarsian Oration*', *HSPh* 103, 407–22.

König, J. (2007), 'Alciphron's Epistolarity', in R. Morello and A.D. Morrison (eds.) 2007, 257–82.

Konstan, D. (1983), *Roman Comedy* (Ithaca and London: Cornell University Press).

Kovacs, D. (1990), 'De Cephisophonte Verna, ut Praehibent, Euripidis', *ZPE* 84, 15–18.

Kuefler, M. (2001), *The Manly Eunuch: Masculinity, Gender Ambiguity, and Christian Ideology in Late Antiquity* (Chicago and London: University of Chicago Press).

Kuin, I.N.I. (2015), 'Playful Piety: Lucian and the Comic in Ancient Religious Experience' (Diss.: New York University).

Kullmann, W., J. Althoff, and M. Asper, eds. (1998), *Gattungen wissenschaftlicher Literatur in der Antike* (Tübingen: Gunter Narr Verlag).

Kutzko, D. (2012), 'In Pursuit of Sophron: Doric Mime and Attic Comedy in Herodas' *Mimiambi*', in K. Bosher 2012a, 367–90.

Kyriakiki, N. (2007), *Aristophanes und Eupolis: zur Geschichte einer dicherischen Rivalität* (Berlin and New York: Walter de Gruyter).

Lada-Richards, I. (2007), Silent Eloquence: Lucian and Pantomime Dancing (London: Bristol Classical Press).

Lada-Richards, I. (2013), '*Mutata corpora*: Ovid's Changing Forms and the Metamorphic Bodies of Pantomime Dancing', *TAPA* 143, 105–52.

Laes, C., C. Goodey, and M.L. Rose, eds. (2013), *Disabilities in Roman Antiquity: Disparate Bodies* A Capite ad Calcem (Leiden: Brill).

Lamari, A. (2014), 'Early Reperformances of Drama in the Fifth Century', *CHS Research Bulletin* 2, no. 2. http://wp.chs.harvard.edu/chs-fellows/2014/06/20/early-reperformances-of-drama-in-the-fifth-century/.

Lape, S. (2004), Reproducing Athens: Menander's Comedy, Democratic Culture, and the *Hellenistic City* (Princeton: Princeton University Press).

Lape, S. (2006), 'The Poetics of the "Komos" – Chorus in Menander's Comedy', *AJP* 127, 89–109.

Lavigne, D. (2008), 'Embodied Poetics in Martial 11', *TAPA* 138, 275–311.

Le Guen, B. (2014), 'The Diffusion of Comedy from the Age of Alexander to the Beginning of the Roman Empire', in M. Fontaine and A.C. Scafuro (eds.), 2014, 359–77.

Leach, E.W. (1971), 'Horace's *Pater Optimus* and Terence's Demea: Autobiographical Fiction and Comedy in *Sermo*, I, 4', *AJP* 92, 616–32.

Ledergerber, P.I. (1905), 'Lucian und die altattische Komödie' (Diss., Freiburg: Einsiedeln).

Legré, L. (1900), *Un philosophe Provençal au temps des Antonins, Favorin d'Arles: sa vie, ses oeuvres, ses contemporains* (Marseilles: Aubertin et Rolle).

Leigh, M. (2004), 'The *Pro Caelio* and Comedy', *CP* 99, 300–35.
Lemarchand, L. (1926), *Dion de Pruse: Les Oeuvres d'avant l'exil* (Paris: J. De Gigord).
Lenz, F.W. and C.A. Behr, eds. (1976), *P. Aelii Aristidis Opera quae exstant omnia,* vol. I, *Orationes* I–XVI (Lugundi Batavorum: Brill).
Leone, P.A.M. (1974), *Claudii Aeliani Epistulae Rusticae* (Milan: Cisalpino-Goliardica).
Lesky, A. (1951), *Aristainetos: Erotische Briefe; Eingeleitet, neu übertragen und erläutert* (Zürich: Artemis).
Liapis, V. (2002), *Menandrou Gnomai Monostichoi: Eisagoge, metaphrase, scholia* (Athens: Stigme).
Lightfoot, J.L. (2003), *Lucian: On the Syrian Goddess* (Oxford: Oxford University Press).
Llewellyn-Jones, L. (2002), 'Eunuchs and the Royal Harem in Achaemenid Persia (559–331 bc)', in S. Tougher (ed.) 2002, 19–49.
Lloyd, G.E.R. (2003), *In the Grip of Disease* (Oxford: Oxford University Press).
Lloyd-Jones, H. (1960), *Menandri Dyscolus* (Oxford: Oxford University Press).
Lowe, N. (2013), 'Comedy and the Pleiad: Alexandrian Tragedians and the Birth of Comic Scholarship', in E. Bakola, L. Prauscello and M. Telò (eds.) 2013, 343–56.
Lowe, N.J. (2000), *The Classical Plot and the Invention of Western Narrative* (Cambridge: Cambridge University Press).
Lowrie, M. (2008), 'Cicero on Caesar or Exemplum and Inability in the *Brutus*', in A. Arweiler and M. Möller (eds.) 2008, 131–54.
Lowrie, M. (2009), *Horace: Odes and Epodes: Oxford Readings in Classical Studies* (Oxford: Oxford University Press).
Luppe, W. (1972), 'Die Zahl die Konkurrenten an den komischen Agnonen zur Zeit des peloponneschen Krieges', *Philologus* 116, 53–75.
Luppe, W. (2000), 'The Rivalry between Aristophanes and Kratinos', in. D. Harvey and J. Wilkins (eds.) 2000, 15–21.
Ma, J. (2007), 'A Horse from Teos: Epigraphical Notes on the Ionian-Hellespontine Association of Dionysiac Artists', in P. Wilson (ed.) 2007, 215–35.
Maaß, E. (1925), 'Eunouchos und Verwandtes', *Rheinisches Museum für Philologie* 74, 432–76.
MacCary, W.T. (1972), 'Menander's Soldiers: Their Names, Roles, and Masks', *AJP* 93, 279–98.
MacLeod, M.D. (1991), *Lucian. A Selection* (Warminster: Aris and Phillips).
Mader, G. (2007), 'This Fake Is Real: Script and Performance at Juvenal 3.86–108', *New England Classical Journal* 34, 36–41.
Magrini, P. (1981), 'Lessico platonico e motivi comici nelle lettere erotiche di Aristeneto', *Prometheus* 7, 146–58.
Makres, A. (2014), 'Dionysiac Festivals in Athens and the Financing of Comic Performances', in M. Fontaine and A.C. Scafuro (eds.) 2014, 70–94.
Manieri, A (2009), *Agoni poetico musicali nella Grecia antica. 1. Beozia. Testi e commenti, 25; Certamina musica graeca, 1* (Pisa: Fabrizia Serra editore).

Mankin, D. (1995), *Horace: Epodes* (Cambridge: Cambridge University Press).
Manuwald, G. (2011), *Roman Republican Theatre* (Cambridge: Cambridge University Press).
Marcovich, M. (1976), Aelian, *Varia Historia* 13.15', *Živa Antika* 26, 49–51.
Marshall, C.W. (1999), 'Some Fifth-Century Masking Conventions', *G&R* 46, 188–202.
Marshall, C.W. (2000), '*Alcestis* and the Problem of Prosatyric Drama', *CJ* 95, 229–38.
Marshall, C.W. (2001), 'The Consequences of Dating the *Cyclops*', in M. Joyal (ed.) 2001, 225–41.
Marshall, C.W. (2006), *The Stagecraft and Performance of Roman Comedy* (Cambridge: Cambridge University Press).
Marshall, C.W. (2012), 'Cratinus, Menander and the Daphne Mosaic', in C.W. Marshall and G. Kovacs (eds.) 2012, 187–96.
Marshall, C.W. (2014), 'Dramatic Technique and Athenian Comedy', in M. Revermann (ed.) 2014, 131–46.
Marshall, C.W. and G. Kovacs, eds. (2012), *No Laughing Matter: Studies in Athenian Comedy* (London: Bristol Classical Press).
Marshall, C.W. and S. van Willigenburg (2004), 'Judging Athenian Dramatic Competitions', *JHS* 124, 90–107.
Marx, F. 1930. 'Plauti Cistellaria Menandrea in Dioscuridis musivo Pompeiano', *RhM* 79, 197–208.
Mason, H.J. (1979), 'Favorinus' Disorder: Reifenstein's Syndrome in Antiquity?', *Janus* 66, 1–13.
Mastromarco, G. (1983), *Commedie di Aristofane* I (Torino: UTET).
May, R. (2006), *Apuleius and Drama: The Ass on the Stage* (Oxford: Oxford University Press).
May, R. (2014), 'Roman Comedy in the Second Sophistic', in M. Fontaine and A. Scafuro (eds.) 2014, 753–66.
Mazal, O. (1968), 'Die Textausgaben der Briefsammlung des Aristainetos', *Gutenberg-Jahrbuch* 43, 206–12.
Mazal, O. (1971), *Aristaeneti Epistularum Libri* II (Stuttgart: Teubner).
Mazal, O. (1977) 'Zur Datierung des Lebenszeit des Epistolographen Aristainetos', *Jahrbuch der Österreichischen Byzantinistik* 26, 1–5.
McCarthy, B. (1934), 'Lucian and Menippus', *YCS* 4, 3–55.
McClure, L. (2003), *Courtesans at Table: Gender and Greek Literary Culture in Athenaeus* (New York: Routledge).
McGill, S. (2005), *Virgil Recomposed: The Mythological and Secular Centos in Antiquity* (Oxford: Oxford University Press).
McKeown, J.C. (1979), 'Augustan Elegy and Mime', *PCPS* 25, 71–84.
McNelis, C. (2012), 'Persius, Juvenal, and Literary History After Horace', in S. Braund and J. Osgood (eds.) 2012, 239–61.
Medaglia, S.M., ed. (2004), *Miscellanea in ricordo di Angelo Raffaelle Sodano* (Naples: Quaderni del Departimento di Scienze dell'Antichità).

Mercier, J. (1610), *Aristainetou Epistolai* (Paris: Marcus Orry).
Mette, H. J. (1977), *Urkunden dramatischer Aufführungen in Griechenland* (Berlin: De Gruyter).
Mignona, E. (1996), 'Narrativa greca e mimo: il romanzo di Achille Tazio', *Studi italiani di filologia classica*, 3rd ser., 14, 232–43.
Miller, M.C. (1999), 'Reexamining Transvestism in Archaic and Classical Athens: The Zewadski Stamnos', *AJA* 103, 223–53.
Miller, P.A. (1994), *Lyric Texts and Lyric Consciousness* (London: Routledge).
Millett, P. (2007), *Theophrastus and His World* (Cambridge: Cambridge University Press).
Mills, B.W. and S.D. Olson, eds. (2012), *Inscriptional Records for the Dramatic Festivals in Athens: IG II2 2318-2325 and Related Texts* (Leiden: Brill).
MMC^3 = Webster 1978 (*Monuments Illustrating Old and Middle Comedy*, 3rd ed.).
MNC^3 = Webster 1995 (*Monuments Illustrating New Comedy*, 3rd ed.).
Moles, J. (1983), 'The Date and Purpose of the Fourth Kingship Oration of Dio Chrysostom', *Classical Antiquity* 2, 251–78.
Monti, A., ed. (2002), *Hindu Masculinities across the Ages: Updating the Past* (Turin: L'Harmattan Italia).
Morello, R. and A.D. Morrison (2007), 'Introduction: What is a letter?' in R. Morello and A.D. Morrison (eds.) 2007, 1–16.
Morgan, T. (1998), *Literate Education in the Hellenistic and Roman Worlds* (Cambridge: Cambridge University Press).
Most, G.W., et al., eds. (2013-ongoing), *Fragmenta Comica* (Heidelberg: Verlag Antike).
Müller, R. (2013), 'Terence in Latin Literature from the Second Century bce to the Second Century ce', in A. Augoustakis and A. Traill (eds.) 2013, 363–79.
Mulliez, D., ed. (1999), *La transmission de l'image dans l'antiquité* (Ateliers, Cahiers de la Maison de la Recherche 21; Lille: Université Charles-de-Gaulle/Lille 3).
Nelson Hawkins, J. (2014), 'The Barking Cure: Horace's Anatomy of Rage in *Epodes* 1, 6, and 16', *AJPh* 135, 57–86.
Nelson Hawkins, J. (Forthcoming), 'Anger, Bile, and the Poet's Body in the Archilochean Tradition', in C. Carey and L. Swift (eds.) Forthcoming.
Nelson, B., A. Freadman, and P. Anderson, eds. (2001), *Telling Performances: Essays on Gender, Narrative, and Performance* (Newark, DE: University of Delaware Press).
Nervegna, S. (2007), 'Staging Scenes or Plays? Theatrical Revivals of Old Greek Drama in Antiquity', *Zeitschrift für Papyrologie und Epigraphik* 162, 14–42.
Nervegna, S. (2010), 'Menander's *Theophoroumene* Between Greece and Rome', *AJP* 131, 23–68.
Nervegna, S. (2013), *Menander in Antiquity: the Contexts of Reception* (Cambridge: Cambridge University Press).
Nervegna, S. (2014a), 'Contexts of Reception in Antiquity', in M. Revermann (ed.) 2014, 387–403.

Nervegna, S. (2014b), 'Greek Culture as Images: Menander's Comedies and their Patrons in the Roman West and the Greek East', in S.D. Olson (ed.) 2014, 346–65.

Nervegna, S. (2014c), 'Graphic Comedy: Menandrean Mosaics and Terentian Miniatures', in M. Fontaine and A. Scafuro (eds.) 2014, 717–34.

Nesselrath, H.-G. (1990), *Die attische mittlere Komödie: ihre Stellung in der antiken Literaturkritik und Literaturgeschichte* (Berlin: Walter de Gruyter).

Nesselrath, H.-G. (2000), 'Eupolis and the Periodization of Old Comedy', in D. Harvey and J. Wilkins (eds.) 2000, 233–46.

Nesselrath, H.-G. (2010), 'Comic Fragments: Transmission and Textual Criticism', in G.W. Dobrov (ed.) 2010, 423–54.

Nesselrth, H.-G. (2014), 'Later Greek Comedy in Later Antiquity', in M. Fontaine and A.C. Scafuro (eds.), 667–79.

Nightingale, A. (1995), *Genres in Dialogue: Plato and the Construct of Philosophy* (Cambridge: Cambridge University Press).

Norwood, G. (1931), *Greek Comedy* (London: Methuen).

Nutton, V. (2009), 'Galen's Library', in C. Gill, T. Whitmarsh, and J. Wilkins (eds.) 2009, 19–34.

Nutton, V. (2013), 'Avoiding Distress', in P.N. Singer (ed.) 2013, 43–106.

Obbink, D. and R. Rutherford, eds. (2011), *Culture in Pieces: Essays on Ancient Texts in Honour of Peter Parsons* (Oxford: Oxford University Press).

O'Flaherty, W.D. (1980), *Women, Androgynes, and Other Mythical Beasts* (Chicago and London: University of Chicago Press).

Ogden, D. (1996), *Greek Bastardy in the Classical and Hellenistic Periods* (Oxford: Clarendon Press).

Olender, M. (1991), 'Aspects of Baubo: Ancient Texts and Contexts', in D. Halperin, J.J. Winkler, and F. Zeitlin (eds.) 1991, 83–114.

Oliensis, E. (1998), *Horace and the Rhetoric of Authority* (Cambridge: Cambridge University Press).

Olson, S.D. (2002), *Aristophanes: Acharnians* (Oxford: Oxford University Press).

Olson, S.D. (2004), *Aristophanes: Thesmophoriazusae* (Oxford: Oxford University Press).

Olson, S.D. (2007), *Broken Laughter: Select fragments of Greek Comedy* (Oxford: Oxford University Press).

Olson, S.D. (2014), *Ancient Comedy and Reception: Essays in honor of Jeffrey Henderson* (Berlin and Boston: Walter de Gruyter).

Omitowoju, R. (2010), 'Performing Traditions: Relations and Relationships in Menander and Tragedy', in A.K. Petridis and S. Papaioannou (eds.) 2010, 125–45.

Önal, M. (2002), *Mosaics of Zeugma* (Istanbul: A Turizm Yayınları).

Önal, M. (2009), *Zeugma Mosaics: A Corpus* (Istanbul: A Turizm Yayınları).

Orfanos, C. (2005), 'La comédie ancienne dans la literature de banquet', *Pallas* 67, 25–33.

Ozanam, A.-M. (1999), *Alciphron: Lettres de pêcheurs, de paysans, de parasites et d'hétaïres* (Paris: Les Belles Lettres).

Paga, J. (2010), 'Deme Theaters in Attica and the Trittys System', *Hesperia* 79, 351–84.
Panayotakis, C. (2010), *Decimus Laberius: The Fragments* (Cambridge: Cambridge University Press).
Panayotakis, C. (2014), 'Hellenistic Mime and its Reception in Rome', in M. Fontaine and A.C. Scafuro (eds.) 2014, 378–96.
Parker, H. (2007), 'Free Women and Male Slaves, or Mandingo Meets the Roman Empire', in A. Serghidou (ed.) 2007, 281–98.
Parsons, P.J. (1971), 'A Greek Satyricon?', *BICS* 18, 53–68.
Parsons, P.J. (1974), '3010: Narrative about Iolaus', *The Oxyrhynchus Papyri* 42, 34–41.
Patzer, A. (1994), 'Sokrates in den Fragmenten der attischen Komödie', in A. Bierl, P. von Möllendorff, S. Vogt, and H. Flashar (ed.) 1994, 50–81.
Pelissero, A. (2002), 'A Sexual Masquerade: Arjuna as a Eunuch in the Mahābhārata', in A. Monti (ed.) 2002, 123–55.
Pelling, C. (1986), 'Synkrisis in Plutarch's Lives', *QGFF* 8, 83–96.
Pelling, C. (2005), 'Synkrisis Revisited', in A. Pérez Jiménez and F. Titchener (eds.) 2005, 325–40.
Peponi, A., ed. (2013), *Performance and Culture in Plato's Laws* (Cambridge: Cambridge University Press).
Pérez Jiménez, A. and F. Titchener, eds. (2005), *Historical and Biographical Values of Plutarch's Works: Studies Devoted to Professor Philip A. Stadter* (Málaga/Logan: Universidad de Málaga/Utah State University).
Pernigotti, C. (2008), *Menandri Sententiae* (Florence: L.S. Olschki).
Perysinakis, I.N. and E. Karakasis, eds. (2014), *Plautine Trends: Studies in Plautine Comedy and Its Reception* (Berlin: Walter de Gruyter).
Petrides, A.K. (2010), 'New Performance', in A.K. Petridis and S. Papaioannou (eds.) 2010, 79–124.
Petrides, A.K. (2014), 'Plautus between Greek Comedy and Atellan Farce: Assessments and Reassessments', in M. Fontaine and A.C. Scafuro (eds.) 2014, 424–43.
Petrides, A.K. and S. Papioannou, eds. (2010), *New Perspectives on Postclassical Comedy* (Newcastle upon Tyne: Cambridge Scholars Publishing).
Petrone, G. (1983), *Teatro antico e inganno: Finzioni plautine* (Palermo: Palumbo Editore).
Petsalis-Diomidis, A. (2008), 'The Body in Landscape; Aristides' *Corpus* in the Light of the *The Sacred Tales*', in W. Harris and B. Holmes (eds.) 2008, 131–50.
Petsalis-Diomidis, A. (2010), *Truly Beyond Wonders: Aelius Aristides and the Cult of Asklepios* (Oxford: Oxford University Press).
Petzl, G. and E. Schwertheim, eds. (2006), *Hadrian und die dionysischen Künstler. Drei in Alexandreia Troas neugefundene Briefe des Kaisers an die Künstler-Vereinigung* (Bonn: Habelt).
Pickard-Cambridge, A. (1968), *The Dramatic Festivals of Athens,* 2nd ed., revised by J. Gould and D.M. Levis (Oxford: Clarendon Press).

Platter, C. (2006), *Aristophanes and the Carnival of Genres* (Baltimore: Johns Hopkins University Press).
Platter, C. (2014), 'Plato's Aristophanes', in S.D. Olson (ed.) 2014, 132–66.
Polt, C.B. (2010), 'Catullus and Roman Dramatic Literature' (Diss.: Chapel Hill).
Porter, J.R. (1999–2000), 'Euripides and Menander: *Epitrepontes*, Act IV', *ICS* 24/25, 157–73.
Porter, J.R. (2007), 'Adultery by the Book: Lysias 1 (On the Murder of Eratosthenes) and Comic Diegesis', in E. Carawan (ed.) 2007, 60–88.
Powell, A., ed. (1992), *Roman Poetry and Propaganda in the Age of Augustus* (Bristol: Bristol Classical Press).
Quadlbauer, F. (1960), 'Die Dichter der Griechischen Komödie im Literarischen Urteil der Antike', *Wiener Studien* 73, 40–82.
Rankin, H.D. (1971), *Petronius the Artist: Essays on the Satyricon and its Author* (The Hague: Martinus Nijhoff).
Rawson, E. (1993), 'The Vulgarity of the Roman Mime', in H.D. Jocelyn and H.V. Hurt (eds.) 1993, 255–60.
Reckford, K.J. (2009), *Recognizing Persius* (Princeton: Princeton University Press).
Rees, E.L.E. (2013), *The Vagina: A Literary and Cultural History* (New York and London: Bloomsbury).
Reich, H. (1894), '*De Alciphronis Longique aetate*' (Diss., Königsberg).
Reich, H. (1903), *Der Mimus*, 2 vols (Berlin: Weidmann).
Reig, M. and X. Riu (2014), *Drama, Philosophy, Politics in Ancient Greece. Contexts and Receptions* (Barcelona: la Universitat de Barcelona).
Revermann, M., ed. (2014), *The Cambridge Companion to Greek Comedy* (Cambridge:
Reynolds, J.M. (1982), *Aphrodisias and Rome. Documents From the Excavations at the Theatre* (London: Society for the Promotion of Roman Studies).
Reynolds, R.W. (1946), 'The Adultery Mime', *CQ* 40, 77–84.
Ribbeck, O. (1888), 'Agroikos, Eine ethologische Studie', *Abhandlungen der philologisch-historische Klasse der Sächsischen Gesellschaft der Wissenschaften* 10, 1–68.
Rich, J.W. and L. Kozak, eds. (2006), *Playing around Aristophanes* (Oxford: Oxbow Books).
Richlin, A. (1992), *The Gardens of Priapus. Sexuality and Aggression in Roman Humor* (Oxford: Oxford University Press).
Richlin, A. (2012), 'School Texts of Persius and Juvenal', in S. Braund and J. Osgood (eds.) 2012, 465–85.
Rieff, P., ed. (1963), *Sexuality and the Psychology of Love* (New York: Collier).
Rihll, T.E. (1995), 'Democracy Denied: Why Ephialtes Attacked the Areiopagus', *JHS* 115, 87–98.
Rimell, V. (2004), *Petronius and the Anatomy of Fiction* (Cambridge: Cambridge University Press).
Rimell, V. (2008), *Martial's Rome: Empire and the Ideology of Epigram* (Cambridge: Cambridge University Press).

Ringrose, K.M. (2003), *The Perfect Servant: Eunuchs and the Social Construction of Gender in Byzantium* (Chicago: University of Chicago Press).
Riu, X. (2005), 'The Comparison between Aristophanes and Menander and the History of Greek Comedy', in M. Jufresa, F. Mestre, P. Gómez, and P. Gilabert (eds.) 2005, 425–30.
Roller, L.E. (1999), *In Search of God the Mother: The Cult of Anatolian Cybele* (Berkeley and Los Angeles: University of California Press).
Rosen, R.M. (1988), *Old Comedy and the Iambographic Tradition* (Atlanta: Scholars Press).
Rosen, R.M. (1998), 'The Gendered Polis in Eupolis' *Cities*', in G. Dobrov (ed.) 1998, 149–76.
Rosen, R.M. (2000), 'Cratinus' *Pytine* and the Construction of the Comic Self', in D. Harvey and J. Wilkins (eds.) 2000, 23–39.
Rosen, R.M. (2006), 'Aristophanes, Old Comedy, and Greek Tragedy', in R. Bushnell (ed.) 2006, 251–68.
Rosen, R.M. (2007), *Making Mockery: The Poetics of Ancient Satire* (Oxford and New York: Oxford University Press).
Rosen, R.M. (2010), 'Galen, Satire and the Compulsion to Instruct', in M. Horstmanshoff and C. van Tilburg (eds.) 2010, 325–42.
Rosen, R.M. (2013), 'Iambos, Comedy and the Question of Generic Affiliation', in E. Bakola, L. Prauscello and M. Telò (eds.) 2013, 81–97.
Rosen, R.M. (2014a), 'Comic *Parrhēsia* and the Paradoxes of Repression', in D.S. Olsen (ed.) 2014, 13–28.
Rosen, R.M. (2014b), 'Efficacité et temporalité de l'invective et de la satire dans la poésie grecque', in *Maudire et mal dire: paroles menaçantes en Grèce ancienne, Cahiers Monde Anciens* 5, 2–13.
Rosen, R.M. (forthcoming 2015a), 'Aristophanes and the Pretense of Synchrony', in J. González (ed.) Forthcoming.
Rosen, R.M. (forthcoming 2015b) 'Aischrology in Old Comedy and the Question of "Ritual Obscenity"', in D. Dutsch and A. Suter (eds.) Forthcoming.
Rosen, R.M. (forthcoming 2015c), 'Symposia and the Formation of Poetic Genre in Aristophanes' *Wasps*', in V. Cazzato, D. Obbink and E. Prodi (eds.) Forthcoming.
Rosen, R.M. and C.C. Keane (2013), 'Greco-Roman Satirical Poetry', in T.K. Hubbard (ed.) 2013, 381–97.
Rosenmeyer, P. (2001), *Ancient Epistolary Fictions: The Letter in Greek Literature* (Cambridge: Cambridge University Press).
Rotstein, A. (2010), *The Idea of Iambos* (Oxford: Oxford University Press).
Roueché, C. (1993), *Performers and Partisans at Aphrodisias in the Roman and Late Roman Periods* (London: Society for the Promotion of Roman Studies).
Rousselle, A. (1988), *Porneia: On Desire and the Body in Antiquity*, tr. F. Pheasant (Oxford: Blackwell).
Rudd, N. (1989), *Horace: Epistles II and Epistle to the Pisones (Ars Poetica)* (Cambridge: Cambridge University Press).

Rudich, V. (1993), *Political Dissidence Under Nero: The Price of Dissimulation* (New York: Routledge).
Ruffell, I. (2014a) 'Old Comedy at Rome: Rhetorical model and Satirical Problem', in S.D. Olson (ed.) 2014, 275–308.
Ruffell, I. (2014b), 'Reception and Performance History of the Oresteia', in *Aeschylus: Oresteia* (London: Bloomsbury): ix–xxii.
Ruffy, M.V. (2011), 'Symposium, Physical and Social Health in Plutarch's *Table Talk*', in F. Klotz and K. Oikonomopoulou (eds.) 2011, 131–60.
Russell, D.A. (1983) *Greek Declamation* (Cambridge: Cambridge University Press).
Russell, D.A. (1983), *Greek Declamation* (Cambridge: Cambridge University Press).
Russell, D.A., ed. (1990), *Antonine Literature* (Oxford: Clarendon Press).
Rusten, J.S., ed. (2011), *The Birth of Comedy: Texts, Documents, and Art from Athenian Comic Competitions, 486–280* (Baltimore: Johns Hopkins University Press).
Saxonhouse, A. (2006), *Free Speech and Democracy in Ancient Athens* (Cambridge: Cambridge University Press).
Schepers, M.A. (1905), *Alciphronis Rhetoris Epistularum Libri IV* (Stuttgart: Teubner).
Schmidt, S. (2009), 'Zum Treffen in Neapel und den *Panhellenia* in der Handriansinschrift aus Alexandreai Troas', *ZPE* 170, 109–112.
Schmitz, C. (2000), *Das Satirische in Juvenals Satiren* (Berlin: Walter de Gruyter).
Schmitz, T. (2004), 'Alciphron's Letters as a Sophistic Text', in B.E. Borg (ed.) 2004, 87–104.
Scholfield, A.F., ed. and tr. (1958–59), *Aelian: On the Characteristics of Animals*. 3 vols. (Cambridge, MA: Loeb Classical Library).
Scodel R., ed. (1993), *Theater and Society in the Classical World* (Ann Arbor: University of Michigan Press).
Seidensticker, B. (1982), *Palintonos harmonia: Studien zu komischen Elementen in der griechischen Tragödie* (Göttingen: Vandenhoeck & Ruprecht).
Serghidou, A., ed. (2007), *Fear of Slaves, Fear of Enslavement in the Ancient Mediterranean. Peur de l'esclave, peur de l'esclavage en Méditerranée ancienne: (discours, représentations, pratiques): actes du XXIXe colloque du Groupe international de recherche sur l'esclavage dans l'Antiquité (GIREA), Rethymnon, 4–7 novembre 2004* (Franche-Comté: Presses universitaires de Franche-Comté).
Shackleton Bailey, D.R. (2001), *Cicero: Letters to Friends*, 3 vols (Cambridge, MA: Harvard University Press).
Shaw, C.A. (2014), *Satyric Play: The Evolution of Greek Comedy and Satyr Drama* (Oxford: Oxford University Press).
Sidwell, K. (1993), 'Authorial Collaboration? Aristophanes' *Knights* and Eupolis', *GRBS* 34, 365–89.
Sidwell, K. (1994), 'Aristophanes' *Acharnians* and Eupolis', *Classica et Mediaevalia* 45, 71–115.
Sidwell, K. (1995), 'Poetic Rivalry and the Caricature of Comic Poets: Cratinus' *Pytine* and Aristophanes' *Wasps*', in A. Griffiths (ed.) 1995, 56–80.

Sidwell, K. (2000), 'Athenaeus, Lucian, and fifth-century comedy', in D. Braund and J. Wilkins (eds.) 2000, 136–52.
Sidwell, K. (2005), *Chattering Courtesans and Other Sardonic Sketches* (London: Penguin Books).
Sidwell, K. (2009a), *Aristophanes the Democrat: The Politics of Satirical Comedy during the Peloponnesian War* (Cambridge: Cambridge University Press).
Sidwell, K. (2009b), 'The Dead Philosophers' Society: New Thoughts on Lucian's *Piscator* and Eupolis' *Demes*', in A. Bartley (ed.) 2009, 109–18.
Sidwell, K. (2014a), 'Fourth-century Comedy before Menander', in M. Revermann (ed.) 2014, 60–78.
Sidwell, K. (2014b), ' "Letting It All Hang Out": Lucian, Old Comedy and the Origins of Roman Satire', in S.D. Olson (ed.) 2014, 259–74.
Sifakis, G.M. (1972), *Parabasis and Animals Choruses* (London: Athlone Press).
Silk, M. (2007), 'Translating/Transposing Aristophanes', in E. Hall and A. Wrigley (eds.) 2007, 287–308.
Singer, P.N. (2013), *Galen: Psychological Works* (Cambridge: Cambridge University Press).
Skinner, M.B. (1993), '*Ego mulier*: The Construction of Male Sexuality in Catullus', *Helios* 20, 107–30.
Slater, N.W. (2014), 'The Evidence of the Zeugma *Synaristosai* Mosaic for Imperial Performance of Menander', in S.D. Olson (ed.) 2014, 366–74.
Slater, N.W., and B. Zimmerman, eds. (1993), *Intertextualität in der griechisch-römischen Komödie* (Stuttgart: Metzlersche & Poeschel).
Slater, W.J. (1991), *Dining in a Classical Context* (Ann Arbor: University of Michigan Press).
Sluiter I. and R. Rosen, eds. (2004), *Free Speech in Classical Antiqtuiy* (Leiden: Brill).
Smith, M.S. (1975), *Cena Trimalchionis* (Oxford: Oxford University Press).
Smith, S.D. (2014), *Man and Animal in Severan Rome: The Literary Imagination of Claudius Aelianus* (Cambridge: Cambridge University Press).
Smith, W. (1985), 'Heroic Models for the Sordid Present: Juvenal's View of Tragedy', *ANRW* 2.33.1, 811–23.
Smith, W.S., ed. (2005), *Satiric Advice on Women and Marriage: From Plautus to Chaucer* (Ann Arbor: University of Michigan Press).
Sommerstein, A.H. (1982), *Aristophanes: Clouds* (Oxford: Aris and Phillips).
Sommerstein, A.H. (1994) *Aristophanes: Thesmophoriazusae* (Warminster: Aris and Phillips).
Sommerstein, A.H. (2000), 'Platon, Eupolis and the "Demagogue-Comedy"', in D. Harvey and J. Wilkins (eds.) 2000, 437–51.
Sommerstein, A.H. (2004), 'Comedy and the unspeakable', in D.L. Cairns and R.A. Knox (eds.) 2004, 205–22.
Sommerstein, A.H. (2010), 'The History of the Text of Aristophanes', in G.W. Dobrov (ed.) 2010, 399–422.

Sommerstein, A.H. (2011), 'Hinc Omnis Pendet? Old Comedy and Roman Satire', *CW* 105.1, 25–38.

Sommerstein, A.H., ed. (2014), *Menander in Contexts* (London: Routledge).

Sonnino, M. (1997), 'Una presunta scena di morte nel Maricante di Eupoli: (fr. 209 K.-A.)', *Eikasmos* 8, 43–60.

Spawforth, A.J.S. (2012), *Greece and the Augustan Cultural Revolution* (Cambridge: Cambridge University Press).

Staden, H. von (1998), 'Gattung und Gedächtnis: Galen über Wahrheit und Lehrdichtung', in W. Kullmann, J. Althoff, and M. Asper (eds.) 1998, 65–94.

Stärk, E. (2002), 'Die Togata', in W. Suerbaum (ed.), *Die archaische Literatur: von den Anfängen bis Sullas Tod*, (*Handbuch der lateinischen Literatur* [*HLL*]; Munich: Beck) 1 §§132–34.

Steffen, V. (1972a), 'De Callippidis et Cnemonis litterarum commercio', in *Studi in onore di Q. Cataudella* (Catania) II, 295–304.

Steffen, V. (1972b), 'Dialog Kallipidesa z Knemonom', *Eos* 60, 255–62.

Stephanis, I.E. (1988), Διονυσιακοὶ τεχνῖται (Heraklion: Panepistemaikes Ekdoseis Kretes).

Stevenson, W. (1995), 'The Rise of Eunuchs in Greco-Roman Antiquity', *Journal of the History of Sexuality* 5, 495–511.

Stillwell, R. (1941), *Antioch-on-the-Orontes. Vol. 3, The Excavations 1937–1939* (Princeton: Princeton University Press).

Stockt, L. van der, ed. (2000), *Rhetorical Theory and Praxis in Plutarch* (Louvain-Namur: Peeters).

Stockton, D. (1982), 'The Death of Ephialtes', *CQ* 32, 227–8.

Storey, I.C. (2002), 'Cutting Comedies', *Drama* 12, 146–67.

Storey, I.C. (2003), *Eupolis, Poet of Old Comedy* (Oxford: Oxford University Press).

Storey, I.C. (2006), 'On First Looking into Kratinos' Dionysalexandros', in J.W. Rich and L. Kozak (eds.) 2006, 115–25.

Storey, I.C. (2010), 'Origins and fifth-century comedy', in G.W. Dobrov (ed.) 2010, 179–225.

Storey, I.C. (2011), *Fragments of Old Comedy*. 3 vols. (Cambridge, MA: Harvard University Press).

Storey, I.C. (2012), 'Angling in Archippos', *BICS* 55.2, 1–19.

Strasser, J.-Y. (2006), 'L'épreuve artistique διὰ πάντων', *Historia* 55, 298–327.

Strasser, J.-Y. (2010), 'Qu'on fouette des concurrents...', *Revue des Études Grecques* 123, 585–622.

Stroup, S. (2003), '*Adulla Virgo*: The Personification of Textual Eloquence in Cicero's *Brutus*', *MD* 50.1, 15–40.

Summa, D. (2008), 'Un Concours de Drames "Anciens" à Athènes', *REG* 121, 479–96.

Swain, S. (1989), 'Favorinus and Hadrian', *Zeitschrift für Papyrologie und Epigraphik* 79, 150–8.

Swain, S., ed. (2000), *Dio Chrysostom: Politics, Letters, and Philosophy* (Oxford: Oxford University Press).
Taplin, O. (1993), *Comic Angels and Other Approaches to Greek Drama Through Vase-Paintings* (Oxford: Clarendon Press).
Taplin, O. (1999), 'Spreading the Word Through Performance', in S. Godlhill and R. Osborne (eds.) 1999, 33–57.
Taplin, O. and R. Wyles, eds. (2010), *The Pronomos Vase and its Context* (Oxford: Oxford University Press).
Thompson, D.W. (1947), *A Glossary of Greek Fishes* (Oxford: Oxford University Press).
Thraede, K. (1970), *Grundzüge griechisch-römischer Briefoptik* (München: Beck).
Thyresson, I. (1964), 'Quatre letters de Claude Élien inspirées par le 'Dyskolos' de Ménandre', *Eranos* 62, 7–35.
Too, Y.L. and N. Livingstone, eds. (1998), *Pedagogy and Power: Rhetorics of Classical Learning* (Cambridge: Cambridge University Press).
Tougher, S., ed. (2002), *Eunuchs in Antiquity and Beyond* (London: Classical Press of Wales and Duckworth).
Tougher, S. (2008), *The Eunuch in Byzantine History and Society* (London and New York: Routledge).
Traill, A. (2001), 'Menander's "Thais" and the Roman Poets', *Phoenix* 55, 284–303.
Traill, A. (2008), *Women and the Comic Plot in Menander* (Cambridge: Cambridge University Press).
Trapp, M.B. (1997), *Maximus of Tyre: the Philosophical Orations* (Oxford: Clarendon Press).
Treu, K. (1973), 'Menander bei Alkiphron', *Schriften zur Geschichte und Kultur der Antike* 6, 207–17.
Tribulato, O. (2014), '"Not even Menander would use this word!" Perceptions of Menander's Language in Greek Lexicography', in A.H. Sommerstein (ed.) 2014, 199–214.
Tronchin, F. (2012a), 'Introduction: Collecting the Eclectic', *Collectors and the Eclectic: New Approaches to Roman Domestic Decoration*, special volume, *Arethusa* 45, 261–82.
Tronchin, F. (2012b), 'Roman Collecting, Decorating, and Eclectic Practice in the Textual Sources', in *Collectors and the Eclectic: New Approaches to Roman Domestic Decoration*, special volume, *Arethusa* 45, 333–45.
Trzaskoma, S.M. (2009), 'Aristophanes in Chariton (*Plu.* 741, *Eq.* 1244, *Eq.* 670)', *Philologus* 153, 351–53.
Trzaskoma, S.M. (2010), 'Callirhoe, Concubinage, and a Corruption in Chariton 2.11.5', *Exemplaria Classica* 14, 205–9.
Trzaskoma, S.M. (2011), 'Aristophanes in Chariton Again (*Plu.* 1127)', *Philologus* 155, 367–68.
Tsirimbas, A. (1936), 'Sprichwörter und sprichwörtlich Redensarten bei den Epistolographen der zweiten Sphistik Alkiphron – Claudius Aelianus' (Diss.: München).

Tsirimbas, D.A. (1950), 'Παροιμίαι καὶ Παροιμιώδεις φράσεις παρὰ τῷ ἐπιστολογράφῳ Ἀρισταινέτῳ', *Platon* 2, 25–85.

Turner, E.G. (1967), 'Ink Drawings', *Oxyrhynchus Papyri* XXXII. London: Egypt Exploration Society, Greco-Roman Memoirs 46, 180–81 and plate XV.

Uden, J. (2006), 'Embracing the Young Man in Love: Catullus 75 and the Comic "Adulescens"', *Antichthon* 40, 19–34.

Uden, J. (2015), *The Invisible Satirist: Juvenal and Second-Century Rome* (Oxford: Oxford University Press).

Ureña Bracero, J. (1993) 'La carta ficticia griega: Los nombres de personajes y el uso del encabeziamento en Alcifrón, Arinéteo y Teofilacto', *Emerita* 61, 267–98.

Van Daele, H. and V. Coulon, eds. (1948), *Aristophane* I. 3rd ed. (Paris: Les Belles Lettres).

van Nijf, O. (2000), 'Athletics, Festivals and Greek Identity in the Roman East', *PCPhS* 45, 176–200.

Van Rooy, C.A. (1965), *Studies in Classical Satire and Related Literary Theory* (Brill: Leiden).

Ventrella, G. (2005), 'L'etopea nella definizione degli antichi retori', in E. Amato and J. Schamp (eds.) 2005, 179–212.

Vieillefond, J.-R. (1929), 'La letter II.1 d'Alciphron et la *Chasse* de Xénophon', *RPh* 55, 354–57.

Vox, O., ed. (2013), *Lettere, mimesi, retorica: Studi sulll'epistolografia letteraria greca di età imperiale e tardo antico* (Lecce: Pensa Multimedia).

Wallace-Hadrill, A. (2008), *Rome's Cultural Revolution* (Cambridge: Cambridge University Press).

Walton, J.M. and P.D. Arnott (1996), *Menander and the Making of Comedy* (London: Greenwood Press).

Warnecke, B. (1906), 'De Alexidis ΟΠΩΡΑ', *Hermes* 41, 158–9.

Watson, L. (2003), *A Commentary on Horace's Epodes* (Oxford: Oxford University Press).

Watson, L. and Watson, P. (2014), *Juvenal, Satire 6* (Cambridge: Cambridge University Press).

Watson, P. (2007), 'Juvenal's *scripta matrona*: Elegiac Resonances in Satire 6', *Mnemosyne* 60, 628–40.

Watson, W. (2012), *The Lost Second Book of Aristotle's Poetics* (Chicago and London: University of Chicago Press).

Webb, R. (2008) *Demons and Dancers: Performance in Late Antiquity* (Cambridge, MA: Harvard University Press).

Webster, T.B.L. (1974), *An Introduction to Menander* (Manchester: Manchester University Press).

Webster, T.B.L. (1978), *Monuments Illustrating Old and Middle Comedy*, 3rd ed. revised and enlarged by J. R. Green. London: *BICS* Supp. 39 [=*MMC*³].

Webster, T.B.L. (1995), *Monuments Illustrating New Comedy Vol. I*, 3rd ed. revised and enlarged by J.R. Green and A. Seeberg (London: Institute of Classical Studies).

Whitby, M., P. Hardie, and M. Whitby, eds. (1987), *Homo Viator* (Bristol: Bristol Classical Press).

Whitehorne, J. (1993), 'The Rapist's Disguise in Menander's *Eunuchus*', in N.W. Slater and B. Zimmermann (eds.) 1993, 122–32.

Whitehorne, J. (2000), 'Menander's "Androgynos": Plot, Personae, and Context', *Hermes* 128, 310–19.

Whitman, C.H. (1964), *Aristophanes and the Comic Hero* (Cambridge, MA: Harvard University Press).

Whitmarsh, T. (1998), 'Reading Power in Roman Greece: The *paideia* of Dio Chrysostom', in Y.L. Too and N. Livingstone (eds.) 1998, 192–213.

Whitmarsh, T. (2001), *Greek Literature and the Roman Empire* (Oxford: Oxford University Press).

Wiles, D. (1991), *The Masks of Menander: Sign and meaning in Greek and Roman Performance* (Cambridge: Cambridge University Press).

Willi, A. (2010), 'Register Variation', in E.J. Bakker (ed.) 2010, 297–310.

Williams, L. (1999), *Hard Core: Power, Pleasure and the 'Frenzy of the Visible'* (Berkeley: University of California Press).

Wilson, N., ed. and tr. (1997), *Aelian, Historical Miscellany* (Cambridge, MA: Loeb Classical Library).

Wilson, N. (2007), *Aristophanea: Studies on the Text of Aristophanes* (Oxford: Oxford University Press).

Wilson, N. (2014a), 'The Transmission of Aristophanes', in M. Fontaine and A.C. Scafuro (eds.) 2014, 655–66.

Wilson, N. (2014b), 'The Transmission of Comic Texts', in M. Revermann (ed.) 2014, 242–32.

Wilson, P. (2000), *The Athenian Institution of the Khoregia: the Chorus, the City, and the Stage* (Cambridge: Cambridge University Press).

Wilson, P., ed. (2007), *The Greek Theatre and Festivals. Documentary Studies* (Oxford: Oxford University Press).

Winkler, M. (1989), 'The Function of Epic in Juvenal's *Satires*', in C. Deroux (ed.) 1989, 414–43.

Wiseman, T.P. (1985), *Catullus and His World: A Reappraisal* (Cambridge: Cambridge University Press).

Woodman, A.J. (1983), 'Juvenal 1 and Horace', *G&R* 30, 81–4.

Woodman, T. and D. Feeney (2002), *Traditions and Contexts in the Poetry of Horace* (Cambridge: Cambridge University Press).

Worman, N. (2008), *Abusive Mouths in Classical Athens* (Cambridge: Cambridge University Press).

Wörrle, M. (1988), *Stadt und Fest im kaiserzeitlichen Kleinasien. Studien zu einer agonistischen Stiftung aus Oinoanda*. Vestigia 39 (Munich: Beck).

Wright, D.H. (2006), *The Lost Late Antique Illustrated Terence* (Vatican City: Bibliotexa Apostolica Vaticana).

Wright, F.W. (1931), *Cicero and the Theater* (Northampton, MA: Smith College).
Wright, M. (2007), 'Comedy and the Trojan War', *CQ* 57, 412–31.
Wright, M. (2012), *The Comedian as Critic: Greek Old Comedy and Poetics* (London: Bloomsbury).
Wyttenbach, W.X. (1797), *Plutarchi Chaeronensis Moralia*, vol. 4 (Oxford: Clarendon Press). <http://books.google.ca/books?id=ipgQAAAAIAAJ>.
Xenophontos, S. (2012), 'Comedy in Plutarch's *Parallel Lives*', *GRBS* 52, 603–31.
Zanetto, G. (1987), 'Un epistolografo al lavoro: le *Lettere* di Aristeneto', *SIFC* 5, 193–211.
Zanetto, G. (2000), 'Plutarco e la commedia', in I. Gallo and C. Moreschini (eds.) 2000, 319–33.
Zimmermann, B. (1998), *Die Griechische Komödie* (Düsseldorf and Zürich: Artemis and Winkler).
Zimmermann, J. (1909), *Luciani quae feruntur Podagra et Ocypus* (Leipzig: Teubner).
Žižek, S. (2004), *Organs without Bodies* (New York: Routledge).

Index

Achilles Tatius 95
actors and performers 69, 118–6
   boys 125–6
   Greeks in Rome 26–8
   guilds of Dionysiac artists 9, 121–6
   in mimes 35
   of the imperial era 124–5
adultery 98–101
Aelian (Claudius Aelianus) 197–216, 238–9
   Rustic Letters, structure 204–13
      1–2: 205–6
      3–6: 206, 208
      7–10: 206–9
      11–12: 208
      13–18: 208–9, 210–12
      19–20: 209
   On the Characteristics of Animals
      10.41: 213–16
   Historical Miscellany 1.18: 202
      2.13: 197–201
Aeschylus 169
Afranius 32–3
Agnoia see Menander, *Perikeiromene*
Alcibiades 4, 91, 141, 198–200
Alciphron 223–8, 239, 251
   as a character in Aristainetos 247
   Letters 1.6.1: 225
      1.15: 229
      2.13: 228
      2.17: 227
      2.32: 251
      2.34: 228
      2.35: 227
      3.22: 228
      3.27: 227
      3.38: 229
      4.2: 225
      4.6: 230
      4.7: 229
      4.8: 230
      4.13: 230–2
      4.17: 229–30
      4.19: 232, 234
Alexis 4, 56, 163, 203, 206
Ameipsias 166, 200, 215
Antiphanes 4
Apollophanes 202
Archilochus 69, 76
Archippos 174
Aristainetos, *Letters* 1.5: 247–50
   1.22: 247–50
   2.3: 239–51
   2.12: 239–51
Aristias 202
Aristides, Aelius 73–4, 106–7, 181–93
   Or. 29 181–93
   Sacred Tales 186–7
Aristophanes 53, 107, 132–7, 141, 163, 202, 206
   Acharnians 45–6, 49–50, 53–4, 81, 132, 148, 172, 175–6, 178
   Birds 164, 178, 201–2
   Clouds 70
      as model for Aelian 197–201, 204
      as model for Alciphron 223, 226, 236
      as model for Aristainetos 240–7, 250–1
      as model for Lucian 164, 167, 178
   Ecclesiazousae 91
   Frogs 151
   in imperial performance 185
   Knights 81, 132, 171–2, 175, 213–14
      scholion *ad* 400: 170
   Lysistrata 50
   paratragedy 169
   Peace 70–1, 81, 206
   Plutus 206, 208–9
   Thesmophoriazusae 46–7, 90–1, 99, 132
   Wasps 53–4, 171, 178, 213
Aristotle 45, 138, 143
   Didaskaliai 5, 6
   [ps.-Aristotle] *Problems* 93

Artemidorus 112
Astydamas 73
Athenaeus 11, 15, 145, 202
Athens, imperial evocations 75-7, 82, 223, 226, 233-4
Augustus 63, 113, 122
Aulus Gellius 5-6, 8, 136, 218, 254

Bakhtin 36
banquets 15-16, 35-6, 145, 249
Baubo 50, 60
Bona Dea 99, 107

Caecilius 29, 136
Cercopes 76
chorus 3, 70-1, 76, 78, 83, 151, 165, 183
Cicero 28, 32, 51-2, 99, 169
Claudius 122
Clodius, Publius 99
Comedy, *see* Middle Comedy, New Comedy, Old Comedy
    ancient scholarship on 10-11
    and religion 188
    as education 71, 100, 190-1
    as 'mirror of life' 25, 34, 37
    at imperial festivals 117-26
    cross-dressing and transvestism in 89-91, 109
    in ancient education 9-10, 16-17
    inscriptional evidence for 117-26
    origins of 3, 76
    representations in art 2, 15-16
    Republican 11, 27-8, 32
costume 89-91, 109
Cratinus/Kratinos 5, 108, 133, 135, 163-4, 168, 178, 199-200, 202, 212, 214
    Archilochoi 77
    Dionysalexandros 133, 174-5
    Wine-Flask (Pytine) 53, 133, 153, 166, 170-2, 178, 200
Courbet, *L'Origine du monde* 59-60, 68

Demosthenes 206
Didymus of Alexandria 145
Dio Chrysostom 69-83, 105-6
    Orations [37]: see Favorinus

Dionysia 3, 5, 9, 19, 49, 149, 165, 173, 199, 217
Diphilus 7-9, 11, 90, 108
Domitian 29, 36

education see comedy, in ancient education
Ephialtes 213-15
Epicharmus 19, 163
epistolarity 204-13, 223-4, 239-50
    as comic plot device 239
    as a genre 205-6, 232-4
ethopoeia 12, 101, 204, 232-3, 239
eunuchs and eunuchism 91-107
    in Achilles Tatius 95
    in ritual 109
    in Hermogenes 98
    in Lucian 95
    in Statius 95
Euripides 29, 69, 72, 148, 169, 237
    Alcestis 6-7
    Autolycus 214
    Bacchae 91, 99
    Danae 72
    favored by Socrates 198-200
    Hecuba 81, 215-16
    Orestes 217
    Skyrioi 91
Eupolis 53, 79, 133, 135, 163, 166, 206, 178, 212
    Autolycus 203, 213-16, 221
    Baptae (Dyers) 4, 8, 91, 141, 164, 177-8, 214
    commentaries 6
    Demes 9, 133, 163, 173-4, 178
    Maricas 71, 176-8, 203, 214
eunuchs 91-4, 98-101, 108

fabula Atellana 27-8
fabula palliata 26-7, 32
fabula togata 25-6, 32-4, 37
Favorinus 89-107
festivals outside Athens
    and imperial cult 124
    Artemisia (Ephesus) 125
    at Ephesus 124
    Demosthenia (Oenoanda) 117-19, 124
    Didymeia (Didyma) 125
    Dionysia (Smyrna) 181, 183

Greater Didymeia (Miletus) 125
Koinon of Asia (Pergamum) 185
Lysimacheia (Aphrodisias) 119–21, 185
Museia (Thespiae) 118–20, 124, 185
Nea Caesarea (Didyma) 125
Olympics 185
Rhomaia (Magnesia) 120–1
schedules and cancellations 123
Freud, Sigmund 60, 220

Galen 17, 47, 134, 145, 158, 176, 202
galli (castrated priests of Cybele) 94–5
genitals
    ambiguous 89
    talking 43–9, 52–9

Hadrian 103, 106, 122–4
hermaphroditism 96–7
Hermogenes 98
Herodas 12
Hippocratic theories 48–9
Hipponax 12
Historiae Augustae 129
Homer 69, 78–9, 148
Horace 12, 29, 40, 43–5, 51–8, 79, 121, 168–9, 171

Iambe 50
Inscriptions
    BGU 4.10 73–4: 122
    CIG 2820 ii: 121
    Corinth VII:3 no. 272: 125
    I. Aphrodisias 12.17, col. ii: 121
        12.29: 121
    I. Didyma 183: 125
    I. Ephesos 24 (= *SIG*³ 867): 124
        27: 124
        1147: 125
        1606: 125–6
    I. Magnesia 88a: 120
        88d i 4: 120–1
    I. Thespies 177: 119–20, 122, 124–5
        172.35–42: 194
    IG II² 2318.201–3: 194
    IG II² 2318.316–18: 194
    IG II² 2323a.39–40: 194
    IG II² 2325.116–38: 219
    IG 7.1773: 117–20, 122, 124
    IG 7.1774–6: 124

IG 7.1776: 122
MAMA 8.418c: 121, 123
    8.420: 194
    8.492: 121
SEG 54: 787: 185–6, 194
Side Kitabeleri (= Bean 1965: 149): 129
'Iolaus Romance' 95
Isaios 206

Julius Caesar 99
Juvenal 25–38, 52, 54, 81

Lenaia 3, 200, 217
lesbianism 96
letters see epistolarity
lex Iulia de adulteriis coercendis 104
Libanius 100–1
libertas 44, 51, 54, see also Old Comedy
    and *parrhēsia*
Longus 100
Lucian 15, 95, 141–4, 147–57, 163–79
    and Aristainetos 247, 256
    Against the Uneducated Book-collector 141, 164
    Anacharsis 168–9
    Dialogues of the Courtesans 96–7
    The Dead Come to Life, or The Fisherman 147–53, 155, 165, 172
    Double Indictment 153–6, 164–7, 169–70
    Eunuch 97–8, 101, 103
    Gout and *Swiftfoot* 15, 182
    Lexiphanes 175–7
    On the Syrian Goddess 95
    You are a Literary Prometheus 167–8
Lucillius 43, 52
Lycophron 11

Marcus Aurelius 141
Martial 55–9
masks 2–3, 7, 26–30, 44, 73, 155, 164, 199–200, 234, 239
Maximus of Tyre 218
[Meleager] (*Anthologia Palatina* 11.223): 104–5
Menander 7–8, 69, 100, 107, 132, 134–7, 145, 163, 202
    among imperial poets 30
    and Caecilius 136

Androgynos 90, 91, 95
  as character in Alciphron 223–4
  as model for Aelian 204–13
  as model for Aristainetos 242, 246, 249
  Dyscolus 204–5, 210–13, 231
  Eunuchus 90
  Georgos 206
  referenced as 'the comic poet' in Lucian 163
  language of 225–6
  maxims 10
  Perikeiromene 228
    Agnoia (Ignorance) 2
    Glykera in Alciphron 223, 225, 232
    Glykera in Aristainetos 247–50
  performance 14–15, 29, 135
  Thais 163, 230
Menippus 155, 167–8, 173
Middle Comedy 4–5
mime 13, 34–7, 40–1, 83, 94, 118, 206
  as model for Juvenal 25, 37
  as successor to New Comedy 113
mimēsis 28, 46, 82, 240–2, 246–50
mosaics 15–16, 120, 179, 194, 232

New Comedy 7–9
  as model for epistolographers 223–4, 239
  at Rome 28–30
  development of 224–5
  in Aelian 202, 207–13
New Comic character types
  hetaira, prostitute 90, 207, 228–4
  pater durus 31, 34, 38
  soldier 228
  young man 228–9

Old Comedy 1–4, 141–57, 181–93, 208
  and invective 52, 76, 150–3, 157, 168, 183
  and *parrhēsia* 44, 50–60, 79, 148
  archaia, as genre term 69, 164, 185–6
  culturally distant from imperial era 142
  in imperial performance 146–7, 159
  original imperial compositions of, 185–6
  Plutarch on 131–7, 144–7
  three poets of 3–4, 12, 17–18, 44, 52, 133, 138, 142, 158
Old Oligarch 136
Oxyrhynchus Papyri
  661: 174
  2476: 122, 123–4
  2610: 122
  2652: 2
  2653: 2
  3010: 95

pantomime 2, 13, 36, 94
parabasis 1, 69–83, 145, 147, 184
parasite 31, 35–6
parabainein 71
performance 14–16, 159, 181–6
  Afranius' *Incendium* 33
  at the Demosthenia, 118–19
  Attelan farces 129
  Euripides 29
  Euripides at Piraeus 198
  Euripides' *Danae* 72
  imperial preference for New over Old Comedy 120
  original imperial comedies 182, 184–5, 192–3
  καινή, meaning original 119–20, 185
  reperformance 5–6, 28–9, 70, 184–5
    of imperial-era plays 121
    palaios, meaning 'restaged' 6, 119–20, 185
  Terence's *Eunuchus* 29
Persius 12, 40, 52
Petronius 44, 53–5, 58
phallus 49–50
Pherecrates 135
Philemon 7–8, 11, 17, 163, 202
philosophy and philosophers 43, 79–80, 97–8, 102, 144, 148–53, 165–6, 173–4
Philostratus 89, 98, 102, 105–6
Phrynichus (*comicus*) 215
physiognomy 93–94
Plato 5, 11, 28, 73, 75, 85, 133, 136–7, 166, 182, 187–92, 197, 217
  Laws 935c–936a: 191–2
  Republic 395e–396a: 190
  Timaeus 91a–c: 47–9

Plato *comicus* 76, 133
Platonius 4
Plautus 7–8, 11, 29–32, 90, 239
Pliny the Younger 1, 10, 32
Plutarch 8, 72, 99, 131–9, 144–7, 157
    Table Talk 74, 144–5, 181
    *The Comparison of Aristophanes
        and Menander* 14–15, 131–9,
        145–6, 181, 226
Polemo of Laodicea 93–4, 102–3
Polemon of Athens 2, 171–2
Pollux 70, 72, 234
Polus 6
pornography 63, 67–8
Prometheus (in Lucian) 167
prosopopoeia 44, 46, 51, 53, 57
prostitute 26, 32, 35, 104, 207, 231,
    251

Quintilian 18, 29–30, 51, 103, 105

Rocky Horror Picture Show 67–8

satyr drama 6, 72–3, 119–20
schools see comedy, as education

scurra 36
Serapis 80
Severus of Alexandria 101
Socrates 76, 80–1, 166, 197–201, 217
Sophocles 72, 202, 215–16
Statius 95
Strato of Sardis 104–5
Strattis 169

Terence, *Eunuchus* 11, 29, 34–5, 90, 95, 101,
    207–8
Theophrastus 11–12
Theopompus 108, 203, 219
Thesmophoria 46, 50, 90,
tragedy 8, 191
Trajan 105, 124
transvestism see Comedy, cross-dressing
    and transvestism in

Varro 46–7
Vergilius Romanus 1, 32, 195

weaving and sex 250–1

Xenophon 208